LANGUAGE AND LITERACY EDUCATION IN A CHALLENGING WORLD

LANGUAGES AND LINGUISTICS

Additional books in this series can be found on Nova's website
under the Series tab.

Additional E-books in this series can be found on Nova's website
under the E-book tab.

EDUCATION IN A COMPETITIVE AND GLOBALIZING WORLD

Additional books in this series can be found on Nova's website
under the Series tab.

Additional E-books in this series can be found on Nova's website
under the E-book tab.

LANGUAGES AND LINGUISTICS

LANGUAGE AND LITERACY EDUCATION IN A CHALLENGING WORLD

THAO LÊ
QUYNH LÊ
AND
MEGAN SHORT
EDITORS

Nova Science Publishers, Inc.
New York

LIBRARY OF CONGRESS CATALOGING-IN-PUBLICATION DATA

Language and literacy education in a challenging world / editors: Thao Lj,
Quynh Lj, Megan Short.
       p. cm.
  Includes bibliographical references and index.
  ISBN 978-1-61761-198-8
  1. English language--Study and teaching--Foreign speakers. 2. Language
and languages--Study and teaching. 3. Literacy--Study and teaching. 4.
Second language acquisition. 5. Language acquisition. 6. Discourse
analysis. I. Le, Thao. II. Lj, Quynh. III. Short, Megan.
  PE1128.A2L2945 2010
  428.2'4--dc22
                                                              2010029766

Published by Nova Science Publishers, Inc. † New York

CONTENTS

PREFACE

Educational success or failure to a great extent depends on language and literacy as it reminds us of the widely quoted statement of Ludwig Wittgenstein "The limits of my language means the limits of my world". Language learning is not just 'learning a language' like learning a computer software or chemistry. Metaphorically language and literacy education is like helping children to embark on a journey of discovery and self-discovery through language. The journey can be inspiring and empowering for some children and it can be disheartening for others as there are many challenges to face, for learners as well as for teachers.

Language and Literacy Education in a Challenging World is a book based on the belief that there are no simple recipes for teachers to use to solve all literacy problems that they and their children experience in a classroom or a program. This is not a pessimistic view, but a challenging perspective as it views language and literacy education as a fascinatingly dynamic and powerful discourse which dignifies human civilisation due to its multidimensional nature and which also poses challenges and problems to be faced.

This book was contributed by a number of selected authors of different educational backgrounds and interests in language and literacy education who have worked with children in their own educational contexts in different parts of the global village. In this book, they want to share their views and experiences with teachers and theorists about language and literacy education in a challenging world.

The world is constantly changing. In fact everything is in a state of flux. Change always involves some risk. However, the probability of success is greater and the risk is less when we listen to the authentic voice of those who have experience and an ongoing commitment to the challenges ahead.

We would like to express our profound appreciation to the chapter authors for their dedication, enthusiasm and inspiration in joining our language and literacy journey. We are very grateful to Nova Science Publishers for their full support for the production of this book.

Thao Lê, Quynh Lê and Megan Short
Editors

PART I

THEORETICAL ISSUES
AND THEIR EDUCATIONAL IMPLICATIONS

In: Language and Literacy Education in a Challenging World   ISBN: 978-1-61761-198-8
Editors: T. Lê, Q. Lê, and M. Short   © 2011 Nova Science Publishers, Inc.

Chapter 1

LINGUISTIC MYSTERY: A CHALLENGE TO LANGUAGE AND LITERACY EDUCATION

Thao Lê, Quynh Lê and Megan Short

ABSTRACT

Native speakers tend to take language for granted as they can speak and use their language naturally. However, when they are asked to explain about some aspects of their language, it turns out to be a difficult or impossible task to do. This phenomenon demonstrates that native speakers have some implicit knowledge and metalinguistic awareness of their mother tongue. However there are many fascinating linguistic aspects of their mother tongue which are still a mystery for them. This chapter introduces some insights gained from linguistics which are useful to literacy teachers theoretically and practically. The chapter also discusses some misconceptions about language structure, language in use and language in education.

Keywords: grammar, implicit knowledge, literacy, logic, misconception, phonics.

INTRODUCTION

Linguistic mystery is fascinating to a curious mind. It arouses curiosity which can lead to transferring implicit knowledge into explicit knowledge, bringing subconscious knowledge to the surface of consciousness, or bringing intuition into rationalisation. This is important in language and literacy education. As we need some insights gained from psychology to help us to understand human behaviour, similarly we need linguistic knowledge to demystify some linguistic mysteries in order to fully appreciate the profundity of human languages. This chapter provides a number of linguistic mysteries for opening a window on understanding the complexity of English and particularly for challenging some misconceptions about English in particular and human language in general.

KNOWING LANGUAGE AND KNOWING ABOUT LANGUAGE

How much do we know about our mother tongue? We can argue that all native speakers of a language "know" their language well, otherwise they cannot engage in verbal communication with one another. Children around the age of five are expected to be able to talk with some degree of fluency with their care-takers about their daily activities unless they experience problems caused by intellectual or linguistic disability or social isolation. The case of Genie, a socially and linguistically deprived child, indicates the importance of communicative interaction in early childhood as she was brought up in severe isolation and, as a consequence her linguistic and cognitive development was severely curtailed (Curtiss, Fromkin, Krashen, Rigler, & Rigler, 1974).

The word "know" in "know language" and "know about language" is a crucial word but it is also an ambiguous one as we can possess knowledge in many different ways and through many different modalities. How we come to have knowledge about the world is shaped by our physical, social, emotional and cultural experiences Chomsky (1968) makes a distinction between implicit and explicit knowledge. All native speakers of English "know" that the meaning of the sentence "dogs chase cats" is different from "cats chase dogs" even though these two sentences have exactly the same words. In other words, native speakers of English "know" that in these two sentences, the initiator or agent of the action should be placed before the verb (i.e. subject) and the receiver of the action should be placed after the verb (i.e. object). Thus, native speakers of English understand the significance of word order in an English sentence as a significant grammatical device. Simply speaking, they "know" English grammar. However if we ask them whether English is a Subject-Verb-Object (SVO) language or not, they may not understand the question, as the concepts "subject", "verb", and "object" are theoretical concepts used in linguistics to describe the grammatical structure of a sentence. Similarly if we ask native speakers of French about word order between noun and adjective in French, they may not tell us. However, they can tell us that "un grand hôtel" (a big hotel) and "un hôtel noire" (a black hotel) are correct. However they may not be able to explain that in French, *adjectives of size* (e.g., big, small, tiny, huge) are positioned before a noun and *adjectives of colour* (e.g., black, red, white) are positioned after a noun. This can be a linguistic mystery for them. The challenge for literacy and language educators is to bridge the divide between the learners' implicit and explicit linguistic knowledge.

LOGIC AND LANGUAGE: MYSTERY AND MISCONCEPTION

Three subjects which were prominent in medieval liberal arts education in the Western world were rhetoric, grammar and logic. It marks a close link between logic, language and communication. Logic is connected to cognition; grammar is connected to the means by which symbols are combined to express thought and rhetoric to the process of communicating purposefully (Joseph, 2002). Thus, language was linked to social and cognitive processes. In the late 1970s, there was a strong incorporation of logic in the formation of linguistic concepts and theories. Chomsky's book *Cartesian linguistics: A chapter in the history of rationalist thought* (1966) highlights the link between linguistic theory, mental process and rationalism. The following two examples illustrate how logic and linguistics work:

Text 1
- There is a dog in the room. (A is in B)
- The room is in the building. (B is in C)
- Therefore there is a dog in the building. (A is in C)

Text 2
- There is a smell in the room.
- The room is in the building.
- Therefore there is a smell in the building.

Text 3
- There is a pain in my head.
- My head is in my hat.
- Therefore there is a pain in my hat.

One would say that text 1 is logical, text 2 is possibly logical and text 3 is illogical. The judgement of linguistic texts in terms of logic is greatly influenced by the semantic property of the lexical items. In text 1, the nouns "dog, room, and building" are physical objects whereas in text 3 the nouns "pain, head, and hat" belong to three different semantic categories. "Pain" is about feeling; "head" is body part, and "hat" is a physical object. Thus, logical judgment depends on the choice of lexical items in a text.

In language and literacy education, linguistic misconception can be caused by inappropriate application of logic on linguistic structure. In English for example, the morpheme "s" is used to mark plural such as one book, two books, a dog and many dogs. Plural marking in English is therefore seen as a logical manifestation of English grammar. However, on this basis one should not conclude that English is more logical than languages which do not apply this logic in plural marking. In Vietnamese, it is "quite logical" to say "one book" and "two book", as Vietnamese speakers would argue that "two book" is linguistically logical as the word "two" indicates "more than one". It is linguistically redundant to add the plural marker "s" to the word "book". This is true with the English word "sheep" which can be a singular noun or a plural noun. It could be said that to make a judgment as to whether something is "logical" is not necessarily a judgment based on theoretical absolutes, and the arbitrary nature of language cannot be explained in terms of logic. The following example illustrates this point.

Text 4
- You are rich, aren't you?
- She is rich, isn't she?
- They are rich, aren't they?

In English it first appears that tag questions are very "logical" as it shows a match between positive in the first component and negative in the second component of the tag questions. However, logic does not always work in grammar as there are other linguistic factors involved. For example, the tag question "I am rich, aren't I" is grammatically correct, whereas "I am rich, amn't I" is not.

LINGUISTIC RULES: MYSTERY AND MISCONCEPTION

When teachers talk about grammar, they tend to talk about rules which show what is wrong and right. Traditionally linguistic rules are greatly valued in language and literacy education. Violation of linguistic rules results in language errors. For example:

Text 5:
- John sing well.
- Tim walked slow.

The first sentence is incorrect as it violates the rule about subject and verb agreement in English. In traditional grammar, if the subject is singular, the verb should be marked with "s". The second sentence is incorrect as an adverb (i.e., slowly) should be used instead of an adjective. In literacy education, there is a tendency to teach learners grammatical rules so that errors can be avoided. Thus, literacy ability is often evaluated in terms of "adherence to grammatical rules" in writing. However it is important to ask the question: Where do linguistic rules come from? Answering this question can shed some light on the way in which literacy is taught.

Linguistic rules come from a variety of sources. Traditional grammar is a primary source which has long provided teachers and students with ideas and practices of English grammar. Many grammatical concepts are derived from traditional grammar such as noun, subject, predicate and subjective mood. Traditional grammar in English stems from the privileging of Latin as a "model language" upon which the rules of English are based. The utilisation of Latin grammatical constructions as a standard for English grammar ignores the utility of the grammatical rules. In this instance, prescriptivism was given a free reign and as a consequence English is studded with "rules" that are not easily contextualised or understood as their origin is Latin. Students are taught grammar and its rules in schools with the hope that this helps them to read and write correctly. However, teachers need to be careful in accepting the value of teaching traditional grammatical rules without due consideration of their hegemony and some misconceptions. The teaching of grammar as a component of language and literacy education is a contested practice for teachers as they negotiate both traditional grammar and the newer grammars. The emergence of functional approaches to grammar teaching drew upon the work of linguists in the 1960s and 1970s and provides teachers with a powerful source for grammar teaching.

In linguistics, rules are often presented in the description of language as a system. Chomsky (1968) argues that rule-governed behaviour, not learning habit, is essential in language use and language learning. According to Chomsky, conditioning and reinforcement are too limited and weak to explain how native speakers can master their mother-tongues so quickly and without conscious effort. When they are exposed to language in early childhood, native speakers internalise linguistic rules in developing their grammar. This is what linguists refer to as "implicit knowledge" of grammar.

The ways in which linguistic rules are examined and described vary, depending on linguists' theories of grammar. Structural linguistics examines rules in terms of overt structure of a sentence. For example:

Text 6:
- Tom is one of the students who *hates* animals.
- Tom is one of the students who *hate* animals.

According to structural linguistics, these two sentences share the same structure. The judgment of grammatical correctness (i.e., the choice of hates or hate) depends on whether the emphasis is placed on the word "one" or the word "students".

Chomsky's early model of transformational grammar pays great attention to the rules which transform a deep structure into a surface structure. Other theories of grammar tend to discuss linguistic rules in terms of their theoretical model of language.

One of the biggest challenges to language and literacy education concerns the two types of rules: descriptive rules and prescriptive rules. The former is what linguists attempt to describe scientifically (and therefore objectively) about a language structure. The latter is often found in many teachers' judgment of linguistic correctness which is based on traditional grammar and social norms.

Text 7:
- *Whom* did you visit yesterday?
- *Who* did you visit yesterday?

According to traditional grammar, the first sentence is correct as "whom" is the object of the verb visit, whereas the second sentence is incorrect as "who" should be used only when it is the subject of a verb as in the sentence "who hit you yesterday?"That is why we must write "To *whom* it may concern", but not "To *who* it may concern". It is interesting to observe that in the current social context of communication, the pronoun "who" tends to be used interchangeably with "whom", even in the spoken language of educated people. A challenge for educators is to ensure that their language and literacy teaching is responsive to the way in which language changes through usage due to its dynamic nature. In exploring issues of correctness in relation to grammatical rules, the English language is continually in a state of flux as new lexical items and grammatical constructions emerge and evolve through the evolution of English as it is used in everyday situations.

The discussion on linguistic rules leads to the current interest in language and literacy education on two kinds of grammar: descriptive grammar and prescriptive grammar. The former describes what a language system *is* and the latter prescribes what it *should* be. According to the latter, one should avoid making the following "errors":

- using a split infinitive:
  These teachers want *to firmly reinforce* the rule.

- Ending a sentence with a preposition:
  Whom did you dance *with*?

- Using "can" for "may":
  Can I sit next to you?

- Using double negative:

   I *don't* eat *nothing*.

- Using question form as an imbedded clause:

   I want to know *who are you.*

It is not easy to convince traditional grammar advocates that sentences such as "I don't eat nothing" and "who do you want to eat with" are grammatically correct. For them, it is not the way educated people use in speaking and writing. Implicit in this judgment is that there is a distinction between standard English and non-standard English and the former is often used as the basis for judging linguistic correctness. This view of linguistic correctness reflects the essence of prescriptive grammar; whereas for linguists, linguistic variation is a common phenomenon in all human languages. Not one variety of speech, whether it is a dialect or a sociolect, is more correct than another as they all present "linguistic realities" in a speech community. However it is worth noting that linguists do not deny that a variety of speech can be more socially prestigious and valued than others. A challenge for language and literacy educators is to ensure that students' social identity is not rejected due to their linguistic background which is, in some way, different to the traditionally perceived "standard English". Secondly, students should be introduced to a variety of ways in which meaning is conveyed in socially appropriate linguistic forms which are favoured in certain social contexts. In other words, their linguistic repertoire should be extended beyond their own linguistic background to broaden their social discourse.

LINGUISTIC ERRORS: MYSTERY AND MISCONCEPTION

In an educational context, errors are normally used to evaluate students' language competence. The most commonly used evaluation tool is a language test and test results are often described in terms of language errors. The less errors students make in a test, the more advanced their achievements. Metaphorically, errors are symbols of linguistic weakness, or worse a linguistic sickness which needs to be cured. On the contrary, from the psycholinguistic perspective, language errors are informative windows on the mental process. They provide insights into learners' active learning in terms of learning behaviour, learning strategies, and learning conditions.

Goodman (1973) treats reading errors as miscues. In his view, errors are important for teachers to understand the reading process. Errors are not arbitrarily made by readers in reading. The following examples indicate the insights gained from examining language errors.

- *Text*: "Jane and her mother walked on a busy road leading to the city centre. Jane walked very quickly but her mother was rather slow".
- *Reader*: "Jane and her mother walked on a busy *street* leading to the city centre. Jane walked very quickly *and* her mother was rather slow".

The words in italics are the reading errors made by the reader. The errors indicate the following features about the reader's reading process:

- The errors do not interfere with the primary meaning of the text.
- Reading is a meaning making process.
- The reader was involved in creative construction, not reading word by word.
- This may be the way competent readers normally do in silent reading.

According to Clark (2002), by listening to children's self-corrections, questions, and language play, teachers realise the extent of their knowledge of language structure. Those linguistic constructions created by language learners provide some interesting and useful insights about their learning. Their active, creative invention of language is amazing and unique as it reflects the learner's cognitive capacities. Lindfors (1991) introduces the concept "creative construction" to characterise this feature of language learning in children. Creative construction occurs both in first and second language learning. Second language learners can be very creative in developing new words in the second language and their creative constructions still conform to the linguistic system of the second language. It is an important aspect of their interlanguage. For instance, in one classroom a student created words "back attack" and "enjoyful" in her writing. In the teacher's comment, these words do not exist in English; therefore they are errors which must be avoided. As a matter of fact, the creation of these "unwanted" words follows consistently English morphology in which the words of the same construction "heart attack" and "respectful" function. If English allows the dichotomy "respectable" and "respectful", it is acceptable to create the dichotomy "enjoyable" and "enjoyful". Poets, novelists, computer scientists and media writers are very good at this way of word formation and their creative construction is often admired, not condemned.

PHONICS AND PHONETICS REVISITED

Phonics has recently re-emerged in current literacy education debates. Advocates of phonics argue that phonics should be vigorously and creatively taught in early literacy education as it helps learners to decode words in a text. However, occasionally we notice the terms "phonics" and "phonetics" are used interchangeably and this could create some confusion to teachers and learners. Though there is a close relationship between phonics and phonetics, their distinction should be made: phonics is about phoneme and grapheme relationship and phonetics is a branch of linguistics.

Phonetics consists of three sub-branches: articulatory phonetics, auditory phonetics and acoustic phonetics. Articulatory phonetics and auditory phonetics are relevant to phonics as the former describes how speech sounds are produced or articulated and auditory phonetics describes how speech sounds are perceived by the ears and the brain.

Phonics is based on the relationship between graphemes and phonemes (commonly known as speech sounds). Grapheme is the representation of phonemes. Below are examples of correspondence between phonemes and graphemes.

Phoneme	Grapheme	Word
/f/	f, ph	fan, phone
/i:/	ee, ea	meet, cheat

/k/   c, k, ch   cat, key, scheme

It is important to note the difference between grapheme and letter. A grapheme may include a single letter or a combination of letters. It would be an ideal if the number of speech sounds and the numbers of letters are the same in English. In this case, the simplest way of representing speech sounds is to assign each letter to match each speech sound. This is a perfect match. However, as English has more speech sounds (phonemes) than the letters of the alphabet, a simple way to handle this problem is to create a grapheme by combining letters such as "th" (as in "thank") and "ie" (as in "lie").

The divisive debates of the 1970s and 1980s regarding the degree to which phonics was utilised in the literacy program have been replaced by an acknowledgement that phonics teaching plays a significant, if not a unitary, role in a balanced literacy program. The challenge for literacy teachers is to have a comprehensive understanding of phonics, not just as an approach to teaching reading and spelling but also as a window into learners' phonological awareness.

CONCLUSION

Language is replete with mystery and this chapter has touched on some aspects of linguistic mystery. In our native language, we tend to take language for granted and feel that in the process of social enculturation we naturally acquire language and develop some awareness of what language is and what language can do for us. Our awakening occurs when we attempt to learn a different language in adulthood and find out the learning journey is full of challenges or when we try with little success to teach someone who suffers sever linguistic disability due to brain damage or neurological disorders. Facing those challenges, we discover that language is a well of mysteries and start to ask ourselves how much do we really know about our mother tongue. Linguists over the years have provided fascinating insights about language which have significant implications and applications in vastly growing areas such as artificial intelligence, communications disorders and language and literacy education. The more deeply linguists explore human language, the more mysteries emerge. For teachers, insights about language and its mystery are not only inspiring to an intellectually curious mind; they are also helpful in examining our linguistic knowledge and challenging our language prejudice.

REFERENCES

Chomsky, Noam (1966). *Cartesian linguistics: A chapter in the history of rationalist thought.* New York: Harper & Row.
Chomsky, Noam (1968). *Language and mind.* New York: Harcourt Brace Jovanovich.
Clark, B. (2002). First- and second-language acquisition in early childhood. The clearinghouse on early education and parenting (CEEP) [Electronic article]. In D. Rothenberg (Ed), *Issues in early childhood education: Curriculum, teacher education, & dissemination of information.* Retrieved April 22, 2010 from *http://ceep.crc. iuc.edu/pubs/katzsym/clark-b.html.*

Curtiss, S., Fromkin, V., Krashen, S., Rigler, D., & Rigler, M. (1974). The linguistic development of Genie. *Language, 50*, 528-554.

Goodman, K. (1973). Miscues: "Windows on the reading process." In F. Gollasch (Ed.) *Language and literacy: The Selected Writings of Kenneth Goodman, Vol. I* (pp. 93–102). Boston: Routledge & Kegan Paul.

Joseph, M. (2002) *The trivium: The liberal arts of logic, grammar, and rhetoric.* Philadelphia: Paul Dry Books Inc.

Lindfors, J. W. (1991). *Children's language and learning* (2nd Ed.). Boston: Allyn and Bacon.

In: Language and Literacy Education in a Challenging World   ISBN: 978-1-61761-198-8
Editors: T. Lê, Q. Lê, and M. Short

Chapter 2

WAR AND PEACE IN LANGUAGE AND LITERACY DISCOURSE

Thao Lê, Quynh Lê and Megan Short

ABSTRACT

The world is seen as a global village in which all the villagers are expected to co-exist peacefully. In reality, the world is also a place where various forces compete for their power, influence and control. The same phenomenon has repeatedly occurred in language and literacy education. This chapter examines different discourses of the literacy discourse where theorists, researchers, teachers, parents and influential others have witnessed waves of war and peace at different levels and contexts.

Key words: accountability, discourse, literacy, phonics, test.

INTRODUCTION

For decades we have witnessed the arrival and departure of many theoretical views, perspectives and approaches in literacy education. Human civilisation in general and education in particular have gained profoundly from the flowering of various ways of making sense of the human world with its intricate complexities and mysteries. However, we have not only witnessed some "battles" among different perspectives on the theoretical front, but also the spill-over in the pedagogical discourse where advocates of one perspective attempt to win over the others who have different views to teaching or have not fully made up their minds about which fence to sit on. While in the theoretical discourse metaphorically theorists "fight" with their power of logical reasoning, communicative expression, and team solidarity, in the pedagogical discourse teachers have to confront different kind of challenges, particularly in terms of literacy politics, community pressure, and personal beliefs.

DISCOURSE AT THE MACRO-LEVEL

Metaphorically, the discourse of literacy education can be seen as calm and inspiring as a beautiful lake in spring where ideas and practices dance constructively together to enhance the lives of school children for a promising future. On the contrary, it can also be seen as a battlefield full of theorists, practitioners, parents and politicians who fight for empowerment, recognition, supremacy and dominance over their opponents. The history of literacy education is one of innovation, contestation and continual shifts in approach and method. The "theory/practice" nexus is, in part, a driver of change in literacy education as theorists and practitioners engage in a discourse that involves the testing of theory in practice within specific social and cultural contexts.

Theorists often use research evidence to back up their claims or counter-claims. It is hard for them to convince teachers, parents and policy makers if they advocate a theory which has no evidence-based research to back them up. Apart from research evidence, the strength of their arguments for or against a theoretical or practical perspective depends a great deal on whom they choose as prominent figures or "leaders" who have established their powerful names in the academic discourse.

Basically there are three levels of influence from a hierarchical pathway. At the top level, we have witnessed with great interest the academic "empires" in education in general and literacy education in particular, which have been generated by influential leaders over the decades, such as B.F Skinner, Noam Chomsky, Michael Halliday, Lev Vygotsky and Jerome Bruner. At the macro-level, their influences tend to be broad and interdisciplinary.

Those figures mentioned above share some common interest in human nature and human learning. Their views can be in total opposition or complementary. Skinner (1957) is well-known for his behaviourist view against innate rules by which organisms learn. On the opposite side of the battle Chomsky (1968) with his mentalist view argues that the mind possesses innately a set of procedures or internally represented processing rules which are deployed in learning. Universal grammar is inherent in the mind of all newborn babies and with such a device children acquire language naturally without great effort and involvement of any designed instruction. Universal grammar is the basis of all human languages. Bruner (1983), with a background in psychology, sees learning as an active process as learners construct new ideas or concepts based upon their background knowledge and personal experience. Thus in learning, learners select and transform information, construct hypotheses, and make decisions, relying on a cognitive structure such as schema and mental models. In language learning, while Chomsky (1968) argues that all children are endowed with Language Acquisition Device (LAD) as a basis on which language acquisition naturally takes place, Bruner (1983) argues that LAD desperately needs LASS (Language Acquisition Support System) as language learning depends heavily on the meaningful and purposeful interaction that caretakers and others close to the child provide. The case of Genie is one of the most extreme cases of social isolation. She was kept in cruel isolation in a Los Angeles suburb till she was discovered at the age of thirteen. Due to the absence of LASS, her language development was severely affected. One can notice some influence of Vygotsky on Bruner's theoretical views on education in general and language learning in particular (Bruner, 1990). According to Vygotsky (1978), social interaction plays a fundamental role in cognitive development which depends on the zone of proximal development (ZPD) which signals a level of development attained when children engage in social behavior.

The great figures discussed above have made a great impact on an interdisciplinary discourse. However specialisation has also taken place depending on the field in which their theories are situated and the influence they have made. Halliday's linguistic theory has influenced language and literacy education for over five decades, particularly in England where his influences started to take place and in Australia where he was appointed the first chair of linguistics at the University of Sydney in the early 1970s (Halliday, 1985). His theory of functional grammar is an integral part of systemic functional linguistics, which has been firmly established as an alternative to other linguistic models. Halliday does not view language as a system of linguistic rules but sees it primarily as a resource for language users. In Halliday's perspective, what language is should be viewed on the basis of what language does. Thus language cannot be divorced from its social and cultural contexts. His influence on literacy education is noticeable in areas such as genre-based curriculum, text analysis, grammar teaching, discourse analysis, and critical discourse analysis. The discourses of literacy education are informed by a range of diverse theoretical explanations for language acquisition, language development and literacy pedagogy. Rather than viewing the contested nature of language and literacy education as an impediment to effective literacy pedagogy, one can argue that the rigorous interchange between theoretical perspectives and practitioner experiences lends immediacy and relevance to the field of language and literacy education.

DISCOURSE OF SPECIFIC INFLUENCE

At a different level we have witnessed the influence of authors who have direct impacts on specific literacy education practices in certain educational discourses, such as Krashen (1987) with his view on second language learning, Frank Smith (2004) with a focus on psycholinguistic approach, Goodman (1973) with an emphasis on the mental process of reading and miscue analysis, Graves (1994) with his well-known process writing approach, Wells (1986) with an emphasis on the role of quality interaction in learning, Luke and Freebody (1990), strong advocates of critical literacy, and Christie and Martin (1997) with an emphasis on the use of Functional Grammar in understanding and analysing learners' texts. The following discussion outlines some of the characteristics of their influences on language and literacy practices.

The emergence and strong influence of the process writing approach and psycholinguistics in literacy education in the 1970's marked a paradigm shift from the traditional teacher-centred curriculum to learner-centred curriculum. From the theoretical perspective, we could attribute the influence of theorists such as Vygotsky, Chomsky and Bruner to this paradigm shift in language and literacy. Learners are no longer seen as a sponge to receive knowledge given by teachers in a transmission model of learning. Learners are active participants in a learning discourse. The shift of focus moves from teaching to learning. Smith (2004) views reading as a psycholinguistic process in which the mind tells the eyes what to read. Accuracy in reading should be viewed differently from fluency in reading. Readers should be encouraged to bring their knowledge and life experience to the task of reading as reading is a meaning making process. Graphophonic cues are important, particularly in the early stage of reading development. However, linguistic and pragmatic cues also facilitate the meaning-making process in reading. In the area of writing development, the process writing approach attracted the attention of teachers as it emphasises the power of text authorship and the intended receivers. Children should be encouraged to write to make sense of their world and to share it with a specific audience which holds meaning for them, rather than write for the teacher.

While it is logical to pay attention to the child as an active participant in the reading and writing process, it is important to realise that the child is a social being in a social discourse. Though teachers should be aware of the mental process of the learners in reading and writing, the social and cultural context should be taken into account as it could exert great influence on literacy practice. It first appears that the genre-based curriculum approach tends to be in conflict with critical literacy as the former insists on deliberately teaching children genres as exposing them to genres is not enough. As genre is staged and goal–directed, children should be taught the generic structure of different genres which empower them to function adequately in society in their reception and replication of a range of different texts. On the other hand, critical literacy encourages learners not to take texts for granted as texts are often loaded with ideologically biased agendas. It first appears that genre and critical literacy are two opposite perspectives as genre advocates want children to learn how to write well in a variety of genres, whereas critical literacy encourages learners to be critical in reading a text; however these two literacy perspectives are complementary in the sense that they provide learners with empowering concepts and tools to create and analyse texts. Genre could be used as a tool to deconstruct texts and it is also useful for examining intertextuality.

DISCOURSE OF LITERACY WAR

Metaphorically language and literacy education can be seen as a war zone in which different battles have been waged between different troops who represent literacy researchers and theorists of different theoretical perspectives, policy makers, politicians and parents of school children. The fierce battles tend to take place in the media where strong language was used to ridicule and attack the opponents.

In 1955, Rudolf Flesch published a book entitled *Why Johnny Can't Read* and blamed the crisis in teaching reading on the "look-say approach". It was one of the bestselling books in literacy education at the time. A week after the publication of his book, the press started to wage war on the literacy debate.

> When Bestselling Author Rudolf Flesch (The Art of Plain Talk) offered to give a friend's twelve-year-old son some "remedial reading," Flesch discovered that the boy was not slow or maladjusted; he had merely been "exposed to an ordinary American school." Author Flesch decided to investigate how reading is taught in the U.S. Last week he published his findings in a 222–page book, *"Why Johnny Can't Read*—and *"What You Can Do About It"*, that will shock many a U.S. parent and educator. (Time, Monday, March 14, 1955)

The battle at that time was between phonics and look-say advocates. Phonics advocates formal teaching of phonics while the so-called "look-say approach" focuses on getting familiar with common words through their shapes and meaning. A decade later, another battle occurred between phonics and the Whole Language perspectives. In 1981, Flesch published a sequel to his book entitled *"Why Johnny Still Can't Read — A New Look at the Scandal of*

Our Schools," which blamed the literacy scandal on the negligence of teaching phonics in schools at the time Whole Language dominated the literacy discourse. While phonics advocates still strongly argue in favour of teaching the relationship between sounds and graphemes, Whole Language does not deny the use of phonics in teaching reading. As the name indicates, it holds the view that the reading process includes a number of linguistic strategies and various cues in order to make sense of the text.

Recently, the literacy war has again surfaced, particularly in the media where "children's literacy performance" is an attractive agenda for public attention. In Australia, the government advocates a return to the basics which include teaching grammar and phonics, and testing of children nationally. The media did not lose the opportunity to join the battle.

> Whether it's a misplaced apostrophe in a student's essay, or an exam question inviting a feminist interpretation of Othello, the teaching of reading and writing is the subject of fierce debates in the media. The debates have reached such intensity in recent years that public confidence in literacy teachers has been undermined and many believe we have a literacy crisis in our schools. (Snyder, The Age, 2008)

In a popular Sydney newspaper in 2005, a heading appeared "Phonics has a phoney role in the literacy wars". The writer opposed the view that phonics is important in reading. She pointed out that "Making the right sounds is phonics, but phonics is not reading. Reading is making sense from the page, not sounds... we do most of our reading in silence: the meaning is on the page, not in the sound. That's why we can read and understand the following, whereas sounding it out would be chaotic and meaningless".

> Aoccdrnig to rscheearch at an Elingsh uinervtisy, it deosn't mttaer in waht oredr the ltteers in a wrod are, the olny iprmoetnt tihng is that the frist and lsat ltteers are in the rghit pclae: you can raed it wouthit a porbelm bcuseae we don't raed ervey lteter but the word as a wlohe.

> So, hey, waht does this say abuot the improtnace of phnoics in raeidng? Prorbalby that phonics ins't very imoptrnat at all. How apcoltapyic is that, in the cuerrnt licetary wars?

It is true that we can read the above text without much effort even though the text includes many words with scrambled letters which do not exist in English. Why can we "read" the text so comfortably? The writer wants to point out that it is because we read for meaning. It is widely accepted that comprehension is the most essential factor of reading. However the given example to show that phonics is "not reading" does have its problem. Firstly, only fluent readers can read that word-scrambled text because they have some knowledge of phonics, which helps them to unscramble the words, for example, the words *"rscheearch", "uinervtisy", "porbelm"* are identified respectively as "research", "university", "problem" even if they are placed in isolation, not in a sentence where semantic and syntactic cues are present. Secondly, beginning readers or weak readers may find it very difficult to read that text because they do not have the phonics knowledge and word knowledge to decode the text (which then interferes with their access to semantic and syntactic implicit knowledge).

In a popular Melbourne newspaper, *The Age* April 14, 2008, a catchy headline "Literacy wars cause collateral damage" reminds readers of the literacy war which has refused to go away. The paper interpreted the wars as a "product of competing views and beliefs about society – what it is, what it has been and what it should become". Interestingly 2008 was the time Ilana Snyder of Monash University published her book entitled *"The Literacy War: Why teaching children to read and write is a battleground in Australia"*. According to Snyder (2008), the bitter disagreements, metaphorically referred to as the literacy war, have caused deep divisions educationally and politically.

One of the main literacy disputes is about the definition of literacy. Different views on how literacy is defined, therefore how it should be taught, draw different frontlines among opposing forces. For instance, the code-orientated views pay great attention to the close link between linguistic features of the written text, whereas critical literacy advocates view literacy in a broader social discourse which involves power, identity, ideology and social values. In other words, those who blame literacy failure due to lack of decoding skills in weak readers would advocate the return of phonics. There are those who think that children to function well in a literate society need to be deliberately taught a range of linguistic genres such as genres of description, argument, report and discussion. For those who look at literacy as discourse, it is important to provide children with ability and skills to critically analyse texts, to deconstruct texts in search of hidden agenda, ideological imposition, and silent voices. Thus, while the literacy war is ravaging on, the question of accountability deserves attention.

DISCOURSE OF LITERACY ACCOUNTABILITY

Bernstein (1990, p.180) introduced the concept "pedagogic device" (PD). According to him, this device provides the intrinsic grammar of pedagogic discourse through distributive rules, recontextualising rules, and rules of evaluation. According to Bernstein, these rules are themselves hierarchically related in the sense that the nature of the distributive rules regulates the recontextualising rules, which in turn regulate the rules of evaluation. These distributive rules regulate the fundamental relationships between power, social groups, forms of consciousness and practice, and their reproduction or production. He states that "we shall define pedagogic discourse as the rule which embeds a discourse of competence (skills of various kinds) into a discourse of social order in such a way that the latter always dominates the former" (Bernstein, 1990, p.183). In the context of literacy education, one can say that the pedagogic device operates both directly and indirectly.

> This framework is useful for locating individuals in terms of the three fields of literacy research, policy and practice that they occupy, understanding their position and place in these fields, and exploring their perspectives in terms of the fields they do and do not occupy. For Bernstein (1990), agencies and organizations constitute the fields of the pedagogic device. Agents of each field struggle for resources and control over the rules for constructing pedagogic practice. In so doing, they take up different positions, some dominating, others dominated; and what and whose agendas prevail represent ongoing concerns. (Harris et al 2007, p. 3)

An examination of language and literacy education discourses in many parts of the English speaking world has indicated mixed emotions among educators and researchers. There are some educators and researchers who are so inspired by powerful figures in a discipline that they commit their whole teaching practices or research to the influence and leadership of those leaders. They are members of a school or group with shared ideology and agenda, for example The New London Group, the language reform group and the Systemic Functional Linguistics Association. There are also research teams that focus on a particular theoretical theme or perspective in language and literacy education such as constructivism in educational multimedia, task-based learning and interaction, critical literacy, and genre curriculum. At the grass root level are practising teachers who are constantly facing challenges of coping with the real world of teaching, interfering politics and the competing theories which attempt to exert some influence on their teaching practice. It is hard or impossible to place language and literacy education in a value-free discourse, as education is socially constructed. Similarly it is naive to believe that language and literacy education is immune from politics. Any new language and literacy curriculum initiative has a shadow of politics looming behind it.

The current call to "return to the basics" in language and literacy education shows a strong indication of the interference of ideology and politics in literacy education. While leading theorists and academics do their best to present their views and implications on the basis of the insights derived from peers' theoretical scrutiny and research evidence to convince practitioners and the academic community, politics operates in a different way. Politicians take the role of advocacy for parents and children to demand "better" education. We often hear politicians citing "real evidence" such as "overwhelming complaints" or 'public outcry" from parents and the media. They use poor test results to demand "appropriate action" to fix the "obvious problems". They tend to shy away from examining whether testing or surveying is the most reliable way of knowing students' literacy abilities or whether there are other ways which can enhance students' literacy achievement, but which cannot be adequately captured by test results. The concept "standard" is often used as the primary indication of success or otherwise in language and literacy education and it provides a convenient basis for mounting the blaming game. While the use of literacy standard is helpful for some parents who actually need it, for others the danger is that "standard" is a slippery concept which can be biased toward a particular discourse, which in turns easily lead to disempowerment of those who have little or no political voice to be seriously taken into consideration.

Accountability designates our responsibility to someone or for some activity. For language and literacy teachers, accountability only makes sense when they have some freedom to make decisions on the best methods that they can teach without being overloaded with pressure to achieve the standard which is politically motivated and which in the worst situation is contrary to their beliefs and valuable teaching experience. Thus, it is important to develop shared accountability in language and literacy education so that individuals are not subject to being crucified due to lack of collaboration, miscommunication, and inconsistencies due to the political climate.

CONCLUSION

Language and literacy education can be metaphorically seen as a journey full of excitements as well as agonies. The excitements include the discovery of a wealth of insights which help us to understand and appreciate more the various features and aspects of language and literacy, particularly the intricate complexity and interconnectedness of different theoretical perspectives and their impacts on teaching practices. It reinforces the view that the loss of such valuable insights could lead to damaging consequences; particularly when the victims are our students who entrust us with their childhood education. The literacy journey is also dotted with agonies as teachers are expected by many stakeholders to do their best for the children while there are constant challenges. For those who treasure the journey, it is an empowering experience, not only for the children they teach but also for themselves as teachers.

REFERENCES

Berstein, B. (1990). *The structure of pedagogic discourse*. London: Routledge.

Bruner, J. (1983). *Child's talk: Learning to use language*. New York: Norton.

Bruner, J. (1990). *Acts of meaning*. Cambridge, MA: Harvard University Press.

Chomsky, N. (1968). *Language and mind*. New York: Harcourt Brace Jovanovich

Flesch, R. (1955). *Why Johnny can't read and what you can do about it*. New York: Harper and Row.

Christie, F. (2002). *Classroom discourse analysis – A functional perspective*. London: Continuum Press.

Christie, F., & Martin, J. (1997). *Genre and institutions: Social processes in the workplace and school*. London: Continuum Press.

Flesch, R. (1981). Why Johnny still can't read: A new look at the scandal of our schools. New York: Harper & Row

Freebody, P., & Luke, A. (1990). Literacies programs: Debates and demands in cultural context. *Prospect: Australian Journal of TESOL, 5*(3), 7–16.

Goodman, K. (1973). Miscues: "Windows on the reading process." In F. Gollasch (Ed.) *Language and literacy: The selected writings of Kenneth Goodman* (pp. 93–102). Vol. I. Boston: Routledge & Kegan Paul.

Graves, Donal (1994). *A fresh look at writing*. Portsmouth: Heinemann.

Halliday, M.A.K (1985). *Introduction to functional grammar*. London: Edward Arnold.

Harris, P., McKenzie, B., Chen, H., Kervin, L., & Fitzsimmons, P. (2007). *Investigating relationships between literacy research, policy, and practice: A critical review of related literature*. ALEA/AATE Annual Conference.

Krashen, Stephen D. (1987). *Principles and practice in second language acquisition*. New York: Prentice-Hall International.

Skinner, B.F. (1957). *Verbal learning*. New York: Appleton-Century-Crofts.

Skinner, B.F. (1971). *Beyond freedom and dignity*. New York: Knopf.

Smith, F. (2004). *Understanding reading: A psycholinguistic analysis to reading and learning*. New Jersey: Taylor and Francis.

Snyder, I. (2008). *The literacy war: Why teaching children to read and write is a battleground in Australia*. Sydney: Unwin & Unwin

Snyder, I. (2008). *Literacy wars cause collateral damage*. The Age 14 April. pp. 1-2.

Time Inc. (Mar 14, 1955). *Education: Why Johnny can't read?* Retrieved April 25, 2010 from *http:// www.time.com/time/magazine/article/0,9171,807107,00.html#ixzz0mBnidILI*

Vygotsky, L.S. (1978). *Mind and society: The development of higher mental processes*. Cambridge, MA: Harvard University Press.

Wells, G. (1986). *The meaning makers: Children learning language and using language to learn*. Portsmouth: Heinemann Educational Books.

In: Language and Literacy Education in a Challenging World   ISBN: 978-1-61761-198-8
Editors: T. Lê, Q. Lê, and M. Short   © 2010 Nova Science Publishers, Inc.

Chapter 3

LINGUISTIC COMPLEXITY AND ITS RELATION TO LANGUAGE AND LITERACY EDUCATION

Thao Lê, Yun Yue and Quynh Lê

ABSTRACT

The notion 'complexity' is inherent in science and mathematics. Children are expected to progress from simple concepts to complex ones and these concepts are often organized in a hierarchical structure. However, it is not so in literacy education as the notion "linguistic complexity" has posed some challenges not only to teachers but also linguists. Intuitively teachers can comfortably identify written texts on the basis of linguistic complexity but there are no clearly defined criteria to guide them so that they can use to monitor children's reading and writing development. This chapter examines some aspects of linguistic complexity and attempts to provide some insights into literacy teaching.

Keywords: complexity, density, grammar, nominalisation, T-Unit.

INTRODUCTION

Linguistic complexity is central in linguistic theories as linguists attempt to describe the complexity of language and to examine how their theoretical models can adequately capture the way in which language works. The insights about linguistic complexity have contributed to new developments in other related research areas such as communication disorders, machine translation, and natural language processing. In the field of language and literacy education, the contribution of linguistics has become an established tradition. The obvious reason is that language permeates almost every aspect of teaching and learning and any insights about the complex nature of language is of great interest to literacy educators. This chapter focuses on syntactic complexity in terms of the following concepts: T-Unit, lexical density, sentence combination, and nominalisation. These concepts have been widely researched in language and literacy education. The main challenge for teachers is how to translate theoretical insights into pedagogical practice.

T-UNIT

Hunt (1965) is the researcher who introduced the term T-unit. It stands for "terminable unit". It is traditionally used to measure children' writing in terms of quantitative maturity. For him, the word "maturity" is intended to designate nothing more than "the observed characteristic of writers in older grades. It has nothing to do with whether older students write better in any general stylistic sense" (Hunt p. 21). For him, T-unit is a useful tool for measuring syntactic maturity in children.

A T-unit includes a (main) clause with or without subordinate clauses. For example,

– Students go home early {**main clause**}, because they must catch a bus on time (**subordinate clause**}.

– When the sun rises {**subordinate clause**}, my mother gets up to prepare breakfast {**main clause**}.

– My teachers invited only those students {**main clause**}, who did well last year {**subordinate clause**}

– We want the car {**main clause**}, which was sold last year to a dancer (**subordinate clause 1**} who did not have a driving licence {**subordinate clause 2**}.

The following texts are broken down into T-units. The symbol # marks the end of each T-unit. By counting the T-units in the texts, Hunt can make some assumptions about writing maturity.

– My dog is Milo. # One day my mother and father walked along a street in town and suddenly saw a pet shop. # They intended to have a look at some animals in a shop. # However, when they entered the pet shop, they could not resist touching a small puppy. # They did not realise that puppies do have magic. # Finally, they walked out with a dog in their hands. #
This text has 68 words, 6 T-units marked with #, average T-unit =11.3 words).

– Learners are tested on their acquisition of syntactic complexity which determines the order of syntactic development from simple sentences to complex ones.#
This text has 22 words, 1 T-Unit.

– Traditional studies in linguistics tend to focus on sentence structure, particularly on written texts. # Modern linguistics has expanded its scope with an emphasis on authentic texts and social situations. # The two areas of modern linguistics which have attracted attention of researchers in linguistics and other disciplines, are genre studies and conversational analysis. # Conversation analysis and genre analysis provide great insights into communicative interaction, particularly on the link between language structure and social meaning. #
This text has 73 words, 4 T-units, average T-unit=18.2 words.

A T-Unit is like a minimal sentence. However, Hunts avoids the use of the word "sentence" as it already has so many different meanings that could cause misunderstanding. He states:

> The word 'sentence' has trouble enough already. A fresh neutral sounding name would be better. These units might be minimal as to length, and each would be grammatically capable of being terminated with a capital letter and a period. (Hunt, 1965, p. 21)

Like any concepts introduced for measuring linguistic complexity, Hunts' T-Unit has received positive and negative feedback. The positive feedback is that it gives teachers and researchers a way to examine children' writing maturity. Teachers often make intuitively some judgement about children's writing in terms of sentence structure. Thus T-Unit is not an unfamiliar concept which is beyond teachers' linguistic knowledge.

> T-unit analysis has been widely applied to measure the overall syntactic complexity of speech and writing samples. It has been used both in cross-sectional descriptive studies and in experimental studies to measure the effect of sentence-combining as a curricular activity designed to enhance normal developmental trends in syntactic maturity. The claim that mean T-unit length is a valid measure of overall syntactic complexity is well supported. (Gaies, 1980, p. 75)

A common criticism of the use of T-unit for measuring sentence complexity is that it can be unreliable as children may not use punctuation and expressions well and researchers have to use their own judgement to make it "fit in" with their T-unit analysis. However it is important to realise that any measurement does not fully capture linguistic complexity; thus a combination of different tools and concepts such as lexical density, nominalisation, and theme analysis should be used to provide useful insights into the nature of text with its multi-dimensional complexity.

LEXICAL DENSITY

Ure's research (1971) on lexical density was based on 30 written and 34 spoken texts in English by native speakers. Lexical density was measured the total number of words with lexical properties divided by the total number of orthographic words in any given text. In a later article, Ure and Ellis (1977, p. 207) provide a more detailed definition, which is "the proportion of words carrying lexical values (members of open-ended sets) to the words with grammatical values (items representing terms in closed sets). In later development of this concept, Halliday and Martin (1993) made the following revision of lexical desnisty:

> This is a measure of the density of information in any passage of text, according to how tightly the lexical items (content words) have been packed into the grammatical structure. It can be measured, in English, as the number of lexical words per clause. (p. 76)

Halliday's version of lexical density puts more emphasis on the meaning of the tool, as it measures the density of information in a text, while Ure's definition shows more concerns about the categorization of lexical words and grammatical words. The differentiation between lexical and grammatical items became an important issue discussed in research dealing with lexical density. Traditionally, nouns, verbs, adjectives and adverbs are the four word classes belonging to lexical item category because they have independent meaning and may be meaningful in isolation, and there are possibilities to add new members of the category. Grammatical items is a restricted category including auxiliary verbs, modals, pronouns, prepositions, determiners and conjunctions. The characteristic of this closed category is that there is no possibility to add new members. They do not have independent lexical meaning and generally serve the grammatical construction of sentence (Jackson & Amvela, 2000; Palmer, 1976). Here are examples of content (or lexical) words and function (or grammatical) word.

- I **know** that they did not **like** my **house**. (3 content words, 6 function words)

- **Effective communicative interaction requires profound linguistic competence** and **intercultural awareness**. (9 content words, 1 function word).

It should be noted that the boundary between lexical and grammatical items is not entirely clear for analysis. For example, the status of the preposition or particle element in phrasal verbs is sometimes difficult to define. Let us look at a phrase verb *take over*, Ure (1971) and Stubbs (1986) count them as two words, one lexical word *take* and one grammatical *over*. Halliday (1985, p. 63) considers the phrasal verb as one lexical item; in other word, he considers a phrasal verb as one semantic unit. According to this perspective, an idiom like *take a bath* would be regarded as one lexical item as well.

Following a categorization devised by Halliday (1985) and later refined by O'Loughlin (1995), nouns, lexical verbs, and adjectives and adverbs of time, place and manner belong to lexical words; grammatical items include verbs *be* and *have*, auxiliaries, determiner, numerals, negative and interrogative adverbs, prepositions, conjunctions, discourse markers, interjections. According to Halliday (2004, p. 655), to measure lexical density, simply divide the number of lexical items by the number of ranking clauses. Instead of using the word "sentence" as a unit for counting lexical density, Halliday uses "clause complex" instead. Halliday argues that high lexical density is typical of formal written text as the expression is more planned. He states:

> In any piece of discourse, there is obviously a great deal of variation in the lexical density from one clause to the next. But there are also some general tendencies. In informal spoken language the lexical density tends to be low: about two lexical words per clause is quite typical. When the language is more planned and more formal, the lexical density is higher; and since writing is usually more planned than speech, written language tends to be somewhat denser than spoken language, often having around four to six lexical words per clause. But in scientific writing the lexical density may go considerably higher. (Halliday, 1993, p.76)

It is interesting to note that there are speakers who "speak like a book" in a formal context as their speech tends to be loaded with high lexical density and other complex syntactic features such as nominalisation and grammatical metaphor. This tends to occur predominantly with those who work in a special field which require public speaking on issues relating to their expertise such as academics, journalists, and scientists.

Halliday also mentions "lexical words" instead of "words", which normally means orthographic words. The following examples show the difference between orthographic words and lexical words:

- Children **look after** their pets.

- John **made up** his mind about not going to school.

Lexical words (e.g., look after, make up) may have more than one orthographic words as they represent a complete meaning of a lexical unit. On this basis, it is logical to treat the following chunks of words as individual lexical units even they are made up of a number of words: in fact, on the one hand, on the other hand.

The division between lexical word and grammatical word (or items in Halliday's use) is important for understanding lexical density. However not every item in English can be easily categorised as lexical or grammatical. While it is noticeable that grammatical words have very high frequency of occurrence in a text (for example, words such as "it", "as", "of" "this" "and" which occur frequently in this chapter) and lexical words have love frequency, there are also some words (e.g., thing, get, almost) which can be either assigned as grammatical or lexical items. Halliday's suggestion is that in any analysis of lexical density, consistency is essential in assigning words to each category. Another solution is that we divide words into three categories: grammatical items, high frequency lexical items, and low frequency lexical items. Thus high frequency lexical items should be given half of the value of the others. (Halliday, 1985, p.65)

It is worth mentioning that lexical density is one of the factors which account for the complexity of a text. There are also texts which do not show much lexical density but can be difficult to write and to read. For example:

- In a discursive mapping model in which all texts and social phenomena are necessarily valid objects of study, the discursive construction of domination does not simply disappear (15 content words and 11 function words)

- Discourse as a social practice is what produces structural differentiation within and between societies and distinguishes one 'order of discourse' from another, and through which different types of formation are endowed with properties of regularity and coherence. (17 content words and 20 function words)

SENTENCE COMBINATION

When children learn writing in early grades and move on to the end of high school, they have constantly been reminded that a sentence should start with a capital letter and end with a full stop or in case a sentence is a question, it should end with a question mark. It first sounds so simple. However, if a child asks: What is a sentence? It is a simple question but the answer can be complicated. This difficulty is recognised by Halliday (1985, p. 66) as he argues that the term 'sentence' has been traditionally used only for written texts, whereas we cannot identify a sentence in the spoken language. Thus he prefers the term 'clause complex' instead of "sentence". However, for teachers who are more familiar with the term 'sentence' in dealing with children' writing, it is helpful to use the term 'sentence' in this chapter.

The term 'clause' can be a challenge to literacy teachers as it can be viewed differently. Chomsky in his early version of transformational grammar avoided the term 'clause' in his linguistic analysis of deep structure and surface structure. Halliday (1985, p. 67) examines the concept "clause" in a complex way in light of his theory of Functional Grammar. A clause is a functional unit with a triple construction of meaning: it functions simultaneously (1) as the representation of the phenomena of experience, as these are interpreted by the members of the culture; (2) as the expression of speech function, through the category of mood; and (3) as the bearer of the message, which is organised in the form of theme plus exposition. He concludes:

> A clause, then, can be defined as the locus of choices in transitivity, mood, and theme. This does not imply that all choices are open to all clauses. But every clause embodies some pattern of section in these three functional components of the grammar. (Halliday, 1985, p.68)

In English a sentence can be a clause or a combination of clauses. Let's start with the following examples

–   The dog barked happily. {1 clause}

–   The dog barked happily when it saw Tim. {2 clauses}

–   The dog barked happily when it saw Tim, who came into the house with dog food {3 clauses}

In traditional grammar, each clause has a finite verb. The number of finite verbs (bold words) corresponds to the number of clauses in a sentence.

Children in their early writing development tend to write simple sentences, which include only one clause. For example:

–   I have a dog.

–   His name is Mylo.

–   He is two years old.

In their writing, when a sentence has two clauses, they are independent clauses joined by the conjunction "and" or "and then". For example:

–   My dog is Mylo {clause 1} **and** he is two years old {clause 2}.

When children progress further in their writing development, they start to write complex sentences, using subordinate clause.

Subordinate clause (SC) is also called dependent clause as it cannot stand alone; it needs a main clause (MC) and adds meaning to it. For example:

–   Children work hard {MC} because they want good marks. {SC}

–   When my mother came home {SC}, we stood at the door. {MC}

–   Because my father was sick {SC}, I cleaned the house {MC} and my brother mowed the lawn. {MC}

A complex sentence structure which is normally seen in advanced writing also consists of embedding clauses. For example, the following sentences have embedding clauses (marked in italics).

–   The man, *who intruded into our house last month*, is our neighbour.

– Those *who disobey their bosses* will be treated badly.

Hunt (1965, 1970) is the pioneer of sentence combining technique, which has been used by teachers to enhance children's syntactic maturity in writing (Cooper & Morain, 1980). Saddler et al (2008) examined the effects of peer-assistance in improving the writing ability of students with learning disability. In their study, they used sentence combining technique to teach sentence-construction skills. They concluded that sentence-combining instruction can be effectively used to improve students' writing skills. Sentence-combining practice should be advantageous for students with learning difficulty because they need to establish intentional control over sentence production.

Basically sentence combining teaching combines different simple sentences into complex ones. For example, children are taught how to make new sentences by combining the following simple sentences into single sentences:

– I was hungry.

– I went to a nearby shop.

– I bought a sandwich.

The results can be shown in a number of combinations:

– As I was hungry, I went to a nearby shop and I bought a sandwich.

– I went to a nearby shop and bought a sandwich as I was hungry.

The two complex sentences generated by using the combination technique still keep the same number of simple sentences. The added elements are the conjunctions 'as' and 'and'. More complex ways are (a) to use embedded clauses and (b) to reduce the number of clauses by means of nominalisation.

NOUN, NOMINALITY AND NOMINALISATION

For children learning how to write complex sentences to express complex ideas, and for second language learners who want to master English writing, the two concepts "nominality" and "nominalisation" are essential. These two concepts are also important for measuring lexical density and readability of a text. To examine these two concepts, let's start with noun as the subject of a sentence:

– Animals live with people.

The noun "animals" is the subject of the verb "live". However a nominal group can also be a subject of a verb in a sentence. For example:

– *Various small domestic animals* live with people.

In this sentence, the nominal group "*various small domestic animals*" is the subject of the verb "live". The noun 'animals' is the head of the nominal group. A head noun can have a nominal group before it (thus called premodifier) and a nominal group after it (thus called postmodifier) as in the following sentence:

- Various small domestic animals with close connection to their environment live with people.
  Premodifier: Various small domestic
  Head noun: animals
  Postmodifier: with close connection to their environment

High lexical density is present in nominality because the nominal group has the ability to embrace a great number of lexical items and build long noun phrases by means of pre-modification, post-modification, or both. A nominal group is "the grammatical unit which allows the widest range of meanings to be expressed" (Thompson, 1996, p. 179). In contrast, the verbal group does not hold the same power. Verbal group tends to be responsible for reflecting grammatical features, such as tense, mood, voice, etc.

Nomonalisation is a feature of lexical density in formal writing. It condenses or packs ideas which are normally expressed in simple clauses into a complex sentence.

a. John *decided* to leave and this upset his parents.
b. John's *decision* to leave upset his parents. (*Nominalisation*)

c. I was *disappointed* when Jane did not *know* anything about grammar.
d. Jane's lack of grammatical *knowledge* filled me with *disappointment*. (*Nominalisation*)

e. Students *argue* that they don't want *to pay* fees because the government *promised* that it would not *charge* fees.
f. Students' *argument* against fee payment is based on the government's *promise* of no fee *charge*. (*Nominalisation*)

Nominalisation is a marker of syntactic complexity in writing and it is also a factor which makes reading comprehension difficult. For example, children may find the following sentence with high nominalisation difficult to comprehend unless it is deconstructed into three separate sentences.

As societies in many parts of this planet become more intricately linked, individuals who engage in communicative interactions between these societies may become more aware of their process of human development.

This complex sentence can be broken down into three simple sentences.

- Societies in many parts of this planet become more intricately linked.

- Individuals engage in communicative interactions between these societies.

- They may become more aware of their process of human development.

In highlighting the complexity of written language in terms of nominality, particularly nominalisation, Halldiay states:

The structure of the modern world and the structure of the language combine together to make the written language what it is: a language with a high lexical, measured in (an informational load) of lexical items per clause, and a strong tendency to encode this lexical content in a nominal form: in head noun, other items (nouns and adjectives) in the nominal group, and the nominalised clauses. It is these nominal structures that give the clause its enormous elasticity. (Halliday, 1986, p.75)

However, it is important to distinguish between lexical density and verbosity. Verbosity should be avoided as it an expressive style that uses excessive or empty words. For example:

Profound learning accommodates persistence of constructivist perspective and generates determination to be creative in numerous human interactions.
This sentence has high lexical density but its meaning is obscure.

Teaching nominalisation can enhance children's synaptic maturity, which is important in reading and writing. It can be done in two ways: combining simple sentences into one complex sentence by using the nominalisation device or deconstruct a complex sentence into simple sentences as discussed above.

CONCLUSION

Linguistics has provided useful theoretical insights about what language is and how language works. Different from traditional grammar which is prescriptive, modern linguistics attempts to be descriptive and explanatory. This chapter examines some fundamental concepts and tools for measuring syntactic complexity, which is present in many aspects of academic writing. Traditionally grammar teaching tends to focus on parts of speech such as noun, verb, adverb, preposition, and pronoun and it is expected that after learning them, children will improve their speaking and writing. There claims and counter-claims about the success of grammar teaching in this tradition. It is argued here that grammar teaching should be extended beyond the scope of traditional grammar to include other linguistic devices provided by modern linguistics could open new windows on literacy education.

REFERENCES

Cooper, T. & Morain, G. (1980). A study of sentence combining techniques for developing written and oral fluency in French. *The French Review, LIII*(3), 411 – 424.

Halliday, M. A. K. (1994). *An introduction to functional grammar* (2nd Ed.). London: Edward Arnold.

Halliday, M. A. K. (1985). *Spoken and written language*. Geelong, Victoria: Deakin University.

Halliday, M.AK. (1993). Some grammatical problems in scientific English. In M.A.K. Halliday and J.R. Martin (Eds): *Writing science: Literacy and discursive power*. London: The Falmer Press.

Halliday, M. A. K. (1994). *An introduction to functional grammar* (2nd Ed.). London: Edward Arnold.

Halliday, M. A. K. (2004). *An introduction to functional grammar* (revised by C. Matthiessen). London: Hodder Arnold.

Hunt, Kellogg (1965) .Grammatical Structures Written at Three Grade Levels. *NCTE Research Report No. 3*. IL: National Council of Teachers of English, Champaign.

Hunt, Kellog (1970). *Syntactic maturity in school children and adults*. Chicago: University of Chicago.

Gaies , S. 1980. T-Unit Analysis in Second Language Research: Applications, Problems and Limitations. *TESOL Quarterly, 14*(1), 53 – 60.

Hammond, J. (1990). Is learning to read the same as learning to speak? . In F. Christie (Ed.), *Literacy for Changing World* (pp. 79 – 117). Hawthorn Victoria: Australian Council for Educational Research.

Jackson, H., & Amvela, E. Z. (2000). *Words, meaning and vocabulary: An introduction to modern English lexicology*. London: Continuum International Publishing Group.

Johansson, V. (2008). Lexical diversity and lexical density in speech and writing: A development perspective. *Working Papers, 53*, 61 – 79.

O'Loughlin, K. (1995). Lexical density in candidate output on direct and semi-direct versions of an oral proficiency test. *Language Testing, 12*, 217 – 237.

Palmer, F. R. (1976). *Semantics*. Cambridge: Cambridge University Press.

Saddler, B., Behforooz, B., Asaro, K. (2008). The effects of peer-assisted sentence combining practice on four young writers with learning disabilities. Learning Disabilities - *A Contemporary Journal, 6*(1), 17 – 31.

Stubbs, M. (1986). Lexical density: A computational technique and some findings. In M. Coulthard (Ed.), *Talking about text* (pp. 27 – 48). Birmingham, University of Birmingham: English Language Research.

Ure, J. (1971). Lexical density and register differentiation. In G. Perren & J. L. M. Trim (Eds.), *Applications of linguistics* (pp. 443 – 452). London: Cambridge University Press.

Ure, J., & Ellis, J. (1977). Register in descriptive linguistics and linguistic sociology. In O. Uribe-Villegas (Ed.), *Issues in sociolinguistics* (pp. 197 – 243). The Hague: Mouton.

Vande Kopple, W. J. (2003). M. A. K. Halliday's continuum of prose styles and the stylistic analysis of scientific texts. *Style, 37*(4), 367 – 381.

Veel, R. (1997). Learning how to mean - scientifically speaking: Apprenticeship into scientific discourse in the secondary school. In F. Christie & J. R. Martin (Eds.), *Genre and institutions: Social processes in the workplace and school* (pp. 161 – 195). London: Cassell.

In: Language and Literacy Education in a Challenging World   ISBN: 978-1-61761-198-8
Editors: T. Lê, Q. Lê, and M. Short   © 2011 Nova Science Publishers, Inc.

Chapter 4

THE INFLUENCE OF THEME THEORY IN THE ASSESSMENT OF ENGLISH COMPOSITIONS

Jingxia Liu and Thao Lê

ABSTRACT

Theme and rheme are the two important concepts in Systemic Functional Linguistics, which constitute Theme Theory. Based on Theme Theory, this chapter gives a thematic analysis to 60 sample compositions written by Chinese students in CET-4 examinations. By the analysis, we find that different scored compositions have different distributions of themes and thematic progressions. There are more types of theme and thematic progressions in high-score compositions than in low-score compositions. This shows that high-score group of the students is more skillful in organizing their compositions. The chapter indicates that the application of thematic analysis is useful in grading English compositions.

Keywords: theme, thematic progression, text, assessment, systemic functional linguistics.

INTRODUCTION

Writing reflects how well a student of English as a foreign language has mastered that language (Zou Shen, 1998, p. 61). Empirical evidences also show the close relationship between writing skill and language ability (Yang Huizhong & C. Weir, 1998, p. 148). Thus, popular English tests such as TOEFL, GRE, IELTS, as well as some domestic tests of CET-4/6 take English writing as an indispensable part of evaluating the comprehensive abilities of English learners. Take CET for example. If the score for the writing part is 0, a candidate will fail no matter how high the total score is. This is not the case for the listening or reading components. One of the challenging issues in testing writing is the assessing criteria, which are not universally accepted. However, factors such as choice of words, appropriateness of language and the fluency of idea are commonly used to assess writing. Generally, factors which attract the attention of testers include vocabulary and grammar, and composition coherence of a text. Recently, theme analysis has been used to assess English composition writing. Based on the analysis of 60 CET-4 compositions, the chapter discusses how theme analysis can be productively used in assessing English compositions.

THEME ANALYSIS

The Studies on the Concepts of Theme and Rheme

The terms theme and rheme could be dated back to the Prague school of functional structuralism in 1930s and Mathesius was one of its prominent figures. According to Svoboda (2005), Mathesius introduced the idea that the formal analysis of a sentence (subject and predicate – a static phenomenon) should be distinguished from the functional analysis of a sentence ('what is being talked about' and 'what is being said about it'. In his analysis, what is being talked about is the theme (the point of departure), and what is being said about it is the rheme (the core of the message).

Initially Mathesius defined theme as the starting point of utterance and rheme as the core of the utterance. And then he, in 1940, defined theme as the foundation of the utterance which is being said about in the sentence, and rheme as the core which refers to what the speaker says about the former.

Mathesius' very purpose to make researches on theme and rheme is to analyze how information is distributed in the sentence and then to find out the communicative effect of the distribution of known or given information and new information in a discourse. According to him, theme always carries known information, and theme is known or least obvious in the given situation and the starting point from which the speaker proceeds, while rheme is always the carrier of new information, so it is called the core.

> What is being talked about is the theme (východisko, the point of departure), and what is being said about it is the rheme (jádro, the core of the message). The point of departure (theme) is often something known or easily gathered from the context or situation. The core of the message (rheme) is often something new or not known at the moment of communication. The natural way is to proceed from the known to the unknown information, so the linear sequence theme-rheme is a natural way of developing the discourse. (Svoboda, 2005, p.1)

Halliday has vigourously revised the interest and treatment of theme in his study of theme. Halliday (1985) categorizes theme into three types: simple theme, multiple theme and clausal theme.

Simple theme: If the theme of a sentence consists of just only one structural element, it is called simple theme. For example:

> The duke (T) // has given my aunt that teapot (R).

Multiple theme: It refers to more than one structural element as the theme of a sentence. Multiple theme includes three structural elements, which are respectively called topical theme (experiential theme), interpersonal theme and textual theme. The three kinds of themes correspond to the three components of Halliday's theory of metafunctions: ideational, interpersonal and textual. Halliday (1985) held that a sentence is, at one and the same time, a representation of experience, an interactive and a message. For example:

Not surprisingly (T-Int), then (T-Tex), its operations (T-Exp)// were viewed with admiration (R).

Clausal theme: A clause serves as theme in the complex sentence, which is constituted by a head (dominant) clause plus a modifying (dependent) clause, and this clause is called clausal theme. For example:

If winter comes (T)// can spring be far behind (R)?

Halliday (1970) held different views about the relation between theme-rheme structure and given-new information structure from Matheius'. He stated that:

> Although they are related, given+new and theme+rheme are not the same thing. The theme is what I, the speaker choose to take as my point of departure. The given is what you, the listener, already know about or have accessible to you. Theme+rheme is speaker-oriented, while given+new is listener-oriented. (p. 299)

In most cases, there is a parallel equivalence between theme and given on the one hand and between rheme and new on the other. However, there is no perfect correlation between them. Given and new information is context based. One can only decide which part of a message is new and which part is given within a linguistic or situational context.

Other descriptions on the concept of theme in general and its place in the theory of Systemic Functional Linguistics can be found in Jimenez Julia (1986), Downing (1991), Martin (1994), Eggins (1994), Berry (1996), Downing and Locke (2002). Downing (1991) discussed marked and unmarked theme in different mood structures, and concluded that, although the thematic element in all of them is the point of departure, is not always "what the clause is about". This is because theme is identified with first position in the sentence, and English, in the unmarked case, has a strict word order.

The discussion so far has concentrated on different views and definitions of the notion of theme and rheme in general. The following discussion focuses on an account of thematic progressions

Thematic Progressions

Danes (1974) postulated four models of thematic progression (TP) and claimed that they can be used in various combinations in any discourse. By the term "thematic progression", he meant "the choice and ordering of utterance themes, their mutual concatenation hierarchy, as well as their relation to the hyper-themes of the superior text unit (such as paragraph, chapter, etc.), to the whole text, and to the situation. Thematic progression might be viewed as the skeleton of the plot". (Danes, 1974, p.114)

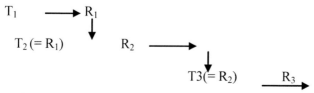

Figure 1: Simple linear TP (Danes, 1974, p.118)

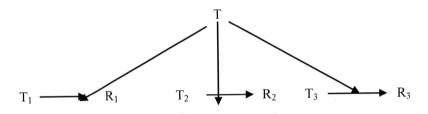

Figure 2: TP with a constant theme (Danes, 1974, p.118)

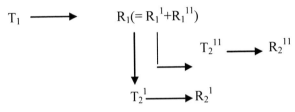

Figure 3: TP with derived themes (Danes, 1974, p.119)

$$T_1 \longrightarrow R_1(= R_1{}^1 + R_1{}^{11})$$
$$T_2{}^{11} \longrightarrow R_2{}^{11}$$
$$T_2{}^1 \longrightarrow R_2{}^1$$

Figure 4: TP with a split rheme (Danes, 1974, p.120)

Thematic progression is concerned with relatedness: where themes come from, and how they relate to previous themes and rhemes. Danes considers thematic progression to be one of the representations of connexity in a text: one of the ways in which a text displays coherence.

On the basis of Danes' models, Huang Yan (1985) gives seven models of Thematic Progression, and Huang Guowen (1988) generalizes six models, all of which frequently appear in the ordinary use of English.

For this chapter, we decide to concentrate on Danes' models.

THE ANALYSIS ON THE APPLICATION OF THEME THEORY IN THE ASSESSMENT OF ENGLISH COMPOSITIONS

Data Collection

The data for analysis are collected from the sample compositions of CET-4, which was initiated in 1987 and continues until now and is held twice every year. CET-4 is a standard test as the nation-wide College English Test in China. It is one of the most authoritative and extensive examinations in China. The participants constitute the majority of the Chinese college students. The sample compositions of CET-4 are chosen from 1995 to 2005. The total score of writing in the exam is 15. The compositions are divided into five ratings, 14 points, 11 points, 8 points, 5 points and 2 points. Because there are so many grammatical and structural mistakes in the 2-point compositions, they will be left out in our research, and our focus will be on the first four scales compositions. We randomly choose 15 compositions of each rating scale. Thus, this chapter is based on 60 compositions.

Research questions

Our research questions are as follows:

1. Are the different scored compositions presented in the different uses of theme types and TP patterns?

2. How does theme theory affect the scoring of the compositions?

3. How do good writers use theme types and TP patterns effectively to achieve textual coherence?

Data processing

Since the focus of our research is to analyse and discuss the thematic structure of students' writing, other problems, such as grammatical and spelling errors in these sample compositions are not considered. The analysis of the data mainly follows 4 steps:

1. Finding the theme and rheme of each clause in every composition, categorize the themes and sum up the times of each theme type.

2. Investigating the TP patterns in each composition; calculate the number of the times of different TP patterns.

3. Dividing all the 60 compositions into two groups: high-score group (11-14 points) and low-score group (5-8 points).

4. Comparing the differences in the use of theme types and TP patterns between the two groups based on the established theme types and TP patterns.

Data analysis

Distribution of theme types in different scored compositions
The number of the themes and theme types is presented in Table 1.
Here we categorise theme into 3 types: simple theme, multiple theme and clausal theme. Meanwhile, according to the function of elements in clause, we identify experiential (topical) theme, interpersonal theme and textual theme. When a clause only has one structural element as theme, the theme must be experiential theme (Halliday, 1985, p. 52). Thus we place simple theme and experiential theme together.

Table 1 – Number and percentage of types of themes in different scored compositions

Category of theme		Different scored compositions			
		14 points	**11 points**	**8 points**	**5 points**
Simple Theme (Experiential Theme)		25 (13.5%)	30 (18.5%)	46 (35.4%)	69 (57%)
Multiple Theme	Experiential Theme	55 (29.8%)	55 (33.7%)	50 (38.5%)	31 (25.6%)
	Textual Theme	58 (31.6%)	42 (25.7%)	20 (15.3%)	13 (10.7%)
	Interpersonal Theme	6 (3.3%)	8 (4.9%)	3 (2.3%)	2 (1.7%)
Clausal Theme		40 (21.8%)	28 (17.2%)	11 (8.5%)	6 (5%)
Total		184	163	130	121

The findings displayed in Table 1 indicate that the distribution of theme types in the four scored compositions is different. Among all the compositions, 14-score compositions use the most themes. On the contrary, 5-score compositions use the least. It shows that there is a relationship between writing achievements and thematic structures of texts. However, the differences between 14-score and 11-score compositions are not distinct. It is true about the differences between 8-score and 5-score compositions. For the convenience of comparison, we divide all the compositions into two groups: high-score group (11-14 points) and low-score group (5-8 points). Table 2 is the comparison of high-score and low-score compositions in terms of the number of theme and theme types.

Table 2 - Number and percentage of types of themes in high-score and low-score groups

Category of theme		High-score group (11-14 points)	Low-score group (5-8 points)
Simple Theme (Experiential Theme)		55 (15.9%)	115 (45.8%)
Multiple Theme	Experiential Theme	110 (31.7%)	81 (32.2%)
	Textual Theme	100 (28.8%)	33 (13.2%)
	Interpersonal Theme	14 (4%)	5 (2%)
Clausal Theme		68 (19.6%)	17 (6.8%)
Total		347	251

Both of the two groups use the three types of themes. However, the three types of themes are distributed differently in different groups. The percentage of simple theme in low-score group is higher than that of high-score group. The percentages of multiple theme and clausal theme in high-score group are greatly higher than those in low-score group. We can find that low-score group prefers to choose simple sentence structure in writing and high-score group is better at using different sentence structure.

In terms of the function of theme, experiential theme is used most. This is not surprising, as experiential theme is obligatory theme that contributes to the development of a text. The difference exists due to the fact that high-score group uses more textual themes and interpersonal themes than those in low-score group. This shows that high-score group is more skillful in making their compositions logical and coherent because both textual elements and interpersonal elements do important cohesive work in relating the clause to its context.

Distribution of thematic progressions in different scored compositions

The analysis of thematic progressions is based on Danes' models. By careful calculating the thematic progressions in different scored compositions, we get the following table.

Table 3 – Number and percentage of different tp patterns in different scored compositions

Category of theme	Different scored compositions			
	14 points	11 points	8 points	5 points
Linear TP Pattern	61 (39.8%)	50 (40%)	32 (37.6%)	22 (37.3%)
Constant TP Pattern	52 (33.9%)	46 (36.8%)	40 (47%)	32 (54.2%)
Derived TP Pattern	30 (19.9%)	21 (16.8%)	10 (11.8%)	5 (8.5%)
Rheme-split Pattern	10 (6.4%)	8 (6.4%)	3 (3.6%)	0 (0%)
Total	153	125	85	59

Just like the distribution of theme types in different scored compositions, 14-score compositions use the most TP patterns and 5-score compositions the least. From Table 3 we can also find that linear and constant thematic progression patterns occur frequently in all compositions. This is not surprising, because Danes refers to them as basic patterns, and Dubois (1986) similarly characterizes them as canonical types, from which other patterns are derived.

Rheme-split pattern only occupies a small part in all compositions. This is may be simply accidental, for our data is not large. It seems probable that rheme-split pattern is less likely to occur in our data by virtue of the fact that these compositions from CET-4 are relatively short because of word limitation.

Also, for the sake of comparison, we simplify the four scales compositions into high-score group and low-score group.

Table 4 - Number and percentage of different TP patterns in high-score group and low-score group

Category of Theme	High-score group (11-14 points)	Low-score group (5-8 points)
Linear TP Pattern	111 (40%)	54 (37.5%)
Constant TP Pattern	98 (35.2%)	72 (50%)
Derived TP Pattern	51 (18.3%)	15 (10.4%)
Rheme-split Pattern	18 (6.5%)	3 (2.1%)
Total	278	144

In high-score group, we find many more types of TP patterns than in low-score group. Besides, for most patterns, the percentages in high-score group are higher than in low-score group. In low-score group, the number of constant TP pattern is the half of the total number of PT patterns in low-score group, and the percentage is 50%, which is higher than 35.2% in high-score group. But the excessive use of this kind of TP pattern easily makes the texts dull. These results show that low-score group has problems in organizing texts.

The analysis on themes and TP patterns in different scored compositions

In this section, we present two sample compositions of CET-4 held in January, 1995 and analyse their themes and thematic progressions. We attempt to show different scored compositions use different theme types and TP patterns, and good writers can use theme types and TP patterns effectively to achieve textual coherence. The two compositions are on the same topic "Advantages of a job interview", and one is scored 14 points and other 8 points. In the composition, each theme is numbered for ease of reference.

Sample one (14 points)

Now, when a person is hunting for a job (T_1), there will always be a job interview and I (T_2) think the job interview has a lot of advantages. It (T_3) is important for both the interviewer and the interviewee. The interviewer and the interviewee (T_4) can know about each other through it.

First the interviewer (T_5) can tell something about the job to the interviewee such as the wage, the work conditions and something else which is relevant to the job. Then the interviewee (T_6) can decide whether the job is really suitable for him. Second, I (T_7) think the job interviewer by good for the interviewee, because, he (T_8) can impress the interviewer by good behavior. He (T_9) can show both his ability and his confidence. Then the interviewer (T_{10}) can figure out whether he is the right person for the job.

In a word, I (T_{11}) think the interview will do good to both the interviewer and the interviewee. By the interview, the interviewee (T_{12}) can find a suitable job and the interviewer (T_{13}) can find a suitable person if both of them make the best of the job interview.

A list of the themes of the composition is as follows:

T_1----Now, when a person is hunting for a job, T_2----and I, T_3----It, T_4----The interviewer and the interviewee, T_5----First the interviewer, T_6----Then the interviewee, T_7----Second, I, T_8----because, he, T_9----He, T_{10}---Then the interviewer, T_{11}----In a word, I, T_{12}-----By the interview, the interviewee, T_{13}---- and the interviewer

When we read the 13 themes of this composition, we know that the composition concerns "interview". In the whole text, we can see that the word is picked up in different forms, such as "interviewer", "interviewee" and "he". We find that in the 13 themes, 8 themes are connected with "interview". This fact reveals that we want to draw the reader's attention to the topic of the text. On the other hand, we choose his themes and vary theme types for special purpose.

As indicated, we use different kinds of theme to avoid dullness and blankness caused by using the same kind of theme, e.g. the clausal theme in sentence 1, the multiple themes in sentences 2, 5, 6, 7, 8, 10, 11, 12, and 13, the simple themes in sentences 3, 4 and 9. In addition, the themes function differently. For example, "By the interview" in sentence 12 is an interpersonal Theme, which implies the mode in the register. In sentences 5, 6, 7, and 10, "First", "Then", "Second" and "Then" are textual elements, which make the text logical and coherent.

The TP patterns of the text are development as follows:

$$T_1 ----R_1 \quad T_4 (=R_3)----R_4 \quad T_7 (=T_2)----R_7$$
$$T_2 ----R_2 \quad T_5 ---- R_5 \quad T_8 (=T_6)----R_8$$
$$T_3 ----R_3 \quad T_6 ---- R_6 \quad T_9 (=T_6, T_8)----R_9$$

$$T_{10} (= T_5)----R_{10} \quad T_{12} (=T_6, T_8, T_9)---R_{12}$$
$$T_{11} (=T_2, T_7)---R_{11} \quad T_{13} (=T_5, T_{10})---R_{13}$$

This composition consists of 3 TP patterns: linear pattern (2 times), constant pattern (7 times), and derived pattern (2 times). Theme 1 introduces the topic of the whole text. The TP patterns in sentences 2, 7 and 11 can be assigned to be constant pattern with the same referent "I" as their themes. In sentences 6, 12 and sentences 8, 9 and sentences 5, 10, 13, again the constant progression, the same themes "the interviewee", "he" and "the interviewer" are used respectively. The thematic progression in sentences 2, 3, 4 is simple linear. Theme 5 (the interviewer) and theme 6 (the interviewee) are derived from theme 4 (the interviewer and the interviewee), so the TP pattern is derived TP pattern.

As can be seen, the sentences of the text are linked together according to the relationship of themes and rhemes of the sentences in TP patterns.

Another sample composition with 8 points on the same topic is given below:

A job interview (T_1) has been popularly in the last few years. It (T_2) has many advantages. The advantages of a job interview (T_3) are the interviewer and interviewee can learn each other. The interviewee (T_4) would be informed much about the company or department. He (T_5) will know, if he had this job, what he would do, what condition he would work in, what he would be paid. The interviewee (T_6) have an opportunity to make a good impression to the interviewer. He (T_7) can show himself in various ways. He (T_8) can show his education level, his ability, his confidence.

So the job interview (T_9) has such many advantages. People (T_{10}) will use it more and more in the future. We (T_{11}) need it for hunting job.

The following is a list of the themes:

T_1----A job interview, T_2-----It, T_3-----The advantages of a job interview, T_4-----The interviewee, T_5-----He, T_6-----The interviewee, T_7------He, T_8-----He, T_9-----So the job interview, T_{10}-----People, T_{11}------We

We can see that all the themes except theme 9 are simple themes. The occurrence of other types of themes is very low. There is only one multiple theme, e.g. theme 9. In this way, the structure of the 8-scored composition tends to be simple. Besides, all together, 10 themes among 11 themes are experiential themes. There is only one textual theme, e.g. theme 9. Because of the lack of textual elements, the experiential themes are not coherent naturally.

There is also evidence of thematic progression. The following is the TP patterns:

$$T_1 ----R_1 \quad T_4 ----R_4 \quad T_7 (=T_4,T_5,T_6)----R_7 \quad T_{10} ----R_{10}$$
$$T_2 (=T_1)----R_2 \quad T_5 (=T_4)---- R_5 \quad T_8 (=T_4,T_5,T_6,T_7)----R_8 \quad T_{11}----R_{11}$$
$$T_3 (=R_2)----R_3 \quad T_6 (=T_4, T_5)---- R_6 \quad T_9 (=T_1,T_2)----R_9$$

The TP pattern between sentences 1 to 2, and 4 to 8, is constant pattern, and sentences 2 to 3 simple linear, 3 to 4 derived pattern. However, it is not difficult to find we use constant pattern in most cases, with the same referent in the continuous sentences. So the whole text appears boring in the organization of the structure. Besides, theme 4 (the interviewee) is derived from rheme 3 (the interviewer and interviewee), but in the following only "the interviewee" is focused, no any mention of "the interviewer". Additionally, some themes are not involved in any TP patterns, e.g., the themes 10 and 11.

FINDINGS

The above analysis has revealed that themes and thematic progressions are distributed differently in different scored compositions. The percentage of simple theme in low-score group (45.8%) is greatly higher than that in high-score group (15.9%). The percentages of the other types of theme in low-score group are lower than those in high-score group, e.g. 47.4% of multiple theme in low-score group, 64.5% of multiple theme in high-score group, and 6.8% of clausal theme in low-score group, 19.6% of clausal theme in high-score group. This shows that low-score group tends to use simple sentence structure while high-score group is better at using different theme types to achieve a variety of sentence structure. Besides, more textual themes (28.8%) are found in high-score group, while the percentage of textual theme in low-score group is only 13.2%. The use of more textual elements makes the high-score compositions develop more smoothly. In terms of thematic progressions, more types of PT patterns are detected in the high-score group than in the low-score group, though simple linear TP pattern and constant pattern occur frequently in the two scored compositions, which are the basic patterns for text construction. This proves that high-score achievers are more skillful in organizing their compositions through the reasonable choices of TP pattern.

From the corpus-based study, we find that the high-score compositions rely largely on the success of the thematic structure. The application of thematic analysis can help us find the problems existing in students' writing, esp. with the structure of writing. Although this method can not handle every aspect of English writing, e.g. sounds, words and expressions, it's one of the important methods for us to judge that a piece of writing is coherent or incoherent.

CONCLUSION

In this chapter, we have attempted to analyze 60 English compositions written by some Chinese students. The results of the analysis reveal that themes and TP patterns are distributed differently in different scored compositions. There're more types of theme and thematic progressions in high-score compositions than in low-score compositions. This shows that high-score group is more skillful in organizing their compositions. Besides, more textual elements are found in high-score compositions, which is a very important factor to achieve textual coherence in high-score compositions. We find that the high-score compositions rely largely on the success of the thematic structure. The chapter confirms that the application of thematic analysis is one of the important methods in grading English compositions. Theme Theory is the theoretical foundation for this method.

REFERENCES

Danes, F. (1974). Functional sentence perspective and the organization of the text. In F. Danes (Ed.). *Papers on functional sentence perspective* (pp. 114-120). Prague: Academia.

Downing, Angela (1991). An alternative approach to theme: A systemic- functional perspective. *Word*, *42*(2), 119-143.

Halliday, M.A.K. (1970). *New horizons in linguistics*. Harmondsworth: Penguin Books.

Halliday, M.A.K. (1985). *An Introduction to Functional Grammar* (pp.38 – 52). London: Edward Arnold.

Mathesius, V. (1939). « O tak zvaném aktuálním čl´n´ní v´ty » [On the so-called actual bipartition of the sentence]. *Slovo a slovesnost*, *5*, 171-174.

Svoboda, A. (2005). An ABC of functional sentence perspective. Retrieved 10 April, 2010 from http://web.iol.cz/alesvo/vyuka/An_ABC_of_FSP.pdf

Yang, H & Weir, C. (1998). *Validation study of the national college English test*. Shanghai: Shanghai Foreign Language Education Press.

Zou, Shen. (1998). *English language testing: Some theoretical and practical considerations*. Shanghai: Shanghai Foreign Language Education Press.

In: Language and Literacy Education in a Challenging World   ISBN: 978-1-61761-198-8
Editors: T. Lê, Q. Lê, and M. Short   © 2011 Nova Science Publishers, Inc.

Chapter 5

THE CATEGORIES OF LEARNING THEORIES IN A HOLISTIC PERSPECTIVE AND FOREIGN LANGUAGE EDUCATION

*Muhlise Coşgun Ögeyik, Nur Cebeci, Sinem Doğruer
and Esin Akyay*

ABSTRACT

The basic agenda of a learning situation includes learners and educators to deal with the essential conditions of learning. Learners need to learn for getting information in any field by interacting with various sources such as educators, materials, other learners, educational policies, world knowledge, learning tasks and experiences. In this complicated process, the pedagogical concerns of educators are based on the basic questions "What do learners need to know?" and "How can they accomplish learning?" In order to identify the issue of learning as regards those questions, the contents of courses are designed and teaching strategies are determined.

From the first half of the 20th century onwards, some learning theories have been put forward, and teaching methods and course designs have been shaped as consistent with those theories. Three main sets of those learning theories which are behaviourism, cognitivism, and constructivism are the focus of this chapter. These learning theories are defined and compared as an opening pathway to a holistic view for learning and teaching settings.

Keywords: learning theories, behaviorism, cognitivism, constructivism, foreign language education.

INTRODUCTION

For the most part, there are three categories or philosophical frameworks under the topic of learning theories, namely behaviorism, cognitivism, and constructivism, which have been put forward since the first half of the 20th century. The emphasis of behaviorism is on the objectively observable aspects of learning, while the emphasis of cognitive theories is to look beyond behavior to explain brain-based learning. Another perspective in the cognitive movement was to connect environment and human development in a productive way. However, like behaviorism, pure cognitivism alone is not appropriate for learning. In order to gain knowledge and skills, human beings should be regarded as neither an animal to be conditioned or as isolated thinkers. Constructivism views learning as a process in which learner actively constructs or builds new ideas or concepts. In other words, learning involves constructing one's own knowledge from one's own experiences. That is to say, learning is a very personal endeavour. This chapter deals with those three categories of learning theory in detail by focusing on their strong and weak points and compares them in a holistically.

BEHAVIORISM

Behaviorism emerged as a psychological theory of learning in the first half of the 20th century. The major principle of the behaviorist theory is based on the analyses of the observable human behavior in stimulus-response interaction. Learning, for this theory, takes place when there is a response which follows by specific stimuli; in other words, learning is shaped by a link between stimuli and response. Therefore, behaviorists deal with the discovery of the basic laws of learning by observing the responses given to the stimuli. Principally, the behaviorist theory of stimulus-response learning was particularly developed from the operant conditioning model of Skinner (1976) who considers learning behavior to be the establishment of habits as a result of reinforcement and reward. In this sense, behaviorism deals with the processes built upon stimuli-response connections. The process of stimulus-response interaction is very much obvious in Pavlov's experiment: it suggests that learning is a result of stimuli and reflexive responses. In his classic experiment, food powder was placed in a dog's mouth (unconditioned stimulus) and salivation was produced (unconditioned reflex); when an arbitrary neutral stimulus was paired repeatedly with the food, it came to produce salivation in its own right (conditioned reflex) (Kymissis & Poulson, 1990). During this process, learners are assumed to figure out associations on the particular process of behavior; thus, these associations gain effectiveness as frequently as they are repeated. As a consequence, repetition has a very fundamental role in gaining the required skills and permanency during the learning process. Thus, this theory views the mind as a "black box" in the sense that response to stimulus can be observed quantitatively, totally ignoring the possibility of thought processes occurring in the mind (Mergel, 1998). In this sense, learning largely occurs due to environmental stimuli.

According to the behaviorist perspective, learning involves the acquisition of new behavior and causes a transformation in the learners' behavior. That is to say, all learning, whether verbal or non-verbal, takes place through the same underlying processes (Lightbown & Spada, 1999). If so, the learner is expected to produce correct responses by imitation, practice, and habit formation. Skinner (1976) insists that habit formation is a structuralist principle: to acquire a habit is merely to become accustomed to behaving in a given way. Behaviorists shape behavior by means of positive or negative support in the learning period which increases the possibility of a habitual act. Particularly, in Skinner's theory, human behavior can be shaped by rewards and punishments. In this sense, behaviorism seeks not merely to understand human behavior but to predict and control it (Roy, 2005).

BEHAVIORISM AND FOREIGN LANGUAGE TEACHING

In relation to language learning, language is seen as a behavior just like other behaviors, and thus it is learned. Richard and Rodgers (2001) state that to apply behaviorist theory to language learning is to identify the organism as the foreign language learner, the behavior as verbal behavior, the stimulus as what is taught or presented of the foreign language, the response as the learner's reaction to the stimulus, and the reinforcement as the extrinsic approval and praise of teacher or fellow learners or the intrinsic self-satisfaction of target language use. As a psychological theory, behaviorism provided its principles to audio-lingualism, notably in terms of the requirement of external stimuli in the learning process. In this view, the audio-lingual method is a language teaching methodology that links linguistic and learning theory: structuralism and behaviorism. Its psychological basis is behaviorism which interprets language learning in terms of stimulus and response, operant conditioning, and reinforcement with an emphasis on successful error-free learning (Liu & Shi, 2007). In a sense, audio-lingualism regards language as a habit formation since target language patterns are learnt through dialogue and drills. At this point, the role of repetition becomes significant for the fact that the more something is repeated, the more powerful the habit becomes and as a result, learning occurs. In short, the audio-lingual method stressed the practice and repetition of what has been learnt in the classroom through forming habits (Meng, 2009). For strengthening and forming correct habits, feedback is provided by positive or negative reinforcements. In this approach, listening and speaking skills are attached more importance than other skills. Accuracy in language teaching is succeeded by imitation, repetition, reinforcements and habit formation. However, this method does not deal with mental processes, as language is accepted as a habitual fact and creativity or innovation in language is disregarded.

COGNITIVISM

During the 1960s, the perspective of behaviorism was considered to be inadequate for psychological theories of learning as the behaviorists ignored the activity inside the learner's mind. While behaviorists supported the idea that learning occurs when there are observable changes in behavior, cognitivists were in favor of thought processes driving the behavior. Thus, cognitivist theories emerged as a reaction against the previously dominant behaviorist paradigm, which focused on observable behavior and the response of humans to environmental stimuli (Hartley, 1998). In general terms, cognitivism deals with the internal mental processes of the mind and focuses on exploring how these processes might possibly be used to provide effective learning. Since cognition is an intellectual process by which knowledge is gained from perception or ideas, cognitivists are primarily concerned with insight and understanding. Individuals are perceived not as passive and shaped by their environment but as capable of actively shaping the environment (Lightbrown & Spada, 2003). Accordingly, the focus of cognitivism is on the internal process of acquiring, understanding, and retaining learning. If so, learning results from inferences, expectations and making connections with the prior knowledge. In a general sense, cognitivism is completely concerned with an internal, symbolic mental processing system that focuses on learning schemas and that focuses on how the brain receives, internalizes, and recalls information

(Leonard, 2002). Accordingly, cognitive structures and processes such as memory, perception, problem-solving, comprehension, attention, and concept- learning are significant concepts in terms of understanding the learning process.

At the beginning of the 20th century, the ideas put forth for exploring the role of psychological process in a holistic way represent the base of cognitive theory. Gestalt theory, one of those theories, had a chief role for describing cognitive psychology. The core of the theory contributes to understanding perception and problem solving. It explores the functions of brain through the patterns perceived by human beings rather than through of behaviours. Another theory put forward by Piaget (1965) insists that human development can be outlined in terms of functions and cognitive structures. The functions of which purpose constructs internal cognitive structures are identical for everyone and stay unchanged throughout our lives. The structures, in contrast, change repeatedly as the child grows (Vatsa, Haith, & Miller,1995). Piaget defines a child's knowledge as schemas which are the mental representation of an associated set of perceptions, ideas, and/or actions, thus schemata is considered to be the basic building blocks of thinking (Woolfolk, 1987). He also identified four stages in terms of cognitive development: sensorimotor, preoperational, concrete operational and formal operations. Through the experiments he did on children's thought process, he stated that the acquisition of new skills is gained when these stages are successfully completed.

During the 1950s, Chomsky put forward his views, especially in terms of language development. He states that the language acquisition mechanism derivates from innate processes. Children have an innate capacity when constructing language, and all children share the same internal constraints which characterize narrowly the grammar they are going to construct (Chomsky, 1977). Moreover, other cognitive theorists such as Bruner (1968) and Ausubel (1968), though they studied different perspectives, also discussed the way how people learn. Ausubel (1968) studied the importance of prior knowledge which was disregarded by behaviorism, whereas Bruner (1968) stressed the importance of learning processes and studied how people learn from their environment. In his theory, Bruner stated three stages for intellectual development: enactive which is related to actions, iconics which is connected to pictures, and lastly the symbolic which refers to words and numbers. He claimed that children think through these stages as actions, pictures and words or numbers are the tools used by people in their environment in accordance with interactions and performing tasks. Based on the ideas put forward by cognitive theorists, it can be said that individuals are actively involved in the learning process in terms of cognitive learning theories. The learning process involves linking information that has been learned before with new information being learned.

COGNITIVE APPROACHES AND FOREIGN LANGUAGE TEACHING

According to cognitive approach, language learning is viewed as rule acquisition, not habit formation. Therefore, deep structure of language rather than surface structure, with the Chomskyan revolution in linguistics, gained importance. This gave rise to cognitive code learning which was developed by Carroll and Chastain in the 1960s. Cognitive code learning was a reaction to the strictly behaviorist practices of the audiolingual method. The theory attaches more importance to the learner's understanding of the structure of the foreign language than to the facility in using that structure, since it is believed that provided the learner has a proper degree of cognitive control over the structures of the language; facility will develop automatically with use of the language in meaningful situations (Brown, 2001).

In 1955, Curran developed the counseling-learning/community language learning (C-L/CLL) approach as an alternative approach in which teachers place primary emphasis on affect and cognition. C-L/CLL is inner directed, meaning oriented, and learner-centered. As Curran believed negative feelings affect learning, a whole person learning process and trusting relationships should be developed. Therefore, learners are viewed as whole persons, and should be given the opportunity to generate the language they would like to learn (Richard & Rodgers, 2001). Another approach is silent way which respects the capacity of learners to work out language problems and recall information on their own without any verbal behavior by receiving minimal help from teacher (Celce-Murcia & McIntosh, 1989). This approach stresses that learning, rather than teaching, should be the primary focus.

As outlined through the cognitive approaches in second language teaching, more emphasis is given to cognitive process of learners in the teaching process. Learning by repetition or conditioning is rejected, as mechanical learning is not the main focus, instead, the mental power of learners is taken into consideration. In cognitive psychology, mistakes and errors are accepted as important steps for gaining a deeper and more accurate understanding of life (Pellegrino, Chudowsky, & Glaser, 2001). This is a significant component related to education, since it helps teachers create meaningful classroom activities in accordance with their learners' needs and develop appropriate ways in order to provide a supportive learning environment.

CONSTRUCTIVISM

As a philosophy of learning, constructivism offers the idea of directed living in which learners can find real world and practical situations. These learning situations have to occur in a social context where learners join in manipulating materials through collaborative and discovery learning (Matthews, 2003).Thus, education cannot be designed for focusing on merely repetitive and rote memorisation by ignoring the social context.Instead, learners are encouraged to be productive and creative. In this context, learners have to go through stages to understand the basic phenomena and discover the knowledge on their own. Through this, understanding is built up step by step in the course of active involvement of learner.

Vygotsky (1962) claims that children learn scientific concepts out of a tension between their everyday notions and adult concepts; thus, children memorise what adults say through adult assistance while constructing knowledge, and they use the concept and link this use to the idea as first presented to them. In educational settings, teachers serve as mediators who encourage learners to formulate their own level of understanding. Each learner has a base level of knowledge, but they can increase it by practising what they know well and adding to it. The social interaction between the learner, teacher and other learners reinforces their knowledge (Goldberg, 2002). As a result, constructivism, rather than a theory of learning, can be accepted as a way of looking at the world which allows multiple interpretations and a perspective which can explain complex and abstract phenomenon while guiding our actions.

CONSTRUCTIVISM AND FOREIGN LANGUAGE LEARNING

Constructivism appeared as a reaction to the traditional educational approach widely practised in the eighteenth and nineteenth centuries in Europe and America. Constructivism can be described as more holistic and less mechanistic than traditional way of instruction theories. In traditional education, teachers are able to predict the outcomes of the instruction and they determine what occurs in the classroom. Yet, they do not predict what the learners will do in the classroom. Although teachers determine learning outcomes for learners, traditional education is not successful in preparing learners to be critical thinkers (Roblyer, Edwards & Havriluk, 1997). Fortunately, in the constructivist classroom, the focus tends to shift from teacher to learner. The classroom is no longer a place where teacher transmits knowledge to passive learners who wait like empty vessels to be filled. In the constructivist model, learners are encouraged to participate in their own process of learning. Since constructivism promotes a learner's free exploration within a given framework or structure, the teacher acts as a facilitator who encourages learners to discover principles for themselves and to construct knowledge by working to solve realistic problems. Thus, a constructivist approach teaches learners to discover their own answers and produce their own concepts and interpretations (Marlowe and Page, 2005). In addition, a constructivist approach includes interactive and collaborative learning in a learner-centered environment.

The paradigm of constructivism involves the intersection of ideas of different theorists, school policy, focal points, and disciplinary approaches (Richardson, 2003). Therefore, various instructional designs inspired by constructivism have been proposed. Gagnon and Collay (2001) mentioned six important elements in constructive learning design as: situation, groupings, bridge, questions, exhibit, and reflections. These elements are designed to help teacher planning and to clarify reflection about the process of learning. Teachers develop situations for learners to explain, select a process for groupings of materials and learners, build a bridge between what learners already know and what they want them to learn, anticipate questions to ask and answer without giving away an explanation, encourage learners to record their thinking by sharing it with others, and solicit learners' reflections about their learning. These elements are crucial in the process of application and learning in the class since they omit referring to objectives or outcomes. Teachers are expected to have these objectives clarified and determined by the district curriculum or the textbook they are using in their classroom. Thus, they need to think more about accomplishing it than about writing it again.

In the area of foreign language/L2 education, constructivism is mostly associated with the use of technology in the classroom (Chuang and Rosenbusch, 2005; McDonough, 2001; Ruschoff and Ritter, 2001). This relationship between computer and constructivist learning is the result of the technology which enables learners' almost unlimited access to information that they need in order to do research and test their ideas.

Another instructional model developed by Bybee (2002) is called "the 5E model" which stands for engage, explore, explain, elaborate, and evaluate. In the "engage" stage, learners first encounter and identify the instructional task. They are given a chance to make connections between past and present learning experiences in order to build a ground for the following activities. In the exploration stage, learners have the opportunity to get directly involved in situations and materials. The "explain" stage encourages learners to put abstract experience into a verbal form. Language which has a crucial importance in this stage provides motivation for sequencing events into a logical format. Communication occurs between peers, the facilitator, or within the learner himself. Thus, learners support each other's understanding with group work as they express their observations, ideas, questions and hypotheses in detail. In stage four, "elaborate", learners work out the concepts they have learned in detail and make connections to other related concepts in order to apply their understandings to the world around them. "Evaluate", the fifth "E", is an on-going diagnostic process that allows the teacher to determine if the learner has attained understanding of the concepts and knowledge. Evaluation and assessment can occur at all points along the continuum of the instructional process. Evaluation in this model gives the idea of a continuous process in constructivist assessment. In a traditional classroom, assessment of learning is viewed as separate from teaching and occurs almost entirely through testing. Brooks and Brooks (1993) describe assessment in a constructivist classroom as an ongoing process in which learners and teachers are active. In a constructivist classroom, assessment of learning is interwoven with teaching and occurs through a number of ways such as observation, exhibitions and portfolios. Teachers can examine the learners' thinking process by asking them to provide a solution to a problem and then defend their decision and ideas. The teaching approaches and methods consistent with some goals which are namely communicative language teaching, the natural approach, cooperative language learning, content based instruction, task-based language teaching and genre-based pedagogy.

CHALLENGES OF LEARNING THEORIES

In behaviorist theory, learners are restricted with stimulus-response chains or with predicted behaviors. If so, learner behaves passive due to merely responding to the environmental stimuli.. The deepest and most complex reason for behaviorism's decline in influence is its commitment to the thesis that behavior can be explained without reference to non-behavioral mental (cognitive, representational, or interpretative) activity (Graham, 2007). When a person is exposed to language education utilizing a behaviorist approach, s/he may have late language mastery for practicing a set of mechanical patterns and drills. Repetition and practising drills may lead learners to reach the threshold level, which is to be gained in order for being creative in language. At this level, the language learner is not creative and cannot use the language properly in new situations. It is, then, obvious that the intrinsic learning will be delayed, owing to the late acquisition of threshold level and previously settled set of rules and drills (Demirezen, 1988). In other words, basic linguistic patterns would not be enough for communication in the long-term period, although practising them provides immediate and accurate speech at the beginning of the language learning process (Brown, 2001).

The cognitivists are generally interested in the process which tries to explain the deep structure of human mind. Although cognitivists claim that new information is linked with the previous knowledge by human beings, what they ignore is that learning is influenced by external factors, and it is inadequate to deal merely with the inner thought process. Innate genetic differences which cause different learning abilities are also ignored. Some people may be innately better at learning some language skills than others, so a proper degree of cognitive control over language cannot be expected by all learners. In addition, since cognitive theory represents experiences and mental functions as measurements, it ignores the context where the meaning of these measurements occurs.

Constructivism has been clarified as a productive paradigm which helps learners take responsibility for their own thoughts, feelings, attitudes, and perceptions to foster their understanding and learning. On the other hand, it leads to some problems in the application phase. Although the desire for such an education has a long history, constructivist reforms have not led to a comprehensive and coherent reform of educational practice in the schools for some reasons. The challenges can be gathered under three headings as teacher challenges, learner challenges and institutional challenges. A teacher's role in constructivism is to assist the construction of powerful knowledge rather than explicit knowledge and information (Reid, 1993; Tharp & Gallimore, 1989). Therefore, the teacher's role may change since s/he has to give up the title of being an expert to become a facilitator which can be very difficult for some teachers. It requires practice and experience. Learners discuss and question more in the classroom which may increase the noise level in the classroom. Furthermore, the teacher may need to make changes in their teaching style and search for a new methodology to strengthen the foundation of the constructivist learning philosophy. Secondly, learners' roles will change since it may take time to change long-formed habits. They will understand that multiple answers are expected and this may challenge the student to document and defend their thinking. They will begin to take an active part in their own assessment of their knowledge and in the assessment of the learning situation. The last challenge refers to the institutions in which constructivist philosophy may be applied. Once the constructivist learning environment is initiated, the institution must engage in continual evaluation of the process. Administration and teacher duties must shift from supervision and control to guidance and support. In addition, the assessment in constructivist learning is against the existing assessment which may have been built on standardized measurement. In this sense, constructivism calls for a reconsideration of evaluation and grading procedures.

A HOLISTIC APPROACH TO LEARNING THEORIES IN FOREIGN LANGUAGE TEACHING

Despite their challenges, the learning theories discussed in this chapter offer different explanations of learning. The theories can be logically evaluated as a cause-effect relationship within the framework of multicultural philosophy. Behaviourism as a learning theory is somewhat easy to understand because it relies only on observable behaviour and describes some types of behaviour. Its positive and negative reinforcement techniques can be very effective in foreign language education settings where learners have difficulty in understanding or where human disorders are treated. By conditioning learners with learning disabilities, responding to a stimulus can be obtained. However, behaviourism disregards all kinds of learning and mental activities. Therefore, educators can plan an appropriate curriculum enhancing learners' conditioning behaviours and focusing on stimulus-response interactions.

Cognitive theory stresses that much learning involves associations established through contiguity and repetition. So the importance of reinforcement is acknowledged for providing feedback about the correctness of responses over its role as a motivator. It views learning as involving the acquisition or reorganization of the cognitive structures through which humans store information. Its reinforcement techniques can be appropriate for enhancing learners' logical and conceptual growth in foreign language learning. By emphasizing the fundamental concepts, learners can learn maturing concepts and retrieve the information for use.

Constructivism, which is a philosophy of learning, emphasizes learning model as a way of generating mental models and individual rules by making sense of experiences. Learning, therefore, is simply the process of adjusting existing mental models to accommodate new experiences. In this sense, learning is a pathway to meaning as a whole and as parts. Individuals construct their own meaning by searching for information on the relevant or interrelated area by analysing, interpreting, or predicting. Thus, they can evaluate their own performances and learning progress.

Table 1 – Learning theories in a holistic view

Learning theories		Behaviorism	Cognitive	Constructivism
Purpose	FLL	Verbal behavior, conditioning	Meaning, understanding, innate knowledge	Socially constructed meaning making, collaborative learning
Course focus	FLL	Learning process is designed by instructor	Problem solving by the management of instructor, cognitive structures by storing information	Instructor mentors for individual or peer interaction in a social construction
Learner	FLL	Responding stimuli in a passive way	Storing and retrieving information	Creating, analyzing, and criticizing knowledge in an active way
Advantages	FLL	Integrating learners into conditioning activities to teach complex structures	Integrating learners into interactive problem solving	Integrating learners into constructive, analytic, creative, dialogic, interactive, social learning process
Disadvantages	FLL	Neglects the mental activity, creativity, social construction and causes late language mastery	It is inadequate to deal merely with the inner thought process.	It may take time to change long-formed habits and necessitates teachers' willingness to support the principles of constructivist pedagogy
Implications	FLL	Learners have stimuli for promoting learning	Learners deal with maturing conceptual learning individually	Learners involve in real experiences and value the previous ones by analyzing, criticizing, synthesizing

When all those three main learning theories are taken into account, some implications for instructional designs of those theories on foreign language learning (FLL) can be viewed in a holistic way.

In this holistic view, the learning theories are complementary. The weakness of one theory is addressed by the other. Thus, each theory has a role to play in foreign language learning regarding the status of learner. When learners are instructed in threshold level where the language patterns are difficult to grasp, behaviourist learning theory can be followed in the instruction process by enhancing stimuli-response chain. Particularly, some learners with learning disabilities, through such instruction, can be integrated into conditioning activities to teach structures for verbal behaviour and conditioning. Thus, they may have stimuli for promoting learning.

In a cognitivist approach, learners may be integrated into problem solving processes individually by storing and retrieving given information of instructor. The strengthening techniques used for enhancing learners' logical and conceptual growth in foreign language learning process can be employed to reflect and evaluate the internal representation of the learners, and thus the external reality and the processes of knowing, in other words, the internal mechanism of human thought can be examined.

In constructivism, socially structured collaborative learning is expected from learner.. Learners are encouraged to make connections between their previous experiences and new knowledge by evaluating their own performances and learning progress. Learners are encouraged to discover principles for themselves and to construct knowledge by working to solve realistic problems. It should be recognized that there is no such thing as knowledge "out there" independent of the knower, but only knowledge which is constructed while learning (Goldberg, 2002). Constructivism offers learner-centered learning with an emphasis on experiences and knowledge construction.

CONCLUSION

This chapter deals with three main sets of learning theories which are behaviorism, cognitivism, and constructivism. The purpose is to examine and evaluate the weak and strong points of each theory and to put them in a multicultural philosophy. Thus by discussing older and new concepts within the framework of those theories, a holistic perspective is presented as a pathway for education settings.

When learning theories are examined in detail, it can be deduced that the emphasis of each theory is on different aspects of learning Therefore, the theories, as a whole, are appropriate for learners with different characteristics. In other words, only one theory is not satisfactory to explain learning attitudes of individuals with dissimilar talents. Since learning is a very personal endeavour, learners need to be cared in a variety of ways. In this view, a holistic perspective of the theories can be brought into play in education process without accepting only one theory as more supreme than the others. In summary, those learning theories provide a comprehensive model for educational assessment of learners. Furthermore, a broader rationale for their system contains many important implications for assessment design, education practice and policy.

REFERENCES

Ausubel, D.P. (1968). *Educational psychology: A cognitive view*. New York: Holt, Rinehart & Winston.

Brooks, J. G. & Brooks, M. G. (1993*). In search of understanding: The case for constructivist classrooms*. Alexandria, VA: Association for Supervision and Curriculum Development.

Brown, H. D. (2001). Teaching by principles: An interactive approach to language pedagogy. New York: Longman.

Bruner, J. S. (1968) *Toward a theory of instruction.* New York: W. W. Norton & Company.

Bybee, R. W. (2002). Scientific inquiry, learner learning, and the science curriculum. In R. W. Bybee (Ed.). *Learning Science and the Science of Learning,* (pp. 25-36). Arlington, VA: NSTA Press.

Council for Cultural Cooperation (2002). *Common European framework of reference for languages: Learning, teaching, assessment.* Cambridge: Cambridge University Press.

Celce-Murcia, D. & McIntosh, L. (1989). *Teaching English as a second or a foreign language.* Rowley: MA: Newbury House.

Chomsky N.(1977). *Essays on form and interpretation.* Amsterdam: Elsevier Science Ltd.

Chuang, H. & Rosenbusch, M. H. (2005). Use of digital video technology in an elementary school foreign language methods course. *British Journal of Educational Technology.* 36(5), 869-80.

Demirezen M. (1988). Behaviourist theory and language learning. *Hacettepe Üniversitesi Eğitim Fakültesi Dergisi, 3,* 135 – 140.

Gagnon, G. W. & Collay, M. (2001). *Designing for learning: Six elements in constructivist classrooms.* USA: Corwin Press.

Goldberg, M. F. (2002). *15 School questions and discussion: From class size, standards, and school safety to leadership and more.* Lanham, MD: Scarecrow.

Graham G. (2007). *Behaviourism*: *The Stanford Encyclopedia of Philosophy.* RetrievedDecember 20, 2009 from *http://plato.stanford.edu/entries/behaviourism/.*

Hartley, J. (1998). *Learning and studying. A research perspective*, London: Routledge.

Kymissis E. & Poulson C. L. (1990). The history of imitation in learning theory: The Language acquisition process. *Journal of the Experimental Analysis of Behaviour. 54*(2), 113-127.

Leonard, D. C. (2002). *Learning theories, A to Z.* Santa Barbara: Greenwood Press.

Lightbrown P. M. & Spada N. (2003). *How languages are learned.* Oxford: Oxford University Press.

Liu Q & Shi J. (2007). An analysis of language teaching approaches and methods, effectiveness and weakness. *US-China Education Review,4*(1),69-71.

Marlowe, B. A. and Page, M. L. (2005). *Creating and sustaining the constructivist classroom* (2nd ed.).Thousand Oaks, CA: Corwin Press.

Matthews, W. J. (2003). Constructivism in the classroom: Epistemology, history, and empirical evidence. *Teacher Education Quarterly.* 30(3), 51-64.

McDonough, S. K. (2001). Way beyond drill and practice: Foreign language lab activities in support of constructivist learning. *International Journal of Media. 28*(1)*,* 75-81.

Meng J. (2009). *The Relationship between linguistics and language teaching*. Asian Social Science, *5*(12). Retrieved December 18, 2009 from *http://www.ccsenet.org/ournal/index.php/ass/article/viewFile/4553/3887.*

Mergel B. (1998). *Instructional design & learning theory*. Retrieved December 16, 2009 from *http://www.usask.ca/education/coursework/802papers/mergel/brenda.htm.*

Newmann, F. M. (1993). Beyond common sense in educational restructuring: The issues of content and linkage. *Educational Research, 22*(2), 4-13.

Ögeyik, M.C. (2008). *English language teacher education and language related fields*. The 5th International Conference. The Language: A Phenomenon without Frontiers, Varna.

Pellegrino, J. W., Chudowsky, N., & Glaser, R. (2001). *Knowing what students know: The science and design of educational assessment*. Washington, DC: National Academy Press.

Piaget, J. (1973). *To understand is to invent*. New York: Grossman.

Piaget, J. (1965). The language and Thought of the Child New York: World Publishing Co.

Reid, D. K. (1993). Another vision of "visions and revisions." *Remedial. Special. Education. 14(4),*16,25.

Richards J. C. & Rodgers T. S. (2004). *Approaches and methods in language teaching*. 2[nd]Edition. Cambridge University Press: Cambridge.

Richardson, V. (2003). Constructivist pedagogy. *Teachers College Record*. 105(9), 1623–1640.

Roblyer, M.D., Edwards, J. & Havriluk, M.A. (1997). *Integrating educational technology into teaching*. Upper Saddle River, New Jersey: Prentice-Hall.

Roy J. 2005. *Soul shapers: A better plan for parents and educators*. Maryland: Review and Herald Publishing Association.

Ruschoff, B. & Ritter, M. (2001). Technology-enhanced language learning: Construction of knowledge and template-based learning in the foreign language classroom. *Computer Assisted Language Learning. 14*(4), 219-232.

Skinner, B. F. (1976). *About behaviourism*. New York: Vintage Books.

Tharp, R. G., & Gallimore, R. (1989). *Rousing minds to life: Teaching, learning, and schooling in context*. New York, NY: Cambridge University Press.

Vasta, R., Haith, M.. & Miller, S. (1995). *Child psychology*. New York: John Whiley & Sons.

Vygotsky, L. (1962). *Thought and Language*. Cambridge: MIT Press.

Woolfolk, A.E. (1987). *Educational psychology* (3rd Ed). Englewood Cliffs, NJ: Prentice-Hall.

In: Language and Literacy Education in a Challenging World   ISBN: 978-1-61761-198-8
Editors: T. Lê, Q. Lê, and M. Short   © 2011 Nova Science Publishers, Inc.

Chapter 6

MICRO AND MACRO SOCIALIZATIONS IN EAL EDUCATION: CURRICULUM AND CLASSROOM ENVIRONMENT FROM THE PERSPECTIVE OF VYGOTSKY'S QUANTUM PSYCHOLOGY OF LANGUAGE

Charlotte Hua Liu

ABSTRACT

Examining language education as a microcosm of social dialectics, this paper discusses Vygotsky's quantum psychology of language mediation in relation to the social impact of EAL education in contemporary multicultural societies. To be able to conceptualize micro-macro connectivity in socialization and change, it argues for the integration of language functions and the development of conscious awareness, which needs to be reflected in both EAL curriculum and the classroom discourse environment. In terms of curriculum, it accentuates the importance of teaching scientific concepts and the written speech. With regards to classroom discourse environment, it proposes reflective resonation between teacher and students as the central mechanism as well as origin of development through socialization. Where language and thinking are integrated at both curriculum and socialization levels, EAL education operates in the '1+1>2' model, as opposed to the '1+1=2' or '1+1<2' model. In the former, inter-linguistic and inter-functional generalization and awareness develop as specific benefits promised by multilingual proficiency. Finally, specific implications are offered for constructing and reflecting on EAL curriculum and the classroom discourse environment.

Keywords: EAL education, Vygotsky, quantum psychology of language, micro and macro socialization in language education, '1+1>2' model, curriculum, classroom discourse environment.

INTRODUCTION

As the process of globalization intensifies, the English language has increasingly come to symbolize social prestige internationally (Pennycook, 1994). In many native as well as non-native speaking countries, proficiency in the English language provides access to social, cultural and educational capitals. In this context, however, it is observed that education, including language education, "preserves structural relations between social groups" (Bernstein, 1996, p.11). In Australia, language education for minority groups has also been stated to recycle ideological influences (Bullivant, 1995). Research on language as social capital thus does not seem to translate to research on the social impact of language education.

To address this disconnection in knowledge, a reconsideration of the social function of language and its educational enactment is in order. Particularly, it is important to understand the function of language that underlies change, human agency and social mobility. It is also important to understand the characteristics and mechanism of language in socialization that enables change and development. With this understanding, it will then be possible to make sense of the social consequences of educational processes. It will be possible to view classrooms or schools as microcosms connected to the ecological whole of society in general.

To understand change and its social origin, researchers must first abandon the view of education as an epiphenomenon of social and ideological structures. Currently, research on the social impact of language classrooms commonly perceives socialization at the micro level as replication or extension of socialization at the macro level. This mechanical definition of the research problem effectively deflects researchers' attention away from classrooms as a unique social ecological setting (Allright, 1998). From the outset, the mechanical definition of the research problem prevents us from understanding classrooms as the origin of change, development and social renewal.

To comprehend the origin of change and development originated in any social, educational setting, be it families, classrooms, schools or workplaces, our understanding of language needs to satisfy two interrelated conditions. First, our description needs to reflect language functions both within and outside the social organization. That is, we seek to define the language functions that uniformly portray the quality of socializations across different settings. In this sense, language functions across settings contribute to an internal plane of human experiences. Second, language functions need to be studied in light of its enablement of qualitative change in structural awareness rather than a quantitative sum of experiences that do not connect. That is, language use in socialization needs to be understood in terms of its contribution to individual freedom and transcendence from social constraints. With such understanding of language in socialization, educational research will then shed light on the internal, authentic connection between micro and macro social structures and organizations. This understanding of the connection between language functions and individual development will also enlighten educational practitioners in their professional engagement.

Thus, replacing the current causal, mechanical paradigm in studying social impacts of education and language education in particular, there now needs to be a new paradigm, where micro and macro structures are connected in light of the qualitative nature rather than the quantitative sum of socialization experiences. In relation, it is proposed that Vygotsky's theories of language-mediated socialization and development presents a quantum view of change in society. In brief, with regards to socialization and relationships at all levels, it depicts a mechanism of resonation rather than simplistic replication. Enabling this resonation is the view of language not as an independent container of meaning but as a mediator of internal dynamics, with which verbalization continually interacts.

On language education as a microcosm of social dialectics, this chapter begins with a brief introduction to Vygotsky's quantum psychology and its key notion of interactive resonation, the origin and mechanism of social change (Section I). In order to shed light on specific implications for social research and language classroom practices, Section II engages in a review of the connection between language and the development of thinking and conscious awareness. This leads to the proposal of EAL teaching for psychological development rather than linguistic acquisition alone, emphasizing the importance of instructions in disciplinary concepts and the written speech. For research on interpersonal relations, the notion of social environment is also redefined. Section III discusses EAL education for empowering minority learners. It puts forward a "1+1>2" model, where L1 and L2 develop interdependently, leading to a higher-level abstraction and generalization. The social advantages of inter-linguistic code switching are also discussed. Finally, Section IV offers specific implications for constructing as well as interpreting EAL curriculum and the classroom discourse environment.

A QUANTUM PSYCHOLOGY OF LANGUAGE AND EDUCATION

Parallel to the disconnection of educational sociology with the psychology of individual development is the mismatch between mechanical macrophysics and quantum physics. For comprehending the world of external matters, macrophysics can only predict the movements of huge masses of particles but is powerless in depicting the trajectories of singular particles. Similarly, the mechanical educational sociological theories, permeating various aspects and levels of policy and decision making, often seem to be at odds with the intricacies of growth psychology. Sociological investigations of developmental trends of social cohorts are well versed in the perpetuation of structural inequality and the mystique of change at either social or individual levels.

In the physical world, Heisenberg's uncertainty principle stipulates that, as soon as the observation of subatomic particles begins, the scientist enters into an interaction with the objects of observation, which interferes with the movement of the objects in a way that is beyond experimental control and manipulation. The principle of unpredictability applies equally to the study of the human world. The human psyche is a universe of multiple, heterogeneous components which are perpetually in interaction with each other. Individuals in society are, consciously or unconsciously, constantly observing, monitoring, and adapting their own thinking and behaviour. Internal interaction as a mechanism underlies any level of sense-making, regardless of one's awareness of it. This uncertainty of the human psyche is essentially the reason for the mismatch between mechanical investigations to date of language, education and change at the macro and micro levels.

In a quantum psychology, therefore, the focus of research must be shifted from the quantitative sum of language and social experiences to their qualitative nature and structure. This essentially involves understanding the structure of interfunctional interactions as they are mediated in speech and social exchange (Liu, 2008). It is the insight into this structural operation in language and socialization that allows for a comprehension of reflective self-regulation, the core construct in human agency. To this end, Vygotsky's dialectic psychology promises the possibility of reconciliation, so far unattained, between the studies of societal and individual trajectories of change.

In this dialectic view of micro- and macro-socialization, education does not cause empowerment by external means (be it the semantics or semiotics of speech) but triggers social or interpsychological connectedness, the subject of psycho-semiotic study of language mediation (Liu, 2008). Interpsychological encounter resonates with individuals' drive for intrapsychological change, which, in turn, influences the quality of social processes. Social relationship thus gives rise to the increasing capacity to communicate intrapersonally. The dialectics, denoting an interactive resonation between individual students and their classroom environments, applies equally to understanding the relationship between smaller social units and the larger settings they are embedded in. The social consequences of language education are, therefore, comprehended in the rings of ripples of social, i.e., interpsychological resonation.

In the following sections, discussions will be devoted, respectively, to Vygotsky's theories on the connection between language and conscious awareness; his position on language education; EAL education from a transformative perspective, namely, the '1+1>2' model; and specific implications for constructing and reflecting on curriculum and classroom discourse environment.

LANGUAGE AND LANGUAGE EDUCATION

Language Mediated Development

For Vygotsky, language mastery is the mechanism of human development; it is not only the pathway to individual internalization of the social, cultural and historical, it is also the enabler of individual transformation through internalization. Language as a symbolic and psychological tool, which allows for such development, has two fundamental characteristics.

First, language is dual in nature -- every word contains an external and an internal plane of meaning. It mediates, simultaneously, processes of social and intrapersonal meaning making. In authentic and growth-enabling communications, the inter- and intra-psychological processes are interdependent and interactive. Mastery of a language, therefore, entails not simply the production of linguistically correct use of speech, but more importantly the ability to engage in verbal thinking in the language.

Secondly, language facilitates verbal thinking in its symbolic, rather than semantic or semiotic, capacity.

> The word does not relate to a single object, but to an *entire group or class of objects*. Therefore, every word is a concealed generalization. From a psychological perspective, word meaning is first and foremost a *generalization* (Vygotsky, 1987, p.47, original emphases).

Because every word relates to a group of objects, and word meaning always represents an individual conceptual abstraction, the reality represented in individual cognitions by language is now qualitatively different from the reality reflected in immediate sensations and primary perceptions. Language serves to organize for the human mind a conceptualization of the objective world that is both interpersonally meaningful and intrapersonally symbolic. Language mastery has revolutionary impacts on thinking and reflection.

Scientific Concepts and Conscious Awareness in EAL Education

Among the basic tasks of the psychology of school instruction is to clarify this internal logic, the internal course of development that is called to life by a particular course of instruction ... School instruction and the adult's collaboration with the child in solving problems must manifest meaningfulness and lead to the understanding of structural relations (Vygotsky, 1987, p. 208, p.210).

School instruction in EAL should not be driven by the need to reproduce in learners' native speaker-like spontaneity. Instead, it must aim to develop scientific concepts and inter-linguistic awareness.

The strength of the scientific concept lies in the higher characteristics of concepts, in conscious awareness and volition. In contrast, this is the weakness of the child's everyday concept. The strength of the everyday concept lies in spontaneous, situationally meaningful, concrete applications, that is, in the sphere of experience and the empirical. ... Scientific concepts restructure and raise spontaneous concepts to a higher level, forming their zone of proximal development. ... instruction in scientific concepts plays a decisive role in the child's mental development" (Vygotsky, 1987, p.220).

Scientific concepts and spontaneous concepts have completely opposite developmental directions and pathways. Whilst spontaneous concepts originate from daily, immediate experiences, scientific concepts reflect the internal logic of knowledge and thinking, systematically constructed in the classroom. In language learning, students' awareness of the speech system and of themselves as learners is to guide the development of spontaneous and colloquial operation with the language. In EAL and any other additional language education, scientific conceptual thinking of the English language predates spontaneous concepts.

Scientific concepts in language education may involve the thinking and communicative operations with linguistic, semantic, semiotic and genre constructs, which describe the higher characteristics of speech and its social usage. Internalized as thinking and communicative instruments, such constructs enable learning-to-learn capacities. They also build inter-linguistic connections between the operant language(s) and the target language, making possible abstraction and generalization.

Written and Oral Language

Also mediating the development of scientific concepts in language is the written speech. The instruction of writing should guide rather than lag behind thinking development.

It could be argued that if written speech requires volition, abstraction, and other functions that have not yet matured in the school child, we need to delay instruction until these functions begin to mature. Practical experience demonstrates, however, that instruction in writing is among the most important subjects in the child's early school career and that it elicits the development of functions that have not yet matured. Thus, when we say that instruction should rely on the zone of proximal development rather than on mature functions, ... we are ... freeing ourselves from an old delusion that implies that development must complete its cycles for instruction to move forward (Vygotsky, 1987, p.211).

If oral language is a first-order generalization of reality, Vygotsky argues, written language is a second-order abstraction. The latter mediates "verbal thinking". Compared to oral language, the "sensual aspect of language" (Vygotsky, 1987, p.203), written language lacks the following: sounds and tones that transmit implicit meanings, situational and contextual cues, and an interlocutor from whom immediate and constant prompts are gained in extending the conversation. On the other hand, written language, 'directed by consciousness and intention almost from the outset' (Vygotsky, 1987, p.204), requires integral understanding and planning of the content as a structural whole.

> Written speech is the algebra of speech. The process of learning algebra does not repeat that of arithmetic. It is a new and higher plane in the development of abstract mathematical thought that is constructed over and rises above arithmetic thinking. In the same way, the algebra of speech (i.e., written speech) introduces the child to an abstract plane of speech that is constructed over the developed system of oral speech (Vygotsky, 1987, p.203).

Vygotsky's writings on scientific and spontaneous concepts and written and oral speech have important implications for sociological investigations of EAL education in multicultural societies. Studies of the social significance of language education must take into account the developmental nature of pedagogic content, classroom interaction and activities. Teaching programs which evolve around spontaneous production of speech and those that establish conceptual operation, self-awareness and inter-systemic generalization have qualitative differences in both developmental and socio-ideological consequences. While the latter works to empower individual change and conscious awareness of minority populations; the former restricts students' mental development, reinforces and perpetuates existing weakness in spontaneity of the target language, and effectively subordinates multilingual operation to English superiority. Social studies that fail to address the developmental nature of teaching programs are deficient for understanding the connection between micro- and macro-socializations in EAL education.

Social Environment in Education

With regards to classroom teaching, it is well-known that Vygotsky emphasizes the importance of interpersonal interaction and socialization. Owing to surface readings of this postulation of the social environment, Vygotsky is popularly branded as the father of the social constructivist school of thinking. For language learning, the latter typically accentuates spontaneous and automatic use through sustained immersion and implicit instructions. "The proposal is that language is learned with a minimal amount of explicit intervention and a maximum amount of undirected participation and immersion in language" (Christie, 1995, p.10). Language productions in the classroom are often elicited by the immediate situation of speech transaction, not volitional awareness of the functions of language.

Allwright (1998, p.130) describes the interesting classroom discoursal dilemma which plagues particularly language teaching: "a simple conflictual relationship between social and pedagogical pressures", "wherein teachers and learners might delude themselves, and each other, that 'all must be well pedagogically if all is apparently well socially'". Where the everyday, social world reproduced within the classroom is believed to make learning 'real' and 'relevant', socialization is emphasized to the detriment of conceptual and academic development.

InVygotsky's position, meaningful socialization that is the origin of reflective development does not refer to the truthful mimicry of the everyday, spontaneous interaction. By contrast, social relationship essentially entails two interrelated dimensions: a) complete integration of conceptual and social processes, and socialization not only *about* but also *with* conceptual operation; and b) in teacher-student interaction, the teacher operates with scientific concepts, or the ideal form in language studies, first in thinking and then in communicating with students. Authentic classroom interaction begins with the teacher's discussion of his/her own thinking structure or process, modeling and engaging with his/her intrapsychological communication. This triggers the resonation of thinking operation in his/her audience, and initiates internal reflection within the individual student (Liu, 2008). Thus, the teacher engages students in conceptual operation not in a causal, external manner but in an internal and acausal manner. Together, the two dimensions define authentic interpsychological encounter. Both teacher and students communicate as thinking and developing individuals. Only in this sense does socialization serve as the source, rather than the mere backdrop, "of all the specifically human characteristics of consciousness that develop in the child" (Vygotsky, 1987, p.210).

To understand the connection between micro- and macro- social phenomena in education, including language education, the definition of authentic socialization is core. To understand change at individual as well as societal levels, the casual, resonating mechanism of socialization now needs to replace the direct, causal and external explanatory model.

EAL EDUCATION: THE "1+1>2" MODEL

The Interdependence of L1 and L2

Deep rooted in Vygotsky's educational psychology is the belief that learning in all scientific disciplines contributes to a formal aspect of development, i.e., the development of generalization, volitional operation and conscious awareness. Instruction of scientific concepts "influence the development of the higher mental functions in a manner that exceeds the limits of the specific content and material of each subject" (Vygotsky, 1987, p.208).

> There is significant commonality in the mental foundations underlying instruction in the various school subjects that is alone sufficient to insure the potential for the influence of one subject on the other (i.e., there is a formal aspect to each school subject) … In attaining conscious awareness of cases, the child masters a structure that is transferred to other domains that are not directly linked with cases or grammar; … the mental functions are interdependent and interconnected. … Because of the foundation which is common to all the higher mental functions, the development of voluntary attention and logical memory, of abstract thinking and scientific imagination, occurs as a complex unified process. The common foundation for all the higher mental functions is consciousness and mastery (Vygotsky, 1987, p.208).

Unlike spontaneous concepts developed through individuals' daily, concrete experiences with the environment, scientific concepts that define a disciplinary area function in such a manner that they interact structurally with the individual's mental organization as a whole.

While spontaneous concepts are developed through specific, immediate and situational experiences; scientific concepts as internalized instruments enable the (re)organization of thinking and conscious awareness at a structural level.

As heterogeneous developmental paths, however, spontaneous and scientific concepts rely on one another for functional vigor and developmental sustainability. The interdependence of spontaneous and scientific concepts is likened to the relationship between L1 and L2 (Vygotsky, 1987). "[T]here is a *mutual dependence* between these two paths of development. The conscious and intentional learning of a foreign language is obviously dependent on a certain level of development in the native language" (Vygotsky, 1987, p.221, original emphasis).

Comparable to spontaneous concepts is the immediate, word-world relationship between L1 and the objective reality. In L2, the relationship between language and thinking is mediated by L1. The word-world relationships in L1 provide formal foundations for the development of abstract, symbolic word-word relationships in L2. Such word-word relationships underlie the awareness and generalization of language as symbolic as well as psychological functioning systems. The transfer from L1 to L2, as Cummins points out, is by no means limited to semantic, i.e., word-world knowledge, but presents itself in higher-order thinking skills. "[S]ubject matter knowledge, higher-order thinking skills, reading strategies, writing composition skills etc. developed through the medium of L1 transfer or become available to L2 given sufficient exposure and motivation" (Cummins, 1984, p.144).

On the other hand, mastery of an additional language has formal impacts on learners' existing speech systems. The mastery of L2 objectifies the primary connection between L1 and reality. As a result, the relation between the external features of language, such as sounds, spellings, and sentence structures, etc., and the meaning aspects becomes less direct. The immediacy in such relation is reduced. Such interdependent development between speech systems is not a matter of addition but one of qualitative change in terms of the way reality is organized in the conceptual system.

Scientific conceptual development, contributing to the formal aspects of learning and the interdependence between languages as psychological systems have important implications for EAL education. EAL education cannot set for itself the same goal as in L1 development, namely, word-world relationships. EAL education is to enable the development of inter-linguistic abstraction, generalization and conscious awareness. It needs to drive and guide the structural (re)organization of thinking that was previously mediated by L1. The additional language education evolving around the formal aspect of the subject is what is referred to as the '1+1>2' model, contrasted with the '1+1=2' model or the '1+1<2' model. In the latter cases, with L1 perceived to distract or interfere with development in L2, EAL instructions are based on its isolated operation from existing speech function systems. Because of the segregation of speech as thinking systems, instruction in EAL inevitably remain at the surface, semantic, coding-decoding level of language operation. In accordance, instruction is subordinated to producing native-like proficiency and fails to contribute to the general development of thinking and consciousness.

Inter-linguistic Code Switching as Social Symbolic Power

In studying the social symbolic power of language, one may rightly point out the artificiality of the social prestige attached to one form of language use such as the standardised English as opposed to other dialects of 'Englishes'. But it would not be justifiable to contend, for reasons of social justice and equality, that there needs only be individual options of any one form or dialect of language use in their educational pursuits, at the discard of multiplicity. At a social level, this version of "multiculturalism" or "multilingualism" indeed implies social separatism (Radtke, 2001). At the individual cognitive level, it effectively prevents the development of higher-order abstraction and conscious awareness resulting from inter-linguistic transfer. Delpit (2002) describes her daughter's ability to "switch" between the standard and black versions of Englishes. Such ability of "code switching", or in other words, the cognitive flexibility in psycho-semiotic capacities, may well be a key to individual empowerment and social realization of multiculturalism.

IMPLICATIONS FOR CURRICULUM AND CLASSROOM DISCOURSE ENVIRONMENT

Implications for Curriculum

In the case of migrant or international students in Australia, many have already received formal schooling in the English language system. With grammatical rules and the written speech often being the foci of foreign language education (Byram, 1989) in their home countries, these EAL learners' comparative strength is their evolving consciousness of the linguistic system, or the scientific conceptual understanding of the language. Their weakness, compared to native speakers, lies in the ability to communicate fluently and spontaneously. For language education to empower social change in minority groups, classroom teaching should aim to enhance inter-linguistic and inter-functional reflectivity and awareness as specific benefits of multilingual proficiency, not to reproduce native-like speech spontaneity. With additional and native languages developing in opposite directions, spontaneity in the additional language is to develop later than and under the guidance of the structural, conceptual understanding of the speech system.

For the EAL curriculum, this has several implications. First, for developing awareness of structural, systemic functions, implicit immersion in everyday speech transactions is not sufficient. Conscious instructions of the linguistic, semantic, semiotic and genre features of the English language, are essential. Second, because of the relation between the written speech and the development of reflective awareness, teaching reading, writing and critical literacy skills is also crucial. Particularly, learners need to be engaged in understanding how the written speech (in reading and writing) is used to mediate thinking, reflecting, problem solving, and creating. In understanding the thinking function of the written speech, it is of paramount importance that learners not be constrained to the semantic or semiotic level of coding and decoding of isolated words and phrases. Instead, they need to be encouraged to reflect and analyze, in the ongoing unfolding of the language and the construction of textual context, the inter-relationship of meaning units. Accordingly, they must be encouraged to adopt the tools of language in enabling their own thinking process.

Implications for Classroom Discourse Environment

Vygotsky's claim of social relationship being the origin of thinking development has several important implications for understanding and constructing the discourse environment in language classrooms. Generally, this means that language and disciplinary concepts should not be taught *about* but be taught *with* in classroom interaction. In other words, curriculum content should not be merely objects of teaching and learning but needs to be authentic communicative instruments utilized in teacher-student and student-student exchanges. Language is used to relate simultaneously to one's own thinking and to the external listener, rather than to prescribe knowing and understanding.

For instance, one often hears the EAL teacher making statements in the classroom such as 'The word, X, means this' and 'This sentence doesn't mean …'. The absolute prescriptions of the meaning of speech, as a purely objective and externally verified entity, effectively situate the teacher as an 'insider' and unsurpassable authority and the student an 'outsider'. Contrasted is the discourse environment where meaning is jointly shared, negotiated and collectively enabled. Characteristic of such an environment would be statements such as 'When I read this, it makes me think of / reminds me of…'; 'Reading this, I feel …'; and 'The word in this context seems to me to suggest …'. These descriptions of the teacher's own thinking and interaction with the text are then used as initiations for students' sharing. Alternatively, students are invited to initiate the dialogue with 'What do you think is meant by …?'; 'Why do you think it says …?'; 'Would you put it differently?' or 'What could you say if the story changes like this?'. Incorporating the students' subsequent responses, the teacher thinks aloud, sharing and requesting confirmation for his/her interpretation of the students' speech.

Demonstrated in these exchanges is the educational belief that the teaching of meaningful use of language must first involve its social modeling. Also illustrated is the belief that the thinking function of language originates from the interpersonal relationship established within the exchange of verbal thinking.

Secondly, concepts that linguists employ in describing the internal system and principles of the language should also be used in classroom directions, questions and discussions. In many classrooms where linguistic characteristics of the English language are explicitly taught, they are defined and identified in texts as objects of studies. Students then invariably do grammatical exercises designed to intensify students' retention of such concepts. But other than the artificial situation where the concepts are talked about as isolated constructs, they are not used interpersonally between teacher and students or between peers as tools of communication. In contrast to this is the classroom discourse environment where concepts are not only consciously taught but they also acquire meaning from interpersonal interaction. Scientific constructs that define the discipline of studies permeate the quintessential initiation--response--follow-up discourse structure. A culture is established for multidirectional transactions with scientific concepts, involving teacher-class, teacher-student, student-student, and student-class exchanges.

Finally, using EAL to mediate conscious awareness means allowing students 'into the plot' and to partake in negotiating the metacognitive aspects of classroom and curriculum activities. To begin with, teachers need to openly discuss and articulate activity structures, including their rationales, goals or objectives, teacher and student roles, corresponding procedures, and evaluation standards, etc. More often than is desirable, teachers in EAL classrooms give directions for detailed, particular, isolated actions or behaviour deemed to indicate "learning", while failing to address the general activity context or pedagogic relevance. Such behavior-oriented directions are believed to be explicit teaching that minimizes chaos and miscomprehension. Often, behavioral directions in such forms as "Take out your notebooks and write this down", "Spell this", "Don't write about the weather", or "Write about the weather" drown whatever desire students may have to own their learning. Classes conducted exclusively with these detailed, specific and prescriptive directions can resemble a one-man puppet show, with the teacher alone being in the know of the logic and trajectory in teaching and learning.

In contrast, what Bernstein (1996) refers to as the regulative discourse, as opposed to the academic discourse, needs to involve teacher and students alike in the joint processes of planning, organizing, and regulating participation. As regulative discourse is externalized and shared by teacher and students, this is, in time, internalized for self-aware and self-regulative learning.

CONCLUSION

In summary, this chapter examines language education as a microcosm of social dialectics. It extends Vygotsky's quantum psychology of language mediation in understanding the social impact of EAL education in contemporary multicultural societies. To be able to conceptualize micro-macro connectivity in socialization and change, it argues for the integration of language functions and the development of conscious awareness, which needs to be reflected in both EAL curriculum and classroom discourse environment. In terms of curriculum, it accentuates the importance of teaching scientific concepts and the written speech. With regards to classroom discourse environment, it proposes reflective resonation between teacher and students as the central mechanism as well as origin of development through socialization. As the central mechanism of development in society, reflective resonation gives rise to the unpredictability of individual transcendence.

Where language and thinking are integrated at both curriculum and socialization levels, EAL education operates in the '1+1>2' model, as opposed to the '1+1=2' or '1+1<2' model. In the former, inter-linguistic and inter-functional generalization and awareness develop as specific benefits promised by multilingual proficiency.

This chapter challenges classroom practitioners and educational researchers alike to operate in the new paradigm with the functional integration of language and conceptual thinking. Specifically, it highlights the importance of EAL classroom practice to be mediated by the educator's internal dynamics. It challenges for mutual growth in EAL learners and practitioners alike. For social research of language education in multicultural societies, Vygotsky's quantum psychology of language mediation challenges for a vision that unites micro- and macro-socializations in terms of the qualitative nature rather than the quantitative sum of social experiences. Corresponding with this is a view of language not as the independent container of meaning but as mediator of internal dynamics with which language interacts. In general, the chapter challenges for the connectivity between: a) teaching and learning; b) education and change; and c) changes at micro and macro levels of society.

REFERENCES

Allwright, D. (1998). Contextual factors in classroom language learning: An overview. In K. Malmkjaer & J. Williams (Eds.), *Context in language learning and language understanding* (pp. 115 – 134). Cambridge: Cambridge University Press.

Bernstein, B. (1996). *Pedagogy, symbolic control and identity: Theory, research, critique.* London, Washington DC: Taylor and Francis Publishers.

Bullivant, B. M. (1995). Ideological influences on linguistic and cultural empowerment: an Australian example. In J. W. Tollefson (Ed.), *Power and inequality in language education* (pp. 59 – 72). Cambridge: Cambridge University Press.

Byram, M. (1989). *Cultural studies in foreign language education.* Clevedon and Philadelphia: Multilingual Matters Ltd.

Christie, F. (1995). An interview with Frances Christie. *Fine Print. 17*(2), 9 – 13.

Cummins, J. (1984). *Bilingualism and special education: issues in assessment and pedagogy.* Clevedon and Philadelphia: Multilingual Matters Ltd., England.

Delpit, L. (2002). No kinda sense. In Delpit, L. & Dowdy, J. K. (Eds.), *The skin that we speak* (pp. 31 – 48). New York: New Press.

Liu, C. H. (2002). *Classroom environment, metacognition, and transfer of mathematical learning: A social contextual and interactionist perspective* (Masters thesis). South Australia: University of Adelaide.

Liu, C. H. & Matthews, R. (2005). Vygotsky's philosophy: constructivism and its criticisms examined. *International Education Journal. 6*(3), 386-399.

Liu, C. H. (2008). A *Vygotskyan educational psycho-semiotic perspective of interpsychology in classroom teaching and teacher socialization: Theories, instrument, and interpretive analyses* (Doctoral dissertation). South Australia: University of Adelaide.

Pennycook, A. (1994). *The cultural politics of English as an international language.* London: Longman.

Vygotsky, L. S. (1987). *Problems of general psychology – Collected works of L. S. Vygotsky* (Volume 1). New York & London: Plenum Press.

Vygotsky, L. S. (1997). *History of the Development of Higher Mental Functions – Collected works of L. S. Vygotsky* (Volume 4). New York & London: Plenum Press.

PART II

LANGUAGE AND LITERACY EDUCATION IN CONTEXT

In: Language and Literacy Education in a Challenging World   ISBN: 978-1-61761-198-8
Editors: T. Lê, Q. Lê, and M. Short

Chapter 7

PRIMARY SCHOOL TEACHERS' VIEWS ON GRAMMAR AND LITERACY TEACHING

Thao Lê, Paul Throssell, Lauren Hoban and Sally Milbourne

ABSTRACT

Grammar is an important aspect of literacy education. Linguists have provided useful insights into the nature of grammar. Current literacy discussions pay great attention to the role of grammar in education. Different perspectives on grammar and grammar teaching are discussed. As teachers are the key players in literacy education, a study was conducted to examine their views on grammar and literacy teaching. This chapter discusses the study and its findings.

Keywords: awareness, development, grammar, language, linguistics literacy.

INTRODUCTION

Grammar teaching has been a widely discussed topic in literacy education at various levels and in different contexts: school, government, community and the media. There are claims and counter-claims by researchers and policy makers about children's literacy achievement and their knowledge of grammar. As teachers are the most essential factor in driving the literacy agenda, it is important to know how they think and feel about grammar and literacy in the current context of literacy education. This chapter reports a qualitative study on primary school teachers' views on grammar and literacy.

GRAMMAR AND LITERACY

What do we mean by the term grammar? Byrnes and Wasik (2009, p.134) cite Saffran's 2003 description that grammar, "…pertains to using word order and inflections to describe 'who did what to whom'". Grammar can be described as the study of the rules which determine the permissible sequences of morphemes (units of meaning) in the sentences that make up any given language (Barrett, 1999, p.3). Crystal states succinctly "the aim of grammar is to give structure to meaning" (2006, p.185).

Grammar functions as a pattern or code that enables us to connect words in such a way as to create intentional meaning. Byrnes and Wasik (2009) discuss the importance of grammar in children's need to know how to create multiword structures that are likely to be interpreted as intended, and that are judged as acceptable to listeners.

There have been different ideas about what features of language are actually included in the concept of grammar. In linguistics grammar is often used to include everything speakers know about their language, including: phonology; semantics; morphology; syntax; and the lexicon (Ministry of Education, Western Australia, 1992). This meaning is used for the current study. Difficulties arise in reviewing the literature on grammar due to conflicting meanings of the term. Authors may use the term grammar to talk purely about syntax, as in Saffran's description, to talk about linguistic features generally, or to talk about any group of linguistic features.

Crystal (2006) identifies two broad categories of teaching grammar based on the purpose each serves. A prescriptive grammar lays down rules governing the socially correct use of grammar. A descriptive grammar describes "the form, meaning and grammatical rules of a language without making any evaluative judgments about their use (p.231). He also describes generational changes in grammar teaching in Britain, changes that can be seen in all English speaking nations, and reflects the three language teaching approaches previously described in this review: people educated before the 1960s learned traditional grammar and emerged with a "set of techniques for analysing sentences" and strong views on correct and incorrect usage (p.230); those schooled between the 1960s and 1990s engaged with language and society, learned "little or no grammar" and emerged with "little understanding of grammatical terminology" (p.231); and those who went to school after the mid 1990s "would have found a resurgence of interest in grammar, as part of the new National Curriculum... avoiding the old prescriptive biases" (p.231).

Traditional grammar teaching commonly used in schools before the 1960s provides explicit instruction in the linguistic elements of language. It is still in use in contexts where detailed and expert use of grammar is essential. These contexts include second language teaching, applied linguistics and speech pathology education.

Examples of other types of grammar include transformational generative grammar (Allen & Van Buren, 1975), and systemic functional grammar developed by M K Halliday which aims to develop an awareness of the functional organisation of language (Tucker, 2002). Halliday's focus is on understanding and explaining what language enables us to do in the everyday world (Harris et al, 2006).

More important than the many types of grammar in existence is the importance of grammar to the development of literacy in children. Babies with normal hearing and without neuro-developmental disorders naturally acquire the language they hear everyday, internalizing the grammar of that language. By thirty months of age children are well on the way to mastering the grammatical system of their native language (Byrnes & Wasik, 2009). Tomasello and Brooks (1999) comment on the relationship between the child's lexicon size and their grammatical competence, "grammatical function words start appearing soon after the child's vocabulary reaches 400 words" (p. 173).

Young children naturally learn spoken language and the grammar of that language, however reading and writing are quite different and have to be taught and painstakingly learned (Crystal, 2006). Knowledge of language including grammar, and the ability to think and talk about language (metalinguistics) is vitally important in learning to read and write.

THE STUDY

A study was conducted in Tasmania, Australia with primary school teachers. The main aim was to examine their views on grammar and grammar teaching. The study had three specific objects:

1. To examine primary school teachers' views on the significance of grammar in literacy education.

2. To examine their views on aspects of linguistic knowledge that primary teachers should have.

3. To examine their views on how grammar should be taught.

The participants were primary school teachers who were teaching in Tasmania during the time the study was conducted. Two primary schools in the northern part of Tasmania and two primary schools in the south were targeted. However, participants from other schools who were happy to participate were also accepted as this could broaden the geographical backgrounds of the participants.

The study used questionnaire and interview for data collection. Participants were offered alternative methods for participating in an interview: face-to-face, phone, and email. Most participants preferred the on-line approach.

DATA ANALYSIS AND RESULTS

This chapter focuses on the interview data only. Data analysis was conducted by identifying themes which were relevant to the research aim and the three specific objectives, which were about primary school teachers' view on: the significance of grammar in literacy education, aspects of linguistic knowledge that primary teachers should have, and how grammar should be taught.

The themes were then examined in light of the existing literature on this topic to identify where findings supported the literature and where new findings emerged, and what implications this might have on grammar and literacy teaching. The following themes were identified as the result of the analysis of the interview data.

Essential Aspects of Language and Literacy Knowledge for Teachers

All participating teachers identified explicit knowledge of language and literacy as being important, with responses including: a sound background in language and literacy; the ability to speak, write and edit correctly; knowledge of the structure and features of language; fundamentals of language; grammar, vocabulary and punctuation; sentence types; simple, compound and complex sentence structure; sound knowledge of phonemic awareness; rules of spelling; the origin and modification of words, and the ability to identify mistakes and correct them.

They also identified the following aspects: changed and modified, parts of speech and how we use them to write and speak interesting, meaningful communications; how to accurately construct grammatically correct sentences; grammar, sentence structure and vocabulary extension; solid comprehension and good grammar skills.

Two of the teachers identified the importance of reading and literature, with responses including: knowledge of Australian literature and significant literature from other countries, as well as contemporary children's literature, and; the ability to promote reading in fun, engaging ways and to encourage enjoyment of books.

One teacher identified the importance of an understanding of text types, the purposes of different types of text and the significance of audience and genre.

Aspects of Language and Literacy for Improvement

All participants identified that teachers need improvement in explicit knowledge of language with responses including: spelling; general language knowledge, root words, broader vocabulary, nouns, verbs, adverbs and adjectives and how knowing about them enables better communication of ideas; how and when to teach genres and grammar stages; how to explicitly teach children to write well constructed sentences, elements of text types and; updating knowledge in spelling and grammar skills.

The teachers identified gaps in teacher's knowledge about language.

- 'Some teachers have limited appreciation of language and literature.'

- 'Some are lacking basic knowledge and skill in writing/teaching grammatically correct texts, because they were not taught it.'

- 'We struggle to teach what we have not been taught explicitly. No grammar was taught in my teacher training course.'

Two participants discussed how to achieve improved language and literacy knowledge among teachers. One suggested that one-off methods do not work and teachers are more accepting of outside influences than co-worker's information, and someone should come to school for a sustained period (6 months) to promote whole school involvement including grade expectations that fit with the new curriculum. The other suggested peer mentoring in a non-threatening manner or PD (professional development), however lack of time and the fact that primary teachers are under a great deal of pressure were cited as impediments to this approach.

What do teachers want to learn more about language and literacy? Three teachers identified linguistic concepts including: the formalities of structures and features of written language, and different text types; how to explicitly teach grammar to children, and; grammar and development of vocabulary within sentence structures.

Two wanted to learn how to help students, with the following responses:

- 'To identify ways to help students communicate their thinking effectively, to work out what is missing when this fails and help them rectify this.'

- 'How to help strugglers: strategies; ideas, and; engagement.'

Two teachers were interested in learning teaching strategies, including:

- 'New and invigorating ways to teach and present structures and features of written language.'
- 'Up to date fun ways to teach grammar.'

The Role of Grammar in Literacy Teaching

Does grammar play an important part in literacy teaching? All participants agreed that grammar is an essential part of literacy education. The reasons given are:

- 'This is becoming more evident of late. There seems to have been a gap in the dedicated teaching of grammar and this is reflected in the fact that our younger teachers are asking for more support in this area. To be effective, grammar should be an ongoing part of the curriculum and be taught from Early Childhood through to Tertiary level.'
- 'When we are trying to teach kids to write in a more interesting way it isn't enough to tell them "put in more describing words" (although MANY teachers do exactly that). Unless you are able to identify which words can be described and what sort of words can BE describing words the whole process is a muddy pit.'
- 'If our children are being assessed on it via National assessment then it's unacceptable for us to ignore it.'

Grammar Teaching Strategies

How do teachers teach grammar? The responses to this question revealed a number of common strategies:

- Teaching whole class and small group and/or individual, depending on the situation and the students. Incidental opportunities for teaching grammar were also mentioned.
- Starting with whole class lessons then moving on to related activities for individuals or groups.
- Using small steps, keeping it simple and not covering too much at one time.
- Consolidating learning covering repeated lessons, worksheets, oral practice, role play, drama, computer activities, conferencing and students sharing their own writing.
- Linking grammar teaching to the current writing focus of the class.

- Using every opportunity to share examples from available literature such as the class novel, newsletters and the students' own work.

- Teaching short and sharp grammar sessions.

- Providing quick practice tasks, fast feedback and being able to identify grammar rules in everyday use.

- Teaching grammar in context.

DISCUSSION

This study identifies a number of themes that reflect the literature on this topic. These include: the importance of teacher's linguistic knowledge; the importance of grammar to literacy teaching; a lack of linguistic knowledge among some teachers, and the need to improve this, and the use of explicit grammar teaching methods.

The participants commented that teachers need to know about the structure and features of language, citing various elements such as spelling, vocabulary, parts of speech, punctuation, sentence types, morphology, phonemic awareness and genres. This reflects findings from a number of recent studies including Center, Freeman and Robertson (2001), Buckland and Fraser (2008), Moats (2009), and Brady et al (2009) which suggest that explicit literacy teaching, by knowledgeable teachers is more effective than a whole language approach.

Several teachers also commented on the need to be able to identify and correct students' mistakes and to identify problems with reading and writing and remediate these. In order to do this, teachers must have a sound knowledge of grammar. The National Inquiry into Literacy Teaching Report (2008) notes that problem readers benefit from explicit teaching of the structure and function of language, which requires a high level of linguistic knowledge by teachers.

All interviewees agreed that grammar is an important part of literacy teaching. A stance supported by the literature. Byrnes and Wasik (2009) note the importance of grammar to children's ability to create intelligible, acceptable multiword structures. Crystal (2006) considers that speaking and listening are learned naturally, but that reading and writing, including their grammar, have to be taught. Studies have also noted the importance of metalinguistic awareness to literacy (Garton & Pratt, 1998; Moats, 2009). This ability to observe and reflect on language requires knowledge of the structure and functions of language, that is, grammar.

Some teachers have a limited knowledge of linguistic awareness. This finding accords with both the research literature and with changes in the literacy curriculum over the past thirty to forty years. A comparative study by Andrews (1999) examining studies of the previous ten years revealed generally inadequate levels of grammatical knowledge among teachers. More recently Moats (2009) found that teachers rarely had enough coursework in the structure of English to inform their instruction. This lack of coursework reflects the whole-language approach to literacy employed by Western education programs from the 1960s until the late 1990s – and still used in some contexts.

The interview participants spoke of using explicit methods of grammar teaching. This reflects recent approaches to literacy, for example the Australian Government's Statements of Learning (2005) for reading, which defines expected student outcomes including knowledge of the structure and function of texts and language. Such knowledge is difficult to gain without explicit grammar teaching.

CONCLUSION

This study has identified a number of revealing facets of teacher's views on grammar and literacy teaching. It reveals that participants regarded grammar as being of particular importance in the teaching of literacy. The participants clearly believe teachers should be knowledgeable in their linguistic awareness. They expressed definitive views on the way that grammar should be taught but suggested a wide range of strategies for this to occur. In effect this asserts a view that teachers do something explicit to teach grammar without agreement on approaches that should occur for grammar to be taught effectively. They are keen to learn more about grammar and grammar teaching strategies, but are unsure how such training should be conducted in light of time constraints and workloads. Further research of this type has the potential to draw upon the wealth of untapped knowledge possessed by teachers to improve literacy outcomes for students.

REFERENCES

Allen, J. & van Buren, P. (1971). *Chomsky: Selected readings*. London: OUP.

Andrews, S. (1999). 'All these like little name things': A comparative study of language teachers' explicit knowledge of grammar and grammatical terminology. *Language Awareness, 8*(3), 143-159.

Brady, S., Gillis, M., Smith, T, Lavalette, M., Liss-Bronstein, L., Lowe, E., North, W. Russo, E., & Wilder, T. (2009). First grade teachers' knowledge of phonological awareness and code concepts: Examining gains from an intensive form of professional development and corresponding teacher attitudes. *Reading and Writing, 22*, 425 – 455.

Buckland, C., & Fraser, H. (2008). Phonological literacy: Preparing primary teachers for the challenge of a balanced approach to literacy education. *Australian Journal of Language and Literacy, 31*(1), 59 – 73.

Byrnes, J., & Wasik, B. (2009). Language and literacy development: What educators need to know. New York: Guildford Press.

Center, V., Freeman, L., & Robertson, G. (2001).The relative effect of a code-oriented and a meaning-oriented early literacy program on regular and low progress Australian students in Year 1 classrooms which implement reading recovery. *International Journal of Disability, Development and Education, 48*(2), 207 – 232.

Crystal, D. (2006). *How language works*. Camberwell: Penguin.

Garton, A., & Pratt, C. (1998). *Learning to be literate*. Oxford: Blackwell.

Harris, P., Turbill, J., Fitzsimmons, P., & McKenzie, B. (2006). *Reading in the primary school years* (2nd ed). South Melbourne: Thomson.

Ministry of Education, Western Australia (1992). *First steps: Language development. Teaching grammar module.*

Moats, L. (2009). Knowledge foundations for teaching reading and spelling. *Reading and Writing, 22,* 379 – 399.

National Inquiry into Literacy Teaching Report (2008). Retrieved 20 October, 2009 from *http://www.dest.gov.au/nitl/report.htm.*

Statements of Learning for English (2005). *Curriculum corporation.* Retrieved 19 October, 2009 from http://www.mceetya.edu.au/verve/_resources/SOL_English.pdf.

Tomasello, M., & Brooks, P. (1999). Early syntactic development: A construction grammar approach. In M. Barrett (ed.), *The development of language* (pp. 161 – 190). East Sussex: Psychology Press.

Tucker, G. (2002). *Systemic functional linguistics in language education.* Retrieved 20 October, 2009, from *http://www.llas.ac.uk/resources/gpg/103#.*

In: Language and Literacy Education in a Challenging World   ISBN: 978-1-61761-198-8
Editors: T. Lê, Q. Lê, and M. Short   © 2011 Nova Science Publishers, Inc.

Chapter 8

AN EXPLORATION OF TEACHERS' BELIEFS ABOUT GRAMMAR

Megan Short

ABSTRACT

Beliefs play an important role in enabling teachers to engage with the day-to-day complexities of teaching. As complex, cognitive structures through which teachers are able to identify task structures, solutions and process reflection (Nespor, 1987) beliefs play both a filtering and an organising role. The types of beliefs that impact upon teachers' practice include beliefs about content or subject domains and as well as epistemological beliefs, or beliefs about knowledge.

This chapter discusses the role that the beliefs of four early childhood, primary and secondary teachers hold about teaching grammar play in their teaching practice. In a challenging social and political environment, marked with the challenges of rapid technological change, teachers' beliefs about literacy teaching may play an important role in their navigation of these challenges.

Keywords: belief, empowerment, grammar, identity, literacy, parsing, teaching.

INTRODUCTION

Perhaps one of the most compelling reasons for considering the role of teacher beliefs is the predictive character of belief systems. Beliefs are often considered to be most analogous to a person's "true" feelings about "something" and thus are reasonable predictors for behaviour and serve as a means of explaining behaviour, as action and belief are considered to be connected processes (Richardson, 1996; Shavelson & Stern, 1981). Hoffer and Pintrich (1997) considered teacher beliefs to be such a potentially rich source of investigation that they could be one of the most important sources of data on the activity of teaching. The number of studies undertaken that seek to investigate the role that beliefs play in teaching and learning attests to their standing in the research field (Borg, 2003; Bryan, 2003; Calderhead, 1996; Green, 1971; Pajares, 1992; Prawat, 1992; Nespor, 1987; Richardson, 1996). Beliefs, or a set of beliefs, are often thought of as an intrinsic part of a person's identity and the phrase "You are what you believe" has resonated in history and literature for centuries. Heroes, heroines and martyrs are marked by the strength of their beliefs. One only has to think of the lives of Joan of Ark, Martin Luther King and Ghandi and the subsequent difficult choices that each of these individuals made as an expression of instantiation of their personal belief systems to witness the power of a personal belief as choice, judgement and action.

Perhaps it is this very immediate connection that beliefs have to who we are that makes beliefs also, at the same time, so difficult to capture as data for research. How do you identify, measure and conceptualise a belief? A sensible starting point is the question of definition. Philosophy, psychology, anthropology, theology and sociology have contributed discipline specific definitions to the field. As a construct, belief is widely and variously acknowledged defined in a range of ways by researchers (Ableson, 1979; Bryan, 2003; Fenstermacher, 1994; Green, 1971; Kagan, 1992; Nespor 1987; Pajares, 1992; Richardson, 1996; Rokeach, 1960, 1968). Richardson (1996) defined beliefs as, "...a subset of a group of constructs that name, define and describe the structure and content of mental states that are thought to drive a person's actions" (p.102). She also acknowledged that conceptions, perceptions, perspectives, stances, orientations and theories are similar constructs to beliefs (Richardson, 1996, p.102). The conceptual similarity between the construct of belief and those of "perspectives", "views", "perceptions", "conceptions" (to name but a few possible descriptors) has compounded the difficulties faced by researchers who are aiming to afford conceptual clarity to the phenomenon under investigation. Pajares (1992) noted that what are known as attitudes, values, perceptions, theories and images are more accurately known as beliefs. To identify any empirical structure of belief is beyond the scope of this chapter. It is, however, important to consider findings from research into the arena of teacher belief – especially as the construct of belief is a fundamental focus for this chapter and its response to the question; "How might the beliefs about literacy education influence teachers' literacy teaching practice?"

THE CHARACTERISTICS OF BELIEF

The construct of belief is multifaceted and defies easy definition. The meaning of belief has been explored in a diverse range of disciplines and fields of inquiry such as cognitive psychology (Abelson, 1979), sociology (Dixon, 1980), anthropology (Hahn & Kleinman, 1983) and philosophy (Rorty, 1999). There are, however, various characteristics of beliefs that can serve as guides for the present study into teachers' beliefs about grammar. Pajares (1992) and Nespor (1987) offer a suite of characteristics of beliefs that form a framework for this chapter. It is argued in this chapter that beliefs are considered to be constructed as a system. Two characteristics, "non-consensuality" and "unboundedness'" identified by Green (1971), are supportive of the proposal that beliefs are constructed and housed within a system. Four further characteristics of beliefs – "existential presumption", "alternativity", "affective and evaluative components" and "episodic structure'" – are valuable in distinguishing beliefs from knowledge (Nespor, 1987, p. 318). In addition, several other characteristics are important for the context of the present study- "'not all beliefs are equally important to the individual", "to be stable and resistant to change", "to be constructed in a social context", "to be formed early in life" and "to help us to understand the world".

BELIEFS ARE CONSTRUCTED AS A SYSTEM

The architecture of the beliefs that individuals hold is regarded by many researchers to be a system (Abelson, 1979; Bryan, 2003; Cooney, Shealy & Arvold, 1998; Green, 1971; Kagan, 1992; Pajares, 1992; Nespor, 1987; Richardson, 1996; Rokeach, 1960, 1972;). The proposition that beliefs are an integral aspect of teaching practice relies partly on the notion that if beliefs were unitary or unattached to other beliefs, it would be difficult to consider the way in which they related to the complex activity of teaching. The act of teaching requires some consistent and stable foundation from which teachers make decisions and through which they reflect on their practice. For the purpose of this chapter, beliefs are not random, unassigned, disconnected thoughts or concepts that we access in order to make judgements or decisions but are situated within a structure in that they are able to be organised, developed, stored, altered and retrieved. Green (1971) develops a sound argument for the connectedness of beliefs in that it seems improbable that a belief can exist on its own without reference or logical linkage to other beliefs. The conception of beliefs of comprising a system calls into relief the way in which the system itself is structured as sets or groups of beliefs that have some type of relationship with each other. As elements of our cognitions, we are unable to perceive them directly and therefore our belief systems and their construction are, to some extent, unknowable. However, researchers across various disciplines have speculated on the structure of the belief system (Abelson, 1979; Green, 1971; Nespor, 1987; Rokeach 1960) and some important findings from these studies have emerged.

In attempting to provide a picture of what a belief system may look like, Green (1971) identified three elements that comprise a belief system. They include a quasi-logical strength, a psychological strength and the arrangement of beliefs in clusters (Green, 1971, p. 47). A significant point made by Green is that the means by which beliefs are held is more instructive to the field of inquiry into beliefs than what the beliefs are about. The relationship that beliefs in a system have to each other is important as this arrangement of beliefs indicates how the belief system is structured. In possessing "quasi-logical" qualities, the way in which beliefs are structured within a belief system is considered by Green to be logical, but only to a point. The affective and intensely personal and subjective quality of beliefs limits their capacity to display fully logical qualities. Rather, beliefs are logical not from any objective logical measure, but rather the logical quality to which Green is referring is best understood as the nature of the relationships between the beliefs. Green distinguishes between primary and derivative beliefs. Primary beliefs are such that their existence does not rely on any other belief. They are "a belief...for which he [sic] can give no further reason, a belief which uses nonetheless as a reason for other beliefs" (Green, 1971, p. 43). These "other beliefs" are derivative, that is, they are derived from the primary beliefs.

The point made by Green that the relationship between primary and derivative beliefs can change. Primary beliefs may develop into derivative beliefs and derivative beliefs may then become primary. The possibility that beliefs may change their quasi-logical status is, according to Green, significant in terms of the pivotal role that beliefs play in the process of teaching (Green, 1971, p. 45).

Beliefs can also be conceived of in terms of their importance to the holder of the belief. Green makes the distinction that some beliefs are more important than others, yet the importance ascribed to the belief is not due to the quasi-logical quality of the belief. Rather, beliefs are important because of their psychological strength. Green refers to beliefs with a strong psychological strength as "central" and to beliefs whose psychological strength is less pronounced as "peripheral".

The notion that belief structures can accommodate inconsistent beliefs is illustrated using Green's psychological and quasi-logical metaphors. A belief "can be logically derivative, but psychologically central or it may be logically primary and psychologically peripheral" (1971, p. 45). This inconsistency in beliefs does not pose any threat to the integrity of the belief system itself as long as the two sets (clusters) of beliefs are not contrasted to each other.

The importance of proximity for beliefs highlights the third element in Green's exploration of belief structures. Contradictory or illogical sets of beliefs are able to be held because beliefs are held in "clusters" (Green, 1971, p. 47). Housing a set of beliefs in a cluster protects the beliefs from interrogation from other sets of beliefs. Clustering is an isolating and insulating process, a consequence of which may be that possible change or questioning of beliefs is more difficult because incompatible sets of belief are cloistered and seldom enter in a dialogue that might cause cognitive dissonance.

TEACHERS' BELIEFS ABOUT GRAMMAR

Four Australian teachers, each from a different teaching background and with a different length of teaching experience were interviewed about their beliefs about teaching grammar via a semi-structured interview. Purposeful selection of the participants was utilised to allow for a range of experience and views. The selection of teacher participants was drawn from early childhood, primary and secondary specialisation. The interviewees also represented diversity in terms of their age and teaching experience in that two teachers were classified as "early career" teachers and two teachers were classified as "mid" or "late" career teachers. The interviewees discussed in this chapter are: Alice, an early childhood teacher with thirty years teaching experience; Stephanie, a primary teacher with twenty seven years teaching experience; Angela, a high school social studies, numeracy and English teacher with six years teaching experience and Cathy, an early childhood teacher with three years teaching experience.

DESCRIBING GRAMMAR

When asked to define grammar, the teachers presented definitions foregrounding the theme of grammar as functional and purposeful in assisting language users to communicate. The focus was on the social and linguistic needs of the learner to have the capacity to communicate in a wide range of ways in diverse situations, as expressed in the following extracts:

> Grammar is a tool. It's not an end and it's just a means to an end. It is a tool and I only see it that way. (Alice, early childhood teacher)

> Grammar is about learning to communicate and understand people and so it really needs to be not just written, but it's visual and spoken and you should be given an opportunity to do all those sorts of things. (Angela, high-school teacher)

Few considerations of the complexities inherent in defining grammar (Yarrow, 2007) were evident in the responses given by the teachers. Each teacher interviewed was confident in their definition of grammar as one that they recognised in their own teaching practice. In this way, the teachers differed from research undertaken with pre-service teachers (Short, 2009). In the pre-service teacher study, the pre-service teachers in their discussion of grammar provided a diversity of opinion as to the linguistic, social, developmental and pedagogic definitions of grammar and there was a considerable amount of uncertainty and trepidation in the process of defining grammar. The definitions from the teachers were substantially weighted towards grammar as a part of language that is usefully described in an educational context as functional. Accordingly, their definitions of grammar highlighted the way in which grammar is taught as one of several "tools" to aid students' literacy and language development.

Differences between the pre-service teacher cohort and the teachers discussed in this chapter, in terms of teaching experience, can perhaps partially explain the difference in emphasis in defining grammar. Pre-service teachers are staking out their territory and attempting, from a broad range of theories and perspectives and approaches to consolidate a position in relation to their subject and content knowledge. They are developing pedagogic relationships towards subject matter and establishing what they know about a subject, how they view a subject as well as thinking about how best to teach that subject in their future teaching. Conversely, teachers have developed personal understandings of the boundaries of grammar as defined in practice, rather than as defined in a theoretical or abstract way. The experiences of the teachers are perhaps less directed by their immediate personal experience of learning the subject and perhaps informed more immediately by their knowledge of what grammar "looks like" in literacy and language education. It may also be that the concerns of teachers are less inclined towards the theoretical and tend towards thinking about what grammar means for their students. If, as Angela reinforces, grammar is "…about learning to communicate and understand people", then her thinking about grammar will be focused on developing communicative and grammatical competence in her students. What grammar "is", is of less importance that what grammar "does".

In reflecting on their understanding of grammar, some of the teachers described how their beliefs about grammar had changed throughout their career. Alice's beliefs about grammar shifted from a belief that the rules of traditional grammar were "gospel" to a belief that language is constantly undergoing change and that grammar is also changing in response to broader social, political, historical and linguistic changes:

> I think it's interesting that I went through a stage where [correct grammar] was sort of a gospel, that it had to be like that. And over the years I've felt differently. I suppose when you're younger and you learn about language, you think that language is set in concrete. Especially seeing language develop as a teacher, what comes out of students' mouths, you really understand how evolving and fluid and organic language is. (Alice, early childhood teacher)

The change in Alice's belief about grammar is a description of a change from a prescriptive approach to a descriptive and functional approach. In her own words, the catalysts for this change were her experiences of working with children, observing how children explore and develop linguistic and communicative competence. Alice also describes how her beliefs about language were also impacted through hearing about the way in which Shakespeare contributed to our language:

> But somewhere along the line I picked up the fact that Shakespeare with his expressive power created thousands of new words which have become part of our language but were never there before the 1600's. So it's fine to create new words and that's how languages develop. The way we view our language now is just a snapshot in time. (Alice, early childhood teacher)

The understandings that contributed to Alice's change in her beliefs about grammar could be considered to be themed together as "knowledge about language" (KAL). Knowledge about language has been described by Harper and Rennie (2008) as:

> ...a concept that relates to all aspects of linguistic form. It relates to knowledge about the sounds of a language, such as knowledge about the phonological and phonemic systems and how these systems relate to print (graphophonics) as well as to knowledge about the words in a language, word meanings (semantics) and the origins of words (etymologies). A major aspect of KAL, especially in the context of schooling, is knowledge about grammar...sociolinguistic knowledge, or knowledge about the different language varieties used in a speech community and their contexts of use. (p. 23)

The role that knowledge about language plays in the development of a teacher's beliefs about language is an important and interesting question. Fillmore and Snow (2002) argue that possessing knowledge about language is essential knowledge for teachers if they are to teach effectively and argue that many teachers "...lack this knowledge because they have not had the professional preparation they need" (p. 8). Through the accumulation of knowledge about language, developed from her literacy teaching practice, her own personal schooling experience and her on-going curiosity about how children develop linguistic competence, Alice can articulate a belief system about teaching grammar that includes diverse conceptual positions. It could be argued that the grounding that Alice received in grammar in her early years of schooling provided her with valuable knowledge that she was able to draw upon, and question, in her teaching practice.

PAST EXPERIENCES OF GRAMMAR AS A STUDENT

Prior experience is considered by a number of researchers to have a significant impact on beliefs, and subsequently, behaviour (Kagan 1992; Nespor, 1987; Richardson, 1996). Every interviewee was asked to describe how their own experiences of learning grammar at school had influenced them in terms of their orientation to teaching grammar, their knowledge about grammar and their personal feelings towards grammar. The experiences of the interviewees' grammar teaching in their own schooling could be divided into the two categories of explicit and implicit grammar teaching. Stephanie, Alice and Angela have distinct memories of learning grammar through discrete, explicit textbook driven lessons. Of interest is the recollection of Angela, an early career teacher in her mid 30s whose schooling occurred in the 1970s and the early 1980s: When asked about her own experiences of learning grammar at school, Angela recalled that the lessons consisted of:

> Lots of rules and sheets and not that sort of whole language approach. Not learning it in that sort of....there was very much a right and wrong sort of grammar and not learning it by

exposure and just being made to attempt it, with no explanation. It was more mathematical and logical. I came across a book that a colleague teacher was using and I got a bit of a shock because it's what I used at school and I flicked through it and it was. Numbers 1-6 on each page was just the same format and different rules about words, like 'ly' words. (Angela, high school teacher)

The realisation that an older colleague was using a textbook that Angela remembered using as a student opens up some interesting issues about grammar teaching. One of the points that could be made is the tradition of grammar teaching that relies on the use of textbooks to guide instruction which replicates the teacher's own experience of grammar learning as a student. The implication for Angela was that the teacher was taking too narrow an approach:

I didn't think that it was "bad", don't get me wrong, but it just shocked me to see the same book cover that I remembered...it made me think about whether it was OK or not to keep using something that was at least twenty years old. Maybe with grammar, some things just don't change. But then, even if grammar doesn't change, the students do – it made me think about the things that I did in my teaching that I took straight from my own school days. (Angela, high-school teacher)

The parsing of sentences is one grammar practice that is rarely taught in Tasmanian primary classrooms in 2009. However, the practice of parsing sentences was recalled by Alice as being one of her strongest recollections of learning grammar at school:

I remember we had to do a process called parsing where you ruled up a double page and put the nouns across the top all the different parts of the sentence structure, the subject, the verb, the participles, and all the different clauses and phrases. I think I quite enjoyed that because it was a discrete skill and I think I probably filed that away and it's something that I've referred back to all through my writing and reading life. I don't think I really remember any formal grammar apart from talking about the part of speech, the nouns and all the rest of it, but I really have a strong memory of the parsing. (Alice, early childhood teacher)

The use of parsing is strongly connected to the era of traditional grammar teaching and a practice among those learning experiences that were criticised for being disconnected from authentic learning, discrete, and of little value for students' writing development. However, the memories that Alice holds towards parsing sentences are, for the most part, positive. Being able to dissect a sentence into its grammatical components provided Alice with a sense of "empowerment":

I think it was almost a feeling of empowerment. You were almost in control of the language that you had as a receptive mode, and then in an expressive mode as well, you could then say it was whether it was "me or I" because you could think logically of why it would be that way. (Alice, early childhood teacher)

The experiences that Alice had of having the tools to understand how English "works" has supported her interest in language throughout her life, and has influenced her own perspectives on language teaching and learning. Christie (1990) notes that many in-service teachers, currently working in classrooms, had a traditional grammar background and this experience may provide this group of teachers with a metalanguage for teaching grammar that younger teachers may not have access to. Traditional grammar does not necessarily entail a limited understanding or awareness of the features and structures of language. It should be acknowledged that although the methods of teaching grammar in a traditional sense were teacher centred, the structural explanations of grammar provided valuable technical knowledge for students. The traditional grammar background that Alice remembers contributed to her "knowledge about language" and, as such, contributed to her teacher knowledge in the form of pedagogic content knowledge (Shulman, 1986). Alice notes that "I probably filed that away and it's something that I've referred back to all through my writing and reading life."

Alice considers parsing to be an inappropriate language experience for students in 2009:

> I don't think that people need that degree of structure because it's enforced in something from the 1960's onto the 21st century which is ridiculous. Our world has changed the way we express ourselves so much, we do things electronically, and I think that it's marvellous, though at one stage that would have worried me. (Alice, early childhood teacher)

Although Alice acknowledges the benefits gained from her grammar instruction in her schooling, she considers that the traditional approach is not appropriate in light of the ascendant shared understandings about how children learn and our recognition that language and literacy must prepare students for adult life in a world of "multiliteracies". The notion that having the right "tools" for communicating well is a foundational belief that Alice holds about language and literacy teaching. As a metaphor, the conceptualisation of grammar as a "tool" suggests a belief that the function of grammar is to enable language to "work".

Stephanie's recollections of learning grammar share some commonalities with Alice and Angela in that she recalls discrete lessons based around a textbook:

> It wasn't a very exciting book. But I think we were taught quite a lot of things that maybe over the last 30 years people haven't been taught in primary school at least anyway. There was a specific amount of work that actually had to be covered and perhaps a lot of children wouldn't have caught on, but quite a lot perhaps did. It's not an ideal way. But at least there was a content of what you were actually taught and I think that might have clicked for a little while. (Stephanie, primary teacher)

Stephanie's mention of content as being part of the grammar lesson could be read as a comment on subsequent teaching approaches such as the "whole language" approach in which the "content" aspect of the learning experience was embedded in the context of the lesson. Similar to Alice's recognition that the traditional grammar she experienced provided her with benefits, Stephanie is also recognising that explicit content can also be beneficial. The recollections of learning grammar are for Angela, Stephanie and Alice significantly more memorable than the recollection that Cathy has of learning grammar.

The recollections of Cathy contrast significantly with the other teachers. She did not have any memories of explicit grammar teaching. Cathy, as the youngest of the teachers interviewed, completed her primary and secondary schooling in the late 1980s and 1990s. The dominant pedagogical approaches in those decades were heavily influenced by the whole language approach (Newman, 1985). Spiegel (1992) qualifies this general language and literacy pedagogical approach by noting that at the same time there was also a consideration of the value of explicit teaching. Cathy, when asked about her own experiences of schooling and grammar teaching in particular recalls that:

> I don't actually ever really remember being explicitly taught grammar as a lesson. It was always part of whatever writing or reading or whatever. Definitely, there weren't any grammar text books, never. (Cathy, early childhood teacher)

The knowledge that Cathy connects back to her schooling experience in terms of grammar is only able to be described in a limited way. Stephanie and Alice, as a contrast, are able to provide detailed and systematic descriptions of the lessons that involved grammar can describe their feelings as they remember them from their childhood and identify the influence that their childhood grammar lessons had on their subsequent teaching practice. In contrast to these detailed descriptions from Stephanie and Alice, Cathy sums up the grammatical knowledge that she recalls from her childhood as:

> I knew the basics like verbs, nouns, adjectives, adverbs. But when you start going to other things I probably wouldn't know them now to be honest. It's probably not that I don't know them, but it's knowledge that I don't have any memories of getting and I don't know how much I draw on it now. (Cathy, early childhood teacher)

Investigating how a perception of having little grammar instruction in a person's own schooling experience can impact upon their teaching practice is of interest to our discussion of teacher beliefs about grammar. What impact does a traditional grammar background have on a teacher's capacity or preparedness to teach grammar as opposed to a whole language background? From the responses of the interviewees, there appears to be an acknowledgement on the part of the teachers who had a traditional grammar background that the explicit teaching that was a hallmark of their schooling experience provided them with knowledge that they drew upon in their own teaching practice.

BELIEFS ABOUT GRAMMAR AS PART OF A TEACHERS' BELIEF SYSTEM

The proposition that primary beliefs occupy an important role in the construction of belief systems was suggested by Abelson (1979), Green (1979) and Rokeach (1960; 1968). The teachers described in this chapter presented clearly articulated belief systems. Of importance is also the relationship between primary beliefs and derivative beliefs, the later being considered to possess a lesser influence on the belief system. Emerging from the teacher interviews was the identification of the relationship between primary beliefs, derivative beliefs and teaching practice. The primary beliefs of two interviewees (Stephanie and Alice) were observed as driving the teaching practice of the teachers. It could be argued that one means by which the primary belief of the teacher was connected to teaching practice was the enactment of a several derivative beliefs. In one example, the primary belief of "respect for the student" was also connected to derivative beliefs that informed practice such as the valuing of a student's spoken language when choosing to correct their grammar and ensuring that the student was present and engaged in a dialogue with the teacher when correcting their written grammar.

Another point that emerged from the interviews with the teachers was an indication that the beliefs of the teachers in relation to grammar teaching were subject to change throughout their career. One of the reported characteristics of teacher beliefs is that they are resistant to change, especially if the beliefs are formed at a young age (Abelson, 1979; Clark, 1988; Lewis, 1990; Munby, 1982; Nespor, 1987; Nisbett & Ross, 1980; Pajares, 1992; Posner, Strike, Hewson & Gertzog, 1982; Rokeach, 1968). However, the teachers indicated that their beliefs about grammar, the role of the teacher and how students learn had changed over the course of their careers. This finding is a valuable one as it provides an insight into the way in which teachers negotiate a range of competing discourses, develop their teacher identities and accommodate changes in their social, pedagogical and institutional landscape, are, to a greater or lesser extent, mirrored in their belief systems.

A valuable addition to this finding of teacher belief change is an exploration of the precursors and mechanisms for these changes in beliefs. The contributing factors for belief change for the teachers were identified as personal dissatisfaction with a particular situation or event and social, pedagogical and curricular changes. Borko and Putnam's (1986) model of conceptual change provides an explanatory framework for this change. An example provided by a teacher, Alice, outlined how she felt uneasy over a period of time with the way in which the teacher was considered to be the "giver" of knowledge and the child was a passive recipient of the teacher's knowledge. She describes how her beliefs about the role of the teacher changed, and with this change in her teacher identity, a change occurred in her teaching practice. The change that she described had an impact on her teaching of grammar in that the positioning of the teacher did not align with a traditional grammar approach. The needs of the student for a functional and pragmatic understanding of grammar as a "tool" was privileged over the need of the teacher for traditional levels of control over the content and the way in which the classroom operated. As her beliefs changed, so too did her practice. For Stephanie, teacher, changes in her teaching of grammar changed as a result of broader curriculum changes in the shift from traditional grammar to a more functional approach.

A particularly important finding is the way in which both Alice and Stephanie's teaching practice was not directed solely from curricular directives or teaching "fads" but from their own personal reflections on what best suited the needs of their students. Stephanie and Alice, in their descriptions of belief change both indicated that they chose from a range of discourses and developed unique teaching approaches. An example provided was the way in which at the height of the "whole language" literacy approach, they also perceived a need for some explicit grammar teaching and adjusted their practice accordingly, even when this may not have been in keeping with accepted literacy teaching at that time. The role played by their primary beliefs was important in that their primary beliefs were supports for change. In this light, their primary beliefs could be viewed as "touchstones" from which a range of pedagogical decisions were made. From these changes, it is suggested that the mechanisms for belief change are deeply personal and involve not simply a "quick change" or following a fad, but are the result of serious reflection that leads to pedagogical and personal transformation.

CONCLUSION

In this chapter, our discussion of teachers' beliefs about grammar teaching indicates that grammar "matters" as an integral component of their language and literacy program. Their beliefs about grammar are identified as connected to primary beliefs about the purpose and value of education and encompass a sense of social empowerment as they view grammar as a means to fuller participation in social contexts outside of the classroom. Their stories of grammar teaching touch on personal pedagogical choices they have made to include grammar in their teaching practice as it aligned to their beliefs about education, knowledge and teaching itself. For each of the teachers, grammar is important yet problematic. The challenge, then, as indicated by these teachers is to consider the manifold and difficult challenges that grammar education presents in the hope of providing for the conditions required for meaningful literacy and grammar education.

REFERENCES

Abelson, R. (1979). Differences between belief systems and knowledge systems. *Cognitive Science: A Multidisciplinary Journal, 3*(4), 355 – 366.

Borg, S. (2003). Teacher cognition in language teaching: A review of research on what language teachers think, know, believe, and do. *Language Teacher, 36*, 81 – 109.

Borko, H., & Putnam, R. (1996). Learning to teach. In D. Berliner, & Califee, R. (Ed.), *Handbook of educational psychology*, (pp. 673 – 708). New York: Macmillan Library Reference.

Bryan, L. (2003). Nestedness of beliefs: Examining a prospective elementary teacher's belief system about science teaching and learning. *Journal of Research in Science Teaching. 40*, 835 – 868.

Calderhead, J. (1996). Teachers': beliefs and knowledge. In D. Berliner, & Califee, R. (Eds.), *Handbook of educational psychology*, (pp. 709 – 725). New York: Macmillan Library Reference

Christie, F. (1990). *Literacy for a changing world.* Hawthorn, VIC: Australian Council for Educational Research

Cooney, T., Shealy, B., & Arvold, B. (1988). Conceptualising belief structures of preservice secondary mathematics teachers. *Journal for Research in Mathematics Education, 29*(3), 306 – 322.

Dixon, K. (1980). *The sociology of belief.* London: Routledge Kegan Paul

Fenstermacher, G. (1994). The knower and the known: The nature of knowledge in research on teaching. *Review of Research in Education, 20*, 3-56.

Fillmore, L., & Snow, C. (2002).What teachers need to know about language. In C. Temple Adger, C. Snow, & D. Christian (Eds.). *What teachers need to know about language* (pp. 7 – 55). ERIC Clearinghouse on Languages and Linguistics.

Green, T. (1971). *The activities of teaching.* New York: McGraw Hill Book Company.

Hahn, R., & Kleinman, A. (1983). Belief as pathogen, belief as medicine: "voodoo death" and the "placebo phenomenon" in anthropological perspective. *Medical Anthropology Quarterly, 14*(4), 3 – 19.

Harper, H., &Rennie, J. (2008). "I had to go out and get myself a book on grammar": A study of pre-service teachers' knowledge about language. *The Australian Journal of Language and Literacy, 32*(1), 22 – 37.

Hoffer, B., & Pintrich, P. (1997). The development of epistemological theories: Beliefs about knowledge and knowing and their relation to learning. *Review of Educational Research, 67*(1), 88 – 140

Kagan, D. (1992). Implication of research on teacher belief. *Educational Psychologist, 27*(1), 65 – 90.

Nespor, J. (1987). The role of beliefs in the practice of teaching. *Journal of Curriculum Studies, 19*(4), 317 – 328.

Newman, J. (1985). *Whole language: Theory in use.* Portsmouth, New Hampshire: Heinemann Educational Books, Inc.

Pajares,. M. (1992). Teachers' beliefs and educational research: Cleaning up a messy construct. *Review of Educational Research, 62,* 307 – 332.

Prawat, R. (2003). Is realism a better belief than than nominalism? In J. Raths, & McAninch, A. (Ed.), *Teacher beliefs and classroom performance: The impact of teacher education* (pp. 65 – 97). Greenwich, Connecticut: Information Age Publishing.

Richardson, V. (1996). The role of attitudes and beliefs in learning to teach. In J. Sikula, Buttery, T., & Guyton, E. (Ed.), *Handbook of research on teacher education,* (pp. 102 – 119). New York: Simon & Schuster Macmillan.

Rokeach, M. (1960). *The open and closed mind.* New York Basic Books, Inc. Publishers.

Rokeach, M. (1968). *Beliefs, attitudes and values: A theory of organisation and change.* San Francisco: Jossey-Bass Publishers

Rorty, R. (1999). *Philosophy and social hope.* London: Penguin.

Shavelson, R., & Stern, P. (1981). Research on teachers' pedagogical thoughts, judgements, decisions and behaviour. *Review of Educational Research, 51*(4), 455 – 498.

Shulman, L. (1986). Those who understand: Knowledge growth in teaching. *Educational Researcher, 15*(2), 4 – 14.

Short, M. (2009). Performance anxieties: Teacher identity and the teaching of grammar. In T. Le, Le, Q., & M. Short (Eds.), *Critical discourse analysis: An interdisciplinary perspective,* (pp. 151 – 163). New York: Nova Science Publishers.

Spiegel, D. (1992). Blending whole language and systematic direct instruction. *Reading Teacher, 46*(1), 38 – 44.

Yarrow, R. (2007). How do students feel about grammar? The framework and its implications for teaching and learning. *Changing English, 14* (2), 175 – 186.

In: Language and Literacy Education in a Challenging World   ISBN: 978-1-61761-198-8
Editors: T. Lê, Q. Lê, and M. Short   © 2011 Nova Science Publishers, Inc.

Chapter 9

CHALLENGES IN LEADING FOR LITERACY IN SCHOOLS

Geraldine Castleton, Timothy Moss and Sally Milbourne

ABSTRACT

The teaching of literacy and students' literacy performance in schools is a high stakes topic, capturing more professional, political and community attention than any other area of the school curriculum. This scrutiny brings with it many challenges for those in leadership roles in systems and schools, particularly if these roles include a responsibility for leading for literacy. This chapter explores the challenges of leadership in schools arguing for the role of distributed leadership that sees expertise and responsibility distributed among staff rather than residing just within the principal. It then explores the particular characteristics of leadership for literacy before examining a selection of school literacy plans as sites of leadership for literacy to discuss the specific challenges that are faced by schools and leaders within schools as they work to achieve optimum literacy outcomes for their students.

Keywords: literacy, schooling, literacy leadership, teacher professional learning.

INTRODUCTION

This chapter begins with a discussion on the significance of literacy for individuals as well as for nations before considering the centrality of literacy to schooling. In arguing that the teaching and learning of reading, writing and literacy is one of the primary purposes of schooling, the chapter moves to consider the challenges that achieving these purposes bring for leaders and teachers in schools. It then turns to school literacy plans as a site for identifying and interpreting the challenges of leading for literacy before concluding with key messages that this exercise provides for those charged with the responsibility of ensuring optimum literacy outcomes are achieved for all students.

THE SIGNIFICANCE OF LITERACY

Few areas of the curriculum or of broader discussions about the nature of schooling receive as much attention as literacy, and in particular to what is often perceived to be the main goal of literacy, namely teaching students to read and write. According to Freebody (2007) a consequence of this importance is that the body of research around the topics of the "teaching and learning of reading, writing and literacy probably account for one of the largest and most diverse bodies of research in all of the social and behavioural sciences" (p.3).

Not only has the teaching of reading and writing been a focal point for professional research and discussion but it also has a long history of involving more than its share of media-fed community debate, which frequently frame up literacy as being in a state of crisis (Belfiore et al, 2004; Freebody, 2007; Louden et al 2005; Snyder, 2008). The heated concern expressed through these debates demonstrate that much more is at stake than the acquisition of skills associated with reading and writing.

Some of this concern at least comes from the recognition that literacy competence is central to learning across the curriculum and consequently critical for individual's success in contemporary society (Clay, 2006; Dugdale & Clark, 2008; Nichols, Rupley & Rasinski, 2009; Kirsch, de Jong, Lafontaine, McQueen, Mendelovits, & Monseur, 2002). Contemporary definitions of literacy which define it as more than the ability to read and write, enable understanding of how literacy has the power to impact on individual's economic well-being, aspirations, family life, health, and civic/cultural engagement (Chevalier & Feinstein, 2006; De Walt et al, 2004; Dugdale & Clark, 2008; Vacca, 2004 in Reschly2010). Dugdale and Clark (2008), for example, argue that individuals with well developed literacy levels reach higher levels of educational attainment, achieve better outcomes in the labour market, are more likely to have access to technology, less likely to receive state benefits, more likely to own their own home, and be more involved in democratic processes such as voting. In contrast, individuals' low literacy skills are associated with social exclusion (Dugdale & Clark, 2008; Kirsch et al, 2002), with such people being more likely to be living in poverty, to be unemployed or experiencing long and frequent periods of time out of the labour market, more likely to reside in overcrowded housing, and less likely to own their own home (Dugdale & Clark, 2008). Furthermore, Vacca, (2004, in Reschly, 2010, p. 68) argues that mastery of literacy skills is a significant factor in addressing the very high rate of recidivism among prison populations.

It is with these concerns in mind that UNESCO defines literacy as a human right, a tool of personal empowerment and a means for social and human development. Educational opportunities depend on literacy (UNESCO, 1995-2010). It argues that literacy is at the heart of basic education for all, and essential for eradicating poverty, reducing child mortality, curbing population growth, achieving gender equality and ensuring sustainable development, peace and democracy.

What is captured in the argument presented by UNESCO is the importance of literacy not only in the lives of individuals but also its significance for the cultural, social and economic well-being of nations. From this standpoint literacy is often inappropriately reduced to represent a functional, employment-related skill, with workers' limited literacy skills presented as a prevailing cause of nations' poor economic performance (Castleton,2006; Comings & Soricone, 2007; Gee et al, 1996; Hull & Grubb, 1999; Taylor, 2008). Without limiting its significance at a national and international level, and not undermining the importance of workers' literacy skills in a competitive global economy, literacy remains fundamentally of most significance to individuals. Kazemek cites Brandt (2001) and reminds us that:

> [h]ow and what we read and write are shaped by who we are, where we find ourselves at various times in life, and the ever-changing demands of the wider economic and social world. As Brand (2001) observed, "Multiple literacy practices are also a sign of stratification and struggle" (p.8) (2004, p.450).

LITERACY AND SCHOOLING

It has become a case of stating the obvious to claim that defining literacy is a complex task. This complexity is evident in the claims that every-day life has become increasingly literacy-dependent, and that the nature, extent and composition of literacy capabilities has become progressively more sophisticated and multifaceted over time. Arguing that contemporary definitions of literacy have been informed by contributions of scholars working within different but complementary discipline bases that include anthropology, linguistics, cognitive and behavioural psychology, as well as feminist social and critical theories, Freebody (2007) usefully defines literacy as "an open-textured concept. It refers to how people use and produce symbolic materials fluently and effectively. It is also about how they put available technologies of production and dissemination to the practical ends of communicating productively, responsively and responsibly" (p. 9).

Returning to the argument that literacy competence is central to learning across the curriculum, and the consequent need for the teaching of literacy to be evidence-based, Freebody (2007, p.12) has argued that literacy research "is an activity carried out in the midst of at least five moving targets". He defines these targets as:

- The changing technologies through which literate communication is used, and how those technologies rework and re-present the knowledge to be learned and the ways of displaying that knowledge (Jonassen & Hyug, 2001);

- The changing pathways that young people face, including recent rapid reformations of the labour markets in many countries and the pressures that puts on learning; currently this is manifest in manual and semi-skilled work in the manufacturing and agriculture sectors drying up and symbolic/analytic, managerial and technical sectors increasing (Reich, 2001);

- Changing patterns of learning, with new tensions between the academic and vocational balances in the school curriculum (Bransford & Schwartz, 1999);

- The changing cultural and linguistic composition of Australian homes and classrooms, and the particular implications this has for literacy teaching and learning (Cope & Kalantzis, 1996);

- The changing nature of work organisations including schools, as reflected in the flat structure, mobile skill-base restructuring characteristic of Post-Taylorist developments, as modelled on the OECD Futures Scenarios for Schooling website, and in the new logic of "accountable educational provision". (p.12).

Those charged with the teaching of literacy must also be cognisant of these same moving, futures-oriented targets, a point that affirms the complexity of what is involved in effective literacy teaching. While Freebody (20070 wrote with Australian schools and children in mind, these targets, which can be interpreted as goals for literacy in schooling, are relevant around the globe. Teachers and schools therefore need to know how to address the challenges associated with incorporating these "moving targets" into the aims, design, implementation and evaluation of their teaching programs. Much of the responsibility associated with these challenges therefore falls to leaders in schools, which includes not only school principals or head teachers but also other key staff charged with leadership roles, and specifically those with responsibilities for leading literacy in their schools

LEADING FOR SCHOOLING

When referring to schools, the term 'leadership' has typically been interpreted as meaning the principal or head teacher, though this view has been changing over recent years with increased emphasis on the notion of 'distributed leadership' (Gronn, 2000; Spillane, 2005) that defines leadership as a more shared responsibility across a school staff. Much of the current literature on the topic of distributed leadership examines the links between this form of leadership and student educational outcomes.

Robinson (2008), for example describes two main concepts of distributed leadership. The first refers to distributed leadership as task distribution in which leadership is apparent in the performance of certain functions or tasks spread across a group with greater effect on student outcomes being created through wider distribution patterns rather than through the conventional hierarchical patterns of leadership. According to Robinson (2008) a further characteristic is that such leadership needs to be supported by a strong evidence base of practices and tasks that actually lead to improved student outcomes. Robinson's (2008) second concept refers to the processes associated with distributed leadership. In particular, its interest is in those influencing processes that result in followers' changed thoughts and/or actions which, in turn, lead to change in student outcomes.

Graczewski, Knudson, & Holtzman (2008) suggest that principals need distributed leadership in order to achieve staff buy-in, an essential aspect which can result in achieving greater benefit from the collective expertise. The advantage of achieving this form of leadership is that it can lead to maintaining and increasing student outcomes, cultivating ownership and agency of staff, developing a shared vision and maximising sustainability of ongoing efforts. In supporting these characteristics identified by Graczewski and colleagues (2008), Penlington, Kington & Day (2008), further propose that greater clarity around a distributed leadership role leads to increased effectiveness. Nettles and Herrington (2007) also acknowledge the significance of distributed leadership as a means of fostering stakeholder involvement, one of the critical factors of effective school leadership. Fullan, Cuttress & Kilcher (2005) identify the need to focus on leadership for change as a key driver for making change in schools effective and long lasting. They also argue that for leadership to be effective, it must be spread throughout the organisation, and note the mark of a successful principal as being how many leaders they leave behind them when they go.

THE IMPORTANCE OF VISION AND GOAL SETTING IN SCHOOLS

Within a model of distributed leadership a pivotal roles of a principal is that of setting a strategic vision, ensuring clarity of communication of this vision with stakeholders and of establishing the relevance of that vision to the school context (Penlington, Kington & Day; 2008). Furthermore, according to Leithwood and Jantzi (2006), setting directions by building school vision, developing specific goals and priorities, holding high performance expectations is one of three broad categories of leadership practices which impact positively on student outcomes.

Dinham (2005) combines vision with expectations and a culture of success as one of a set of fundamental attributes and practices which contribute to outstanding educational outcomes. He states this is achieved through

- having a long-term agenda and vision and work towards;

- setting meaningful achievable goals rather than short-term targets;

- identifying and nurturing the 'seeds' for change and school improvement;

- seeing the big picture and communicating it to staff

- having and communicating high expectations of self and others;

- establishing a positive physical environment;

- recognising student and staff achievement;

- promoting the school; and

- distributing leadership.

BUILDING CAPACITY FOR SUSTAINABILITY

For distributed leadership to be effective and sustainable it is essential that appropriate attention is given to building stakeholder capacity. Murphy (2004), for example, identifies building capacity (knowledge, responsibility, skill) of teachers as one of ten functions for successful leadership. Two dimensions must be attended to, with the first being human and intellectual achieved through ongoing professional learning for staff. The second dimension is social and is achieved through developing learning communities, strong school-home partnerships, and creating a safe, purposeful, structured and caring school climate.

With regard to the human and intellectual dimension, Penlington, Kington & Day (2008) note that as well as building capacity in general (using succession planning, internal promotion to positions within schools, and providing support and guidance for leaders within schools), it is also important to adopt a strategic approach to developing teaching capacity. This is achieved by a focus emphasis on teacher professional learning that is aligned with school-wide priorities and emphasises the value of in-house professional learning. This line of argument is consistent with Hattie's (2003) contention that, when talking all factors that impact on student learning into consideration, it is teachers that make the difference. He goes further to maintain, however, that it is not just any teachers that make the difference, but expert teachers. By arguing for building capacity in schools through teacher professional learning the case is made for building that capacity which leads teachers to be expert teachers (Hattie, 2003), but also for building the collective expertise of all members of the school community. Fullan, Cuttress & Kilcher (2005) further contend that building capacity is a key driver for sustainability and involves not only enabling people to develop new skills, knowledge and competencies, but also encompasses increasing people's collective power to move forward through the use of policies, strategies, resources and actions.

LEADING FOR LITERACY

In concert with the impetus given to leadership within schools over recent years has been growing pressure on schools and systems to raise students' literacy performance. This has resulted in a growing interest and consequent body of literature on the type of leadership that engenders improved literacy outcomes in schools (e.g., Dole, 2004; Education Queensland, 2000; Sharratt & Fullan, 2006; Murphy, 2004). Although writers take up different themes in their analysis of leading for literacy, there is general agreement that achieving high levels of student literacy outcomes requires strong and effective leadership. Such an approach is characterised by the dimensions of distributed leadership already presented, which take on a particular form when applied to leading for literacy.

When applying this principle to leading for literacy Sharratt and Fullan (2006) contend that it is the role of leadership to model and live the shared beliefs and understandings about literacy that underpin a school literacy program, ensuring that the school implements ongoing self-evaluation, and maintains the focus on literacy improvement. The emphasis given to this characteristic is consistent with the work of Luke, Freebody and Land (Education Queensland 2000) who have similarly identified strong administrative and key teacher leadership as essential features of effective whole-school literacy programs that document how these roles are defined and which particular tasks and responsibilities are assigned to them.

There is further agreement in the literature first of all about the need for a strong focus on enhancing teacher expertise in effective literacy teaching, and secondly on the role of professional learning in ensuring this expertise (Dole, 2004; Gilrane, Roberts and Russell (2008); Murphy, 2004; Sharrat & Fullan, 2006). Murphy (2004), for example, identified fostering staff development and promoting communities of learners as one of the ten key functions of literacy leadership in schools. Dole (2004) also defines expertise as a shared rather than as an individual commodity, and in framing it this way presents a changing notion of expertise as residing within a community of learners rather than being held individually. Effective literacy leadership couples the previously mentioned characteristics of shared beliefs and understandings with this emphasis on developing communities of learners with shared expertise to then lead in the development and delivery of a literacy program that is contextually appropriate for the learners in their school. Murphy (2004) cites Wenger (1998) in arguing that the most effective learning for teacher takes place within a community of learners and contends that schools with high student achievement in literacy are characterised by teacher participation in a variety of professional communities, along with a high level of teacher agency, a strong commitment to the teaching profession and a deep respect for lifelong learning. The author also sees parents and the wider community as participants in these communities of learners, arguing for strong school-home partnerships within which all partners have clearly defined role and responsibilities. In addition to the typical role parents play in reading with their children at home, these roles include the need for parents and the community to hold high expectations for the work and performance of students, thereby reinforcing the academic expectations of the school. Taking on these additional roles requires close collaboration between parents and school and allow members of the community of learners to share in the recognition and celebration of success in literacy (Murphy, 2004).

In returning to the importance of professional learning for teachers, and of teacher agency, the role for school leaders is in enabling this agency by focusing on skilling teachers in evidence-based effective literacy pedagogy. A further focus needs to be on the use of systematic and empirical sources of evidence of students' literacy achievements that include the use of teacher-developed literacy assessment tasks and protocols. This focus needs to be linked to clear and measurable key performance indicators that are closely aligned to those aspects of literacy achievement that have been defined as areas of need.

One site where challenges for leading literacy can clearly be seen and interpreted is within the formal documentation and planning that schools (and school leaders specifically) produce. One such document is the school literacy plan, which articulates the school vision for literacy learning, and provides a foundation for the implementation of literacy strategies. In addition to this explicit information, these plans also potentially provide evidence of a school's understanding of what is involved in leading for literacy, the challenges and opportunities likely to be experienced, and how the school intends to enact this leadership and overcome these challenges.

SCHOOL LITERACY PLANS AS A SITE OF LEADING FOR LITERACY

The school literacy plans analysed below were collected as part of a larger ongoing research project evaluating the effectiveness of a large-scale educational initiative which aims to significantly increase the number of children who complete primary school with functional literacy skills (DEEWR, 2008). In keeping with the literature on raising students' literacy achievement, the initiative has a particular focus on strengthening leadership roles in literacy within schools, supporting whole school approaches to literacy, and building teacher capacity. As such, the initiative and the research evaluating it provide opportunities for understanding more about leading for literacy in schools.

The research evaluation involved collecting data from 36 schools, of varying sizes and contexts. Along with literacy plans, data were collected from a wide variety of stakeholders within each school context, including students (testing – within the school, and through national literacy testing results, surveys), parents (surveys), teachers (surveys and interviews), and principals (surveys and interviews). In addition, case studies were undertaken within a number of schools, to provide a more detailed 'picture' of literacy learning and leadership. The school literacy plans collected provide a vehicle for the analysis of each school's understanding of the processes involved in literacy learning, their intentions in terms of providing leadership for literacy within the classroom and school community, their articulation of the needs of their educational community, and the intended mechanisms for the evaluation of their efforts to improve student outcomes in this area. While all of the 36 schools were required to prepare and submit their school literacy plans to their regional office, they were not provided with any guidelines as to the content or purpose of this document. The variability that resulted was taken into account when interpreting and evaluating these documents.

PLANNING FOR LEADING FOR LITERACY

In order to interpret and evaluate the literacy plans, it was necessary to develop a set of analytical criteria, based on the features of effective whole-school literacy programs. As discussed earlier, literature in this field (Education Queenland, 2000; Sharratt & Fullan, 2006; Murphy, 2004) suggests that there are a number of features that are commonly found within effective programs. Of this literature, The Literate Futures (Education Queenland, 2000) project was considered most compatible with the school literacy plans provided by the 36 schools. That project report identified the following as particularly important: strong administrative and key teacher leadership, with theoretically grounded expertise in literacy education; substantial school-level investment in professional development; a coordinated focus on teaching; encouragement of broad, multi-method instructional approaches; a rapid and continual exchange of information and data about students; use of student data to set targets; a shared vision of literacy; and, a high degree of parental involvement.

Based on this research, the literacy plans were analysed against the following ten criteria:

- vision of literacy and literacy learning (how clearly this was articulated within the plan);

- approach to literacy and literacy learning (how the plan reflected a balanced approach, as indicated in curriculum documents);

- key leadership roles and responsibilities for literacy (how these roles were defined/described and ascribed particular tasks/responsibilities);

- commitment to and involvement in sustained professional development (what professional development activities were included, and how this was linked to identified need);

- coordinated focus on pedagogy across the school (how the school's pedagogical approach to literacy was articulated, in the plan, and across the school community);

- broad multi-method instructional programs (clear information about what is taught within literacy time);

- clear communication of information and data about student achievement (how the school planned to embed a culture of information exchange);

- use of data to inform instruction and set targets (how clearly the plan showed links between collection of data and its use in subsequent planning);

- community and parental involvement (how clearly this involvement was defined, and what roles were assigned to community members and parents within the planning);

- clear and measurable key performance indicators (how the school aimed to monitor the literacy activity within the school, and how they would know these initiatives had been successful).

For each of the ten criteria, schools were individually ranked on a four-point scale (1 = limited evidence, 2 = developing evidence, 3 = clear evidence, 4 = extensive evidence), with areas of particular strength and/or in need of further development noted. This process allowed for a detailed overall assessment of each school's planning, in terms of the degree to which the plans aligned with commonly-accepted principles of effective literacy approaches. The degree to which the 36 plans did align with these principles, enable an insight into how schools are taking up the challenge of leading for literacy.

KEY CHALLENGES IN LEADING FOR LITERACY

Across the criteria described above, several areas of strength emerged within the literacy plans. These included a clear emphasis on sustained professional development activities, an important characteristic of leading for literacy identified by Murphy (2004) and others (e.g., Dole, 2004) and discussed earlier in this chapter. The plans typically showed a strong focus on parental involvement, often with clearly articulated roles and responsibilities, again capturing priorities highlighted by Murphy (2004) and by the Education Queensland project (2000).

However, even within these areas of strength, there were clear opportunities for further development. With regard to professional learning, for example, although all schools identified the activities that they would offer for staff, only one school explicitly linked these activities to an audit of staff professional learning needs. This clearly highlights the importance of schools determining the current levels of expertise and knowledge of their staff before undertaking professional learning activities, in other words, using teachers' current skills and capabilities as a starting point. Further, there was little emphasis on the sustainability of such professional development activities – how staff would be supported over time in implementing what they had learnt, for example. The link between developing teacher capacity and sustainability is argued by Penlington and colleagues (2008) and also by Fullan and others (2005) who contend that building capacity for sustainability is a key driver for lasting and effective changes in schools.

With regard to parental involvement, many schools articulated how parents could support literacy development within the home environment, but very few considered how this involvement might expand to incorporate parental/community involvement *within* the school. In developing a point made by Penlington and colleagues (2008), it is argued that greater parental and community involvement in schools, and in particular in literacy teaching and learning, could assist in cultivating a shared ownership of outcomes, and agency in producing outcomes among staff and community members..

For the purpose of exploring literacy leadership in schools, the third criterion employed in the analysis (key leadership roles and responsibilities) is of particular relevance. Results in relation to this area provided insights into the challenges of leading for literacy learning. Almost all of the 36 schools involved in the project included in their plans the establishment of literacy leaders/coordinators, and project teams. However, the degree to which these roles were assigned specific responsibilities, and the provision of associated performance indicators, varied significantly. Only five schools provided strong evidence of literacy leadership, articulating these roles within their schools clearly and consistently. One such school articulated a need to build strong leadership from within the teaching staff, provided school time for that group (referred to as the Literacy Task Team) to identify its own goals, linked the work of the group to clearly defined strategies, and provided a clear timeframe for this need to be addressed. Even within this school, though, no evaluation was planned against this team – it was unclear how the team would know when it had achieved its goals, or to what extent.

A second school identified the key element of its literacy leadership as a "Focus on teacher learning and pedagogy through the development of learning/planning teams" – and linked the work of these planning teams explicitly to what was being taught, professional learning activities, the establishment of school-based standards of exemplary practice, and a requirement for teams to engage in action research to extend and refine teachers' repertoires of practice. This therefore presented clarity in terms of how the leadership group would actually work within classrooms to identify and improve teaching practice, and how their performance would be evaluated (which was also linked to student achievement), as well as presenting a well-developed plan for teacher capacity-building – showing consideration of the sustainability of the approach. Leadership roles for this school were thus very closely linked to individual classrooms – as the plan notes, the focus is "to support the classroom teacher in taking the primary responsibility for the learning of all children in the class. This includes enabling connections between the classroom program and targeted support provided by support specialists".

Across all five schools that showed clear evidence of leadership roles and responsibilities for literacy, then, the common features were: A strong connection between leadership positions/roles and classroom teaching (often identifying leaders as being classroom teachers with some time out of class, or being released from other leadership roles to enable more time in classrooms); specific detail of how leaders would actually work that would lead to improvement of practices within the school community as a whole; and, importantly, clear descriptions of how the performance of leaders would be monitored and/or evaluated. These examples provide evidence of the clarity around leadership roles that in turn lead to increased effectiveness (Penlington, Kington & Day, 2008).

Eighteen of the schools whose literacy plans were analysed showed limited or no evidence of consideration of key leadership roles/responsibilities – with most of these failing to describe clearly the accountability of any leadership roles presented. As such, accountability was the key element that distinguished those plans described above from those that did not articulate leadership for literacy at a school level as effectively. Some of these schools identified outcomes such as "a strong focus on sharing good practice", but did not go on to describe how this would be achieved, who would be responsible, or what indicators of this focus might be, that would enable the school to know that it had been achieved. Other schools identified literacy leaders from outside of the school community – one school, for example, wrote that "we will be using [literacy specialist] to facilitate literacy improvement" – but did not identify specific indicators of improvement, or discuss the specific roles that this leader would take on within the school. A third group of schools provided overall indications of improvement, but did not link these to specific personnel, or present these indicators in a form that would enable measurement. For example, one school wrote that their goals included to "value add to literacy outcomes for all students" and "positive attitude to literacy learning by students".

One factor that may have impacted on the capacity of schools to clearly identify appropriate indicators of success was that very few schools offered any insight into how the school community chose to define literacy, or their vision for literacy learning. Such a statement of vision would assist in enabling schools to determine appropriate indicators of success, and therefore define and delineate the roles and responsibilities required by all stakeholders to achieve this. Only one school provided a clear articulation of beliefs about literacy, focusing on the importance of explicit and systematic teaching, the use of a range of approaches, and other such beliefs about teaching. Interestingly, this school also presented the most comprehensive and sophisticated schedule of assessment, showing very clearly how these beliefs would be translated through classroom practice into measurable outcomes, and who would be accountable throughout this process.

One final issue in relation to the articulation of leadership roles and responsibilities within the school literacy plans emerged near the end of the first year of the initiative, during a forum where preliminary findings from the evaluation were presented to key staff from each school and the system involved. After discussing the analysis of literacy plans, a number of participants expressed concern that the plans did not adequately represent the activities that their schools had been involved with – in a sense, they had 'moved on', and the plans did not adequately reflect what had happened, or was happening, within their contexts. In this sense, then, the plans at these schools were not functioning as 'working/living documents' – rather, they had been completed early in the year and not revisited. A concern that arises from this is the degree to which the outcomes and performance measures identified in these early planning documents might still apply – how useful would these plans actually be in assessing the school's success, and/or setting future targets? This represents a clear tension for those involved in leading literacy in schools – to what extent are plans to be completed and filed away, as opposed to being used as a basis for ongoing documentation of progress and change?

The analysis of literacy plans, then, revealed a number of significant issues and challenges that schools must take into account when articulating their vision of leadership, and just as importantly, when implementing this vision.

CONCLUSION

There is general agreement (e.g., Education Queenland, 2000; Dole 2004; Sharratt & Fullan, 2006, Murphy, 2004) on what is required in order for a whole-school approach to literacy to succeed. One important factor in this success is strong administrative and teacher leadership. However, the analysis reported above revealed that there are a number of challenges that impact on schools' capacity to provide this leadership. One such challenge involves the style of leadership to be provided. Sharratt & Fullan (2006) argue for a style that is collaborative in nature, allowing for the distribution of responsibilities and maintaining a strong focus on self-evaluation and continuous improvement at a classroom and school-level. A related challenge is that of achieving a shared vision, ensuring what Gracezewiski and colleagues (2008) define to as staff buy-in. It is this shared ownership that contributes to the sustainability of an initiative or approach, so that momentum is gained beyond the immediate actions of the person or people performing the leadership role.

Another challenge linked to leading for literacy in schools is knowing how to define success and set appropriate targets. As Dinham (2005) points out, not only must there be strong leadership to effect change in schools, but that those taking on such roles must be setting and working toward achieving meaningful goals rather than short-term targets. In order for such goals to be meaningful and relevant, though, it is important that success is understood and valued by the school community as a whole, achieved through a shared vision discussed above.

A final significant challenge that emerged from the analysis of the school literacy plans and from the literature is the importance of sustainability and how schools can best plan to achieve this through its investment in building not only teacher capacity and expertise but also that of its community. To return to Murphy's (2004) point that building capacity that leads to sustainability involves attending to both human and intellectual dimensions as well as social dimensions, it is argued that it is through the combination of these dimensions in communities of practice (Wenger, 1998) that share in the recognition and celebration of success in literacy that sustainability is achieved.

ACKNOWLEDGMENTS

This chapter draws on research funded by the Department of Education, Tasmania through the evaluation of the *Raising the Bar, Closing the Gap* Project.

REFERENCES

Belfiore, M., Defoe, T., Folinsbee, S., Hunter, J., & Jackson, N (2004). *Reading work: Literacies in the new workplace.* Mahwah NJ: Lawrence Erlbaum Associates.

Castleton, G. (2006). Putting language, literacy and learning to work. In G. Castleton, R. Gerber & H. Pillay (Eds.), *Improving workplace learning: Emerging international perspectives* (pp. 135 – 151). New York: Nova Science.

Clay, M. (2006). *Literacy lessons designed for individuals part one: Why? When? How?* Auckland, NZ: Heinemann Education.

Comings, J., & Soricone, L. (2007). *Adult literacy research: Opportunities and challenges.* Cambridge, Mass: National Centre for the Study of Adult Learning and Literacy, Harvard Graduate School of Education.

Chevalier, A., & Feinstein, L. (2006) *Sheepskin or Prozac: The causal effect of education on mental health. Discussion Paper.* London: Centre for Research on the Wider Benefits of Learning.

De Maeyer, S., Rymenans, R., Van Petegem, P., van den Berg, H. & Rijlaarsdam, G. (2007). Educational leadership and pupil achievement: The choice of a valid conceptual model to test effects in school effectiveness research. *School Effectiveness and School Improvement, 18*(2), 125 – 145.

DeWalt, D., Berkman, N., Sheridan, S. Lohr, K. & Pignone, M. (2004). Literacy and health outcomes: A systematic review of the literature. *Journal of General Internal Medicine, 9*(12),1228 – 1249.

Department of Education, employment and Workplace Relations (DEEWR) (2008). *Raising the bar and closing the gap initiative.* Retrieved January 22, 2010, from *http://pilots.educationau.edu.au/node/561.*

Dinham, S. (2007). *Authoritative leadership, action learning and student accomplishment.* ACER: Melbourne.

Dinham, S. (2005). Principal leadership for outstanding educational outcomes. *Journal of Educational Administration, 43*(4/5), 338 – 356.

Dole, R. (2004). The changing role of the reading specialist in school reform. *The Reading Teacher, 57*(5) 462 – 471.

Dugdale,G. & Clark, C (2008). *Literacy changes lives: An advocacy resource.* UK: National Literacy Trust.

Education Queensland (2000). *Literate futures: Report of the literacy review for Queensland state schools.* Brisbane: Queensland government, Education Queensland.

Elmore, R. (2005). Accountable leadership. *The Educational Forum. 69*(2), 134 – 142.

Freebody, P. (2007). *Literacy education in school: Research perspectives from the past, for the future.* Australian Education Review. Camberwell, Victoria: Australian Council for Education Research.

Fullan, M., Cuttress, C. & Kilcher, A. (2005). 8 Forces for leaders of change. *Journal of Staff Development, 26*(4), 54 – 64.

Gee, J. Hull, G. & Lankshear, C. (1996). *The new work order.* Sydney: Allen & Unwin.

Gilrane, C., Roberts, M. & Russell, L. (2008). Building a community in which everyone teaches, learns and reads: A case study. *The Journal of Educational Research, 101*(6), 333 – 349.

Graczewski, C., Knudson, J. & Holtzman, D. (2008). Instructional leadership in practice: What does it look like and what influence does it have? *Journal of Education for Students Placed at Risk, 14*(1), 72 – 96.

Gronn, P. (2000) Distributed Properties: A new architecture for leadership. *Educational Management and Administration, 28*(3), 317-338.

Gurr, D., Drysdale, L. & Mulford, B. (2006). Models of successful principal leadership. *School Leadership and Management, 26*(4), 371 – 395.

Hallinger, P. & Heck, R. (1998). Exploring the principal's contribution to school effectiveness: 1980-1995. *School Effectiveness and School Improvement, 9*(2), 157 – 191.

Hattie, J. (2003) Teachers make a difference: What is the research evidence? *Conference Proceedings Australian Council for Educational Research.* Retrieved April 10 from *http://www.emr.vic.edu.au/Downloads/English%20and%20Maths%20Leader%20Professional%20Learning/Leaders%20and%20Data%20Collections/teachers_make_a_difference.pdf*

Hull. G., & Grubb, N. (1999). Literacy skills and work. In D. Wagner, R. Venezky & B. Street (Eds.), *Literacy: An International Handbook* (pp. 311 – 417). Boulder Co: Westview Press.

Kazemek, F. (2004). Living a literate life. *Journal of Adolescent & Adult iLteracy, 47*(60), 448 – 452.

Kirsch, I., de Jong, J., Lafontaine, D., McQueen, J., Mendelovits, J. & Monseur, C.   (2002). *Reading for change: Performance and engagement across countries - results from PISA 2000.* Retrieved May 15, 2009 from *http://titania.sourceoecd.org.ezproxy. utas.edu.au/vl=3496166/cl=12/nw=1/rpsv/cgi-bin/fulltextew.pl?prpsv=/ij/oecdthemes/ 99980029/v2002n10/s1/p1l.idx*

Leithwood, K. & Jantzi, D. (2006). Transformational school leadership for large-scale reform: Effects on students, teachers and their classroom practices. *School Effectiveness and School Improvement, 17*(2), 201 – 227.

Leithwood, K. & Riehl, C. (2003). *What do we already know about successful school leadership?* Paper presented at the American Educational Research Annual Conference, Chicago, April 21 – 25.

Knuth, R. & Banks, M. (2006). The essential leadership model. *NASSP Bulletin 90*(1), 4 – 18.

Leithwood. K., Day, C., Sammons, P., Harris, A. & Hopkins, D. (2007). *Successful school leadership: what it is and how it influences pupil learning*; NCSL. http://www.nationalcollege.org.uk/index/leadershiplibrary.htm.

Leithwood. K., Day, C., Sammons, P., Harris, A. & Hopkins, D. (2006). Seven strong claims about successful school leadership, NCSL. Retrieved April 20, 2010 from *http://www.nationalcollege.org.uk/index/leadershiplibrary.htm.*

Louden et al (2005). Teachers' hands: Effective literacy teaching practices in the early years of schooling. *Australian Journal of Language and Literacy* (special edition), *28*(3).

Murphy, J. (2004). Leadership for literacy: A framework for policy and practice. *School Effectiveness & School Improvement, 15*(1), 65 – 96.

Nettles, S. & Herrington, C. (2007). Revisiting the importance of the direct effects of school leadership on student achievement: The implication of school improvement policy. *Peabody Journal of Education, 82*(4), 724 – 736.

Nichols, W. Rupley, W. & Rasinski, T. (2009). Fluency in learning to read for meaning: Going beyond repeated readings [Electronic version]. *Literacy Research and Instruction, 48*(1), 1 – 13. Retrieved April 05, 2009, from *http://www.informaworld. com/ 10.1080/19388070802161906*

Penlington, C., Kington, A. & Day, C. (2008). Leadership in improving schools: A qualitative perspective. *School Leadership & Management, 28*(1), 65 – 82

Reschly, A. (2010) Reading and School completion: Critical connections and Matthew effects. *Reading & Writing Quarterly, 26*, 67 – 90.

Robinson, V. (2008). Forging the links between distributed leadership and educational outcomes. *Journal of Educational Administration, 46*(2), 241 – 256.

Sharratt, L., Fullan, M. (2006). Accomplishing district wide reform. *Journal of School Leadership, 16*, 583 – 595.

Snyder, I (2008). The literacy wars: Why teaching children to read and write is a battleground in Australia. Sydney: Allen & Unwin.

Spillane, J. (2005). Distributed Leadership. *Educational Forum, 69*, 143 – 150.

Taylor, N. (2008). Metaphors, discourse and identity in adult literacy policy. *Literacy, 42*, 131 – 136.

UNESCO, 1995-2010. *Literacy.* Retrieved April 20, 2010 from *http://www.unesco.org/ en/literacy.*

Wenger, E. (1998). *Communities of practice: Learning, meaning and identity.* Cambridge: Cambridge University Press.

Zammit, K., Sinclair, C., Cole, B., Singh, M., Costley, D., a'Court, L & Rushton, K. (2007). *Teaching and leading for quality Australian schools: A review and synthesis of research-based knowledge.* Teaching Australia.

In: Language and Literacy Education in a Challenging World   ISBN: 978-1-61761-198-8
Editors: T. Lê, Q. Lê, and M. Short   © 2011 Nova Science Publishers, Inc.

Chapter 10

THE USE OF LANGUAGE IN THE MATHEMATICS CLASSROOM

Rosemary Callingham and Judith Falle

ABSTRACT

Despite the mantra of "all teachers are teachers of literacy", the importance of language is often overlooked in the mathematics classroom. In this chapter, different ways in which teachers might approach language development in mathematics will be considered. In particular, the importance of students having a mathematical register that goes beyond vocabulary use to indicate their growing understanding of mathematical concepts is explored. In both spoken and written text, teachers' use of mathematical language can help or hinder students' understanding. Conversely, careful attention by the teacher to students' spoken and written language can provide pointers to students' misconceptions, confidence and developing understanding. The implications for teaching are considered.

Keywords: mathematics, mathematical vocabulary, conceptual development, language.

INTRODUCTION

Mathematical language develops early. Pre-school children readily engage in number songs, such as "Five little ducks went out one day", and hence begin to learn the language of numbers and counting. They compare heights, "I'm taller than you", appreciate fairness, "Jamie's half is bigger than my half", and describe position, "The cat is behind the tree". All of these activities are the foundations for a language of mathematics, an essential mathematical register that they will draw on while learning mathematics formally in the classroom.

Register "is the set of meanings, the configuration of semantic patterns, that are typically drawn upon under the specified conditions, along with the words and structures that are used in the realization of these meanings" (Halliday, 1978, p. 23). The extent to which a speaker uses privileged words, the fluency and elegance of the prose, and the confidence, or otherwise, conveyed by voice and gesture constitute the register of discourse.

As children progress through school the language of the mathematics classroom becomes increasingly complex and the ideas more abstract. Gradually the vocabulary shifts from natural language to specialist words, not met with in everyday talk. The sentence structures become more complicated, and there is the added difficulty of decoding "word problems". As the mathematics becomes increasingly abstract, the language used to describe the ideas and processes is progressively denser. There is also the dilemma of having to move between words and a symbolic representation of the concept, that itself may take several forms.

Teachers play a major role in achieving this transition from natural language to a mathematical register. They must model correct language, explicitly teach the specialist mathematical meanings of words such as average, random, equals and fraction, and encourage students to use a language that is not part of their out-of-school experience. This task does not appear to be too different from the daily work of teachers in all other subjects. There are some aspects of mathematical language, however, and how students use it, that add to the difficulty of developing a mathematical register and vocabulary. In this chapter, some challenges associated with the development and use of language in the mathematics classroom will be considered in relation to students' mathematical register in terms of their acquisition of appropriate vocabulary, and the grammatical and syntactical structure of their discourse.

DEVELOPMENTAL ASPECTS OF LANGUAGE AND MATHEMATICS

Language is crucial to cognitive development (Goswami & Bryant, 2007), and this is true in mathematics as in every other field of endeavour. Counting appears to be a fundamental activity that appears in some form in every culture (Bishop, 1991), and this activity provides a foundation for mathematical development. Very young children show an increasing dependence on verbal skills for counting rather than relying on visual comparisons (Brannon & Van de Walle, 2001) and children with specific language delay often demonstrate impaired counting and computational skills (Donlan, Cowen, Newton & Lloyd, 2007). Studies such as these indicate that language is fundamental to number development.

Once children enter formal schooling, mathematical language becomes even more important. Children are now exposed to a variety of words that have a specific meaning in mathematics, which may be very different to that in their daily lives. In addition, they need to master a new representational format which may be described in several different ways with words, but which has specific and precise mathematical meaning. For example, the mathematical symbol "+" is one that children in kindergarten may be familiar with, but the mathematical idea may be expressed as "plus", "more than", "and" or "add", depending on the context of the problem, adding to the challenge of developing a particular vocabulary. Similarly, the concept of subtraction is another that children meet early in their schooling. The mathematical operation may take the form of "how many more", "take away" and "difference between". For example, children may be asked "Lee has 6 marbles and Mo has 10 marbles. How many more marbles does Mo have than Lee?" Alternatively, they could be asked, "Mo has 10 marbles. He gives 6 marbles to Lee. How many marbles does Mo have now?" Finally, the same operation could be posed as "What is the difference between the number of marbles if Lee has 6 marbles and Mo has 10 marbles?" Each of these can be represented mathematically as $10 - 6$. Although different linguistically, the same mathematical operation is implied, adding to the challenge for students. Additionally, arithmetic operators act as relational signs, in similar ways to the use of conjunctions and conditional clauses in natural language. Students have to interpret from the context whether to carry out a computation (3 + 5 results in 8) or to read the symbols as a mathematical entity (3 + 5 represents a number).

The development of young students' mathematics is often identified by their acquisition of appropriate language associated with the mathematics. To communicate their growing understanding, young students may act out learning experiences, produce images that represent mathematical ideas, and talk about their emergent understanding. They do not necessarily have the appropriate vocabulary with which to communicate their ideas, nor are their concepts fully formed. Language and the associated mathematical ideas are interconnected (Sfard, 2001), and the development of both is a process of complex interplay between the two. The challenge for teachers is to identify students' appropriate developmental levels so that they can provide access to increasingly complex language and mathematical concepts.

These links between language and mathematical concepts are less clearly marked with older students and, as the mathematics becomes increasingly abstract, opportunities for concrete experiences become rarer. Learning theories suggest, however, that novices of any age rely on immediate, or remembered, experiences to which new ideas can be conceptually attached, which requires language. When encountering entirely new contexts, even experienced mathematicians revert to thinking rather naïvely about unfamiliar ideas (National Council of Teachers of Mathematics, 2000). It is a struggle to acquire, or adopt, the vocabulary appropriate to the new context, and in parallel, it is equally difficult to convey thinking to others – either those who are more expert, or fellow novices. Such struggles are commonplace in the secondary mathematics classroom, and teachers need to provide opportunities for students to challenge their own thinking and that of others through the development of a specialised written and spoken vocabulary. Students who have developed linguistic competence that enables them to engage in everyday dialogue, may not appear to struggle to find words to explain their thinking, and may adopt easily the conventional vocabulary used by their teachers. Fluent use of everyday language, or even mathematical vocabulary, does not, however, guarantee understanding of mathematical concepts.

An example drawn from interviews with students discussing their thinking when completing introductory manipulative algebra questions illustrates this point. Two students, one of whom scored highly on a test of algebra, the other who performed poorly, both stated that brackets in an expression meant "to do it first", a common everyday expression attached to the role of a bracket in symbolic mathematical sentences. The first student correctly answered all test items containing brackets. The second answered none correctly. The "do it first" statement about the role of brackets in mathematical expressions appears to be understood differently by the two students. Hearing the same language from both, but seeing the application of their understanding differ suggests that words alone are not sufficient to guarantee understanding (Falle, 2007).

Another example drawn from special education reinforces this view. Asked to write the number sentence from a picture that showed three-quarters and one-half, a high-functioning student with autism spectrum disorder correctly wrote $\frac{3}{4} + \frac{1}{2}$. When asked to describe what he had written, however, he said "three four add one two", indicating that despite his ability to write the mathematical representation correctly he appeared to have limited understanding of the fraction concept (Seah, 2009). It is a challenge for students to link effectively language and mathematical ideas – one informs the other.

THE CHALLENGE OF MATHEMATICAL VOCABULARY

Meanings are given to words by persons according to individual experience. The challenge for teachers is to ensure that the precise meanings ascribed to words or phrases in mathematics are quite distinctly understood by students. Learning new words can be a matter of associating particular mathematical ideas with a label. A simple case is that of students learning that some figures are to be called triangles, others, squares or rectangles. At its most unsophisticated this is labelling particular shapes according to their appearance. However, the label itself obtains deeper meaning as students learn to identify properties of individual geometric figures, and to see connections between figures and their properties. It then becomes problematic for the teacher to discern whether a student is responding simply to the appearance of a figure, or has a deep understanding that the figure is what it is because of its properties, using the label as a shorthand or code for a complex of ideas.

On the other hand, words of precise mathematical meaning are often used rather more vaguely, even incorrectly, in everyday discourse, including common classroom practice. *Equal,* for example, often comes to mean "the result" or "the answer" to a computation, and students associate the sign "=" with obtaining an answer. The more powerful and exact mathematical meaning of "equivalence" becomes lost through early arithmetic experiences such as "five plus three makes…?" *Sum* is another, all too often used to denote any sort of computation instead of the result, strictly, of addition.

Presenting particular difficulties are those words in common use which mathematics has privileged. For example, *similar* is well understood in everyday parlance as meaning "sharing some common features", "looking like". In mathematics its use is restricted to describing geometric figures having the same proportions. Students who have heard and used the word in their everyday conversation might have little difficulty in accepting it as heard in a mathematics lesson but they do not always understand its precise and restricted use in a mathematical sense. The mathematical meanings given to everyday words need to be carefully constructed by teachers.

Acquisition of the technical vocabulary associated with mathematics is important, and associated with increasing understanding of mathematical ideas. However, students' own attempts to find words that convey their thinking might often be more revealing of their understanding than their use of conventionally accepted words or phrases. The language of space is complex, often having Greek or Latin origins, and this can create difficulties for some students. This exchange happened in a middle-years classroom after a series of lessons addressing 3D objects:

Student: We live on a circle, don't we?

Teacher: Are you sure? If we cut the earth in half we'd see a circle… Do we live on a circle?

Student: Hang on, no, it's a [long pause] It's a cubic circle.

This student was clearly demonstrating conceptual understanding of a sphere, but didn't have the technical term at his disposal. Moments like these are "teachable moments" for connecting students' understanding with the appropriate language through modelling the correct word, and following up the naïve explanation.

Acquisition and use of the accepted terminologies, although necessary for clear and distinct understanding of mathematics and for communication, is not sufficient on its own. The ways in which words are used to convey ideas can indicate the extent to which the ideas are understood or accepted. Teachers consciously listen to what their students say, but are often unconsciously influenced by the ways in which students frame their utterances. Teachers focus on the content of their students' discourse – seeking confirmation of the extent of knowledge acquired or recalled by a student.

Pragmatic analysis of student utterances or student writing (Bills & Gray, 2001; Boero, Douek, & Ferrari, 2002; Rowland, 2000) reveals that the quality of the language used also serves as an indicator of depth of knowledge. Informal, everyday language, interspersed with hesitancies, unnecessary words such as "like", "you know" "I think", sometimes verbose, offered as a statement of what the individual would or did do ("I added") often indicates a lack of confidence on the part of the student. Such linguistic features suggest that students are challenged by the ideas about which they are speaking or writing.

Conceptual development of a mathematical idea is paralleled by, and interconnected with, language development from an everyday, informal register to the appropriate mathematical register. New concepts with which students struggle are accompanied by a change in register, with students returning to an informal register at the early stage of concept development. As the ideas begin to be better understood the register of students' speech or writing begins to develop a more formal tone.

CHALLENGES FOR EDUCATIONAL PRACTICE

The interconnectedness of mathematics and language provides challenges for curriculum writers and teachers. Some of these challenges are examined in this section.

Challenges for Curriculum Writers

The importance of language is recognised in mathematics curricula around the world. Communication is one of the process strands in the mathematics curriculum in the United States (NCTM, 1989, 2000), in many Australian states (e.g., Board of Studies, NSW, 2002) and the importance of language is explicit in descriptions of what this requires:

Communication plays an important role in helping children construct links between their informal, intuitive notions and the abstract language and symbolism of mathematics; it also plays a key role in helping children make important connections among physical, pictorial, graphic, symbolic, verbal, and mental representations of mathematical ideas (NCTM, 1989, 26).

Similarly, the New South Wales K-6 Mathematics Syllabus (Board of Studies, NSW, 2002) includes an outcome statement that states "Students develop and use appropriate language and representations to formulate and express mathematical ideas" (p. 21), and includes a set of standards for different stages of schooling.

The language *of* mathematics and language *for* mathematics both develop as mathematical understanding increases. Language moves from the informal, everyday register to the more formal, mathematical register as understanding moves from a single experience grounded in the real world through many experiences from which abstractions and consequent generalisations are made to disembodied, decontextualised mathematical ideas. Complicating this move is the increasing disengagement of the language used from its everyday meaning.

Mathematics would appear to be unique in its conceptual structure. Some fundamental ideas such as counting and the foundations of measurement may occur informally outside the classroom, and have an informal language associated with them. In the classroom, however, the language becomes more complex as the mathematical concepts are developed. Even the four basic arithmetic operations of addition, subtraction, multiplication and division are conceptually difficult when they are translated into formal mathematics, compounded by the many every day meanings that may be associated with each operation. A balance needs to be struck between procedure and concept and the associated language development can provide a marker, giving students the wherewithal to articulate their thinking, and describing the processes needed to manipulate the mathematics successfully.

The facts and procedures associated with the formal mathematics need to be automated so that they become tools that enable further mathematics to be explored. This is the language *of* mathematics. The relationship between conceptual understanding of the foundational ideas and the need for automaticity of basic facts provides one challenge for curriculum developers. Without a fundamental mathematical "vocabulary" of basic facts, students are limited in their mathematical opportunities. Without understanding the conceptual bases for these facts and procedures, they are also limited, and language is a key to the development of concepts.

This tension is repeated throughout the mathematics curriculum as it develops across the years of schooling. In the later years of schooling, for example, the same tension is observed between the rules and procedures for differentiation and integration, and the conceptual underpinnings.

Language, therefore, is critical to the mathematics curriculum, and serves dual purposes. Natural language provides a means towards conceptual understanding and, as the mathematics becomes more complex, also one way of expressing that understanding: language *for* mathematics. At the same time, a mathematical register develops that has a vocabulary that is increasingly symbolic and abstract: the language *of* mathematics. Both of these aspects need to be acknowledged explicitly in modern mathematics curricula.

Challenges for Classroom Teachers

Although thinking can occur without language, language is needed to formulate and communicate more complex ideas. The quality of students' language, whether written or spoken, can serve as an indication of the quality of their understanding of mathematical ideas. Talking or writing about thinking enables those ideas to be clarified both personally, and so that others might better understand. This is the mathematical discourse in which students, and professional mathematicians, engage. When students operate in a discursive environment, their spoken language has to develop in order that they make themselves clear to others. By clarifying their own language, students clarify their thoughts. Once spoken ideas are better organised, written records become useful additional ways of developing the appropriate register. This can become a collaborative effort that then helps with individual construction of personal explanations.

The challenge for teachers is to identify students' levels of understanding so that instruction can be more closely tailored to the students' needs. This task is not trivial, and may be made more difficult by students' apparent successful use of mathematical language. One approach to this issue is to use Newman Error Analysis (Newman, 1977, 1983).

The error analysis technique is most often applied to "word problems" but can, potentially, be used in any situation where mathematical meaning is wrapped in text. A five-step process is used to identify exactly where the student is having difficulty in solving the problem. The steps are as follows:

1. To identify reading errors: "Read the question to me. If you don't know a word tell me."

2. To identify comprehension errors: "Tell me, what the question asked you to do."

3. To identify transformation errors: "Now tell me what method you used to find the answer."

4. To identify process skills' errors: "Now go over each step of your working, and tell me what you were thinking."

5. To identify encoding errors, which is an inability to express an answer in an acceptable form: "Tell me, what is the answer to the question? Point to your answer."

A variety of research studies indicates that overwhelmingly students have most difficulty at Step 3, the Transformation stage, when they need to move from the written words to a mathematical sentence or process (Clements & Ellerton, 1992).

Gawned (1990) proposed a socio-psycho-linguistic model of language development in mathematics. The model progresses through four stages: 1. Real-world language; 2. Language of the classroom; 3. Specific components; and 4. Construction of meaning in mathematics. This model indicates the complexity of the inter-relationship between language and mathematics, especially at stage 3, Specific Components, which addresses several aspects of developing mathematical language: Language of Reasoning, Activity Specific Language, Language of the Mathematics Curriculum and Literacy of Mathematics. This step appears to be comparable to Step 3 in the Newman analysis.

These findings indicate that when students do not fully comprehend mathematical vocabulary they cannot make the links between the formal language of a word problem and their mathematical knowledge. Such difficulties in transformation are deeper than natural language comprehension because the student *can* explain what the word problem requires. It is the boundary between the two forms of language, formal written text in the mother tongue and the language of mathematics, which creates the confusion. Teachers need to focus on the nature and structure of the initial text and help students make the links between that and the structure of the mathematical language that they need to solve the word problem.

In mathematics, communication takes the forms of both written and spoken words. In the written form, symbols are often used to communicate mathematical ideas almost to exclusion of other representations. The meaning-dense symbolic language of mathematics requires students to associate the looser structures of everyday speech with the restricted syntactical structures of mathematical expressions. Mathematical symbols encapsulate the precise meanings of mathematical terms. Written symbolic mathematical expressions lack the contextual clues of normal speech that help remove ambiguity. Appreciation of the structure of these mathematical expressions is essential to understanding the subtleties of different mathematical meanings.

The natural language itself, however, can lead to confusion because of the complex structure of the written language needed for mathematics. Take the classic problem: "There are six times as many students as professors. Write an equation that expresses this relationship." Teachers as well as high school students tend to write $6S = P$ instead of the correct $6P = S$. Mapping directly onto the written language creates an error in the mathematical sentence (Abedi, Lord & Plummer, 1997). The initial sentence has to be decoded in a very specific way for it to make sense mathematically. The complexity and density of the language creates particular challenges for teachers as they aim to develop mathematical understanding. To write using the formal conventions of mathematics requires students to have the ideas well formed. Teachers do not usually require students to produce at first pass a complete, correct piece of writing in their natural tongue. The language of mathematics is not a natural tongue, and hence producing "finished" mathematics in the very first instance imposes a large cognitive load on the student. This can interfere with students' mathematical thinking and the development of understanding.

If "communication …is almost tantamount to thinking itself" (Sfard, 2001, p.13), then discursive practices in the classroom must serve to foster and to reveal the mathematical thinking of pupils. Fostering mathematical thinking involves students acquiring the terminology and the language patterns necessary to formulate mathematical concepts, and to communicate these with others, and also with themselves. Humans learn to speak before they can read, or write. Speech is transient but provides an immediacy of thought, and occurs with perhaps less cognitive effort than having to think both of the mathematics and also of how to write the mathematics, especially when having to comply with formal conventions of mathematical writing.

Teachers have to decide which of these activities is most important at any particular time. Is students' mathematical thinking and conjecturing to be the focus? Is their recording of their mathematics to be the centre of attention? Is it important that they use the correct notation and vocabulary? These aspects of clear mathematical communication are all important, but not necessarily simultaneously, and the challenge for teachers is that in a single classroom all of these may be significant and necessary for different students.

Teachers also need to be aware of their own language use. Bills and Gray (2001) found that students tended to use the teacher's voice as they gained greater understanding of the mathematics. However, they may also simply echo words or phrases the teacher uses, with only a vague notion of the deep meaning. Of particular danger is the use of metaphor by teachers to explain mathematical ideas. Firstly, students can interpret the metaphor literally. The mathematical idea of "cancelling", for example is often explained as "crossing off" numbers or letters that "look the same". Interpreted literally, this metaphor can lead to incorrect actions by students who have not conceptualised the mathematical meaning of division. Students whose mathematics is better developed appear to see the mathematical meaning in the metaphors. Students whose mathematical understanding is naïve do not see the mathematics in the metaphor. Consequently, they are limited to simple examples and unable to generalise or make incorrect extensions. Pimm (1987), for example, describes a student extrapolating from a "right angle", to a "left angle" when the direction of the angle was reversed. In addition, the limited experiences afforded students who may see only examples that provide a simple illustration of a mathematical idea, but rarely have the opportunity to encounter non-examples, does not allow the language *of* mathematics to be developed by language *for* mathematics. Non-examples provide a problematic environment, opportunities for debate and subsequent clarification of important mathematical concepts; and further opportunities for teachers to eavesdrop on students' conversations.

SOME APPROACHES TO DEVELOPING LANGUAGE SKILLS IN MATHEMATICS

In this section some ways in which teachers have successfully helped their students develop mathematical language are considered. In many instances these approaches not only help students develop an appropriate vocabulary but also promote the meta-cognitive thinking that helps mathematical development.

Writing in order to learn has long been advocated. Boscolo and Mason (2001, p. 85) stated "writing can improve students' learning by promoting active knowledge construction, requiring them to be involved in transforming rather than a process of reproducing". One approach to encouraging writing in the mathematics classroom is to use journals to provide students with ways of recording their mathematical thoughts. Journals need carefully crafted questions on which students might reflect – questions that have a mathematical focus, and that serve to develop the mathematical register. Such questions might be better addressed in journal writing if they are firstly the subject of classroom discussion that develops the language and protocols of explanation, as distinct from simple recounting of what was done (Mousely & Marks, 1991).

It is not uncommon for students initially to resist writing a mathematical journal. Comments such as "This is maths not English" are frequent. Persistence, however, does bring benefits. A student in a Year 9 low-ability class at the start of the journaling experience wrote, "Why are we doing this?" After two weeks in which the focus in the classroom was problem solving using a variety of mathematical tools, he wrote in his journal "I think my brain is beginning to work. I solved three problems today". At the end of the unit, in which the problem solving approach had been used with Pythagoras' theorem he contributed a page of writing describing in detail how he and a friend had worked together to complete a new problem that required using the inverse Pythagorean relationship, a skill that students in this kind of class rarely achieved.

Allowing students to explain their thinking using any language that they have available also provides teaching opportunities. There is a temptation for teachers to step in and explain a procedure but this can short circuit developing understanding. For example, students undertaking an early algebra task called "Street Party" were asked what would happen to the number of people that could be seated as a table was gradually extended by adding in small square tables. The final question was "How would you find out the number of tables needed for any number of people?" The correct mathematical equation is $T = 2(P + 1)$. Allowing students to explain their thinking in a variety of ways, however, provides additional useful information to teachers. For example, one student wrote "You just have to draw the number of tables and count how many people can sit at the amount of tables that are need[ed]". This student had successfully solved all the earlier problems suggesting that she had a good understanding of the process involved. When pushed to a generalisation, however, she reverted to a naïve idea that demonstrated that the underlying algebraic relationship was not clear (Callingham, 2003).

Another approach to linking natural language with mathematical language is through the use of children's literature as a stimulus for mathematical discussion (e.g., Whitin & Whitin, 2004). Many delightful children's books are available that serve to provide worthwhile mathematical material. Some are deliberately mathematical, such as *Anno's Mysterious Multiplying Jar* (Anno, 1983) which has become a classic of its type. Others can be used to develop mathematical ideas such as *Counting on Frank* (Clement, 1990). All are visually appealing and intrinsically motivating for children to become engaged in mathematics. For older students too there are suitable mathematical books. One classic is *Flatland* (Abbott, 1944) which deals with the geometry of two- and three- dimensional space. As a spin off, children can produce their own mathematical stories. By reading or listening to appropriate stories, children have opportunities to transform natural language into mathematical forms if this activity is promoted by the teacher.

CONCLUSION

The relationship between mathematics and language is not simple. Mathematics has its own privileged use of natural language as well as its own unique vocabulary and syntax. Research suggests that natural language alone will not be sufficient to develop deep understanding of mathematical concepts. As mathematical concepts become more abstract, a new register is required that becomes increasingly divorced from natural language, but that initially requires natural language for its expression. This paradox should be addressed in curricula and its resolution become an important and explicit part of classroom experience. Ultimately the aim is to construct mathematical meaning in ways that allow students to develop their mathematical skills and understanding to progress towards whatever level of mathematical endeavour they wish to pursue. The challenge of this task should not be underestimated.

REFERENCES

Abbott, E. A. (1944). *Flatland.* Oxford: Basil Blackwell.

Abedi, J., Lord, C. & Plummer, J. R. (1997). *Final report of language background as a variable in NAEP mathematics performance.* Los Angeles, CA: National Centre for Research on Evaluation, Standards and Student testing.

Anno, M. (1983). *Anno's mysterious multiplying jar.* New York: Penguin.

Bills, C., & Gray, E. (2001). The "particular", "generic" and "general" in young children's mental calculations. In M. van Heuval-Panhuizen (Ed.), *Proceedings of the 25th Annual Conference of the International Group for the Psychology of Mathematics Education,* (pp. 153 – 160). Utrecht: PME.

Bishop, A. (1991). *Mathematical enculturation*. Dordrecht: Kluwer Academic.

Board of Studies, NSW (2002). *Mathematics K-6 syllabus*. Sydney: Board of Studies.

Boero, P., Douek, N., & Ferrari, P. (2002). Developing mastery of natural language: Approaches to theoretical aspects of mathematics. In L.D. English (Ed.), *Handbook of International Research in Mathematics Education* (pp. 241 – 267). Mahwah, NJ: Lawrence Erlbaum.

Boscolo, P. & Mason, L. (2001). Writing to learn, writing to transfer. In P. Tynjala, L. Mason, & K. Lonka (Eds.), *Writing as a learning tool. Dordrecht*. The Netherlands: Kluwer Academic Publishers.

Brannon, E.M. & Van de Walle, G.A. (2001) The development of ordinal numerical competence in young children. *Cognitive Psychology 43*(1), 53 – 81.

Callingham, R. (2003). Improving mathematical outcomes in the middle years. Keynote address. In B. Clarke, A. Bishop, R. Cameron, H. Forgasz & W. T. Seah (Eds.) *Making mathematicians*. (Proceedings of the 40th Annual Conference of the Mathematical Association of Victoria. pp. 76 – 88), Melbourne: Mathematical Association of Victoria.

Clement, R. (1990). *Counting on Frank.* Sydney: Harper Collins.

Clements, M. A., & Ellerton, N. F. (1992). Overemphasising process skills in school mathematics: Newman analysis data from five countries. In W. Geeslin & K. Graham (Eds.), *Proceedings of the Sixteenth International Conference on the Psychology of Mathematics Education* (Vol. 1, pp. 145 – 152). Durham, New Hampshire: International Group for the Psychology of Mathematics Education.

Donlan C., Cowan, R., Newton, E. J. & Lloyd, D. (2007). The role of language in mathematical development: Evidence from children with specific language impairments. *Cognition* 103, 23 – 33.

Falle, J. (2007). Students' tendency to conjoin terms: An inhibition to their development of algebra. In J. Watson & K. Beswick (Eds.) *Mathematics: Essential research, essential practice*. (Proceedings of the 30th annual conference of the Mathematics Education Research Group of Australasia, pp. 285 – 294) Hobart: MERGA.Gawned, S. (1990). An emerging model of the language of mathematics. In J. Bickmore-Brand (Ed.), *Language in mathematics* (pp. 27 – 42). Melbourne: Australian Reading Association.

Goswami, U. & Bryant, P. (2007). Children's cognitive development and learning. Primary review research survey 2/1a. Cambridge: University of Cambridge.

Halliday, M.A.K. (1978). *Language as social semiotic: The social interpretation of language and meaning.* Baltimore: University Park Press.

Mousley, J., & Marks, G. (1991). *Discourses in mathematics*. Melbourne: Deakin University Press.

National Council of Teachers of Mathematics (NCTM). (1989). *Curriculum and Evaluation Standards for School Mathematics*. Reston, VA: National Council of Teachers of Mathematics.

National Council of Teachers of Mathematics (NCTM). (2000). *Principles and Standards for School Mathematics*. Reston, VA: National Council of Teachers of Mathematics.

Newman, M. A. (1977). An analysis of sixth-grade pupils' errors on written mathematical tasks. *Victorian Institute for Educational Research Bulletin, 39*, 31 – 43.

Newman, M. A. (1983). *Strategies for diagnosis and remediation*. Sydney: Harcourt, Brace Jovanovich.

Pimm, D. (1987). *Speaking mathematically: Communication in mathematics classrooms.* London: Routledge & Kegan Paul.

Rowland, T. (2000*). The Pragmatics of Mathematics Education: Vagueness in Mathematical Discourse.* London: Falmer Press.

Seah, R. (2009). The development of fraction ideas among students with disabilities. In R. Hunter, B. Bicknell, & T. Burgess (Eds.), *Crossing divides* (Proceedings of the 32nd annual conference of the Mathematics Education Research Group of Australasia), 8pp. [CDROM]. Palmerston North, NZ: MERGA.

Sfard, A. (2001). There is more to discourse than meets the ears: looking at thinking as communicating to learn more about mathematical learning. *Educational Studies in Mathematics, 46*, 13 -57

Whitin, P. & Whitin, D. (2004). *New visions for linking literature and mathematics.* Urbana, IL: National Council of Teachers of English.

In: Language and Literacy Education in a Challenging World   ISBN: 978-1-61761-198-8
Editors: T. Lê, Q. Lê, and M. Short   © 2011 Nova Science Publishers, Inc.

Chapter 11

RESPONDING TO THE CHALLENGE OF TRANSITIONING CHILDREN INTO EFFECTIVE LITERACY

Ian Hay and Ruth Fielding-Barnsley

ABSTRACT

This chapter reviews the types of responses teachers need to make when faced with the challenges associated with designing programs that accommodate the dynamic and interactive links between children's language, phonological skill, and reading development. Some of the key issues explored are procedures to enhance children's language development, decoding, and word recognition skills along with programming strategies that can facilitate children's early reading development. The links between children's reading and writing are explored as well as the links between children's social behaviour and their language and literacy proficiency. The authors outline how teachers can improve their children's language and literacy development by enhancing their dialogue and instructional procedures with the children in their classrooms, based on shared reading activities and Marion Blank's four levels of dialogue. The new challenge for teachers is how to apply Blank's psycholinguistics levels into their individual and group work with students of all ages. Blank's four levels of dialogue and questioning are: (i) dealing with directly supplied information (matching the experiences); (ii) classification (selective analysis of the experience); (iii) reorganisation (reordering the experience); and (iv) abstraction and inference (reasoning about the experience). This chapter outlines how high frequency words and language can be better related to improve children's comprehension of text. The chapter also deals with some of the challenges faced by parents and their children in the early years of their literacy development and outlines how to respond to these challenges.

Keywords: language, literacy, reading, social behaviour, children, comprehension, socio economic status (SES), shared reading.

INTRODUCTION

The main purpose of this chapter is to review procedures that can facilitate the reading development of children. In particular, it is written to help teachers respond to the new challenges associated with incorporating applied psycholinguistics elements into their work with individual students and groups of students of all ages. The theoretical framework for these psycholinguistics elements is drawn from a body of research that argues: that there is a strong reciprocal relationship between the structures and the purposes of the language used in spoken and written texts (Nation, 2005); that early reading interventions need to be multidimensional and multifaceted (Neuman & Dickson, 2001); that children's phonological, alphabetical and language skills are highly correlated (Adams, 1990); and that there is a link between children's language and social development (Sénéchal, 2006).

When children are advanced in their language development they are more likely to settle into school and classroom routines, to develop school attachment and to form positive peer social interactions involving advanced play and problem solving communication (Lindsay, Dockrel, & Strand, 2007). That is, children's social interactions have an influence on the development of children's language by creating opportunities for dialogue. The argument is, language encourages children's social interactions and social interactions encourage children's language development. From this perspective, the three elements of: (i) children's language proficiency; (ii) children's social skills proficiency; and (iii) children's behaviour control proficiency are considered to be related because they stem from a common underlying cognitive source that manifests all three proficiencies (Goswami & Bryant, 2007).

The challenge for teachers is, they need to understand that the core cognitive proficiency of both language and academic development is the child's working memory along with processing speed and capacity (Goswami & Bryant, 2007). From this perspective, children's attention related behaviours, language, and social development cannot be easily separated from their developing cognitive skills to store, organise, and retrieve information from long-term memory (Paul, 2007). The claim is that children with language delays often struggle with peer interactions, attention tasks, and in social dialogue situations because they cannot quickly or efficiently process or attend to all of the linguistic and non-verbal information needed to interact appropriately with their teachers, their peers, and others.

Children's alphabet letter name and sound knowledge and phonological awareness (e.g., the awareness of the sound units, such as syllables and phonemes in spoken words) are known to facilitate rapid decoding and are important predictors of reading success but these are not the only predictors of reading success (Adams, 1990). Some of the other predictors are children's concept of print, expressive vocabulary, sentence/story recall skills, and receptive and expressive language. These elements are interactive, such that an enhancement in one can have a direct and/or indirect influence on another of the elements.

In terms of reading, the challenge for teachers is that many of the children who have deficits in both phonological awareness and language skills also have more difficulty in transitioning into reading and maintaining the same level of reading acquisition as their peers (Byrne, Fielding-Barnsley, & Ashley, 2000). Thus, in the population of students with reading difficulties, language delays are a cause of reading delays, and the lack of reading skills has an ongoing negative influence on the students' vocabulary and language development.

ENHANCING EARLY LANGUAGE DEVELOPMENT

The challenge for children with early reading delays is that they need more exposure to and more practice with both expressive and receptive areas of language, such as vocabulary development and syntactic and semantic development, as well as greater dialogical interactions that engage and extend the children's level of language complexity (Hay et al., 2007). It has been argued that children's language development directly and indirectly fuels the development of children's phonological and phoneme awareness. Deficits in phonological awareness usually follow directly as a consequence of children's slow vocabulary development (a classic marker of language delay). Similarly, the claim is that the majority of children with language delays suffer a double disorder, in the sense that the operation of both their reading pathways via phonological (decoding) and semantic (meaning) are compromised.

Teachers can improve children's language and literacy development by enhancing their dialogue and instructional procedures with children in their classrooms. This is based on the notion that language is both learned and used in a communicative setting, often involving an older person and the child. From this perspective Marion Blank and her colleagues (Blank & Franklin, 1980; Blank, Rose, & Berlin, 2003) have proposed four levels of dialogue complexity, where the children are active participants in the learning interchanges. In such a communicative context the teacher initiates and shapes the dialogue so that the students respond at a more appropriate and advancing level of linguistic complexity.

Initially developed for the early years of school, Blank's system of coding and analysing dialogue has application to students in the higher grades. Blank's sub-elements are outlined in Tables 1, 2 and 3. At the lowest level of complexity or first level, the student is required to respond to language concerning salient perceptions (e.g., to the question, *what is this?*), with a focus on vocabulary development, moving to the second level, the organization of information stage, where the key questions investigate how objects, events, or issues are classified. This organisation and classification of the information particularly helps facilitate students' encoding and retrieval of information into and from their long-term memory. Even basic teacher questions, such as "which letter is the first, middle, or final sound in the word "hat" " are linguistically complex instructions to follow, if the child is still unable to organise information into a sequence. The third level is focussed on reorganising or adding to the information, based on what an individual already knows of the topic, which is the linking of the information to higher order reasoning (e.g., *what else do you know about that?*). The fourth level deals with the abstract, and at this level the language demands involve reflecting upon or restructuring perceptions (e.g., the question, *what do you think will happen if - - -?*).

It is incorrect to assume that a child can deal with the higher order teacher dialogue questions, before the earlier levels of language proficiency are mastered. For example, a Year 1 child still working at the vocabulary and classification stage of Blank's levels of discourse, is confused by a teacher talking of "good and bad" foods, if that child still does not know the names of the common fruits and vegetables and most of his/her language experience of "good or bad" deal with being co-operative with his/her parents. Questions about food being good or bad are level four questions, and the teacher needs to work with the child at the earlier, more foundation levels and to build up to the abstract level of questioning and dialogue. The evidence is that teachers who have used Blank's cognitive-based system of dialogue assessment and responses in their classrooms significantly enhanced their children's level of language development and consequently their reading development (Hay et al., 2007).

Table 1– Blank's Four Levels of Language Complexity and Proficiency Related to Teacher Discourse and Questioning (Blank et al., 2003)

Level of Complexity & Proficiency	Language Complexity to the Experience	Example of Teacher Discourse
1	Directly Supplied Information (Matching experiences)	What do you see?
2	Classification (Selective analysis of experience)	Group the shapes by colour.
3	Reorganisation (Reordering the experience)	Re-tell me the story
4	Abstraction and Inference (Reasoning about experience)	What made it happen?

Table 2 – Scale for Coding Utterances (level I) based on Blank and Franklin (1980)

Sample Processes	Examples of Utterances
Level I. Matching experience	
a. Identifying objects by sight, sound or touch	"That's a car" (upon hearing a car)
b. Imitating utterances of other speakers	"It's all right" (after someone has just said that phrase).
c. Labelling actions or events	"She's sitting."
d. Employing social routines	"Bye-bye."
e. Requesting attention	"Mummy!"
f. Requesting desired objects	"I want a piece of fruit."

Table 3 – Scale for Coding Utterances (levels II, III & IV) based on Blank and Franklin (1980)

Sample Processes	Examples of Utterances
Level II. Selective analysis of experience	
a. Noting attributes	"I want a blue ball."
b. Noting possession	"This is mum's hat."
c. Noting location	"It's in the bedroom."
d. Comparing objects	"This doll is prettier than this one."
e. Identifying the function of objects	"What can you use to cut things with?"
f. Integrating objects, actions and events	"She is sitting on the grass."
Level III. Reordering experience	
a. Sequencing material or events	"I'll put this one first and then this one second."
b. Defining objects or events by exclusion	"Where else could we go, besides to the movies?"
c. Role-taking	"What would you say if you were a puppy?"
d. Establishing conditional relationships (that are not causally related)	"He finished his lunch, so he can go and play."
e. Talking about language (metalinguistics)	"I wonder if you can tell me what 'boys' hats' means?"
f. Formulating a generalisation about a set of events (similarity)	"They're all so soft" (touching cotton, wool, a blanket and velvet).
g. Describing social conventions	"It's impolite to sing at the table; the table is a place for conversations."
Level IV. Reasoning about experience	
a. Formulating a solution to a problem	"How could we find out if the shop is open?"
b. Justifying a decision	"You only need one spoon of sugar because it's a small cup."
c. Identifying the causes of an event	"The bus is going slow 'because there's too much traffic in the way."
d. Explaining the construction of objects	"Why is the wheel made of rubber?"
e. Explaining an inference drawn from an observation	"You can tell the puppies are happy because of their wagging tails."

ENGAGEMENT

Engaging children and students with both narrative and non-narrative reading resources is an essential component of a rich literacy program. For example, this engagement can be via magazines, newspapers, or books, or well as having the students read and write their own stories, or use and develop texts associated with the internet and other media (Cooney & Hay, 2005). Once engagement is initiated the teacher, parent, or tutor has a starting point. This is an ongoing process where the teacher models and demonstrates how the words are pronounced and what they mean, uses the words in context, reads along with the student to encourage the student to read independently, and then encourages the student to review and reflect on what he/she has read.

Children's engagement in reading has to start early and the indications are that there is significant variability in the amount of early shared reading occurring in different homes. For example, Hay and Fielding-Barnsley (2006) reported that book reading occurred as seldom as five times per year with some low-income families. Such findings have underpinned the need for the development of literacy programs that aim to encourage parent-child book reading in all homes and for early childhood teachers to ensure that they incorporate significant language and vocabulary development within their regular program, especially for children from families where English proficiency is an issue.

One of the main unresolved challenges associated with children's early literacy development is clarifying when a child is ready to engage with formal classroom reading instruction. Unfortunately this challenge is unlikely to be easily resolved (Marrow & Tracey, 2007) in part, because of the variability in language functioning of children of the same chronological age, but who come from different socio-economic status and home backgrounds. Utilising a cut off point of a language age of 5 years 6 months for expressive language as assessed by the *Hundred Picture Naming Test* (HPNT; Fisher & Glennister, 1992), Hay and Fielding-Barnsley (2009) reported that approximately 15% of the children in a large cross sectional sample (*N*=457), failed to achieve this criteria. However, there was significant variation by schools' SES rating. In low SES schools, 1 in 4 children (25%) was below the basic language benchmark. This dropped to 1 in 12 children (8%) in middle SES schools, while no children entering in high SES schools were below the benchmark standard of 5 years 6 months. A similar pattern was identified for the children's receptive language proficiency as assessed by the *Peabody Picture Vocabulary Test- Revised* (PPVT-R; Dunn & Dunn, 1981). In low SES schools, around 1 in 3 children (31%) were below the 5 years 6 month expressive language benchmark, this reduced to 1 in 5 children (18%) in middle SES schools, and no children entered the high SES schools below the 5 year 6 month benchmark. Hay and Fielding-Barnsley (2009) also investigated the class teachers' rating of the children's in-class behaviours. They found that the children's ability to: remember daily tasks; organise tasks; wait their turn; and engage in tasks that require effort were highly correlated with the child's initial reading achievement. This relationship is not all that unexpected given the theoretical argument that children's attention related behaviours, language, and social development cannot be easily separated from their developing and maturing cognitive skills to store, organise, and retrieve information from long-term memory.

Such findings demonstrate a clear requirement for teachers, working in the early years of schooling to respond to the child's language and learning needs by modifying and adapting their programs of instruction to accommodate children's background and diversity factors within their classroom. In particular, children with language delays need more exposure to and more practice with both expressive and receptive areas of language, such as vocabulary development, phonological awareness, syntactic and semantic development, as well as the manipulation of oral and print text information, and greater amounts of dialogical interactions. The implications for teachers are that children who have language delays are also more likely to need more teacher cueing and prompting as they engage in the learning tasks, as well as instructional periods that are shorter in duration, but more frequent, compared with their peers without literacy or language delays. Teachers also need to keep their language of instruction at a suitable level of complexity and clarification to better accommodate the children's speed of oral language processing but also to give the children opportunities to extend and advance their language development.

To help engage children, the classroom learning environment needs to be motivating with teachers providing meaningful feedback within a quality early childhood experience. The evidence is that quality early childhood experiences include oral language experiences that focus on gestural expression, verbal and non-verbal expression, vocabulary development, building background knowledge, and listening to others talk to understand and comprehend what they say.

The challenge is, teachers need to foster with their children the types of oral language interactions that enable their children to engage and benefit from the ever advancing formal instructional demands of the classroom. This involves the teacher engaging individual (dyadic) and small group interactions. In a dialogic reading situation, the other person is asked to engage in a dialogue with the child about the content and context of the text and allow the child to direct and share in the conversations associated with the text and the pictures. The more experienced reader is encouraged to model and expand on the child's dialogue and encourage the student to practise this linguistically enhanced dialogue. Thus, the student improves in vocabulary knowledge, syntactic (the rules/patterns of language) knowledge and semantic (word meaning) knowledge, as well as in the social skills of turn taking, waiting, and listening, and the conventions associated with reading text (pragmatics). There are two significant benefits associated with dialogical reading. The first benefit is that the child/student is better able to read along with and to direct the caregiver/teacher when re-reading familiar text. The second benefit is that reading is established as a purposeful social activity. In time, this purposeful activity may enable the individual to read so he/she can, for example, play a computer based game, text friends on a mobile phone, read for fun and share this reading with another. Purposeful reading helps to motivate students of all ages and facilitates their confidence and involvement in their own reading acquisition process.

To foster this social engagement, Elias, Hay, Homel, and Freiberg (2006) worked with children's parents who generated shared reading books based on pictures taken by their children using a digital camera. Initially only sentence length text was developed per full page of illustration, but over time the text length increased. In those homes where English was the second language, the parents' first language was also included as part of text. At the outset, few words were used as text with a focus on encouraging parent child bonding, child engagement and wait time. The challenge was to keep the parents focused on having them talk about the pictures and the words, model the read text, have the children read along with the parents, have the children re-read the text, and then to review the words and the task. Over time these home made reading books engaged both the child and the parent in a purposeful activity and so they became the re-reading books of choice for the children. Too often parents become anxious when reading with their child and directly and indirectly this anxiety about reading is transferred to the child. The challenge is "calming" the parents and informing them that this is about enjoying quality time with their child, and not about achieving instant accuracy from their child in terms of reading. Many of these dialogic support strategies have also been successfully incorporated into training programs for tutors who work with a range of students including adolescents who are reluctant readers or who have reading difficulties (Woolley & Hay, 2004).

DECODING

Adams (1990) wrote that there is a positive relationship between children's performance in phoneme judgement tasks and their progress in alphabet knowledge and learning to read and spell words. This necessity for decoding is understandable given that the beginning reader has to learn to decode thousands of words that are visually unfamiliar and to commit those visual patterns to memory. It is also a lifelong skill. For readers of all ages, all new words are visually unfamiliar when encountered for the first time and so decoding continues to be necessary. Novice readers usually start to recognise the word by identifying and blending its phonological (sound) elements and comparing the sound pattern to the sound patterns of words in their spoken vocabulary (Fielding-Barnsley & Purdie, 2003). Such a process can be taught to the young reader, and this process is often revisited when older readers have to operate with a new set of words, such as when they learn a foreign language, or curriculum specific vocabulary, such as science vocabulary and concepts. Improvements in children's phonological skills usually increase their ability to identify single words and enhance their spelling skills. In terms of teaching strategies, when confronted with an unfamiliar word, the child should first be encouraged to look into the word for familiar letter and spelling patterns, and then to use context as back up support to confirm hypotheses as to what that word might be, e.g., make is /m/ plus *ake,* as cake is /c/ plus *ake.* This approach helps to explain why reading comprehension of young children is highly correlated with decoding skills in the early school years, but by Year 5 the students' ability to use the context of the text to derive meaning also plays an important role in the prediction of the students' comprehension proficiency (Woolley & Hay, 2007).

As part of the initial process of having children learn to read, the school and the home can work together to enhance children's early literacy. Often this has involved parents reading to and with their children using selected books. In the early stages teachers and parents need to be encouraged to select books that have a high rhyme content in the words and to select books for the development of children's alphabet knowledge, alliteration (phonemic awareness), and rich vocabulary. Included within this set of books should be alphabet books, which are made up of pages for each capital letter and example words with corresponding pictures. In particular, Murray, Stahl, and Ivey (1996) have noted that children achieved greater gains in decoding and phoneme awareness and alphabet knowledge when they used alphabet books with example words to demonstrate the sounds associated with the letters. This is because alphabet books provide children with the opportunity to link phoneme awareness with alphabet knowledge, because of phonemic information of the first letter's name, such as /s/ for seal, for sand, and for six. For children with early difficulties in phonemic awareness and sounding out letters there needs to be a greater linkage between the writing of words and letters and the saying of the words. This is a challenge, but the process of writing alphabet letters, practising phonological spelling, copying and saying words, also enhances the children's basic decoding and phonemic awareness skills.

Reading and writing are interactive skills and children's initial writing and spelling of words are often highly phonological, such as writing "kan" for "can." The challenge for parents is that they may be disappointed in such phonological spelling attempts, for they fail to understand that such word attempts represent the child's level of mastery of the process of converting spoken sounds to written symbols, and their ability to connect their developing decoding skills to both a reading and writing context. These "inaccuracies" also reflect some of the irregularities of the English language and in a dialogical interaction these "incorrect" phonological spellings can be explained and talked about in a supportive social environment so that the students know when and where to use the different spelling of words in different contexts, for example "here" and "hear".

WORD RECOGNITION

Efficient readers use a variety of orthographic data to recognise word units, such as individual letters, letter clusters, morphemes, word stems, and word patterns. In the process of rapid word recognition, rather than converting the letter group into a sequence of sounds, blending the sounds, and matching them to a known spoken pattern, readers retrieve stored information simultaneously about how a word looks and sounds. The challenge for the student is that limited word recognition and fluency are possible causes of young readers' lack of comprehension because at the early stages of learning to read, children use all of their working memory capacity to decode the symbols and text units and thus meaning is lost at the expense of decoding. For a child to free up working memory in order to be more engaged in comprehension, the automatic processing of orthographic information is required. This automaticity of word recognition allows children to devote the majority of their memory resources to understanding the text and acquiring new concepts and information. As already stated, the more children are exposed to print, the more likely they are to develop this visual orthographic representation, to automatise this information, and retrieve words from their long-term memory word bank. The argument is that children's success with alphabetical knowledge, vocabulary, phonological awareness, and decoding skills are interactive, such that an enhancement in one reading skill area can have a direct and/or indirect influence on a related reading skill (Hay & Fielding-Barnsley, 2009).

To enhance automaticity of word recognition, practice and over-learning are often required by some students. Rather than isolated drill, however, this needs to be embedded in motivating activities that include reading high interest text, games and activities. Once a child has knowledge of the separate words the focus shifts, when reading aloud, to grouping words together as phrasing. Phrasing needs to be practised on known text, as new, unfamiliar text requires the use of monitoring and self-correcting strategies that slow down the reading process and the acquisition of meaning. Assisting the child to read the words is helping to "set the child up" for success with reading. To facilitate the process of developing a child's word bank, Spencer and Hay (1998) have identified a contemporary Australian list of 400 high frequency reading words that appear in children's early reading books, of which the first 50 are presented in Table 4.

Table 4 – First 50 Words of the 400 Spencer and Hay (1998) Australian Reading Word List

the	you	see	cat	get
a	look	he	they	house
I	can	for	out	where
is	we	go	at	down
said	come	am	what	ran
and	up	little	dog	of
my	it	this	she	old
in	me	will	mother	all
to	big	no	are	too
here	went	on	with	like

Within the first 150 words of the Spencer and Hay list, pronouns, such as: she, he, us, me, him, and her; as well as words associated with the tense of verbs such as: come, came, and comes were well represented. Pronouns are pivotal to the reader's comprehension of text and even if the child is able to pronounce the pronoun, the teacher still needs to evaluate the reader's understanding of to whom the pronoun refers, in relationship to the text. Problems associated with pronouns and the tenses of verbs are often common difficulties for children with reading difficulties. The challenge for the teachers is to explain to children who are at the beginning stages of reading, how verbs and pronouns change in relationship to the tense and structure of the sentence.

When the child is learning a new word it is recommended that the teacher first introduce the word in context and within the meaning of the sentence, and then talk to the child about the word as a unit. During the focus on the word unit stage, the child may need to orally rehearse the word and clearly visualise it away from other background text, with the teacher reviewing whether the child understands the word, its usage and structural features before returning the word back into the passage where it is again reviewed. Thus, the teaching of high frequency reading words should not be an end in itself, but rather one means of achieving greater comprehension of text (Woolley & Hay, 2004).

To assist young children's motivation and confidence to engage with words, they often need opportunities to work and play with words, where there is a focus on enjoyment and social peer interactions (e.g., board games, card games like matching, and computer word games). In addition, the child also builds confidence by interacting with a personal group of words, letters and texts that they know how to read and write. This 'playing' promotes the learning of these words and enhances the prospect that the children will gain pleasure from reading. Because many sight words are commonly used to connect other words together, a list of short meaningful phrases/ sentences can also be incorporated into the child's reading program, rather than just single sight words (e.g., the phrase "come over here", after the child recognises and understands the meaning of the word "come").

CLASSROOM INSTRUCTION

The challenge for children and students is that teachers often move through the teaching of reading to children too quickly for many pupils with reduced aptitude and confidence in their language and reading abilities (Monie & Hay, 2008). In part, this may reflect the need for teachers to follow authorised, national curriculum programs. The issue is that many teachers make few significant adjustments for the literacy levels of children with reading problems, apart from giving the children some books that contain text that is at a lower reading age, than their classroom peers (Hay & Fielding-Barnsley, 2007). The concern is that this level of classroom reading program adjustment is not sufficient, given that one of the main differences between children with reading difficulties and those without is the amount of time it takes the children to complete a range of classroom activities and the number of trials before they achieve success. Thus, the frequency and duration of instruction impacts on the students' ability to understand and master the skills associated with reading (Byrne et al., 2000). Consequently, if it takes children with academic difficulties longer to master a task, teachers have to consider using educational resources and methods that will keep students motivated, focused, and on-task for a longer period of time. The challenge is that students who are slower at mastering foundation reading knowledge and concepts are going to require more of everything: more explicit instruction, more opportunities to practice, and more general assistance.

CONCLUSION

In conclusion, this chapter has been written to help teachers better respond to the new challenges associated with incorporating applied psycholinguistic elements into their work with individual students and groups of students of all ages. The evidence is that teachers working with young children in the domain of reading need to be aware of the dynamic and interactive links between children's language, phonological awareness, word recognition and reading development. Such links help to explain the predictive importance of a range of reading variables, including children's concepts of print, expressive vocabulary, sentence/story recall skills, and receptive and expressive language, along with the children's phonological awareness and their alphabetic letter naming and sounding skills. Children start to transition into literacy as soon as they become speakers and listeners, and the evidence is that children's transition into formal reading is significantly predicated on the ability of their teachers to design multidimensional and at times structured programs.

ACKNOWLEDGMENTS

This chapter was written based on research funded from an Australian Research Council Discovery Grant DP0666577 to Professor Ian Hay, Associate Professor Ruth Fielding-Barnsley and Professor Adrian Ashman.

REFERENCES

Adams, M.J. (1990). *Beginning to read.* Boston: MIT Press.

Blank, M., & Franklin, E. (1980). Dialogue with preschoolers: A cognitive-based system of assessment. *Applied Psycholinguistics, 1*(227), 150.

Blank, M., Rose, S.A., & Berlin, L.J. (2003). *Preschool Language Assessment Instrument: The language of learning in practice* (2nd ed.). Austin, TX: Pro Ed.

Byrne, B., Fielding-Barnsley, R., & Ashley, L. (2000). Effects of preschool phoneme identity after six years: Outcome level distinguished from rate of response. *Journal of Educational Psychology, 92,* 659 – 667.

Cooney, C., & Hay, I. (2005). Internet-based literacy development for middle school students with reading difficulties. *Literacy Learning: The Middle Years, 13,* 36 – 44.

Dunn, L. M., & Dunn, L. (1997). *Peabody Picture Vocabulary Test, Version 3.* Circles Pines, MI: American Guidance Services.

Elias, G., Hay, I., Homel, R., & Freiberg, K. (2006). Enhancing parent-child book reading in a disadvantaged community. *Australian Journal of Early Childhood, 31,* 20 – 25.

Fisher, J., & Glenister, J. M. (1992). *The hundred pictures naming test.* Hawthorn, Vic: Australian Council for Educational Research.

Goswami, U., & Bryant, P. (2007). *Children's cognitive development and learning: Primary review research survey 2/1a,* Cambridge: University of Cambridge Faculty of Education.

Hay, I., Elias, G., Fielding-Barnsley, R., Homel, R., & Frieberg, K. (2007). Language delays, reading delays and learning difficulties: Interactive elements requiring multidimensional programming, *Journal of Learning Disabilities, 40,* 400 – 409.

Hay, I., & Fielding-Barnsley, R. (2006). Enhancing the early literacy development of children at risk for reading difficulties. *Australian Journal of Learning Disabilities, 3,* 117-124.

Hay, I., & Fielding-Barnsley, R. (2007). Facilitating children's emergent literacy using home shared reading: A comparison of two literacy models. *Australian Journal of Language and Literacy, 3,* 191 – 202.

Hay, I., & Fielding-Barnsley, R. (2009). Competencies that underpin children's transition into early literacy. *Australian Journal of Language and Literacy, 32,* 148 – 162.

Lindsay, G., Dockrel, J.E., & Strand, S. (2007). Longitudinal patterns of behaviour problems in children with specific speech and language difficulties: Child and contextual factors. *British Journal of Educational Psychology, 77,* 811 – 828.

Monie, K., & Hay, I. (2008). Secondary school and transitions. In A. Ashman & J. Elkins, (Eds.), *Education for inclusion and diversity* (pp. 305 – 338). Sydney: Pearson, Australia.

Morrow, L. M., & Tracey, D.H. (2007). Best practices in early literacy development in preschool, kindergarten, and first grade. In L. B., Gambrell, L.M. Morrow, & M.

Pressley (Eds.), *Best practices in literacy education* (3rd ed.) (pp. 57 – 82). New York: Guilford Press.

Murray, B.A., Stahl, S.A., & Ivey, M.G. (1996). Developing phoneme awareness through alphabet books. *Reading and Writing: An Interdisciplinary Journal,* 8, 307-322.

Nation, K. (2005). Connections between language and reading in children with poor reading comprehension. In H.W. Catts, & A.G. Kamhi. (Eds.), *The connection between language and reading disabilities* (pp. 55 – 75). Mahwah, NJ: Erlbaum.

Neuman, S.B., & Dickson, D.K. (Eds.). (2001). *Handbook of early literacy research.* New York: Guilford Press.

Paul, R. (2007). *Language disorders: From infancy through adolescence* (3rd ed.). St. Louis, MI: Mosby.

Sénéchal, M. (2006). Testing the home literacy model: Parent involvement in kindergarten is differently related to grade 4 reading comprehension, fluency and reading for pleasure. *Scientific Studies of Reading, 10,* 59 – 87.

Spencer, R., & Hay, I. (1998). Initial reading schemes and their high frequency words. *Australian Journal of Language and Literacy, 21,* 222 – 233.

Woolley, G., & Hay, I. (2004). Strategies to improve reading comprehension. In R. Knight & W. Scott (Eds.), *Learning difficulties: Multiple perspectives* (pp. 82 – 98). Frenchs Forest, NSW: Pearson Education, Australia.

Woolley, G., & Hay, I. (2007). Reading intervention: The benefits of using trained tutors. *Australian Journal of Language and Literacy, 30,* 9 – 20.

In: Language and Literacy Education in a Challenging World   ISBN: 978-1-61761-198-8
Editors: T. Lê, Q. Lê, and M. Short   © 2011 Nova Science Publishers, Inc.

Chapter 12

CLASSROOM DISCOURSE: A CRITICAL ANALYSIS OF MALAY LANGUAGE LESSON

Idris Aman and Rosniah Mustaffa

ABSTRACT

Research on the teaching and learning process of the Malay language in the classroom usually focuses on the method, content, strategy, and teaching aids. Contrary to this phenomenon, this study views the process from the discourse analysis perspective called pedagogic discourse analysis. The discussion is based on several hours of teaching-learning case study conducted in a secondary school classroom, which emphasizes integrated curriculum, in an attempt to understand the unseen social processes, i.e. teacher dominance in discourse. This study reveals that teacher dominance is concealed in turn-taking system, types of questions posed by the teacher, discourse control and the overall structure of the discourse. These types of classroom discourse have their implications to the implementation of the National Education Philosophy, which places emphasis on each student's potential. In spite of this, the nature of the learning process that takes place in the classroom hardly focused on students' thinking skills. This is indeed contrary to the objectives of the teaching and learning of the Malay Language whereby the major emphasis of the Integrated Curriculum for Secondary School is learner-centred, with thinking skills infused across the curriculum. In this respect, students should be given the opportunities to exercise their critical and creative potentials. For the analysis, this chapter adapts Fairclough's (1992; 1995) Critical Discourse Analysis framework.

Keywords: classroom discourse, Malay language lesson, secondary school, integrated curriculum, teacher dominance.

INTRODUCTION

Classroom discourse refers to the type of language use (*parole* or performance) that is found in classroom situations. This student-teacher discourse is also referred to as pedagogic discourse, and it is different in form and function from language used in other situations due to the distinct social roles of students, teachers and the activities they are engaged in (Richards, Platt & Platt, 1992, p. 52). Analysis of classroom discourse is useful when examining the effectiveness of teaching methods and the types of student-teacher interaction (Richards *et. al.* 1992, p. 111). According to Chouliaraki (1998, p. 10), textual features or pedagogic discourse contribute towards an understanding of the relation between pedagogy and its practice. An analysis of classroom discourse produced by Sinclair & Coulthard (1975) in Britain gained prominence as the Birmingham model and was named after the university both linguists were attached to. Their research attempted to examine the structure of classroom discourse (McCarthy, 1991, pp. 6 - 12).[1]

Classroom discourse seems to offer autonomy and opportunity for understanding teaching and learning interactions between student-teacher and student-student. On a superficial level it appears pedagogically to be a social process that is *par excellence*. Such classroom discourse makes learning more fun, student participation more active and teaching-learning activities moreeffective. Moreover, such situations also allow teachers to fine-tune their speech according to students' progress. Chouliaraki (1998), whose work is based upon the pedagogic theories of Barne & Todd (1977), Bruner (1983; 1986) and Barnes (1992), assert that fine-tuning is essential in learning since it improves students' understanding.

However, classroom discourse is usually analysed and understood in a transparent context, namely as the collective space where an individual interacts, discusses knowledge in a specific subject or matters that are "out there" (Chouliaraki, 1998, p. 7), similar to the works of Sinclair & Coulthard (1975). The social process and practice taking place in a classroom discourse seldom becomes the focus of analysis. Hence, contrary to this phenomenon we posit that in the context of this study two social practices, namely power and control, are embedded in or hidden within a classroom discourse based upon an integrative curriculum. Many speakers, especially teachers, are unaware of this notion. In other words, classroom discourse is dominated by teachers by virtue of their teaching status. This issue reflects Chouliaraki's view (1998, p. 7) that emphasises the school as a substitute or medium for the reproduction of social power in particular, class, gender and race. In the context of this study, the three identified concepts also implicate social status. As such, classroom discourse lacks the ability to achieve the pedagogic aims of an integrative curriculum. This is due to classroom discourse having primarily interactive functions that marginalise knowledge inputs or thinking abilities. Besides, in such classroom discourse the priority is on teacher teaching that allows collectively minimal student involvement as compared to their intellectual needs. This kind of discourse is not beneficial to students and having this awareness can initiate improvements.

To expound the above idea, this chapter begins by explaining the concept of classroom discourse in the contexts of an integrative curriculum, primarily in the teaching and learning of Malay language (Bahasa Melayu). Examples of, as well as discussions on findings will follow the explanations on the theoretical concept applied to the understanding and clarification of the issue at hand, namely the critical discourse analysis[2] as proposed by Norman Fairclough.

---

[1] They discovered the structure of classroom discourse is consisted of 5 descending units beginning with LESSON, TRANSACTION, EXCHANGE, MOVE and ACT. An upper unit is built upon a lower one, for instance a lesson is built upon several transactions, which in turn are the product of several exchanges. The exchange unit is usually marked by an informative, imperative or enquiry where in every element a statement and request or command is made and a question asked, usually by the teacher.

[2] Critical discourse analysis, popularly abbreviated to CDA

CONCEPT OF CLASSROOM DISCOURSE IN AN INTEGRATIVE CURRICULUM CONTEXT

The integrative curriculum of the Malaysian education system (in both primary and secondary levels)[3] is implemented to improve the quality of education by placing emphasis on holistic and integrative individual potentials. It is the objective of this curriculum that students' intellectual, spiritual, emotional and physical potentials are developed so as to produce well-balanced individuals who can, not only adapt themselves in, but also contribute towards a harmonious and prosperous society and country (see Shahril@Charil & Habib, 1999, p. 83). To achieve this philosophical objective, planning for Malay language education in the contexts of an integrative curriculum, is motivated by the following needs: improving of language skills for effective communication; improving as well as expanding of the proficiency and practice of Malay language as the country's official language; developing and enhancing of intellectual as well as rational, critical and creative thinking; procuring of knowledge and developing as well as applying these skills in daily lives; possessing self-confidence that can contribute towards self and society (see Shahril@Charil & Habib ,1999; Mok, 1996). In view of the contemporary developments and challenges, for instance the current increase in access to information, rapid progress of science and technology as well as the effects of globalisation, the Malaysian Education Ministry has been challenged to review the Malay language subject within the Integrative Curriculum for Primary School (ICPS) and Integrative Curriculum for Secondary School (ICSS). As a result of revisions, adaptations have been made to the aims of the syllabus, namely to produce individuals who are literate in information and communicative technology, capable of exploring new knowledge and possessing the ability to communicate effectively in multiple socio-cultural conditions (Zahirah, 2001, p. 12).

In this context, the concept of classroom discourse in the integrative curriculum Malay language subject deals with discourse that emphasises student-centred teaching and learning as students play active roles in a variety of activities. This means teachers are encouraged to plan numerous activities and teaching aids suitable for their students' abilities and interests (Shahril@Charil & Habib, 1999, pp. 72-73).

While executing a Malay language lesson, a crucial component for the teacher to give emphasis to is thinking skills; this is in addition to the incorporation of the skills of other core subject literary readings in addition to the concept of Malay language across disciplines. To achieve high level thinking skills, teaching and learning activities need to stimulate students into thinking and discussing logically, rationally and objectively (Malaysian Ministry of Education, 1992 p. 6). In short, the form of classroom discourse to be utilised so as to achieve the above objectives is one that is student-centred or one in which each student takes part actively in the teaching and learning. In such a context, a teacher becomes a facilitator, counsellor, manager, planner, guide, and evaluator and helps mould their students' personality. Teachers need to plan their teaching and learning materials carefully in order to provide students with opportunities to enhance their analytical and logical skills, besides the

---

[3] The New Curriculum for Primary Schools was first implemented in 1983 and was revised in 1988 as the Integrative Curriculum for Primary Schools (ICPS) or Kurikulum Bersepadu Sekolah Rendah (KBSR). Integrative Curriculum for Secondary Schools (ICSS) or Kurikulum Bersepadu Sekolah Menengah (KBSM) was implemented on 1989 (see Mok 1996: 147-8).

abilities to reason, summarise and produce sound and effective ideas for speech and writing. Teachers need to be aware that students are not empty vessels; they instead possess abilities and talents that await discovery and perceptive nurturing by their teachers (Malaysian Ministry of Education 1992, pp. 17-19).

To achieve those objectives, Zahirah (2000, p. 9) lists three language skills listed in the Malay language syllabus which teachers can utilise to direct their teaching and learning activities towards improving students' proficiency in critical and creative thinking skills. These skills are:

a. discussing critically and analytically the comprehensive meanings of the various materials as well as solve problems
b. reading, evaluating and reviewing critically and analytically facts and ideas as well as human, social and cultural values in various prose and poetry
c. producing reviews and criticisms of prose and poetry

Hence, classroom discourse practice in the integrative curriculum context needs to be heterogeneous or, in other words, varied in nature.

CRITICAL DISCOURSE ANALYSIS AS A THEORETICAL FRAMEWORK TO EXAMINE CLASSROOM DISCOURSE

Critical discourse analysis (CDA) provides the theoretical framework for this study. In this theory, analysis of discourse is not merely transparent[4]; it is instead a perceptive and committed approach that includes examining the web of social processes implicated in the discourse. According to Fairclough & Wodak (1997, p. 258), "CDA sees itself not as dispassionate and objective social science, but as engaged and committed". In other words, the theory considers discourse as a social process. Language, or discourse, which is inclusive of its own as well as representational nature, is an aspect of social process (Chouliaraki, 2000, p. 297).

Accepting discourse as a social practice means having to reveal the covert nature of social process embedded in discourse. Discourse is not merely a linguistic category or communicative medium, rather, it is a mediation between social structure and process cultural practice (Fairclough & Wodak,1997). As a social process, discourse is linked intricately to the socio-cultural context from which it operates. It is neither produced, nor can it function, in a vacuum. It is instead a contextual discourse, one which is embedded within social and institutional systems of ideology.

Social practice refers to actual acts of human activity, utterances or writing. Orientations of social practice include economical, political, cultural and ideological (Fairclough, 1992, p. 66). Nonetheless, many speakers are unaware of such practices and analysts may have problems identifying them (Hodge & Kress 1993, p. 210). This theory proposes that a close

[4] In this context, transparent refers to an examination of the nature of linguistic discourse merely through its textual and/or discursive features without considering other underlying features inherent in discourse, namely practice, process and social issues.

and systematic analysis of discourse can reveal the nature of social practice in discourse. Critical discourse analysis examines the social practices of individuals or institutions that involve concerns such as the use and abuse of power, hegemony, ideological operations, social change as well as conflict, domination, race and leadership (Wodak 1996; van Dijk, 1991; Aman, 2001; Fairclough, 1992).

Critical discourse analysis and its practitioners can contribute towards enriching or transforming discourse practice patterns and unhealthy or negative social processes that have been identified. For instance, when the identified and analysed patterns and features of pedagogic discourse reflect dialectic association with undeveloped or ineffective education[5] process, analysts are in fact bringing this finding to the attention of society, specifically those implicated in education. As such, improvements or adjustments to the discourse can be conducted by those concerned, while policy makers may, for example, adapt teacher training curriculum. Clearly, critical discourse analysis is a form of social practice too (Fairclough & Wodak 1997, p. 279).

This next section discusses the theoretical underpinnings of Norman Fairclough's critical discourse analysis and his systemic approach to, and method in analysis for its application in this study. Fairclough's descriptions of textual features and definitions of the processes in discourse practice are more comprehensive than other scholars[6], making his a dominant theory in the analysis of social processes in discourse.

Fairclough (1992, pp. 63-64; 1995a, pp.131-132; Fairclough & Wodak, 1997, p.258) deems it important to accept discourse as a social process because (a) discourse reflects an action, in which the way a man acts or reacts towards the world, and especially each other, may be a form of representation, (b) there is a dialectic relationship between discourse and social structure, in which social structure determines and creates social process. On the one hand, discourse is not only produced by social structures (for instance, class and social relationships in society or institution), it also produces them. On the other hand, discourse also contributes to shape, just as it is also shaped by, dimensions within social structures (such as social relationship and identity). In short, when analysing discourse, social factors that are embedded within it determine its own production and need to be taken into account. The analysis should not merely concentrate on studying structural or behavioural linguistics, as is the norm in pragmatics.

Discourse simultaneously constructs (i) social identity of a subject, namely social position, and character type; (ii) social relationship between people; and (iii) knowledge systems and beliefs, in various degrees of importance depending on situations. The description, interpretation and explanation of discourse as a social process also require language theories that emphasise on the multi-purpose nature of language. The three simultaneous constructs mentioned are intricately linked to four language functions, namely identity, relationship, ideational and textual. Identity functions are related to the ways social identities are constructed by discourse. Relationship functions refer to the manner in which social relationships between participants is negotiated. Ideational functions concern the ways texts reflect not only the world but also its processes, entities and connections. Textual

---

[5] Education is a social process too.
[6] There are other discourse analysts who have proposed other theoretical frameworks in critical discourse analysis with different approaches to and methods for analysis, namely van Dijk, Wodak, Billig etc.

functions, on the other hand, refer to linguistic information and social situations that are outside of the text (Fairclough, 1992, p. 65).[7]

The underlying principles in Fairclough's critical discourses analysis theory are its descriptive, interpretative and explanative approaches towards discourse. They are not just based upon linguistics, but links are also simultaneously made to relevant social thinking orientations (Fairclough, 1992). Based upon these principles, Fairclough produces a three-dimensional approach to discourse analysis: namely text analysis, discourse practice analysis and social process analysis. He claims his theoretical analysis include three comprehensive ways to read the complex social conditions embedded in discourse which primarily requires interdisciplinary, or at the very least transdiscplinary, skills (Fairclough, 1997).

Textual analysis is a process whereby the forms and meanings of textual discourse are described. Textual form and meaning are interconnected to ideational, interpersonal and textual discourse functions. Textual features that are explicated include textual, clausal grammar and lexical structures. In relation to the objectives and nature of the discourse analysed in this study, explanations are focused on textual structures. In terms of dialogue discourse, textual structure analysis involves a description of interaction control, namely who controls the interaction, turn-taking and structure of change in discourse. A reading of these aspects can provide insights into the knowledge system, beliefs, values or perceptions regarding social relationships and identities that are embedded in discourse (Fairclough, 1992, pp.75-78, 234-237; Fairclough, 1995a, pp. 133-134).

Discourse practice analysis, on the other hand, aims at interpreting the processes of discourse production at the micro level. The interpretation may examine discourse production in relation to whether it has been conventional or creative, the producers of the discourse, the distribution and use of discourse as well as the presence of elements such as interdiscursivity of genre and intertextuality (Fairclough 1992, p. 65, 134).

Meanwhile, social process analysis is concerned with revealing the social issues and practices that are embedded in discourse through its dialectic relationship with the nature of texts and discourse practices, as previously discussed. In short, such analysis aims at revealing the reasons why an addresser produces a particular discourse (Fairclough 1992, pp. 226, 228).[8]

THE DISCOURSE

The discourse used as samples in this chapter is part of the data collected through case and preliminary studies on 10 classroom discourses (or 10 texts) on the Malay Language subject collected from several secondary schools in the state of Selangor.[9] These were collected through direct audio recording while the teachers were teaching in the classrooms. Recordings were transcribed into texts. To simplify the analysis, each utterance is given a number according to clauses. On the whole, the discourse implicates 5 graduate teachers (1

---

[7] Basically, Fairclough's discourse/language functions share similar features with Halliday's language functions, namely textual, interpersonal and ideational. Fairclough separates interpersonal functions into two, identity and relationship even though in his writings he usually draws upon Halliday's three language functions.

[8] For more details refer to Fairclough (1992; 1995a; 1995b; 2000) and Fairclough & Wodak (1997).

[9] The writers believe this number (10) is adequate for case and preliminary studies because for the purpose of critical discourse analysis specifically, it is the discourse that is of concern. Fairclough (1995a) only analysed three texts on university advertisements in his discussion on 'Marketization of public discourse'.

male and 4 female) with at least 5 years of teaching experience. The students involved were the ICSS forms one and two students, male and female, aged 13-14 years old.[10]

INTEGRATIVE CURRICULUM FOR THE MALAY LANGUAGE SUBJECT CLASSROOM DISCOURSE AND TEACHER DOMINATION

The social practice embedded in classroom discourse, which the speakers may not be aware of (and that includes many of us), that is of interest in the present study is teacher domination. Teacher domination, as used in the context of this study, refers to the more prominent teacher roles and actions in classroom teaching and learning process than those of the main targets or subjects (i.e., the students). Such pedagogical practice can be illustrated by its dialectical relationship with several textual elements and relevant classroom discourse practices. The following are qualitative illustrations on the ways teacher domination take place in teacher-student discourse. Discussions begin with textual analysis, followed by those on discourse practice.

CLASSROOM DISCOURSE TEXTUAL ANALYSIS

The focus of this classroom discourse textual analysis is on features of teacher-student interaction. Generally, interactive control in discourse is concerned with ensuring that interaction takes place effectively at specific levels of organisation, for example systems of smooth distribution in turn-taking, topic selection and exchange as well as question-answering (Fairclough, 1992, p. 139). In the classroom discourse analysed, findings reveal specific interactive structures dominated by teachers. Such teacher practice is reflected in the following textual features, namely (a) domination in turn-taking, (b) topic control, (c) closed-questions usage, (d) modelled-answer extraction, and (e) teacher interruption of student-answers.

Domination in Turn-taking

Domination in turn-taking means the system is not necessarily based upon the equal rights and obligation of all speakers in discourse. This dominating phenomena in turn-taking is normally found in institutions that involve the professional, the "insider", or "gatekeeper" interacting with the "public", "client", "outsider" or student (Fairclough, 1992, p. 153). Domination in turn-taking is obvious in the classroom discourse analysed. It happened when most interactions were initiated by the teacher, either through extraction, instruction or information by way of questions, statements or requests. A teacher-initiated utterance received response from the student, and was followed by an acceptance or acknowledgement by the teacher. In other words, the teacher-student interaction was organised according to the teacher-initiated "move" (using Sinclair & Coulthard's concepts), followed by student

---

[10] The elaborations in this study are not references to any individual specifically, but they are to be regarded as institutional discourse.

response/reaction and teacher acceptance. Thus, the interactive movement of this classroom discourse can be structured into 3 parts; Teacher initial-move – Student response – Teacher acceptance (explicit or implicit), or alternatively T-S-T. This structure is reflected in the example (1) below.

Example 1:

T (teacher)   : [061] O.K.berapakah jumlah pekerja pada tahun 1985?
                (O.K. What is the total number of workers in 1985?)
S (student)   : [062] *(Buzzing – unclear)*
T   : [063] O.K. 5 juta 6 ratus orang,manakala tahun 1990,1990,aa6
                (O.K. 5 million 6 hundred people, meanwhile in 1990, 1990, aa 6)
S   : [064] juta 500 ribu
                (million 500 thousand.)

....

T   : [065] Jadi, adakah berkurang atau meningkat?
                (So, is there an increase or decrease?)
S   : [066] Meningkat
                (Increase.)
T   : [067] Meningkat
                (Increase.)

....

T   : [068] Sebanyak
                (How much.)
S   : [069] Sembilan ratus ribu
                (Nine hundred thousand.)
T   : [070] O.K. Sembilan ratus ribu
                (O.K. Nine hundred thousand.)
              : [071] Enam dengan lima di situ.
                (Six and five there.)
S   : [072] *(unclear)*
T   : [073] O.K. Bagus ya. Aa macam itu
                (O.K. good, yes, aa just like that.)

....

T   : [074] Tapi itu masih isi tersurat atau tersirat?
                (But is that an explicit or implicit content?)
S   : [075] Tersurat
                (Explicit.)
T   : [076] Masih isi tersurat lagi, OK
                (It is still an explicit detail, O.K.)
T   : [077] Aa. Jadi, jadi senang tak nak buat isi tersurat?
                (Aa, so, so is it easy to make an explicit detail?)
S   : [078] Senang
                (Easy.)
T   : [079] Aa senang kan, semua ada di situ.
                (Aa, easy is it not, all the details are there.)

....

(Text 4, Discussion on Occupational Sectors in Malaysia)

The example above has five exchanges (each marked with dotted lines). Moves in each exchange are initiated by the teacher, followed by response from the student and then acknowledgement/comment from the teacher. For example, in the first exchange, the teacher began a move by asking a question in [061], and this was followed by the student's move [062] as response to teacher's question, even though in the form of buzzing. In [063], teacher made an acknowledgement move by re-emphasising the answer given by the student in the previous move. A similar pattern was repeated in other exchanges. In exchange three, the teacher began the move by extracting an answer from the student with a request (068], and not by questioning.

Such interaction structure leads to teacher control of the basic organisation of interaction by opening as well as closing every move and accepting the student response/answer. This reflects the existence of control or domination in turn-taking, whereby the student has no chance at all of getting a turn to speak unless given by the teacher through the given questions or requests. In one aspect, this turn-taking system is one method of controlling the flow of discourse, but in another, it unfortunately reflects teacher domination in discourse.

Topic Control

Topic control means the main participant – in this case, the teacher – usually controls topics in discourse, interaction or move. In other words, change to a new topic is made by the main participant.

In the classroom discourse analysed, this textual feature is identified. Topic control takes place when a new topic is proposed as a result of the teacher's question or statement, teacher disregard for student response/answer and also teacher selection in accepting student response. These phenomena are reflected in the following examples.

Example (2):

T   : [164] Sektor mana yang nampak sangat meningkat di situ?
         (Which sector seems to be on the increase there?)
S   : [165] Perkilangan.
         (Manufacturing.)
T   : [166] Sektor per-
         (Which sector? Manu-?)
S   : [167] kilangan
         (facturing)

....

T   : [168] Kenapa agaknya sector perkilangan makin meningkat?
         (Why do you think the manufacturing sector is on the increase?)
S   : [169] Aa..kerana (tak jelas-buzzing)
         (Aa... because (unclear – buzzing)).
T   : [170] Aa, negara kita menuju ke arah negara perindus-
         (Aa, our country is becoming indus-

S   : [171] trian
           (–trial)
           : [172] (Tak jelas)
           (Unclear)
T   : [173] Banyak, contohnya kilang-kilang banyak dibuka,kan?
           (Many, for example many factories have been built, right?)
....
T   : [174] Di Bandar Baru Bangi ini saja, ada berapa buah kilang, siapa tahu?
           (In Bandar Baru Bangi, how many factories are there, anybody knows?)
S   : [175] 10 kot
           (Maybe 10.)
T   : [176] 10!
           (10!)
S   : [177] Lebih
           (More.)
T   : [178] Lebih daripada itu
           (More than that.)
(Text 4)

In example (2), which had three exchanges, the teacher determined the topic in every exchange. All three topics were decided through the questions in the teacher's initial moves, namely [164], [168] and [174]. In the first exchange, the topic concerned an occupational sector that was on the increase. In the second, it concerned the reasons for the increase of the manufacturing sector and the third exchange concerned the number of factories in Bandar Baru Bangi.

Teacher disregard for student response can also be detected in example (3) below. The student provided response [186] by completing teacher statement [185], but that response was disregarded by the teacher when the teacher instead gave a set answer followed by a tag question [187]. The student was undeterred and continued giving responses, [188] to [191], three times, including making repeated interruptions marked by vertical lines in the data as in [188]. The actions were disregarded by the teacher.[11]

Example (3):

T   : [183] O.K.Mungkin jalan raya itu jalan raya apa?
           (O.K. maybe it's the road, the road is -)
S   : [184] *(Unclear/buzzing)*
T   : [185] Sempit, jalan raya yang sempit atau yang jalan raya yang tak
               ada   tanda,
           (Narrow, narrow roads or streets without road-signs,)
S   : [186] lampu
           (lights)
T   : [187] Papan tanda tertentu, ya tak?
           (Proper road-signs,right?)
S   : [188]   Tak ada lampu boleh juga!

---
[11] For interaction interruption or turn-taking, refer example (3).

    (No lights, it's still possible.)
     [189] Gelap cikgu!
    (Darkness, teacher!)
    : [190] *(buzzing)*
    : [191] Tak ada lampu gelap, cikgu.
    (It's dark without lights, teacher.)

T   : [192] Awak punya takrif kebanyakan,aa kemalangan ini kalau awak tengok lapuran dari aa, cawangan trafik polis diraja itu, awak tengok, kemalangan ini berlaku di jalan apa?
    (Your understanding of, most, aa, accidents, if you check the report from aa, that royal police traffic branch, you see, accidents happen on which type of roads?)

....

(Text 3)

Close-question Usage

A prominent textual feature identified in this pedagogic discourse is the use of closed questions by the teacher. Closed questions are questions that use question-words, such as "right/yes-no", "is there", "where to", "who" or "what", which merely require straight answers or just confirmation. They do not require answers that provide opinions or the type of answers that require thinking. The use of open questions that begin with question words such as "why", "how" or "explain" are limited. The following examples show the use of closed questioning in the analysed discourse.

Example (4):

T   : [210] O.K .Selain SPBT apa?
    (O.K. what else besides SPBT?)
S   : [211] Biasiswa.
    (Scholarship)
T   : [212] Biasiswa, betul?
    (Scholarship, right?)
S   : [213] Betul.
    (Right)
T   : [214] Biasiswa untuk orang-orang yang berkelayakan sahaja
    (Scholarships are only for the deserving.)

....

T   :[215] Kemudian, rayuan apa, sekarang ni,kamu nak adakan kem atau pun kita nak bina surau?
    (Then, what kind of appeal, now, you want to have a camp or do we build a surau?)
S   : [216] *(Buzzing-unclear)*
T   : [217] Betul?
    (Is it correct?)
S   : [218] Betul.

(Correct)

....

T	: [219] Kita perlukan apa?
	(What do we need?)
S	: [220] Duit
	(Money)
T	: [221] Duit derma
	(Money from donation)

....

T	: [222] Derma kita mesti mohon melalui surat,
	(For donations, we must request through what letters,)
S	: [223] rasmi
	(official)
T	: [224] Surat rayuan, rayuan der,
	(Letter of appeal, appeal for don-)
S	: [225] ma.
	(–nation)
T	: [226] ma.
	(–nation)

....

(Text 7)

In the discourse analysed, even though open questions were also utilised, there were instances when the teacher answered the question himself. The teacher did not provide time for the student to think and offer their own opinion.

Example (5):

T	: [172] Saya nampak acara Hari Guru ini, ramai yang terlibat ialah pelajar- pelajar.
	(I noticed in this Teachers' Day event, there are many students involved.)
	: [173] Betul tak?
	(Is that right?)
S	: [174] Betul
	(Right)
T	: [175] Cikgu buat kerja…
	(Teachers do some work... (unclear))
	: [176] Cikgu buat dek.
	(Teachers do nothing.)
S	: [177] Betul, betul
	(Right, right)
T	: [178] Ada point lagi?
	(Any more points?)

(Text 1)

In example (5), the use of close-question is in [173], namely 'Betul tak?' (*Is that right?*). It was used by the teacher merely to inform the students of an important point that was to be stated in that move early in [172]. Thus, the question *Is that right?* only functions as a confirmation request for the student, as clearly seen in the student response [174] (i.e., *Right*). Utilisation of such questions merely shows interaction taking place without the application of thinking skills.

By asking closed questions, the teacher does not provide opportunity for students to speak more or express their opinions. This is because the teacher has limited the expected student response/answer to just one or two words. Such situations signal the teacher taking control of the discourse.

Designed Answer Extraction

In example (6), the extraction of student response according to teacher design can be detected in teacher discourse [127] and [131]. In [127], students were only requested to provide as response to the last two syllables for the word "industry"; in [127] the teacher had already provided as guide for the student the set answer or the intended word. In example (7), this feature can be identified in move two (i.e., in [093] and [096]).

Example (6):

T   : [125] Negara kita masih negara pertanian, faham?.
             (Our country is still an agricultural country, understand?)
             : [126] Itu sebab, pertanian lebih tinggi, faham?
             (That is reason why agriculture is higher, understand?)
             : [127] Barulah sekarang negara kita maju dalam bidang perindus-
             (Only now, our country is developed in terms of ind-)
S   : [128] - trian
             (-dustry)
....
T   : [129] Negara kita terkenal dengan apa?
             (Our country is famous for?)
S   : [130] *(Unclear)*
T   : [131] Pengeluar kelapa sawit, dan juga..
             (Producer of palm, and also..)
S   : [132] getah
             (rubber)
T   : [133] Getah
             (Rubber)
....
(Text 4)

Example (7):
T   : [090] Pengeboman apa?
             (What was bombed?)
S   : [091] WTC
             (WTC)

T   : [092] Aa, WTC di New York
           (Aa, WTC in New York)

....

           : [093] Jadi,aa,mereka ,aa pelancong-pelancong takut untuk menaiki kapal,
           (So, aa, they, aa, tourists are afraid to fly on the air)
S   : [094] terbang
           (plane)
T   : [095] terbang
           (plane)
           : [096] Takut kapal terbang diram-
           (The fear planes will be hij-)
S   : [097] -pas.
           (–jacked)
T   : [098] -pas
           (–jacked)
           : [099] Aa, itu sebabnya
           (Aa, that is why).

....

(Text 4)

Teacher Interruption of Student-Answers

Interruption of student answer is another textual element which dialectically reflects teacher domination during the teacher's performance of his/her pedagogic duties. In such instances, the teacher interrupted and showed impatience for the student to stop speaking or give response to the question or statement extraction. Interruption came in the form of the teacher's own answer to the question posed. In other words, the teacher did not provide time for the student to complete his turn to speak. Such textual features mean the teacher has denied the opportunities for the students to be active and effective in the discourse.

Example (8):

T   : [308] Baik, sebagai penutup, penutup apa nak tulis?
           (Right, as conclusion, what do you write as conclusion?)
S   : [309] *(Buzzing)*
           : [310] Ingatkan pemandu (tak jelas)
           (Remind drivers (unclear))
T   : [311] Awak boleh kata sebagai penutup, banyak, O.K. banyak
           kemalangan jalan raya berlaku di Malaysia pada setiap tahun dan
           ini memerlukan langkah-langkah apa,
           *(You can say as conclusion, many, O.K. many road accidents happen
           in Malaysia every year and what kind of measures are required,)*
S   : [312] Langkah-langkah keselamatan
           (Safety measures)
T   : [313] Langkah-langkah keselamatan dari semua pihak ya,
           termasuk pengguna jalan raya itu sendiri dan siapa,

(Safety measures from all those concerned, yes, including road users and who)

       : [314] Pihak,

(which body,)

S   : [315] berkuasa

(government.)

T   : [316] Pihak berkuasa atau pihak kerajaan, ya tak.

(Governing body or the government, right,)

       : [317] Maksudnya, pengguna jalan raya itu perlu berhati-hati di jalan   raya, mematuhi peraturan-peraturan di jalan raya,O.K.

(This means road users have to be cautious on the road, follow all the traffic rules, O.K?)

....

(Text 3)

Example (9):

T   : [049] Apa tajuk jadual yang diberi?

         (What title is given to the chart?)

S   : [050] Kemalangan jalan raya… (buzzing/tak jelas)

         (Road accidents… (buzzing, unclear)).

T   : [051] O.K. jadual menunjukkan jumlah Kemalangan yang berlaku pada tahun 2000 di Malaysia.

         (O.K. the chart shows the total number of accidents in 2000 in Malaysia.)

....

(Text 3)

Examples of interruption shown in (8) and (9) are marked by vertical lines. In (8), teacher interruption occurred in [311], where the teacher did not acknowledge the student's response and instead proceeded to produce an alternative answer. In (9), this feature is identified in [051]; the teacher was too impatient to wait for students to complete their group response[12] and interrupted them by providing the answer.

The textual features discussed above indicate the manifestation of teacher domination in the classroom discourse analysed. The following section examines teacher domination from a discourse practice perspective.

CLASSROOM DISCOURSE PRACTICES

Discourse practice analysis involves a macro-level interpretation of, not only the production of discourse, but also its producers (Fairclough, 1992, p. 65 & p.134). Analysis reveals the pedagogic discourse examined in this study has been produced conventionally, in which conventional practice indicates the act of production has centred on the teacher, and

---

[12] The group response is produced due to the nature of the teacher's questioning; the teacher opened the question to the whole class instead of identifying individual students to answer. This phenomenon is discussed in 5.2. Individuality in pedagogic discourse has its own benefits; Chouliaraki (1998) had addressed this issue.

not the student. A teacher-centred practice reflects, among others, a more dominant teacher-role as compared to student interrupted responses and the approach to question-making by the teacher. The following sections discuss the aforementioned practices identified in this study.

Teacher Answers Own Question

In this situation, teachers answer their own question rather than allowing student to answer. This practice is identified in (10) and (11). In (10), the teacher provided questions in [143] and [144] but proceeded to answer them himself/herself in [145]. Teacher-question in [146] was again self-answered in [147]. In (11), teacher-question in [294] was self-answered in [295]. Student responses in [296] and [297] were repeated ignored by the teacher before proceeding to the next move.

Example (10):

T   : [143] Dalam ucapan itu, apa lagi ada?
                  (What else is there in that speech?)
               : [144] Ucapan siapa?
                  (Whose speech?)
               : [145] Ucapan… Kadang-kadang Pengetua.
                  (Speech... sometimes by the Principal.)
               : [146] Kadang-kadang cikgu lain membaca ucapan oleh siapa?
                  (Sometimes other teachers will read whose speech text?)
               : [146] Menteri Pendidikan.
                  (The Minister of Education.)
               : [147] Lagi satu ucapan Pengarah Pendidikan.
                  (Another speech, the Director of Education.)
               : [148] Betul tak?
                  (Is that right?)
               : [149] Ucapan teks yang disediakan, cikgu yang baca.
                  (The teacher read the speech text that was prepared.)

....

(Text 1)

Example (11):
T   : [294] Apa lagi?
                  (What else?)
               : [295] Mungkin dia tidak menyalakan lampu. O.K. supaya dapat dilihat
                  oleh   kenderaan lain, O.K.
                  (Maybe he did not turn-on the headlights, O.K. so that he could be seen by on-coming cars, O.K.)
S   : [296] Dia tak pakai baju hijau.
                  (He wasn't wearing the green shirt.)
               : [297] Dia tak pakai baju cerah, cikgu.
                  (He wasn't wearing a light coloured shirt, teacher.)

: [298] (Buzzing).
    (Buzzing).

....

T   : [299] Lagi, lagi apa?
    (So, anything else?)

....

(Text 3)

Limited Student Involvement

Another feature of a teacher-centred discourse practice is limited student involvement during interaction in classroom discourse production; this phenomenon results in teacher domination. In this study, the limited involvement of the student was triggered by the way the teacher conducted the discourse in the classroom, namely by giving little or no chance at all for the student to be active by offering opinions, asking questions or discussing in groups. Instead, student participation was only limited to answering teacher questions (many of which were close questions, as previously discussed) or confirming teacher's statement. The T-S-T turn-taking system which benefits the teacher (as discussed previously) is a practice that limits student participation.

Prominent Teacher Role

In contrast to the above discussion (b), the discourse analysed in this study reflects prominently the teacher's role and teaching profession. For example, this practice happens when the teacher prefers to offer explanations, descriptions or answers to students rather than allow them to discuss, analyse or summarise in order to seek for their own answers. In other words, the teacher speaks more than the student. Discourse is, thus, centred on the teacher. This practice can be detected in example (12).

Example (12):

T   : [35] Baik, dekat sini cuba kamu tengok.
    (Right, over here, check and see.)
    : [36] Yang pertama, tujuan dia, dia nak cerita fasal kematian sepupu dia.
    ((The first, his reason, he wants to inform the death of his cousin.)
    : [37] Yang kedua, dia pergi kepada penerangan, bagaimana kejadian itu berlaku.
    (Secondly, he proceeds to the description, how the accident happened.
    : [38] Jadi, kalau kamu tulis surat, yang pertama tujuan kamu tulis surat
    (So, if you write a letter, firstly, you a reason for writing.)
    : [39] Yang kedua, kamu pergi kepada isi kedua, apa lagi yang berkaitan dengan yang tadi.
    (Secondly, you proceed to your second point, other issues related to

the previous one.)

: [40] Selalunya dalam surat kiriman ke, apa-apa, kita akan letakkan isi, yang   pertama isi penting.

(Usually in letter writing, we put the main point as the first)

: [41] Yang kedua isi yang kurang penting.

(The second point is one that is less important.)

: [42] Lepas itu sampailah kepada isi yang paling kurang penting lagi.

(Then you can have four other points that are of lesser importance.)

: [43] Yang last sekali ialah…(gangguan-murid lain masuk).

(The last one is… (disturbance – a student enters).)

: [44] Kamu tengok ya, dalam petikan ini semasa dia ceritakan, dia bagi penerangan lanjut.

(You see, in this passage he provides details with descriptions.)

....

T   : [45] Kalau kemalangan, dia akan nyatakan apa benda?

(If it's an accident, what details will he give?)

: [46] Aa, Khairuddin, bila kita cerita tentang kemalangan, apa yang kita nyatakan?

(Aa, Khairuddin, when we talk about an accident, what do we include for details?

S   : [47] Kesedihan?

(Sadness?)

T   : [48] Ha, kesedihan!

(Ha, sadness!)

(Text 2)

In example (12), it is obvious the utterances in the discourse are teacher-centred. The teacher played a central role in this move by providing the explanations and not, for instance, asking students to examine the text and seek their own answers. In this scenario, the teacher's role has more prominence.

The above discussions and explanations reflect the features of teacher domination in relation to discourse practice as found in the classroom discourse analysed in this study. Generally, this aspect is also interconnected to textual elements.

CONCLUSION

Based on the aforementioned discussion on textual features and discourse practice, it can be concluded that the classroom discourse analysed in this study is embedded with teacher domination practice. Teacher domination means the teacher controls not only the discourse but also the students. As a result of this control, the role of the student as the main target of the education process seems to be relegated, and instead it is the teacher who plays the central role.

Such pedagogic discourse is not reflective of the concerns in the integrative curriculum education system. The teaching of the Malay Language subject in the integrative curriculum demands the incorporation of thinking skills among students. To acquire thinking skills that incorporate logic, rationality, analytical skills and objectivity, classroom teaching and learning activities have to be geared to encourage students towards those ends. In other words, a pedagogic discourse that is suitably practiced is one that has to be student-centred, and every student needs to be actively and effectively involved in the teaching and learning process. Among the practices that should be utilised are making students offer their opinions, to summarise, analyse and reason as well as suggest ideas through speaking and writing. The teacher/educator must be sensitive to students. Students have skills and talents that need to be recognised and polished by their teachers (The Ministry of Education 1992, pp. 17-19). The discussions on the negative practices found to be embedded in this example of classroom discourse have good intentions and should be regarded as a contribution from the field of linguistics, especially discourse analysis towards the teaching of Malay language.

REFERENCES

Aman, I. (2001). *Wacana dan kepimpinan: satu analisis terhadap perutusan Perdana Menteri Mahathir Mohamad*. Ph.D thesis. Faculty of Language Studies and Linguistics, Universiti Malaya, Kuala Lumpur.

Chouliaraki, L. (1998). Regulation in "progressive" pedagogic discourse: Individualized teacher-pupil talk. *Discourse & Society* Vol. *9*(1): 5-32.

Chouliaraki, L. (2000). Political discourse in the news: Democratising responsibility or aestheticizing politics? *Discourse & Society*. Vol. *11*(3): 293-314.

Fairclough, N. (1992). *Discourse and social change*. Cambridge: Polity Press.

Fairclough, N. (1995a). *Critical discourse analysis: The critical study of language. London and New York*: Longman.

Fairclough, N. (1995b). *Media discourse*. London: Edward Arnold.

Fairclough, N. (1997). Discourse across disciplines: Discourse analysis in researching social change. *Working paper series 84*. Centre for Language in social life. Lancaster University.

Fairclough, N. (2000). *New Labour, new language?* London and New York: Routledge.

Hodge, R. & Kress, G. (1993). *Language as ideology*. 2nd edition. London and New York: Routledge.

McCarthy, M. (1991). *Discourse analysis for language teachers*. Cambridge: Cambridge University Press.

Ministry of Education Malaysia. (1992). *Asas perkaedahan mengajar bahasa: Siri risalah panduan guru Bahasa Malaysia Kurikulum Bersepadu Sekolah Menengah (KBSM)*. Jilid 1. Kuala Lumpur: Dewan Bahasa dan Pustaka.

Mok, S. S. (1996). *Pendidikan di Malaysia untuk diploma perguruan*. 6th edition. Kuala Lumpur: Kumpulan Budiman Sdn. Bhd.

Richards, J.C., Platt, J., & Platt, H. (1992). *Longman dictionary of language teaching and applied linguistics*. Essex: Longman.

Shahril, Charil, M., & Habib, M. S. (1999). *Isu pendidikan di Malaysia: sorotan dan cabaran*. Kuala Lumpur: Utusan Publications & Distributors Sdn. Bhd.

Van Dijk, T.A. (1991). *Racism and the press*. London and New York: Routledge.

Wodak, R. (1996). *Disorders of discourse*. London and New York: Longman.

Zahirah, A. (2001). *Pendekatan bersepadu dalam pengajaran Bahasa Melayu.* Paper presented at the Seminar Pengajaran dan Pemelajaran Bahasa Melayu Pada Alaf Baru. Kuala Lumpur. Organized by TKNA Network (S) Pte. Ltd., Persatuan Linguistik Malaysia, and Dewan Bahasa dan Pustaka.

In: Language and Literacy Education in a Challenging World
Editors: T. Lê, Q. Lê, and M. Short

ISBN: 978-1-61761-198-8
© 2011 Nova Science Publishers, Inc.

Chapter 13

ENGLISH LANGUAGE EDUCATION AT SCHOOLS IN CHINA: REFORMS AND CHALLENGES

Suxian Zhan

ABSTRACT

English language education is regarded as being a crucial component of the drive to achieve many important national aims. This chapter presents an overview of basic English language education in the Chinese education system. It aims to review reforms and challenges in the development of basic English language education in China. The chapter consists of four parts. The first part sketches policy efforts directed towards improving English language learning and teaching at schools prior to 2001. The second part focuses on the current English language curriculum reform, which was initiated in 2001. The third part investigates challenges facing basic English language education, within the Chinese context of current English language education reform. The last part identifies several key issues that deserve serious attention for interested individuals and organizations in China and beyond.

Keywords: basic English language education, China, English language curriculum reform, task-based approach, contextual factors.

INTRODUCTION

Driven by the national modernization scheme, and the expression of robust national goals for socio-economic growth (Jin & Cortazzi, 2003), English has become a particularly significant aspect of the Chinese school curriculum, because of the national recognition of English as a global language (Nunan, 2003). English language education is now regarded as being a crucial component of the drive to achieve many important national aims. Consequently, the provision of effective English language teaching throughout China has become a priority. Moreover, the current English language curriculum reform, initiated in 2001 as a means of improving school learners' language use, has been deemed a matter of national importance (Ministry of Education, 2001b). This has been brought about because of the perceived weakness of conventional teaching practices in relation to language education.

Nonetheless, the collaborative efforts of teachers, teacher facilitators and the national government prior to 2001, have resulted in impressive progress (Y. A. Wu, 2001). Not only have the numbers of English language learners greatly increased, but the quantity and quality of English language teachers have also increased, primarily because of the provision of pre-service and in-service teacher development programs. Furthermore, there have been considerable achievements in relation to curriculum development, syllabus design, and learning and instruction materials.

However, the interplay of many factors, which have been challenging English language education in the environment of basic education[1] in China, cannot be underestimated. In order to provide a good understanding of either actual or potential challenges, this chapter firstly provides an overview, regarding important efforts, which had been made by the Ministry of Education, curriculum developers and textbook writers before 2001. Secondly, the current English language curriculum reform, which was initiated in 2001, is discussed. Thirdly, those challenges facing English language teaching and learning, within the Chinese context of current English language education reform, are investigated. Finally, various issues are discussed in order that those challenges can be dealt with adequately.

EFFORTS TO IMPROVE ENGLISH LANGUAGE EDUCATION BEFORE 2001

The link between poor student learning outcomes and the traditional mode of instruction was made clear in a 1985 national survey (Ministry of Education, 2002) conducted throughout 15 provinces across China. The results of the survey indicated that pedagogical practice, particularly with respect to English language teaching in secondary schools, was characterised by examination-orientated and textbook-centred, didactic teaching. The survey produced clear evidence of an almost exclusive focus on reading and writing. It also revealed that there was an excessive amount of emphasis on transmitting isolated linguistic items and the memorising of grammatical rules.

It must be remembered, however, that giving priority to grammatical competence, and focusing on teaching isolated language items within a range of teacher-controlled, form-focused activities, was the traditional and normal practice of the grammar-translation method, and audio-lingualism, prior to the 1960s (Larsen-Freeman, 2000). Chronologically, these two methods were introduced into China during the 1950s and 1960s (Adamson, 2004). Since that time they have been predominantly used in the Chinese context, because they appeared to be well suited to the Confucian ideals of education (Jin & Cortazzi, 2003). From a traditional, Confucian point of view (G. W. Hu, 2002a), teachers are the masters of authoritative sources (usually textbooks and classics). The principal role of teachers is to adequately and appropriately transmit information via textbooks. In this role of pedagogy teachers tend to present and analyse book knowledge for students, sometimes excessively emphasising that conveying book knowledge is the ultimate goal of teaching. In line with this transmission model of teaching there has been a belief that students should be wholeheartedly receptive to knowledge conveyed by their teachers or textbooks. Students are expected to respect their

---

[1] In most parts of China, basic education normally consists of nine-year compulsory education (i.e., 6 years' primary schooling and 3 years' junior high school education) and 3 years' senior high school education.

teachers, and they must not challenge that knowledge. Nor are students at liberty to present their own views regarding that knowledge.

However, this traditional mode has undoubtedly fallen short, in relation to achieving the nominated educational goals, which are to fundamentally improve students' communicative abilities (Ministry of Education, 2001b). This deficiency has occurred because the particular abilities of listening and speaking, crucial in learning the English language, have been largely neglected, and as a result, communicative competence has generally been very low (Ministry of Education, 2002). Notwithstanding this generalisation, students' communicative abilities have tended to be better in some economically well-developed regions than was indicated by the Chinese average.

In response to the survey findings, many revisions were made regarding the national syllabus. These revisions were based on the principles of communicative language teaching (Ministry of Education, 2002), which has been prevalent since the 1970s. This teaching approach emphasises the generation of meaning in realistic contexts (Brumfit & Johnson, 1979). Each classroom is regarded as being a simulated social community (Richards, 2005), one in which the teaching and learning processes are interactive. In such a communicative learning process, a series of communicative speech acts should be included in classroom instruction. By means of these speech acts, learners are encouraged to interact with each other, using the target language in an appropriate context.

As a result of the recognised need to create an effective and realistic environment for teaching English in China, in the 1980s, the communicative approach was first introduced into the academic field by a small group of university researchers (Candlin, 1982; W. Z. Hu, 1982; X. J. Li, 1984). Subsequently, the concept of communicative language teaching was incorporated within the 1992 and 1993 national school syllabus documents.

In order to support the 1992 and 1993 syllabus, and help teachers develop their capacity to implement a more communicative approach, the People's Education Press (which is a branch of the Ministry of Education), in collaboration with the international publishing house, Longman, developed textbooks which were orientated toward developing communication (Adamson, 2004). By means of a series of textbooks, a five-step method for the implementation of the communicative approach has been suggested. This approach has been described as being eclectic, because the model integrates the new language teaching ideas with some of the more traditional approaches.

Over time, there have been extensive revisions of the syllabus and many versions of the textbooks, usually with the aim of improving English language education. The syllabus, which was released in 1996, was particularly important, because it was the first national syllabus that was tailored to meet a diversity of regional needs (G. W. Hu, 2002b). In that document the decentralisation of locally developed syllabus and textbooks was reinforced. In some of the more economically well-developed regions, where students were performing better, local educational authorities were allowed to develop their own syllabi and textbooks. Presumably this move was intended to foster innovation in those regions; it also represented policy efforts directed towards a consolidation of the decentralisation process of the current English language curriculum reform initiated in 2001. As a result of providing national syllabus and policy directions for achieving local autonomy, the national government expected that English language education would be improved.

However, in a speech in 1996 by Vice Premier Li (1996) it became apparent that these efforts were not bearing sufficient fruit. The Vice Premier reiterated the importance of

English language education as a means to furthering China's continuing economic development. He maintained that student outcomes were not good enough. Vice Premier Li encouraged teachers to abandon the old and ineffectual modes of instruction and to adopt communicative approaches to teaching that were underpinned by the syllabus and textbooks.

This emphasis on the urgent need for change in language education was borne out by a second national survey in 1999 (Z. D. Zhang & Associates, 2001). The results of this survey revealed that, overall, there had been few gains in students' communicative competencies since the first national survey which had been conducted nearly a decade and a half earlier (Ministry of Education, 2002). The evidence indicated that most teachers were still devoting a great deal of class time to didactically transmitting knowledge, in order to prepare students to cope with examinations, just as they had done in the past. The overall lack of progress was attributed to the failure of teachers to implement the innovations that had been suggested in the syllabus and textbooks.

Many reasons have been offered as explanations for teachers' ineffectual implementation of communicative language teaching in the past initiative prior to 2001. Some researchers (Burnaby & Sun, 1989; Leng, 1997; Yu, 2001) have pointed out that there were very few teachers with adequate levels of English language competency. Few of the struggling teachers had sufficient English language skill, or sociolinguistic competence, and many had scant knowledge about the rules of language use. Those researchers suggested that teachers were unable to provide appropriate input by way of instruction of English language, nor were they able to conduct real communicative activities in their classrooms. Understandably, the teachers felt inadequate because of a lack of sufficient quality of professional development programs that might have helped to enhance their knowledge and understanding about the communicative approach.

Furthermore, the curriculum writers of the 2001 national *English Language Curriculum Standards* (Ministry of Education, 2001b) have suggested that previous syllabus documents have, all too often, not provided sufficient guidance to enable teachers to use the communicative approach (Ministry of Education, 2002). Just as importantly, repeated attempts to provide clarity to teachers, by continually updating and modifying the appropriate syllabus, has tended to confuse teachers rather than assist them (X. Wu, 2005).

Other researchers (see G. W. Hu, 2002a) have argued that even if there had been adequate pre-service or in-service professional development programs, the communicative approach would probably not have been particularly effective, principally because teachers have viewed the idea as being a foreign concept, at odds with Chinese Confucian conceptions of teaching and learning. Indeed, many students too have found the new approach to be a rather alien concept, one that was quite different from their previous enculturation within the traditional Confucian learning environment. Furthermore, despite the more socially equal relationship between teacher and students that the new approach demanded, the new teaching practice differed so much from students' experiences in their other subjects that they often appeared to feel uncomfortable and apprehensive. Additionally, it has been particularly difficult for teachers to conduct interactive communicative activities, and to simultaneously resolve the common discipline issues that are associated with big classes (Leng, 1997). This is a matter of quite general concern, given the high number of large classes in Chinese schools.

Furthermore, teaching resources required to support teachers' implementation of the communicative approach have frequently been identified as being inadequate and of poor quality (Leng, 1997). Because of these shortcomings, and coupled with the other contextual challenges, teachers have generally felt a need to rely almost entirely on textbooks. Understandably, the teachers, in their attempts to retain some authority, have set out to didactically transmit discrete language items, in what they have considered to be an orderly and systematic approach.

The situation, as described to this point, has demonstrated that a teaching environment in the classroom presented almost insurmountable difficulties for the teachers and students. However, it is crucially important to note that beyond the classroom, there were no changes to the exam system, little had been done in the process of assessment that might reflect the changed focus of the syllabus (Burnaby & Sun, 1989). National examinations did not test the communicative competencies that were the basis of the communicative approach. Indeed, the results produced by the official examinations have regularly determined the future career paths of both students and their teachers. Therefore, it is not surprising that teachers, students and parents have been unified in their lack of enthusiasm for the communicative approach. These were forces that combined to support the conventional forms of teaching because they recognised that they were more likely to produce success in the national examinations.

Additionally, other researchers (e.g., Bao, 2006) have observed that a general lack of opportunity to practise English outside the classroom, in most regions of China, has also been an inhibiting factor that has impeded the implementation of the communicative approach. Because of this very considerable limitation, compounded by the other impediments that have already been mentioned, it is hardly surprising that students' communicative competencies have usually been disappointingly low.

There have been, however, some noticeable exceptions to this overall picture, and these exceptions have been largely found in the more economically well-developed regions (Z. D. Zhang & Associates, 2001). The earlier government decision to allow these regions a degree of autonomy to develop syllabus and textbooks that were tailored to meet the local needs of teachers and students, have suggested that the approach could be implemented effectively throughout China. Thus, a level of local autonomy, sufficient to provide initiative and innovation, has appeared to be a partial solution that might help teachers overcome their difficulties. Furthermore, Chinese teachers have been able to demonstrate a capacity to adopt, as well as adapt to what may initially have appeared to be an alien, foreign concept. When the "one-size-fits-all" approach, regarding the implementation of the curriculum, is eventually discarded, and when teachers have access to more appropriate resources, both physical and intellectual, Chinese teachers will be in a much better position to resolve the dilemmas that have confounded their intentions to overcome their contextual circumstances.

THE CURRENT ENGLISH LANGUAGE CURRICULUM REFORM

The observations made in the previous section were considered by the national government when the new national *English Language Curriculum Standards* (Ministry of Education, 2001b) document was developed. The intention of the Ministry of Education was to shift English language teachers from their conventional textbook-centred and teacher-led pedagogy to more progressive, learner-centred approaches. This change process was designed in order to encourage a pedagogy emphasising learners' language use in social practice (Ministry of Education, 2001b).

The curriculum reform team recognised that giving autonomy to the regions could result in improved outcomes for students. Therefore, rather than producing yet another syllabus, the national government released a set of learning, outcomes-based curriculum standards and these formed the foundation of the new curriculum for both primary and secondary schools (Ministry of Education, 2001b). The aim of the national curriculum was to encourage different regions to develop their own syllabus. However, these documents must adhere to the national standards.

Paralleling this move, different regions, in collaboration with foreign publishers, were also encouraged to develop their own textbooks to support their own syllabus. However, the textbooks are required to meet a set of textbook guidelines set out in the curriculum document. These guidelines have helped to ensure that the textbooks would support the intentions of the new curriculum (Ministry of Education, 2001b).

The national examination system was also revised in order to test the sorts of communicative competencies that have been advocated in the new curriculum (Ministry of Education, 2001b). It was necessary that the outcome-based, discrete, point-testing system of assessment should be balanced with a process-based, formative, testing system.

Moreover, in order to provide teachers with a better pedagogical model, a task-based approach to language teaching was introduced in the national curriculum standards (Ministry of Education, 2001b). A task-based approach is regarded as being the natural development from a communicative approach (Richards, 2005), rather than being a substitute for it. According to Skehan (2003), tasks are developed from communicative activities in communicative approach. Thus, a task-based approach is one of the pedagogical intentions within a broad philosophy that supports the communicative approach (Nunan, 1999).

In the companion guide to the curriculum document (Ministry of Education, 2002), the concept of the task-based approach is described as being an approach to language pedagogy in which: "Students are driven or motivated by a specific *task* [author emphasis] to learn English. In the process of performing a task, students learn English. Their learning results are evaluated by the outcomes of their performed task (not by their grades)" (p.105) [author's translation]. Specifically, this approach encourages learner-centred, experiential learning as a means of supplying learners with tasks, and these tasks should link students' new knowledge with their real-life experiences outside classrooms. Teachers are able to support learners, as they interact and negotiate with peers whilst performing tasks.

Although task-based approach has been well understood in many western countries (R. Ellis, 2003; Nunan, 2004; Willis, 1996), it is new in the Chinese context (E. Y. Zhang, 2005). Nevertheless, teachers are required to implement the curriculum through a task-based approach which is embedded in practical teaching. In order to shift teachers from less productive, traditional, teacher-centred practices, curriculum developers have guided teachers to develop the sorts of communicative competencies that have been outlined in the curriculum standards (Ministry of Education, 2001b).

Furthermore, curriculum writers have regarded the task-based approach, with its focus on language authenticity, and its focus on the concept of language as producing real communication, as a way of developing the practical language competencies of students. There has been policy recognition that an improvement in language use has the potential to produce considerable economic benefits (Ministry of Education, 2001b). It may be said that this is a farsighted objective, given the fact that there were, at the time when this objective was conceived, few opportunities for most students in China to practise these skills outside the classroom.

In order to pioneer this process, the Ministry of Education (2001a) has required that English, as a subject, be offered to all primary school students as early as Year 3 (8-year-old children). The purpose of this policy is to establish a good foundation for the teaching of English in secondary schools by engaging children in foreign language education. As an outcome of the new arrangement, the curriculum standards have been integrated across the 12 years of schooling in basic education so as to establish an integrated English language system.

With their newly found autonomy, the different regions of China have been encouraged to work out teacher development program plans that might provide effective support for school English language teachers (Ministry of Education, 2001b). School administrators have been encouraged to develop school-based teacher learning and teacher professional development. It was also decided that schools, textbook writers and other teacher facilitators needed to collaborate. The purpose of collaboration has been to offer the most effective teacher support program that might achieve teacher change as part of the process of curriculum reform.

However, the policy promotion and implementation of the new curriculum through task-based approaches, has generated intense educational debate about the appropriateness and effectiveness of adopting this new language pedagogy in China. This debate has revived many concerns which were raised by researchers during the 1980s, when communicative language teaching was first introduced as the basis of the English syllabus in China (Burnaby & Sun, 1989; G. W. Hu, 2002a; Leng, 1997; Yu, 2001). Similar concerns have also been raised in other parts of the world, for example when communicative approaches or task-based approaches were officially promoted and implemented in Hong Kong (Carless, 2003), Egypt (Gahin & Myhill, 2001), South Korea (D. F. Li, 1998), Thailand (Nonkukhetkhong, 2006), and Vietnam (G. Ellis, 1994), as well as other developing nations (Ho & Wong, 2003).

CHALLENGES POSED BY CONTEXTUAL FACTORS

The intensity of the educational debate has occurred because of the presence of various contextual factors, which are similar to those acknowledged ones when communicative language teaching was first introduced into China. Hence, this appears to be an appropriate place for this debate to be reviewed, and to examine the various challenges which English language education faces during the current language teaching reform process.

In China, two sides, with contrasting views, have engaged in debate over the implementation of the current national English language curriculum. *On the one hand,* the curriculum developers have argued that task-based pedagogy is the most appropriate approach for achieving the curriculum standards (Ministry of Education, 2002). According to the Ministry of Education the new language pedagogy has proved effective in some regions of China. Consequently, the Ministry argues that the adoption of such task-based approaches should be just as effective in other regions of China. As a result, the curriculum developers have succinctly claimed: "The task-based approach, compared to other approaches, is consistent with the ideas of the new curriculum standards and therefore conducive to its implementation" (Ministry of Education, 2002, p. 105) [author's translation].

Many studies support the curriculum developers' views in a variety of different ways. Some researchers have discussed the theoretical basis of this pedagogy (Cheng & Gong, 2005) and its adaptability (Lu, 2006). Those researchers have suggested that the new curriculum is appropriate to the Chinese context because it is underpinned by recently developed theories, and is adaptable to China's social development. Similarly, other researchers (Cheng, 2004; Gong & Luo, 2003) have demonstrated the potential of a variety of different models of implementation to achieve effective task-based approaches to language teaching.

Furthermore, Chinese researchers have initiated studies of the implementation of task-based approaches based on sound theoretical understandings (e.g., Y. N. Hu, 2005). There have also been Chinese attempts to gain an understanding of localized task-based approaches by studying English teaching in local schools (Lu, 2003). However, it is worth noting that many of these studies were enacted as theoretical discussions, rather than empirical research. There has been far more opinion and conjecture, than evidence-based studies founded on rigorous scientific practice producing reliable data.

On the other hand, a prominent Chinese educational expert, Bao (2006), who holds the position of Director of the National Centre for Foreign Language Education and Research in Basic Education, has steadfastly resisted the use of the task-based pedagogy recommended in the new curriculum. He has asserted that teaching English as a foreign language in Chinese schools should be orientated towards the primary goal of improving learners' knowledge and skills, rather than focusing on the practice of sharpening learners' abilities in terms of practical use, as has been recommended within the new curriculum document. According to Bao, China lacks authentic contexts in which English language could be used and practised. Furthermore, Bao has opposed the task-based approach because, as he claims, "it suits neither the Chinese context nor the teaching and learning context specific to China. It cannot be implemented at all … we cannot oppose deduction, grammar and knowledge-transmission" (p. 34) [author's translation].

Although Bao (2006) has vehemently opposed task-based approaches, he has not provided empirical evidence to support his assertions. Nevertheless, his argument has been echoed in other publications by Chinese researchers who have not supported the implementation of the new curriculum and its dependence on a task-based approach. Those researchers have claimed that the use of task-based approaches is inappropriate as a means of implementing the curriculum; apparently such approaches are not functional because of the particular contextual barriers that are supposed to exist in the Chinese context (Gao, 2007). These critics maintain that the specific cultural resistance to task-based teaching is influenced by Confucian beliefs that render the approach alien to the Chinese philosophy of education. However, these critics have not been able to provide empirical evidence to support their case. Their position appears to lack substance.

Notwithstanding the lack of substance in the internal Chinese argument against communicative, task-based approaches, the international literature is replete with empirical data demonstrating that there is potential for contextual barriers to work against the implementation of task-based approaches. In countries such as Cyprus and Chile (Bygate, Cook, Iannou-Georgiou, Jullian, & Morrow, 2004), Hong Kong (Carless, 2003), and in a particular Chinese city in an economically well developed region within China (E. Y. Zhang, 2005). Each of these empirical studies has shown a range of contextual factors that have challenged teachers' implementation of task-based approaches, in one of the following three ways:

1. *Teacher factors* (Bygate et al., 2004; Carless, 2003; E. Y. Zhang, 2005) refer to a composite of a teacher's knowledge, ability, time and workload, as being possible limitations on teachers' overall capacity to implement a task-based approach to language teaching. According to these studies, teachers commonly lack sufficient subject content knowledge, pedagogical content knowledge as well as knowledge of the new curriculum and its pedagogical implementation. Such researchers stress that these limitations tend to inhibit a teacher's understanding and implementation of the new language pedagogy. Furthermore, a heavy teaching workload, and lack of time to conduct task-based activities in classrooms, have also been identified as being barriers against a teacher's ability to engage in the implementation of task-based approaches.

2. *Micro-contextual factors* (Carless, 2003; E. Y. Zhang, 2005) are related to student factors, classroom factors, and other aspects of a teacher's workplace, such as the realisation that students and parents, who have unfavourable attitudes towards task-based approaches, can sustain and even encourage student resistance to new language pedagogy, thereby resulting in a low-level English communicative ability. Cumulatively, these are factors that might well discourage teachers from implementing task-based approaches within their classrooms. Big class sizes, too, add a further challenge, if teachers are to keep classes disciplined whilst interacting with students in a communicative way.

3. *Macro-contextual factors* (E. Y. Zhang, 2005) are socio-cultural aspects that are in evidence beyond a teacher's workplace. One such factor is a new curriculum document, which has been designed as a general guideline for a teacher's implementation, without a clearly defined schedule of activities. The prevalence of poor quality teaching resources, such as inadequate numbers of textbooks, insufficient foreign language teaching facilities, and nonexistent or inadequate in-service professional development activities, have presented challenges to teachers' implementation of the curriculum. Collectively, the impediments have made the task very difficult. Furthermore, there has been a considerable amount of inconsistency between the examination system and the outcomes of a task-based approach. Ultimately, all of these have helped to compound the resistance of teachers, students and their parents to an apparently inappropriate task-based approach to language education in the Chinese socio-cultural context.

These data, derived as they have been from international literature, and one particular economically well-developed area within China, suggest that there is the possibility that contextual factors could be potential barriers that inhibit the potential for English language teachers elsewhere in China to implement the new curriculum through task-based approaches. Additionally, the evidence from these studies is almost uniformly consistent in suggesting that teachers have neither implemented task-based approaches, nor conducted the progressive behavioural practices required in the new Chinese curriculum. Specifically, teachers have tended not to focus on improving students' communicative abilities; all too frequently their teaching has avoided the demand for student-centred communicative tasks.

By contrast, traditional pedagogical practices are still common in most classrooms in China (Gao, 2007; E. Y. Zhang, 2005). Consequently, teachers have tended to concentrate on improving students' abilities of reading and writing. Teachers have tended to stick to what they regard as the tried and true methods of textbook-centred teaching. They have not moved on to developing interactive learning activities, and they have remained firmly stuck in the teacher-centred knowledge transmission mode. Thus, a big gap remains between national policy and teachers' classroom implementation techniques. For a variety of reasons it does seem that the local environment has the potential to result in creating a negative impact of Chinese teachers' efforts to implement the imported concepts of language education.

CONCLUSION

There has been impressive progress in basic English language education in China due to the initiation and implementation of several English language curriculum reforms. However, it has been realised that these reforms have often been impeded by a variety of different challenges in the Chinese context. Faced with these challenges, there is a need to seriously consider at least three issues which have arisen from previous discussions.

The first of these issues relates to how western teaching theories and practices can be effectively introduced into Chinese local conditions and factors. All too often in the process of "borrowing" practices, Chinese socio-cultural factors have often been neglected (G. W. Hu, 2002a), and almost no regard has been taken of the fact that there are considerable regional differences in China. However, this is not to say that "imported" theories or practices should be opposed or abandoned. But there is an inherent danger in "borrowing" without considering local social-cultural factors in relation to the process of "planting" them in the Chinese context. As the Chinese saying goes, good fruits grown in other regions may not grow well in this [different] context. They may even taste differently because of the changed conditions.

As a result, the transplanting of theories and practices imported into a new environment must always be modified to suit the Chinese situation. Borrowing must be accompanied by a process of accommodation. New and alien ideas and concepts will often need to be modified if they are to blend well with local factors. Only in this way can ideas borrowed from other places be realised as action in the local context of the Chinese school system.

There is then a need for interested experts who are well versed in western theories and practices, who are also well aware of Chinese local factors. With such knowledge it may be possible to find a "balanced" way of integrating the best aspects of both systems. Despite some attempts at seeking effective approaches, regarding the teaching of English in the Chinese context, researchers in China, to a large extent, have not significantly established or produced theorisation in relation to English language education in the Chinese context (Y. A. Wu, 2001). Hence, researchers, both in China and overseas who are interested in the Chinese situation, are faced with enormous considerable challenge if they are to establish a theoretical blueprint that is based on empirical research and reliable data.

The second issue relates to how any worthwhile in-service professional development programs can be appropriately and effectively designed and implemented in order that the process of teacher change be achieved. This is not new knowledge that effective curriculum change is inevitably intertwined with teacher development. Even over 30 years ago Stenhouse (1975) stressed the interrelationship between curriculum change and teacher development. Without teacher development, the gap which exists between a planned curriculum and the enacted curriculum can never be narrowed. Thus, the effective implementation of curriculum change depends on whether teachers will change their classroom behaviour (Fullan, 2001).

However, it has been acknowledged that the in-service language teacher professional development programs, which have been provided in China, frequently did not appropriately and effectively address the professional development needs of teachers in the actuality of the classroom (X. Wu, 2005). Therefore, as is the case regarding learners who are involved in student-centred language teaching, teachers, too, need to be treated as professional learners (Hargreaves, 2003) in a client-centred approach to curriculum reform (Cohen, 2002).

The third issue is a concern for the reformation of the national examination system, regarding English language curriculum reform. That is, only when a scientific and practical examination is sought to test learners' communicative abilities, can English language learning and teaching be guided, in tune with the keynote of the curriculum reform. This is because examination always has a strong "backwash" effect on English language education (Taylor, 2005).

Addressing these issues, however, is not an easy task. Indeed, it may only by achieved by collaborative endeavour, from all interested individuals and organisations in China and beyond. Obviously, the most important and urgent scholarly and practical work lies ahead.

ACKNOWLEDGMENTS

I extend my hearty thanks to Dr. Robin Wills and Mr. Gerard Daniel from Charles Sturt University, who patiently edited the whole chapter, offering generous help and valuable suggestions.

REFERENCES

Adamson, B. (2004). *China's English: A history of English in Chinese education*. Hong Kong: Hong Kong University Press.

Bao, T. R. (2006). Dangqian woguo jichu yingyu jiaoyu de shida redian wenti yu duice [Ten hot issues and their solutions in basic English education in China]. *Foreign Language Teaching and Research in Basic Education*(1), 24 – 27.

Brumfit, C., & Johnson, K. (1979). *The communicative approach to language teaching*. Oxford: Oxford University Press.

Burnaby, B., & Sun, Y. (1989). Chinese teachers' view of western language teaching: Context informs paradigm. *TESOL Quarterly, 23*, 219 – 238.

Bygate, M., Cook, G., Iannou-Georgiou, S., Jullian, P., & Morrow, K. (2004). The ELT journal/IATEFL debate: Tasks are nothing new. They're just exercise with a new name. In P. Grundy & International Association of Teachers of English as a Foreign Language. International Conference (Eds.), *IATEFL: 37th international annual conference, Brighton, 22-26 April 2003* (pp. 174-177). Canterbury, Kent: IATEFL.

Candlin, C. N. (1982). Principles and practice in communicative language teaching. *Foreign Language Teaching and Research, 4*, 36 – 44.

Carless, D. (2003). Factors in the implementation of task-based teaching in primary schools. *System, 31*, 485 – 500.

Cheng, X. T. (2004). *Renwuxing yuyan jiaoxue [Task-based language teaching]*. Beijing: Higher Education Publishing House.

Cheng, X. T., & Gong, Y. F. (2005). Yingyu Kecheng biaozhun de lilun jichu [On the theoretical basis of the English Language Curriculum Standards]. *Curriculum, Teaching Material and Method 25*, 66 – 72.

Cohen, R. (2002). School our teachers deserve: A proposal for teacher-centred reform. *Phi Delta Kappan, 83*, 532 – 537.

Ellis, G. (1994). The appropriateness of the communicative approach in Vietnam: An interview study in intercultural communication. *ELT Journal, 36*(2), 73 – 81.

Ellis, R. (2003). *Task-based language learning and teaching*. New York: Oxford University Press.

Fullan, M. (2001). *The new meaning of educational change* (3rd ed.). New York: Teachers College Press.

Gahin, G., & Myhill, D. (2001). The communicative approach in Egypt: Exploring the secrets of the pyramids [Electronic Version]. *TEFL Web Journal, 1*, (n.d.).

Gao, S. (2007). Renwuxing waiyu jiaoxue de juxianxing [On the limitations of task-based language teaching]. *Huazhong Normal University Journal of Postgraduates, 6*, 48 – 52.

Gong, Y. F., & Luo, S. Q. (2003). *Renwuxng yuyan jiaoxue [Task-based language teaching]*. Beijing: People's Education Press.

Hargreaves, A. (2003). Teaching in the knowledge society: Education in the age of insecurity. New York: Teachers College Press.

Ho, W. K., & Wong, R. Y. L. (2003). English Language teaching in east Asia today: Changing policies and practices. Singapore: Times Academic Press.

Hu, G. W. (2002a). Potential cultural resistance to pedagogical imports: The case of communicative language teaching in China. *Language, Culture and Curriculum, 15*, 93 – 105.

Hu, G. W. (2002b). Recent important development in secondary English-language teaching in the People's Republic of China. *Language, Culture and Curriculum, 15*(5), 30-49.

Hu, W. Z. (1982). Jiaoji Jiaoxuefa chutan [Initial studies of communicative language teaching]. *Foreign Language Education, 5*, 15 – 22.

Hu, Y. N. (2005). Yong renwuxing yuyan jiaoxue tujing sheji jiaoxue huodong de shijianxing tansuo [Designing learning activities by using task-based language teaching]. *Foreign Languages Teaching, 2*, 44-48.

Jin, L. X., & Cortazzi, M. (2003). English language teaching in China: A bridge to the future. In W. K. Ho & R. Y. L. Wong (Eds.), *English language teaching in East Asia today: Changing policies and practices* (pp. 131 – 145). Singapore: Times Academic Press.

Larsen-Freeman, D. (2000). *Techniques and principles in language teaching*. New York: Oxford University Press.

Leng, H. (1997). New bottles, old wine: Communicative language teaching in China. *Forum, 35*(4), 38 – 41.

Li, D. F. (1998). "It's always more difficult than you plan and imagine": Teachers' perceived difficulties in introducing the communicative approach in South Korea. *TESOL Quarterly, 32*, 677 – 703.

Li, L. Q. (1996, September 5). Gaijin waiyu jiaoxue fangfa, tigao waiyu jiaoxue shuiping [Changing foreign language teaching methods and improving language teaching]. *China Education Newspaper,* p. 1.

Li, X. J. (1984). In defence of the communicative approach. *ELT Journal, 38*(1), 2 – 13.

Lu, Z. W. (2003). *Zhongxiaoxue yingyu zhenshi renwu jiaoxue shijianlun [Practice of authentic task-based language teaching at primary and secondary schools]*. Beijing: Foreign Language Teaching and Research Press.

Lu, Z. W. (2006). Yingyu kecheng biaozhun jiegou de shehui fazhan shiyingxing bijiao yanjiu [The comparative study of the adaptability of the new curriculum standards to social development]. *Curriculum, Teaching Materials and Method, 26*(5), 87 – 91.

Ministry of Education, P. R. C. (2001a). *Jiaoyubu guanyu jiji tuijin xiaoxue kaishe yingyu kecheng de zhidao yijian [Ministry of Education's directives for actively promoting to offer English at primary schools]*. Beijing: Ministry of Education, China.

Ministry of Education, P. R. C. (2001b). *Yingyu kecheng biaozhun [English language curriculum standards]*. Beijing: Beijing Normal University Publishing House.

Ministry of Education, P. R. C. (2002). *Yingyu kecheng biaozhun jiedu [Interpretations of the English language curriculum standards]*. Beijing: Beijing Normal University Publishing House.

Nonkukhetkhong, K. (2006). *Teachers' perceptions and implementation of the learner-centered approach in teaching English as a foreign language (EFL) in Thai secondary school contexts*. Unpublished doctoral dissertation, University of Queensland – Brisbane.

Nunan, D. (1999). *Second language teaching and learning*. Boston: Heinle & Heinle.

Nunan, D. (2003). The impact of English as a global language on educational policies and practices in the Asia-Pacific region. *TESOL Quarterly, 37*, 589 – 613.

Nunan, D. (2004). *Task-based language teaching*. Cambridge, England: Cambridge University Press.

Richards, J. C. (2005). *Communicative language teaching today*. Singapore: SEAMEO Regional Language Centre.

Skehan, P. (2003). Task-based instruction. *Language Teaching, 36*, 1 –14.

Taylor, L. (2005). Washback and impact. *ELT Journal, 59*(2), 154 – 155.

Willis, J. (1996). A flexible framework for task-based learning. In J. Willis & D. Willis (Eds.), *Challenge and change in language teaching* (pp. 52 – 62). Oxford: Macmillan Heinemann.

Wu, X. (2005). *Teacher change: Issues in in-service EFL teacher education*. Beijing: Foreign Language Teaching and Research Press.

Wu, Y. A. (2001). English language teaching in China: Trends and challenges. *TESOL Quarterly, 35*(1), 191 –194.

Yu, L. M. (2001). Communicative language teaching in China: Progress and resistance. *TESOL Quarterly, 35*(1), 194 –198.

Zhang, E. Y. (2005). *Implementing task-based approach in primary school ELT in mainland China*. Unpublished doctoral dissertation, University of Hong Kong – Hong Kong.

Zhang, Z. D., & Associates (Eds.). (2001). Yingyu jiaoxue de xianzhuang yu fazhan: "Quanguo gaozhong yingyu jiaoxue diaocha yanjiu" jieti baogao zhuanzhu [Current situation and development of English language teaching: Report of national survey of English language teaching at secondary schools]. Beijing: People's Education Press.

In: Language and Literacy Education in a Challenging World   ISBN: 978-1-61761-198-8
Editors: T. Lê, Q. Lê, and M. Short   © 2011 Nova Science Publishers, Inc.

Chapter 14

IS ENGLISH LANGUAGE PROFICIENCY AN APPROPRIATE DISCRIMINATOR FOR ADMISSION INTO HIGHER INSTITUTIONS OF LEARNING?

Clement Dlamini

ABSTRACT

What is meant by English language proficiency? Is language proficiency measured by English language, the subject Grade 12 learners write as the end of year examination? University entry requirements in Swaziland include English language as one of the entry requirements for mathematics related fields of study. In this chapter I argue that the inclusion of this subject in the criteria is not appropriate, especially in mathematics related fields. My argument is based on recent findings that showed that learners who were high achievers in mathematics in Swaziland attained low scores in English language and hence were automatically excluded from the University of Swaziland on the basis of their English language grades. This chapter uses data collected in Swaziland to argue that the use of English language as a gatekeeper may strategically be discriminating against learners whose home language is not English.

Keywords: language proficiency, mathematics high achievers, English language high achievers, social languages, academic languages, entry requirements.

INTRODUCTION

The use of English language as a medium of instruction seems to be gaining momentum with the advent of internet and the technological advances in communication. These advances have led to the world being viewed as a global village. For others, this view of the world calls for the use of a common language. The hegemony of English has been viewed by others as the ideal language for international communication as it is increasingly being used in international conferences and as a *lingua franca* in many countries, even in countries that were not formerly colonised by Britain. For example, countries like Namibia and Rwanda that used Afrikaans and French respectively as medium of instruction have turned to English both as a unifying official language and a prominent language of instruction in schools.

In the Southern African Development Community (SADC) region, a majority of countries have a policy of using English as a medium of instruction in schools and higher education. Even countries in this region that recognise or promote the use of indigenous languages for instruction in schools do not seem to be advocating the use of indigenous languages in tertiary institutions. In South Africa, for example, the African population still associates the use of these languages with inferior education (Mesthrie, 2006; Alexander, 2001). This view is understandable given that in many African countries indigenous languages have not been made what others call a "linguistic capital" (Barwell, 2003; Zevenbergen, 2000), that is, they cannot be exchanged for access to education and employment. This "policy implementation avoidance strategy" is typical of many former Anglo and Franco African colonies (Bamgbose, 1999). Like almost all governments in Africa that use European languages of wider communication (ELoWC), indigenous languages are not used at all in higher education and places of employment. For indigenous Africans these are the crucial places where the recognition of their languages would make the most positive impact in their lives.

While this chapter is not advocating the use of African languages in tertiary institutions and places of employment, it attempts to bring another perspective on issues of equity with regard to the potential policies have for discriminating against indigenous ethnic populations. While I appreciate the fact that a lot still needs to be done to elevate indigenous languages even to the point of using them for secondary school instruction, the argument is on the need to review tertiary institutional language policies for the benefit of learners who take instruction in a second language. In this chapter I present data collected in Swaziland to show that language policies of the University of Swaziland[1] (UNISWA) may be excluding a certain community of indigenous learners. I then show that the use of English language as one of the criteria for admission into mathematics related disciplines may not be appropriate as it excludes high achieving learners in mathematics. Finally, I argue that the use of English as one of the selection criteria is inappropriate for mathematics related fields of study at tertiary institutions.

ENTRY REQUIREMENTS

University entry requirements are used to select applicants or applicants who have a potential of succeeding in programmes for which they have been selected (Zaaiman, 1998). An analysis I have conducted of entry requirements of seven South African universities showed that most of these institutions require a pass in English in the Matric examination in institutions where English is the medium of instruction, and a pass in English or Afrikaans in institutions where these are languages of learning and teaching (see Table 1). For example, the use of English in most universities is justified on the premise that it is "the language of instruction". This justification seems to assume that a pass in Matric English is an indicator for the accepted level of proficiency. Table 1 below illustrates some of the requirements.

---

[1] The University of Swaziland was the only university at the time of data collection.

Table 1– Entry Requirements of Some South African Universities

University	English (Home Language or First Additional Language) as a general requirement	English as a requirement for natural sciences +engineering
University of Western Cape	50-59%	50-59%
University of Cape Town	Placement Test in English for Educational Purposes (PTEEP) – top 20% (with two other tests included)	Required only for Actuarial Sciences (English First Language C (HG) – English Home Language 5 (60-69%))
University of the Free State	min. 50% in your chosen language (b/n English and Afrikaans)	min. 50% in your chosen language (between English and Afrikaans)
University of Johannesburg	50-59%	50-59%
University of KwaZulu Natal	50% or above	50% or above
University of Pretoria	English or Afrikaans (50-59%)	English or Afrikaans (50-59%)
Stellenbosch University	Achieve an aggregate of at least 4 (50-59%) in four subjects designated for university study (of which at least one should be either English or Afrikaans)	50-59%

This is one example of a country where English language is used as an entry requirement in higher institutions of learning. The argument presented here is based on the assumption that the inclusion of English language as an entry requirement in any field presupposes some form of proficiency that is necessary for achievement in disciplines of that field. Put differently, the requirement assumes a strong correlation between achievement in English and achievement in mathematics. The underlying overall assumption is that candidates who do not meet the minimum level of proficiency may not cope with the (language) demands of university disciplines, e.g., mathematics. What exactly are the demands of highly scientific fields like mathematics?

EXPLANATIONS FROM LITERATURE

In the school system, the notion that language proficiency is related to mathematics achievement has been debated for many years (MacGregor and Price, 1999) and is still subject to debate depending on the level of schooling. However, focusing on language proficiency alone can be misleading as there are other factors that can hinder achievement in mathematics. Other factors include the type of immersion programmes used in the school (Garcia, 1997), school management, school resources including qualification of teachers, and other factors. Although it cannot be denied that one cannot be expected to achieve good grades when learning in a language that one is still learning, the literature on this issue has not advanced an adequately convincing argument about how language proficiency is associated with achievement in senior secondary education. At this level learners are supposed to have achieved some proficiency in the language of learning and teaching (LoLT).

In their study, where they explored aspects of language proficiency and algebra learning, MacGregor and Price (1999) assessed learners' metalinguistic awareness and their ability to use algebra. They found that few students with low metalinguistic scores obtained high scores in algebra. The term *metalinguistic awareness* was used to explain the relationship between language proficiency and mathematics achievement. They explained that metalinguistic awareness is a linguistic term which is used to describe the ability of a learner to "reflect on the structural and functional features of text as an object, to make choices and about how to communicate information and to manipulate perceived units of language" (p. 451). This process was likened to an equivalent ability in mathematics, algebra in particular. In the context of algebra they interpreted metalinguistic awareness to mean the ability to show *symbol awareness* and *syntax awareness*. This notion of metalinguistic awareness can be extended to mathematics when viewed as a "language" (Pimm, 1982) with its own grammar (syntax) and letters (symbols). Given that in mathematics, symbolic representations are valued over prose presented texts, the ability to read and represent mathematical text can inextricably be linked to academic achievement in higher education.

Other factors affecting the achievement of second language learners have more to do with assessment. In South Africa, for example, critics of the Trends in International Mathematics and Science Study (TIMSS) which showed poor performance of learners in mathematics focused more on the assessment items. A report on the analysis of two TIMSS studies, TIMSS-1999 (Howie, 2001) and TIMSS-2003 (Dempster, 2007) identified low proficiency in the language of testing as one of the factors that contributed to poor performance in mathematics and science. Commenting about TIMSS-1999, where South Africa participated in 1995, Howie and Petersen (2001) observed that:

> Significant language and communication problems of South African students learning mathematics in second language were revealed by the analysis. Students showed a lack of understanding of mathematics literacy questions and an inability to communicate their answers in instances where they did understand the questions. Students performed particularly badly in questions requiring a written answer (p. 19).

Dempster (2007) supported this view with evidence that suggested that readability factors and/or misconceptions influenced the choices that candidates from African schools[2] made when responding to the TIMSS-2003 items. This analysis is presented verbatim below:

> Text-based strategies could explain the pattern of choice in 14 of the 20 items in which over 40% of learners in African schools selected one incorrect answer. The most common strategy (eight items) consisted of favouring the answer that contained the greatest number of familiar words. Learners rejected answers containing unfamiliar words (p. 47).

---

[2] According to Dempster, African schools are those where most learners were black and spoke English as second language.

What Dempster suggests is that there was some degree of guesswork among second language learners in TIMSS-2003. Nonetheless, a study conducted in South Africa should have taken cognisance of the historical factors that still affect the status of many former "black" or township schools. According to Thompson (1996), cited in Vesely (2000) some shocking statistics reveal that:

> In 1978, when there were five times as many African children as white children in South Africa, only 12,014 Africans passed the matriculation examination or its equivalent, whereas three times as many whites did so... The government spent ten times as much per capita on white students as on African students, and African classes were more than twice as large as white ones (p. 72).

It is now common knowledge in South Africa that former white schools are still the best resourced. Therefore, it is doubtful that English proficiency is a major factor that may be attributed to the underperformance of African learners in South Africa.

Other studies have attributed success in mathematics and science more to knowledge than to the language of learning (Adler, 2001; Gorgorio and Planas, 2001). Adler observed that:

> ...school performance (and by implication, mathematics achievement) is determined by a complex of inter-related factors. Poor performance of bilingual learners thus cannot be attributed to the learner's language proficiencies in isolation of classroom processes shaped as they are by wider social, cultural and political factors that infuse schooling (p. 6)... mathematics is difficult for everyone, irrespective of the learner's main language since problems of understanding have more to do with the mathematics itself than with English as the LoLT (p. 8).

A similar observation was made by Gorgorio and Planas 92001) whose research on immigrants who were learning mathematics in a second language in Catalan (Spain) showed that the conflicts shown by these learners were not always strictly due to a language obstacle.

Another observation relates to the significance of the role of language with regard to mathematical achievement as learners progress with schooling. Two studies by Worswick (2004; 2001) in Canada showed that after years of schooling, there were significant achievement patterns in mathematics for the immigrant children whose parents spoke neither French nor English and that the differences in performance between children whose parents spoke either English or French decreased with years in school at a rate of 2.7 to 4.6 percent. He reports that by the age of 12 years the performance of children whose parents spoke neither English nor French was as high as that of children of Canadian born parents. Worswick's study suggested that although English may hinder performance at the early stages of schooling, as learners gain proficiency in the language of instruction their performance in mathematics is less dependent on language proficiency as a barrier to mathematics achievement. Another evidence of this relationship is drawn from a study that was conducted in Swaziland where second language learners who were assumed to have low proficiency in English and yet were high achievers in mathematics.

LIMITED PROFICIENCY IN THE LoLT AND HIGH ACHIEVEMENT IN MATHEMATICS

I now turn to the findings of this study that showed that limited proficiency in English is not always a barrier to high achievement in mathematics. This is a study that was conducted with learners in an environment that did not support the speaking of English. The learners in this study were in an environment where English is viewed as a foreign language. This environment has been referred by Setati, Adler, Reed and Bapoo (2001) as a Foreign Language Learning Environment (FLLE). This environment is commonly found in rural areas in Southern Africa where the language of teaching is only heard and spoken in the school. These are settings where learners rarely have access to English media such as newspapers and television, hence less support for English as the LoLT. Although the participants in this study were in a semi-urban environment where they had access to English media, they came from families with strong Swazi traditional backgrounds. These are families where the speaking of English is not encouraged. They attended mathematics lessons in a school where English was spoken only in the classroom. These learners belong to the Nguni indigenous tribe, which is the only tribe that constitutes indigenous Swazis.

Indigenous learners, in this study, are those Swazis whose parents or one of their parents is a native Swazi, or those Swazis who can be recognised as belonging to native Swazis. Native Swazis are those who are first language siSwati speakers. Almost all indigenous learners attend either Government or Grant-Aided schools. Almost all Government or Grant-Aided schools do not offer a substitute language subject for siSwati, which is the first language of the learners and which is taught in school as a subject. This means that almost all indigenous learners take siSwati and English as language subjects in school.

Indigenous learners come from a tribe with a rich culture and traditions. A majority of indigenous learners come from home backgrounds that participate in all cultural activities such as *the cutting of the reed* (by virgin girls), *the cutting of the shrub* (by virgin boys) and *the dancing of Incwala* (a celebration marking the end of the year and eating of the first fruit) (Thompson, 2008). In a majority of these homesteads, the speaking of siSwati is favoured. Therefore, learners from these backgrounds only speak English at school or during sessions that are taught in English. Interviews with learners who participated in the study suggested that they only spoke English during classroom sessions. They did not speak English either outside the classroom or at home. To them English is a foreign language. As mentioned earlier, indigenous learners belong to the Nguni group of people which is a larger tribe in Southern Africa that includes the Ndebele, Zulu and Xhosa. People who belong to these tribes and who have a strong affinity with their culture are found in rural areas where English is not spoken at home (Setati et al, 2002). The transcript excerpt below is a testimony to this claim. The excerpt is a conversation with Grade 12 learners in a school in Swaziland who were high achievers in mathematics. High achievers are associated with low English language proficiency (Dlamini, 2008).

Please note the interview was conducted in siSwati. Italicised words indicate translations from the interviewees' main language or a code-switched statement that has been translated to English. "I" is the interviewer, the others (P, C, K, Me and Mp) are the learner participants and "Ls" stands for learners.

I	*Okay I had this question; I just want to know: Which language do you speak outside school?*
Ls	SiSwati.
I	*SiSwati?*
Ls	Yes.
I	*All the time?*
Ls	Yes.
P	*But sometimes I speak English when we are chatting with my brother.*
I	*When you are chatting...? Why?*
P	*Because he always speaks English.*
I	*So you also find yourself speaking English.*
C	*Yes.*
I	*Otherwise you speak siSwati outside school?*
Ls	SiSwati.
C	*I also use English sometimes.*
I	You sometimes use English?
C	Because...
K	*Even the environment you are in contributes. If you are staying with your parents they will be taken aback when you speak English. You will obviously speak siSwati in their presence. You also find that your family members are not educated and so they contribute.*
I	*Okay, what about in school?*
Ls	[Laugh]
Me	*We don't speak English.*
Mp	*Unless there is a teacher around.*

A majority of the indigenous learners in Swaziland took the GCE[3] examinations, a school leaving examination that was used by the University of Swaziland for selecting prospective students. An analysis of their achievement patterns in mathematics and English in the GCE examinations showed a strange pattern.

Achievement patterns

An analysis of the GCE results for mathematics and English for three consecutive years from 2001 to 2003 showed that there was a consistent non-credit[4] pass rate in English language of all the mathematics high achievers[5] in Swaziland. In 2001, 62.6% of the 965 candidates did not gain a credit grade in English language. In 2002 and 2003, 66.0% and 63.9% respectively did not gain credit grades in English language (See Table 2). This analysis suggested that high achievers in mathematics in Swaziland *were low achievers in English language.* Low achievers in tests that measure knowledge of English language are said to be

---

[3] The GCE has now been replaced by the International General Certificate of Secondary Education (IGCSE)

[4] A credit is a C grade or better. The grading system that was used in the GCE O-level was a nine-point scale where 1-6 was a credit grade, 7 and 8 a pass and 9 ungraded fail. Grades 1-6 range from A+ to C-, where A+ is equivalent to 1 and C- to 6.

[5] High achievers in mathematics were those who had obtained a C grade or better.

Limited English proficiency (LEP) learners (Lockwood, 2005). According to Lockwood, LEP learners are those who perform in the bottom quarter to one half in tests that measure knowledge of English language. It follows from this finding that the high achievers in mathematics were LEP learners.

Table 2 – Percentage of high achievers in mathematics who scored less than a credit grade *in English in the O-Level GCE examinations*

Year	Percentage
2001	62.59%
2002	66.01%
2003	63.91%
2006	60.35%

Table 2 shows that more than 60% of mathematics high achievers (when the whole population was taken) did not gain a credit grade in English. I have termed this figure the "exclusion rate" since this is the percentage of learners who were not eligible to pursue mathematics related fields according to the University of Swaziland admission policy, e.g., the Bachelor of Science degree. UNISWA was the only university in Swaziland in 2006. Most of the high achievers in mathematics were also high achievers in other subjects. Below is an analysis of the achievement pattern of learners at BeNguni[6] High School. The school is one with a high population of indigenous learners. Table 3 shows the results of a study conducted in Swaziland in 2006.

Table 3 – Number of total credits gained by BeNguni High School learners

Number of credits	0	1	2	3	4	5	6	7	Total no. of learners	Total no. of credits
No. of maths high achievers	0	0	0	2	9	12	23	18	64	366
No. of English high achievers	0	0	0	5	7	11	9	18	50	278
No. of English high achievers who are poor in maths (with no credit grade in maths)	0	0	0	5	7	8	5	1	26	120

Table 3 shows the number of total credits gained by BeNguni learners. The table shows that 2 mathematics high achievers obtained 3 credit grades, 5 English high achievers and 5 high achievers who were poor in mathematics obtained 3 credit grades each. Out of a total of

[6] BeNguni is a pseudo name of the school where the study was conducted. This is a school where almost all the learners were indigenous Swazis.

186 learners, the 64 high achievers in mathematics had a total of 366 (5.70 credits per candidate) credit grades compared to the 50 high achieves in English who had 278 (5.56 credits per candidate) credit grades (also see Table 4). Furthermore, Table 3 reveals that more high achievers in mathematics had 5 or more credit grades (53) than English high achievers (38). Moreover, 76.9% (20/26) of English high achievers who had no credit in mathematics had less than 6 credit grades[7], with an average of 4.15 credit grades per candidate.

When the performance of BeNguni English high achievers was analysed, the analysis showed that only 48% obtained a credit grade in mathematics (see Table 4). This is an indication that proficiency in English did not seem to play a significant role in enhancing their performance in mathematics. Further analysis showed that mathematics high achievers had more credit grades than English high achievers. Based on this assumption, correlation coefficients between mathematics and English for the entire population of high achievers in mathematics in the country were calculated on the assumption that there may be a strong correlation between English language and mathematics subjects. Correlation coefficients for the entire population of high achievers in mathematics in the country were calculated using the Pearson product-moment correlation formula. Results of these calculations are shown in Table 4.

Table 4 – Correlation between Mathematics and English language

Year	Total number of candidates	Correlation coefficient	% variance in common
2001	965	0.2980	8.9
2002	1217	0.2899	8.4
2003	1114	0.3422	11.7
2006	1849	0.2827	8.0

The above analysis shows that the correlation coefficients were consistently weaker for the periods in which data was provided. The correlation figures between mathematics and English language suggests a weak positive correlation between the mathematics and the English grades of mathematics high achievers in Swaziland. When the correlation coefficients were squared and multiplied by hundred percent the result is what is referred to as the percentage "variance in common". This is an index that measures the percentage of association between two variables. In this case it showed the percentage of association between mathematics achievement and English language achievement. As can be seen in Table 4, the variance in common figures suggest that there is very little influence on the achievement of one subject by the other. The figures presented from Table 2 to 4 imply that English may be a poor predictor of performance in fields that are driven by scientific discourses. These figures provide insights that the assumed association between the two subjects is not always true for some sections of society.

---

[7] The University of Swaziland requires that prospective students should have obtained at least 6 credit grades for admission eligibility. This requirement suggests that English high achievers who were poor in mathematics were not likely to obtain enough grades to fulfill some of the conditions for admission and yet mathematics high achievers were only short of passing English language to be eligible for admission.

While the retention of European languages of wider communication is said to have been viewed by newly independent multilingual nations as neutral languages that would act as a unifying symbol, their other symbolic power was that they became the languages of the indigenous elites (Alexander, 2001; Bamgbose, 1999; Bokamba, 1995; Halai, 2009; Mesthrie, 2006). In some countries, indigenous languages are the recognised official languages alongside English language. In South Africa, for example, where a total of eleven languages are recognised, only one (Afrikaans, which happens to be the primary language of a white tribe) has been developed to the status of a medium of instruction at university level. The underdevelopment of the languages of the population that was previously disadvantaged during colonial times has had a profound effect on Africans in terms of accessing tertiary education.

With regard to the prevalent assumption that proficiency in the language of instruction has a bearing on achievement, Worswick's findings may have some theoretical underpinnings that may explain why ordinary language proficiency did not seem to affect achievement of Swazi indigenous learners in mathematics. The findings by Worswick suggest that the role of language is more profound at the early stages of mathematics learning as second language learners are still learning the language of instruction, and as they advance with their education the role of ordinary languages diminishes and what becomes profound is the language of the discipline.

Another theoretical claim on language and achievement is made by Gee (2005a). Gee makes a distinction between *d*iscourse and *D*iscourse, a distinction that shows the cleavage between language and social practices on one hand and language as an embodiment of social practices on the other. Gee (2005b; 1999) differentiates between the two by using the term *discourse* (with a lower case "d") and *Discourse* (with an upper case "D"). He refers to *discourse* as the language-in-use, e.g., mathematical language and all the actions that go with this language. *Discourse* is defined by Gee (1999) as

> The different ways we humans integrate with non language "stuff" such as different ways of thinking, acting, interacting, valuing, feeling, believing, and using symbols, tools and other objects in the right places at the right time so as to enact and recognize different identities and activities, give material world certain meanings, distribute social goods in a certain way, make certain sorts of meaningful connections in our experience, and privilege certain symbol systems and ways of knowing over others (p. 13).

This notion suggests that mathematical practices and identities constitute the *D*iscourse of mathematics. Gee (2005a) goes further to distinguish between what he calls "lifeworld" and "academic social language". He views a "lifeworld" as "that domain where we speak and act as "ordinary", "everyday", "non-specialist" people" (p. 22). These are the domains where I presume "ordinary English" is mostly used and where second language learners use their home languages. Gee (2005b; 2005a; 1999) extends the description of languages to include what he calls "social languages". He defines social languages as "a way of using language so as to enact a particular socially-situated identity and carry out a particular socially-situated activity." (p. 20). This definition implies that there are numerous social languages. There could be lifeworld social languages and academic social languages. This distinction could mean that the Nguni mathematics high achievers are proficient in mathematical English social languages and not in lifeworld English social languages. Gee (2005a) contends that success in school has a strong relationship with willingness and ability to cope with academic language.

Elsewhere, Gee has also made reference to what he termed "primary discourse" and "secondary discourses" (Gough and Bock 2001). According to Gough and Bock (2001), the secondary discourse requires "a degree of expert knowledge and language to produce and comprehend and is something that is, in rather simplistic terms, learned and refined rather than acquired" (96). Given these two distinctions, English language acquisition can be likened to a secondary discourse which second language learners use to acquire another higher level discourse (referred earlier as the academic social language) that is specific to the disciplines they learn in school. This, therefore, suggests that for second language learners, their language learning trajectory is a continuum, where on the lower end they learn their home language followed by the language of instruction in school and then the academic social language of the discipline on the other.

CONCLUSION

The issue of language will remain sensitive and controversial unless more studies are conducted to provide more insights on the role of language on mathematics achievement. Numerous studies that have been conducted in the past have established the relationship between language proficiency and mathematics achievement on studies where the participants were at their initial stages of learning in a language they were still learning. The study by Worswick (2004; 2001) has provided a strong indication that ordinary language has a strong influence during the early stages of learning and this influence becomes weaker as learners move towards what Gee refers to as "academic social language". The study conducted in Swaziland seems to resonate with Worswick's findings in that it also suggests that low proficiency in the social language of English as a school discipline does not necessarily result in underachievement in mathematics. The weak correlation between English language grades and mathematics grades does not imply a lack of a strong relationship between language and achievement in mathematics but seems to point to a strong relationship between achievement in mathematics and the academic social language of mathematics. Given the exclusion rates of Swazi learners, there is need to establish the extent of the exclusion of second language learners who come from FLLE environments in Southern Africa to inform possible language policy reformulation in higher institutions of learning.

REFERENCES

Adler, J. (2001). *Teaching and learning mathematics in multilingual classrooms*. Dordrecht, Netherlands: Kluwer Academic Publishers.

Alexander, N. (Ed.). (2001). *Bilingual education as a strategy in post-colonial Africa* (1st ed.). Cape Town: University of Cape Town.

Bamgbose, A. (1999). African language development and language planning - Language and development in Africa. *Social Dynamics, 25*(1), 13 – 30.

Barwell, R. (2003). Linguistic discrimination: an issue for research in mathematics education [1]. *For the Learning of Mathematics, 23*(2), 37 – 43.

Bokamba, E. G. (1995). The politics of language planning in Africa: Critical choices for the 21st century. In M. Putz (Ed.), *Discrimination through language in Africa? Perspectives on the Namibian experience,* (pp. 11 – 27). Berlin and New York: Mouton de Gruyter.

Dempster, E. R. (2007). Textual strategies for answering multiple choice questions among South African learners: what can we learn from TIMSS 2003. *African Journal of Research in Mathematics, Science and Technology Education, 11*(1), 47 – 60.

Dlamini, C. (2008). Policies for enhancing success or failure? A glimpse into the language policy dilemma of one bilingual African state. *Pythagoras, 67,* 5-13.

Garcia, O. (1997). Bilingual education. In F. Coulmas (Ed.), *The handbook of sociolingustics* (pp. 405-419). Oxford: Blackwell.

Gee, J. P. (1999). *An introduction to discourse analysis theory and method* (First Ed.). New York and London: Routledge.

Gee, J. P. (2005a). Language in the science classroom: Academic social languages as the heart of school-based literacy. In R. Yerrick, W. Roth; L. Erlbaum (Eds.) *Establishing scientific classroom discourse Communities: multiple voices of teaching and learning research,* (pp 19 – 39). New Jersey: Lawrence Erlbaum Associates, Inc.

Gee, J. P. (2005b). *An introduction to discourse analysis theory and method* (Second Ed.). New York and London: Routledge.

Gorgorio, N., and. Planas, N. (2001). Teaching mathematics in multilingual classrooms. *Educational Studies in Mathematics, 47,* 7 – 33.

Gough, D. N. and Bock, Z. (2001). Alternative perspectives on orality, literacy and education: A view from South Africa. *Journal of Multilingual & Multicultural Development, 22*(2), 95 – 111.

Halai, A. (2009). Politics and practice of learning mathematics in multilingual classrooms: Lessons from Pakistan. In R. Barwell (Ed.), *Multilingualism in mathematics classrooms,* (pp. 47 – 62). Bristol, Buffalo, Toronto: Multilingual Matters.

Howie, S. (2001). Mathematics and science performance in Grade 8 in South Africa 1998/1999. Pretoria: Human Sciences Research Council.

Howie, S., and Pietersen, J. J. (2001). Mathematics literacy of final year students: South African realities. *Studies in Educational Evaluation, 27,* 7 – 25.

Lockwood, K. (2005). *Annotated bibliography* (Vol. 2005). Retrieved March 22, 2006 from *http://mathforum.org.*

MacGregor, M., and Stacey, K. (1999). An exploration of aspects of language proficiency and algebra learning. *Journal of Research in Mathematics Education, 30*(4), 449 – 467.

Mesthrie, R. (2006). Language, transformation and development: a sociolinguistic appraisal of post-apartheid South African language policy and practice. *South African Linguistics and Applied Language Studies, 24*(2), 151 – 163.

Pimm, D. (1982). Mathematics? I speak it fluently. In A. Floyd (Ed.), *Developing mathematical thinking,* (pp. 139 – 150). Wokington: Addison Wesley.

Setati, M., Adler, J., Reed. Y., and Bapoo, A. (2002). Code-switching and other language practices in mathematics, science and English language classrooms in South Africa. In J. Adler, & Y. Reed (Ed.), *Challenges of teacher development,* (pp. 72 – 93). Pretoria: Van Schaik.

Thompson, C. F. (2008). *Swaziland business year book.* Mbabane: Christina Forsyth Thompson.

Vesely, R. (2000*). Multilingual environments for survival: The impact of English on Xhosa-speaking students in Cape Town.* Cape Town: University of Cape Town.

Worswick, C. (2001). School performance of the children of immigrants in Canada, 1994-98. *Statistics Canada No. 11F0019-No.178.*

Worswick, C. (2004). Adaptation and inequality: Children of immigrants in Canadian schools. *Canadian Journal of Economics, 37*(1), 53 – 77.

Zaaiman, H., (1998). Selecting students for mathematics and science: The challenge facing higher education in South Africa. Pretoria, 134 Pretorius Street: HSRC Publishers.

Zevenbergen, R. (2000). "Cracking the Code" of mathematics classrooms: School success as a function of linguistic, social, and cultural background. In J. Boaler (Ed.), *Multiple perspective on mathematics teaching and learning* (1ˢᵗ Ed), pp. 201 – 242. London.

In: Language and Literacy Education in a Challenging World   ISBN: 978-1-61761-198-8
Editors: T. Lê, Q. Lê, and M. Short   © 2011 Nova Science Publishers, Inc.

Chapter 15

THE EFFECT OF LINGUALITY ON METACOGNITIVE AWARENESS OF READING STRATEGIES

Alireza Karbalaei

ABSTRACT

This chapter investigated whether significant differences exist between dominant and balanced bilingual readers in their metacognitive awareness and perceived use of specific strategies when reading for academic purposes in English by using an ex-post facto design. Ninety three undergraduate college students in India (56 dominant vs. 37 balanced) completed an instrument designed to measure their metacognitive awareness of reading strategies after they read some reading comprehension passages. The results indicated that there is no significant difference between dominant and balanced bilingual students in employing metacognitive reading strategies and their sub-categorie . Furthermore, no significant difference was reported in the scores of students with high and low proficiency in their aforementioned strategies. Finally, the interaction between linguality and proficiency was found to be non-significant in using metacognitive reading strategies and their sub-categories indicating that pattern of these strategies scores are similar for both high and low-proficient students without considering the bilinguality background.

Keywords: metacognitive reading strategies, global, problem-solving, and support strategies, dominant and balanced bilingual.

INTRODUCTION

Multilingualism is the natural potential available to every normal human being rather than an unusual exception. Environmental factors may fail to provide the opportunity to learn another language resulting in monolingual speakers: "Given the approach environment, two languages are as normal as two lungs" (Cook, 2001, p. 23); "A theory purporting to account for universal language learnability cannot be considered adequate if it excludes the non-monolingual speakers of this world" (Satterfield, 1999, p. 137).

The ability to speak two languages is often seen as something of a remarkable achievement, particularly in the English-speaking countries. Since 70% of the Earth's population is thought to be bilingual or multilingual (Trask, 1999), there is good reason to believe that bilingualism is the norm for the majority of people around the world.

Defining bilingualism might at first seem self-evident: a bilingual person can speak more than one language. However, defining the term becomes more complicated when one starts to consider what knowing a language actually means and how one defines things such as fluency. Bilinguals' language proficiency may vary considerably from being able to communicate to some extent in a second language, to having considerable skills in both languages (Crystal, 1987, p. 362). Since the speakers' skills in a second language might vary from native-like competence to knowing only a few areas of research, there are different degrees of bilingualism.

Also, several researchers have attempted to define bilingualism with the help of dichotomies and different kinds of scales. Usually they relate to three central criteria in bilingualism: the level of proficiency, means of acquisition, and age of acquisition. The extreme view of bilingualism is mastering both languages with native-like competence, and being able to use either language in any context or situation. This is often referred to as *balanced bilingualism* .i.e. being approximately equally fluent in two languages (Baker, 1996, p.8). On the other hand, *dominant bilinguals* are those who only master their second language (L2) partially but who have native competence in their first language (L1), or as Hamers & Blanc (1989) believe they have superior competence in one of their two languages.

Concerning advantages of bilingualism, research conducted has concluded that bilingualism can have positive effects on individuals, if their competence in one of their L1s is sufficient. Cummins and Swain (1986) reported some advantages existing among bilinguals including better linguistic skills, orientation to linguistic structures, sensitivity to feedback cues, general intellectual development and divergent thinking. In addition, Diaz and Klinger (1991) stated the advantages as being concept formation, classification, creativity, analogical reasoning, meta-linguistic skills and sensitivity to language structure and detail.

Regarding the context in which a person is experiencing his/her second language or more, South Asian bilingualism, in general and Indian bilingualism, in particular provide an excellent progressive, realistic, contemporary, and multicultural windows on the phenomenon of bilingualism. Shaped largely by the natural democratic focus of linguistic, accommodation and assimilation, they reveal the complexity of multiple bilingual language choices and use which is conducive to linguistic diversity and additive bilingualism. There is no denial that language rivalry and conflict are natural consequences of bilingualism. However, contrary to the popular conception, language rivalry in India often does not lead to linguistic and national disintegration. It provides an impetus to the focus of national development and anti-discrimination.

Bilingualism in India is a stable and a natural phenomenon. The acquisition of an additional language does not commonly lead to gradual loss of the first language; the possession of an additional language is like possessing an additional garment, or tool, needed for a different situation or purpose. It is not transient as in the case of migrant communities in some countries like the USA, or where it is an intermediate, temporary phase in the movement from monolingualism in one language to monolingualism in another. It is the expected behavioural norm when languages are in contact, and not an exceptional one.

In the last decade or so knowledge of the breadth of bilingualism has grown. Discussion of bilingualism has concentrated on "the many kinds and degrees of bilingualism and bilingual situations" (Crystal, 2003, p.51), leading to in-depth description of the varied circumstances involved in bilingualism, and anticipating the recent call for understanding the bilingual situation through its context and its purpose (Edwards, 2004). For instance, Sundman (1994) conducted a study in Finnish schools which showed positive results in balanced bilingualism. The balanced bilinguals were also successful in other subjects besides their L1 / writing skills.

On the other hand, the study of metacognition - what readers know about themselves, the task of reading and various reading strategies – has proven to be a fruitful area of investigation. In fact, learners' metacognitive strategies knowledge involves thinking about the reading processes, planning for reading, monitoring comprehension while reading and verifying what is read, as well as specific steps in problem-solving during comprehension (Flavell, 1987; O'Malley & Chamot, 1990; Wenden, 1991; Young & Oxford, 1997). For example, from research focused on mainstream monolingual English speakers, we know that older and more successful readers know more about themselves as learners, that they approach different genre in distinct ways, and that they use more reading strategies (Baker & Brown, 1984; Garner, 1987).

Concerning metacognitive reading strategies of bilinguals, little research has been done by different scholars in this field. For example, in a comparative study of the bilingual reading (Spain- English) of native-language Spanish speakers and native language English speakers, Carrell (1985) drew a conclusion that only the better readers adjusted their reading strategies depending on the text language, and their perceived proficiency in that language. In another study, Jimenez et al. (1995) focused on understanding what eight bilingual Latin/o sixth and seventh grade students in the US knew about their reading processes, use of their reading strategies across two languages, how they used certain strategies while reading, and under what conditions they invoked such strategies. Several important findings were reported. Successful bilingual readers "tended to have a unitary view of reading. Secondly, almost all of the successful bilingual readers demonstrated awareness of several strategies, with some limited actual use of certain strategies. Finally, the successful bilingual readers were aware of the "transference of knowledge" across languages. In other words, they "knew that information and strategies learned or acquired in one language could be used to comprehend text written in another language" (Garcia et al.,1998, p.204).

In addition, positive relationship between target language proficiency and strategy use has been reported in a number of studies. For example, Baker and Brown (1984) determined that proficient readers employ a number of metacognitive strategies during reading that assist them to understand a text. Also, as Oxford and Burry-Stock (1995) indicated, Indian college students having a high proficiency in English reported a significantly higher mean frequency of strategy use than students having a lower proficiency in English. Moreover, successful language learners tended to employ strategies in an orchestrated way, while unsuccessful learners did not (Vandergrift, 2003).

On the other hand, Anderson (1991) investigated the individual differences in using reading strategies and concluded that there was no single set of processing strategies that significantly contributed to success. Both high and low scoring readers appeared to be using the same kinds of strategies, although high scoring students seemed to be applying strategies more efficiently and appropriately in comparison to low scoring ones. Another result which could be drawn from this study was that reading is not only a matter of knowing which strategies to use, but also the reader must know how to successfully apply those strategies.

Taking the prior research into account, these studies have not considered the impact of bilinguality and proficiency on awareness and use of metacognitive reading strategies in an ESL context. Therefore, the following hypotheses are suggested for the current chapter.

1.   Dominant and balanced bilingual students differ significantly in employing metacognitive reading strategies, in general and global, problem-solving, and support reading strategies, in particular.

2.   There is a significant difference between low and high-proficient students in utilizing total metacognitive reading strategies and their sub-categories including global, problem-solving, and support reading strategies.

3.   There will be significant interaction between bilinguality and proficiency in global, problem-solving, and support reading strategies, in particular, and metacognitive reading strategies, in general.

METHODOLOGY

Participants

The participants in this chapter consisted of 93 undergraduate students from three private and public colleges in Mysore, India. These were freshman and sophomore students in full-time study, majoring in English Literature. They had all completed 12 years of schooling and had graduated from high school prior to enrolling in college. These students were between 18 and 28 years of age with the mean of 20 (M=20). The colleges were randomly selected.

A self-evaluation questionnaire on bilinguality was administered and analyzed from which two groups of students were obtained:

Group A: 26 female and 30 male dominant bilinguals
Group B: 17 female and 20 male balanced bilinguals

It should be noted that a *dominant* bilingual is a person who is more proficient in one of the two languages (in most cases native-like). In this study the participants were capable of communicating in Kannada and English but were more dominant in Kannada. On the other hand, a *balanced* bilingual is someone who is more or less equally proficient in both languages, but will not necessarily pass for a native speaker in both languages. These participants' mother tongue was Kannada but were also native-like in English so were regarded as balanced bilinguals. That is, although they are not native speakers in English, they use it in their daily conversations competently. The participants were homogenous in both groups regarding variables such as age, teaching method used by schools, and number of hours dedicated to English instruction.

Materials
In order to meet the purpose of this study, the following instruments were used:

- *Language Proficiency Test (TOEFL):* This test consisted of multiple-choice grammar, vocabulary, and reading questions. Before this test was utilized for the real sample, a pilot study was carried out on 20 students with the intention of testing the reliability of the proficiency test. Its reliability, through the K-R21 formula, came to be 0.75, which confirmed the appropriateness of this test for use in the study.

- *Reading Comprehension Test:* The test of reading comprehension was taken from Kit of Reading Comprehension (Rajinders. 2008). The time allocated to this part of the study was 60 minutes and was determined at the piloting stage. The reading passages used in this chapter included a general content, which were of interest to the students. Also, running through K-R21, it was demonstrated that this reading comprehension test was reliable (0.78) for the goals in this chapter. Subsequently, the test was suitable for this study after the correlation coefficient (0.70) between the TOEFL proficiency test and the test of reading in English was calculated in the pilot study.

- *Background Questionnaire:* A background questionnaire was developed by the investigator for the purpose of eliciting information about the participants including age, gender, place of living, years of studying English, and medium of instruction (see Appendix 1).

- *Metacognitive Awareness of Reading Strategies Inventory (MARSI):* The students' metacognitive awareness of reading strategies was assessed through this instrument, which was designed for measuring adolescent and adult students' awareness and use of reading strategies while reading academic or school-related materials. The MARSI questionnaire (see Appendix 3) measures three broad categories of reading strategies including:

  1. Global Reading Strategies (GLOB), which can be thought of as generalized or global reading strategies aimed at setting the stage for the reading act (for instance, setting purpose for reading, previewing text content, predicting what the text is about, etc.);

  2. Problem-Solving Strategies (PROB), which are localized, focused problem-solving or repair strategies used when problems develop in understanding textual information (for instance, checking one's understanding upon encountering conflicting information, re-reading for better understanding, etc.); and

  3. Support Reading Strategies (SUP), which involve using the support mechanisms or tools aimed at sustaining responsiveness to reading (for instance, use of reference materials like dictionaries and other support systems).

The 30-item questionnaire was validated by Mokhtari and Reichard (2002) using large subject population representing students with equivalent reading abilities ranging from middle school to college. The internal consistency reliability coefficient for its three above subscales ranged from 0.89 to 0.93 and reliability for the total sample was 0.93, showing a reasonably dependable measure of metacognitive awareness of reading strategies. However, to confirm that the questionnaire was reliable for the subjects of this study, it was given to 20 students in the pilot study. Based on the data collected, the reliability coefficient alpha for this questionnaire was calculated to be 0.70.

– *Self-evaluation Proficiency Scale:* This questionnaire was utilized to measure the degree of bilinguality of the subjects, and classify them based on *Dominant* and *Balanced* bilinguals. They were asked to evaluate their abilities on a 4-point scale in the languages popular within the state such as Kannada, English, Hindi, Tamil, Urdu and Telugu. In addition, they were asked to write down any other language they spoke which was not mentioned in the questionnaire. For this, the researcher developed a questionnaire which included five tables; different languages and different skills a person had were provided in each table. Next, students were requested to self-evaluate their level of proficiency in different languages based on 4-point Likert scale varying from excellent (1) to very weak (4) (see Appendix 2). Like other instruments in this chapter, this self-made questionnaire was piloted on 20 students of similar backgrounds in order to determine the internal consistency reliability coefficient which was calculated to be 0.68. In addition, in order to increase the reliability of this questionnaire, other researchers in the respective field were asked their opinions on this questionnaire.

Procedure

The following procedures were adopted in order to meet the objectives of this chapter. First, the background questionnaire and the self-evaluation proficiency scale were given to the subjects after some modifications were made due to recommendations given by the advisors. Next, the participants were divided into two groups consisting of a Dominant and Balanced bilinguals group (see Appendix 3) according to their feedback on receptive items of the self-evaluation report. Third, the proficiency of the participants was determined by TOEFL proficiency test (Mean= 17 & SD= 5.60). Based on the results of this test, subjects whose scores were one standard deviation above the mean were considered as high and those who were one below the mean were regarded as low. This extreme groups design resulted in 37 balanced bilinguals (16 high vs. 21 low) and 56 dominant bilinguals (24 high vs. 32 low). Finally, the subjects were given the metacognitive reading strategies questionnaire after completing the reading comprehension test.

RESULTS AND DISCUSSION

After the data collection, the two-way ANOVA was used to find out the significant difference among variables as shown in the following tables.

The results of the two-way ANOVA in the above table indicate that there is no statistically significant difference between balanced and dominant bilinguals in employing total metacognitive reading strategies and its sub-categories including global, problem-solving, in relation to the first hypothesis as the F value of .974 was insignificant at .05 level. However, dominant bilinguals reported a better mean score than balanced ones (105.13 and 103.12, respectively) in total metacognitve reading strategies and their subcategories.By considering these results, the first hypothesis is rejected for both total reading strategies and their subcategories (global, problem-solving, and support).

Table 1 – Mean scores on global, problem-solving, support, and total metacognitive reading strategies of Dominant and Balanced Bilinguals in high and low-proficient groups

Parameters		Linguality				Total	
	Proficiency	Dominant Bilingual		Balanced Bilingual			
		Mean	SD	Mean	SD	Mean	SD
Global	Low	43.75	5.82	42.00	7.12	43.5	6.36
	High	44.37	7.82	43.50	7.07	44.02	7.45
	Total	44.01	6.69	42.64	7.04	43.47	6.83
Support Problem-Solving	Low	28.06	4.51	29.23	4.83	28.52	4.63
	High	30.08	3.83	28.12	5.38	29.30	4.55
	Total	28.92	4.31	28.75	5.04	28.86	4.59
Problem-solving Support	Low	32.06	4.06	32.19	4.67	32.47	4.27
	High	31.66	5.18	31.12	5.61	31.17	5.30
	Total	31.86	4.53	31.72	5.05	31.82	4.72
Total Reading Strategies	Low	103.87	11.17	103.42	12.74	103.69	11.70
	High	106.12	14.55	102.75	14.09	105.27	14.28
	Total	104.51	12.65	103.12	13.15	104.16	12.81

Regarding the second research hypothesis (students with high and low proficiency are significantly different in employing total metacognitive reading strategies and their subcategories), there was no significant difference between high and low-proficient bilinguals in employing these strategies as the obtained F value of .80 was not significant at .05 level. Though, students with high proficiency reported to use more metacognitive reading strategies in all categories except support strategies in comparison to those of low proficiency with mean scores of these two groups (105.27 vs. 103.69). In other words, low-proficient students in both balanced and dominant bilingual groups had better mean score in support reading strategies than high-proficient ones (32.47 vs. 31.17). This means they use these strategies to compensate for their lack of knowledge or vocabulary. Overall, the second hypothesis was rejected for total metacognitive reading strategies and their sub-categories.

Table 2 – Two-way ANOVA result for mean scores on global, problem-solving, support, and total metacognitive reading strategies scores of Dominant and Balanced Bilinguals with high and low-proficient groups

Parameters	Source of variation	F value	df	P value
Global	Between linguality (A)	.793	1	.376
	Between Proficiency (B)	.520	1	.473
	Interaction (A*B)	.088	1	.767
Problem-solving	Between linguality (A)	.159	1	.691
	Between Proficiency (B)	.214	1	.645
	Interaction (A*B)	2.549	1	.114
Support	Between linguality (A)	.041	1	.840
	Between Proficiency (B)	.508	1	.478
	Interaction (A*B)	.107	1	.745
Total metacognitive strategies	Between linguality (A)	.474	1	.493
	Between Proficiency (B)	.080	1	.778
	Interaction (A*B)	.279	1	.599

Analysing the third hypothesis (there will be significant interaction between linguality and proficiency in metacognitive reading strategies, in general, and global, problem-solving, and support strategies, in particular), there was no significant difference between dominant and balanced bilingual groups and proficiency in employing total metacognitive reading strategies (F=.279; p< 0.599), global strategies (F=.088 ; p< 0.76), problem-solving strategies (F= 2.549 ; p< 0.114), and support strategies (F= .107 ; p< 0.745). This suggests that the patterns of metacognitive reading strategies scores are similar for students with high and low proficiency without considering their bilinguality levels. Therefore, the third hypothesis was rejected for total metacognitive reading strategies as well as their sub-categories.

RECOMMENDATIONS

Data analysis of the study investigated that balanced and dominant bilinguals used the same strategies without considering the role of proficiency, as no significant difference was reported between high and low-proficient students. However, an examination of the mean scores of the type of strategies reported by the participants in this chapter indicated that despite the mean differences noted, both groups of bilingual students invoking a low to moderate strategy awareness level with clear preference for using global strategies, followed by support strategies, and problem-solving strategies. These results are completely different from the study done by Mokhtari and Reichard (2004) in which they studied metacognitive awareness of reading strategies in native (US) and EFL (Moroccan) contexts. In this study, students reported using a moderate to high strategy awareness level with a preference for employing problem-solving, followed by support strategies, and global reading strategies.

In exploring the results of the study, teaching different kinds of metacognitive reading strategies is a necessity for teachers regardless of the students' levels of proficiency and bilinguality. Teaching these was found to positively affect both reading performance and strategy use of language learners of varying abilities (Anderson, 1991; Muniz-Swicegood, 1994; Jimenez, 1997). Anderson (1991) found that after strategy instruction in varying contexts, adult second language learners of varying abilities used similar strategies. Muniz-Swicegood (1994) concluded that the bilingual third grade students receiving instruction outperformed the control group in a reading comprehension test. Also, Jimenez (1997) reported that instruction positively influenced the use of cognitive strategies in seventh grade Latino students of a lower proficiency level. As a result, strategy instruction positively benefits bilingual reading.

Considering the relationship between learners' L2 proficiency and strategy use, various empirical studies have indicated that conscious, "tailored" use of strategies is related to achievement and proficiency, and successful learners use a wider variety of strategies to improve their reading skills and performance (Oxford, 1996, p.xi). However, this study showed that this is not the case for undergraduate bilingual students studying English as a second language. Therefore, teachers can teach these strategies irrespective of the role of proficiency in the classroom.

In conclusion, limited amount of research has focused on documenting the development of metacognitive awareness of reading strategies concerning monolinguality and different levels of bilinguality. In other words, do major differences in metacognitive awareness and use of reading strategies exist among different groups of learners studying English in different contexts? This is a thought-provoking question which should be subjected to systematic research.

CONCLUSION

In this chapter, I wanted to explore the metacognitive awareness and perceived use of reading strategies of balanced and dominant bilinguals at undergraduate level while reading academic materials. The data analysis of this study showed that bilinguality and proficiency as the two dependant variables have no impact on the metacognitive awareness of reading strategies. In other words, there is no significant difference between balanced and dominant bilinguals in employing global, problem-solving, and support metacognitive reading strategies without considering the level of proficiency of the students.

ACKNOWLEDGMENT

This paper was a long time in the writing. But the journey was made easier by the help of Prof K. S. Rajyashree, who had been a constant source of inspiration and encouragement to me in this work. I should also express my thanks to the principals, teachers and students of colleges who helped me in this project cheerfully.

REFERENCES

Anderson, N. (1991). Individual differences in strategy use in second language reading and testing. *Modern Language Journal*, *75*, 460–472.

Baker, C. (1996). *Foundations of bilingual education and bilingualism.* Clevedon: Multilingual Matters.

Baker, L., & Brown, X. (1984). Metacognitive skills and reading. In: R. Barr, M. Kamil, P. Mosenthal, P. Pearson (Eds.), *Handbook of reading research* (vol. II), pp.353-394. White Plains, NY: Longman.

Carrell, P. (1985). Facilitating ESL reading by teaching text structure: Classroom implications and applications. *TESOL Quarterly*, *19*, 441–469.

Cook, V. J. (2001). Using the first language in the classroom. *Canadian Modern Review*, *57*(3), 3-49.

Crystal, D. (1987). *The Cambridge encyclopaedia of language.* Cambridge: Cambridge University Press.

Crystal, D. (2003). Bilingual: A dictionary of linguistics and phonetics. Oxford: Blackwell Publishing.

Cummins, J. & Swain, M. (1986). *Bilingualism in education.* London: Longman.

Diaz, R. M. & Klinger, C. (1991). Towards an explanatory model of the interaction between bilingualism and cognitive development. In Bialystok (ed.), *Most of the chapters in this volume were originally presented in the invited symposium "language acquisition and implications for processing in bilingual children" at the meeting of the society for research in child development*, 1987. (pp. 167 – 192). New York, NY, US: Cambridge University Press.

Edwards, J. (2004). Foundations of bilingualism. In T. K. Bhatia & W. C. Ritchie (Eds.), *The handbook of bilingualism,* (pp. 7 – 31). Oxford: Blackwell Publishing.

Flavell, J. H. (1987). Speculations about the nature and development of metacognition. In F. E. Weinert and R. H. Kluwe (Eds), *Metacognition, motivation and understanding* (pp. 21 – 29). Hillsdale, NJ: Erlbaum.

Garcia, G. E.; Jimenez, R. T.; & Pearson, P. D. (1998). Metacognition, childhood bilingualism, and reading. In D. Hacker, J. Dunlowsky, & A. Graesser (Eds), *Metacognition in educational theory and practice* (pp.193 – 219).Lawrence Erlbaum, Mahwah, NJ.

Garner, R. (1987). *Metacognition and reading comprehension.* Norwood, NJ: Ablex Publishing.

Hamers J. F.; & Blanc, M. H. A. (1989). *Bilinguality and bilingualism.* Cambridge: Cambridge University Press.

Jimenez, R. T. (1997). The strategic reading abilities and potential of five low-literacy Latina/o readers in middle school. *Reading Research Quarterly, 32*, 224 – 243.

Jiminez, R.; Garcia, G.; & Pearson, P. (1996). The reading strategies of bilingual Latina/o students who are successful English readers: opportunities and obstacles. *Reading Research Quarterly*, 31, 90 – 112.

Mokhtari, K.; & Reichard, C. (2000). Investigating the strategic reading processes of first and second language readers in two different cultural contexts. *System, 32*, 379 – 394.

Mokhtari, K. & Reichard, C. (2002). Assessing students' metacognitive awareness of reading strategies. *Journal of Educational Psychology*, *94* (2), 249 – 259.

Muniz-Swicegood, M. (1994). The effects of metacognitive reading strategy training on the reading performance and student reading analysis strategies of third grade bilingual students. *Bilingual Research Journal, 18*(1), 83 – 97.

O'Malley, J. M. & Chamot, A. U. (1990). *Learning strategies in second language acquisition*. Cambridge: Cambridge University Press.

Oxford, R. (1995). Gender differences in language learning styles: What do they mean? In J. M. Reid (Ed.), *Learning styles in EFL/ESL classroom* (pp.195 – 222). New York: Heinle and Heinle.

Oxford, R.; & Burry-Stock, J. (1995). Assessing the use of language learning strategies worldwide with the ESL/EFL version of the strategy inventory for language learning (SILL). *System, 23*, 1–23.

Rajinder, S. D. (2008). *Kit of reading comprehension.* New Delhi: Dhillon Group of Publication.

Satterfield, T. (1999). Bilingual selection of syntactic knowledge: extending the principles and parameters approach. Dordrecht: Kluwer.

Sundman, M. (1994). *Tvåspråkigheten i skolan.* Åbo: Åbo Akademi.

Trask, R. L. (1999). The key concepts in language and linguistics. New York: Routledge.

Vandergrift, L. (2003). Orchestrating strategy use: toward a model of the skilled second language listener. *Language Learning, 53*(3), 463–496.

Wenden, A. L. (1991). *Learner strategies for learner autonomy*. London: Prentice-Hall.

Young, D. J.; & Oxford, R. L. (1997). A gender-related analysis of strategies used to process written input in the native language and a foreign language. *Applied Language Learning, 8* (1), 43–73.

APPENDIX 1

Students pro-forma

Attention: Please answer the questions honestly. We keep them strictly confidential.

1. Name of the student: ………………

2. Age: ……………..

3. Gender……………

4. Name of college……………

5. Class studying:…………………..

6. Medium of instruction: ………………..…….

7. Are you coming from Urban or Rural areas? ……………………………

8. I have ....familiarity with English language.

    a. complete

    b. average

    c. a little

9. How many years have you been studying English except the usual classes in school? ....years ....months

10. What is your purpose of learning English?

    a. To continue education

    b. To travel

    c. To find a good job

    d. To compete with other students

    e. Others (please write)

11. My attitude toward English is....................

    a. positive

    b. negative

    c. no comment

APPENDIX 2

Measurement of degree of bilingualism

Please indicate the language or languages you know, (Table 1) and use with different groups (Table 2 – 5). Please place one of the following numbers in each cell to indicate your competence in these skills of language(s): Excellent=1; Good=2; Weak=3;   Very weak =4

1) Self

Name of language	Understand	Speak	Read	Write
Kannada				
Urdu				
Hindi				
Telugu				
Marathi				
English				
Tamil				
Others(specify):				

2) Language(s) used with Friends

Name of language	Understand	Speak	Read	Write
Kannada				
Urdu				
Hindi				
Telugu				
Marathi				
English				
Tamil				
Others(specify):				

3) Language(s) used with Brothers/Sisters

Name of language	Understand	Speak	Read	Write
Kannada				
Urdu				
Hindi				
Telugu				
Marathi				
English				
Tamil				
Others(specify):				

4) Language(s) used with Parents

Name of language	Understand	Speak	Read	Write
Kannada				
Urdu				
Hindi				
Telugu				
Marathi				

4) Language(s) used with Parents (Continued)

Name of language	Understand	Speak	Read	Write
English				
Tamil				
Others(specify):				

5) Language(s) used with Neighbours

Name of language	Understand	Speak	Read	Write
Kannada				
Urdu				
Hindi				
Telugu				
Marathi				
English				
Tamil				
Others(specify):				

APPENDIX 3

Metacognitive Awareness of Reading Strategies Inventory

Direction: Listed below are statements about what people do when they read academic or school-rated materials such as textbooks or library books. Five numbers follow each statement (1,2,3,4,5), and each number means the following:

- 1 means " I **never or almost never** do this."
- 2 means " I do this **only occasionally.**
- 3 means " I **sometimes** do this."
- 4 means " I **usually** do this."
- 5 means " I **always** or **almost always** do this."

Strategy

1. I have a purpose in mind when I read. **(Glob)**
2. I take notes while reading to help me understand what I read. **(Sup)**

3. I summarize what I read to reflect on important information in the text. **(Sup)**
4. I try to get back on track when I lose concentration. **(Prob)**
5. I underline or circle information in the text to help me remember it. **(Sup)**
6. I use reference materials such as dictionaries to help me understand what I read. **(Sup)**
7. I use tables, figures, and pictures in text to increase my understanding. **(Glob)**
8. I use context clues to help me better understand what I am reading. **(Glob)**
9. I paraphrase (restate ideas in my own words) to better understand what I read. **(Sup)**
10. I guess the meaning of unknown words by separating different parts of a word. **(Prob)**
11. I think about what I know to help me understand what I read. **(Glob)**
12. I preview the text to see what it is about before reading it. **(Glob)**
13. When text becomes difficult, I read aloud to help me understand what I read. **(Sup)**
14. I think about whether the content of the text fits my reading purpose. **(Prob)**
15. I read slowly but carefully to be sure I understand what I am reading. **(Prob)**
16. I discuss what I read with others to check my understanding. **(Sup)**
17. I skim the text first by noting characteristics like length and organization. **(Glob)**
18. I adjust my reading speed according to what I am reading. **(Prob)**
19. I decide what to read closely and what to ignore. **(Glob)**
20. When text becomes difficult, I pay closer attention to what I am reading. **(Prob)**
21. I stop from time to time and think about what I am reading. **(Prob)**
22. I try to picture or visualize information to help remember what I read. **(Prob)**
23. I use typological aids like boldface and italics to identify key information. **(Glob)**
24. I critically analyze and evaluate the information presented in the text. **(Glob)**
25. I go back and forth in the text to find relationship among ideas in it. **(Sup)**
26. I check my understanding when I come across conflicting information. **(Glob)**
27. I try to guess what the material is about when I read. **(Glob)**
28. When text becomes difficult, I reread to increase my understanding. **(Prob)**
29. I ask myself questions I like to have answered in the text. **(Sup)**
30. I check to see if my guesses about the text are right or wrong. **(Glob)**

In: Language and Literacy Education in a Challenging World   ISBN: 978-1-61761-198-8
Editors: T. Lê, Q. Lê, and M. Short   © 2011 Nova Science Publishers, Inc.

Chapter 16

THE CHALLENGE OF READING COMPREHENSION

Ian Hay and Gary Woolley

ABSTRACT

For successful reading comprehension to occur the reader should have the following attributes: background knowledge of the text; fluent word recognition and decoding skills of the words in the text; knowledge of the vocabulary and the meaning of the words in the text; an understanding of how the text is constructed; as well as task persistence. Successful comprehension of text is also linked to the readers' abilities to effectively plan what they are to read, and to review what they have read. Because students' develop their reading comprehension skills over-time, they need to develop the self-confidence and proficiency in knowing how, where, and when to apply a range of comprehension strategies that can be used with different text forms. While these issues will be reviewed in this chapter, the problem is that at the classroom level there is often an over reliance on testing comprehension, rather than teaching students the skills to be better at comprehending texts. The reality is that good reading comprehension is often difficult to teach, particularly if the readers are from disadvantaged backgrounds and they have limited vocabulary, word recognition, memory, or language skills. What is certain is that readers across the grades need effective instruction, feedback, and support to enhance the students' reading comprehension development.

Keywords:comprehension, language, memory, vocabulary, fluency, context, summarization, reading, strategies.

INTRODUCTION

Students' ability to comprehend what they read is at the very core of the reading and education process, and while for some readers this skill is achieved with ease, for many it is a challenge. Any text, be it in a short or long print form or in a multi-media form, is successfully comprehended under certain conditions. That is, successful comprehension is the outcome of the interplay of at least three factors: the skill of the reader, the complexity of the text, and the task demands or purpose for doing the reading. For example, a middle school student may be able to successfully read, understand, and enjoy a book, such as *Harry Potter*, but struggle to make any sense of the content of his or her textbook in science. There are a number of important points as to why this challenge occurs: first, not all texts are read for the same purpose; second not all texts are at the same level of complexity; and third, while many reading skills transfer from one reading situation to another, different reading strategies may need to be engaged if meaning is to be achieved with different texts. The challenge for all teachers is: how can they facilitate the successful comprehension of the texts that their students encounter in their classrooms, be that classroom a grade one classroom, or a grade five classroom, or a grade twelve classroom? [The challenge is also that many teachers underestimate the importance of text comprehension for their students' learning and their students' ability to comprehend the texts in their classrooms. Teachers also underestimate the amount of time and effort they need to spend in supporting and teaching their students to be able to comprehend their in-class reading texts (Ehren, 2009). Addressing these challenges is the purpose of this chapter.

READING IS A MEANING MAKING PROCESS

At the most basic level, effective comprehension of print or multi media text involves the reader being able to do three activities simultaneously: (1) decode the words; (2) know the meaning of those individual words; and (3) be able to reason about the text as a whole. Thus, reading comprehension needs to be seen as a complex and multidimensional process.

Many students with reading comprehension difficulties also show difficulties and delays in their ability to handle expressive language (speaking the language), such as selecting the "right" word in a conversation, as well as having difficulties with their receptive language abilities (being able to listen and understand oral information) (Catts, 2009). Typically, they also have difficulties with the pragmatics of language, such as being able to understand and use metaphors, similes, and alliteration. This strong link between language ability and reading ability is understandable given that reading is the interpretation of the symbolic and written representation of the spoken word. Comprehending the written form of a language is significantly related to the students' vocabulary knowledge in that language. In particular, for children from grade three onwards, the successful comprehension of a read text is highly dependent on both their fluent word recognition skills and on an average or above average vocabulary (their knowledge of word meanings). The absence of one of these attributes is highly predictive of students' poor reading comprehension. For example, there is a significant correlation between oral receptive vocabulary in first grade and students' reading comprehension in their eleventh grade ($r = 0.55$) (Biemiller & Boot, 2005).

WORD LEVEL PROCESSING

Fluent word recognition and decoding skills are assumed to facilitate the good comprehension of texts because they free up the students' working memory. As a consequence the reader can concentrate on gaining meaning at the text level, rather than at the word or alphabet level. For example, when children first learn to sound out words, they are required to use concentrated effort and focused attention in using their newly acquired skills of joining sounds and alphabetical shapes together. Because working memory has limited cognitive "space", meaning is more efficiently processed in larger chunks, such as at the word, phrase and sentence level. The larger the chunk of text being processed into memory the more meaningful the comprehension (Perfetti, 2007). It is also easier for this new "incoming" reading information to be linked with other stored knowledge relevant to the topic being read. Unless teachers are able to adapt their teaching approach and encourage students to read words fluently, heavy demands are made on readers' memory during a slow and tedious word decoding process that requires readers to identify each succeeding word (Nation & Norbury, 2005). While many primary teachers understand this problem, as it is more apparent in the early stages of students' learning to read, the same issue also occurs in the upper grades, particularly if the text contains too many new words of specific meaning that are unknown to the reader. The message that teachers across the grades have to remember is that comprehension of any text is detrimentally affected when the readers' memory capacity becomes overtaxed. Typically, by the time these readers reach the end of a sentence or the end of the passage they have little or no memory of the text information that they identified earlier and so are unable to answer correctly the comprehension questions related to that text. One of the advantages in *re-reading* text is that the increasing familiarity of the material reduces the demands made on memory by the decoding process, thereby allowing students to attend to the meaning of the text.

VOCABULARY

As stated already, students' vocabulary development is essential to their academic development (Ricketts, Nation, & Bishop, 2007). It has been estimated that for most children, their receptive vocabulary at school entry can be somewhere between 5,000 and 10,000 words. However, many children from language-impoverished backgrounds may have up to 4,000 fewer words than their more experienced peers. Children who enter school with limited vocabularies are at risk for reading comprehension difficulties in later primary or middle school. Generally, children starting school with more than adequate vocabularies find reading easy, read more widely, and make better academic progress (Hay & Fielding-Barnsley, 2009). As a consequence, they tend to read more challenging texts and learn new vocabulary as they encounter unfamiliar words. Thus, good readers tend to have fuller and richer vocabularies, because they are able to derive meanings for new or less familiar words from the context. In contrast, children with limited vocabularies generally find reading more difficult, avoid reading, and learn fewer words in context resulting in an ever widening of the comprehension gap between themselves and their more successful reading peers (Stanovich, 1986).

The purpose of reading is to gain meaning from text. A critical issue for teaching is that by the end of third grade most children can "read" and say more words correctly than they can understand in context. The other issue here is that children who start school with a smaller vocabulary "grow" their vocabulary in schools at a slower rate. The evidence is that while the average child gains about 860 root-word meanings per year (around 2.4 new root words per day), for children from disadvantaged communities there is about a 40% drop (with this group only gaining about 1.8 new words per day) (Hart & Risley, 1995). This reduction is assumed to reflect that children with a less developed initial vocabulary benefit less from just listening to words and they need the meaning of words explained more. That is, they benefit from more explicit instruction about the meaning of words and how these words change because of the syntax of the sentence.

This instruction does not always have to occur within a whole class activity and the following is a vocabulary enhancement strategy that is effective in a small group setting. For each student:

- Underline two to four interesting words per paragraph.

- Explain why these words are interesting.

- Talk about these words and their place in the text.

- Look at the word meaning, use alternative words that could be used, consider the word family of these words.

Another helpful strategy is using cloze activities to teach vocabulary. Students can be encouraged to find alternative words to those in the set text, but still maintain the overall meaning of the text passage. Importantly, cloze can also focus on the pronouns used in the texts that some students from disadvantaged backgrounds find difficult to master and so reduce the students' comprehension of the text. Similarly, selected adjectives or adverbs can be taken out of the text and the reader encouraged to substitute other words. Cloze as a whole class reading comprehension activity should not be seen as a testing tool but as an important opportunity for students to play with words and to understand how a range of different words can be added to a text to enrich or change its meaning. For example, a cloze sentence, such as "The _____cat is _____" can produce a range of vocabulary experience, such as: "The forlorned cat is slumbering". This group activity can involve the teacher putting the students' word suggestions on the board so that the other students can see and say the words and to use the different words in an alternative setting. For example, an extension of the work on the word "forlorned" may produce the following: "Forlorned and drenched the two boys headed for the comfort of their home". The critical issue here is that by increasing the students' vocabulary knowledge and their understanding of concepts the students build up their prior experience and background knowledge that is essential for them to comprehend even more difficult texts in the future.

Cloze is also a valuable procedure to introduce the meaning of technical or scientific vocabulary to the students so they can compare and understand these words in relationship with everyday words. The aim here is to have students incorporate into their conversations and writings the more advanced and precise word. For example:

| Everyday word: | work out | suggest | information |
| Technical word: | conclude | hypothesise | data |

Having readers comprehend the vocabulary of science words has a significant impact on the comprehension of that science text. Comprehending science text is often difficult because a new topic in science typically involves a number of unknown concepts and vocabulary. In science texts new words also come in groups that are often nested in new concepts. For example, readers can only fully comprehend the following passage if they understand the meaning of the words "generates", "charge", "possibtive[and] negative particles from a a scientific perspective.

Lightning is a form of electricity that occurs in nature. The movement of air and water droplets in a cloud generates a charge where the positive particles sit near the top of the cloud and the negative particles sit at the bottom. When the cloud meets another cloud, the positive particles from one flow to the negative particles in the other, which is expressed as light (lightning) and sound (thunder).

Because of the density of the above text and the linking of a number of new concepts together, this passage needs significant unpacking and explicit teaching if comprehension is to be achieved. The problem is that unless readers are provided with either an opportunity to engage in an inquiry based science program or are given additional information or support that will build the background to understanding the vocabulary, they are often unable to make meaning from the text or make appropriate inferences from the text passage (Pearson, Hiebert, & Kamil, 2007).

Successful vocabulary instruction needs to occur within the framework of the passage or text being studied (Hay et al., 2007). This may include the direct teaching of selected words, as well as providing background information associated with the text being explored. Text selection is thus an essential issue in terms of encouraging students' reading and comprehension.

In terms of text use in a reading program teachers need to encourage readers to:

- Use texts that are interesting, comprehensible, and sufficiently varied so that the individual can relate to it in terms of interest and motivation.

- Incorporate daily read texts that are personally interesting and *easy to read* so that readers can consolidate their learning of skills and strategies.

- Read *more challenging* texts with support in order to stretch the readers' knowledge and skill repertoire and to establish new prior knowledge for future reading.

One way of selecting texts that incorporate all of the above is to follow the following formula that estimates the reading difficulty of text, in relationship to the individual reader.

- Count 100 words.

- Have the reader start reading aloud and the observer count the reading errors. (If the reader self-corrects do not count it as an error.).

- After reading the 100 words have the reader stop and the observer count the errors.

- If there are 0 to 4 errors the text is at an easy or *independent* reading level, and good for consolidation and reading for pleasure.

- If there are 6 to 10 errors, the text is at the *instructional* level ,and reading and comprehension support is required.

- If there are more than 10 errors the text is too difficult and it is at a *frustration* level, and comprehension and meaning will be lost.

While some commercially available texts are designed to allow students to apply specific word decoding and specific comprehension skills, there is little evidence to support the necessity to exclusively rely on such special instructional texts for this purpose (Reutzel, 2007). In particular, the current corpus of children's books contains numerous samples of authentic texts that provide many of the opportunities students need in terms of decoding, vocabulary development, and comprehension, in a framework of interesting story lines and creative illustrations. It is how teachers use the text as a teaching tool that is the decisive issue. Furthermore, there is little evidence to suggest that having students fill out reading worksheets is equal to teaching students to be better readers or comprehenders using authentic texts. Worksheets and testing sheets may provide practice and diagnostic information but they should not be seen as a substitute for individual dialogue and the student/teacher feedback that is so important in the learning process (Hattie, 2009).

FLUENCY AND COGNITIVE LOAD

To be successful in text comprehension readers need to be able to identify and process the information contained in phrases and sentences and understand the relationships between sentences. They need to understand the purpose of reading a particular text and to be aware if they are failing to meet the requirements of the reading task. Frequently, readers in the middle primary grades struggle to make the transition from learning-to-read to being independent readers, able to read-to-learn and achieve the various demands of the curriculum. As successful readers process text they are active, they skim the text and make predictions, they relate ideas in text to their prior knowledge, they construct images, generate questions, and summaries (Woolley & Hay, 2007). Furthermore, they identify the purpose of the reading task and the main ideas in the text, monitor their ongoing understanding of the story or content (repairing breakdowns when comprehension failures occur), and integrate the content of the text with what they already know. This monitoring is referred to as metacognitive since it refers to the reader/learner "thinking about thinking". When the goals of the reading task are not being met, the successful reader modifies and/or substitutes strategies to remedy the situation (e.g., re-reading).

One of the better known oral reading strategies for facilitating reading fluency is repeated readings whereby the reader re-reads a short text passage until the text flow and fluency is sufficiently developed. Another fluency enhancing strategy is referred to as the "neurological impress method" (NIM) where readers are encouraged to read in conjunction with a more expert reader. The expert reader reads at a faster pace than the novice reader would normally read. The novice reader is encouraged to concentrate on the flow of the text while keeping up with the expert reader as they read orally together. Singing songs from sheets, group oral reading activities, and poetry reciting are other activities that promote reading fluency and expression.

The classroom practice of students reading aloud around the class using the same text is not encouraged, unless significant work has been completed on this text with the students. While such reading aloud may be rewarding for skilled readers, their less skilled peers can be discouraged by this practice because it emphasises their reading inadequacy to their peers. Students do, however, need to experience the pleasure of listening to a variety of texts read aloud and for teachers to frequently model fluent and expressive oral reading. In these situations, the teacher can talk with the students about the story, the events in the story, and the meaning of the words within the texts.

BACKGROUND AND CONTEXT KNOWLEDGE

Readers who possess a rich prior knowledge about a topic being read characteristically have a deeper understanding than their peers with poorer prior knowledge and world experiences. This is because many less skilled readers lack domain-specific knowledge that inhibits the generation of inferences and the construction of meaning. In some cases poor comprehenders may have adequate world and background knowledge but are unable to link their experiences to the particular topic they are reading (Catts, 2009). Usually, when skilled readers encounter a mismatch between unfamiliar story information and their background knowledge, they may seek to make the closest match to form a suitable analogy. For example, knowing the word "energy" in everyday use is about "vigor" and "liveliness", when the word is used in a science text an appropriate inference is that the word "energy" is about "power". The issue is that less skilled readers may not make appropriate inferences based on their available prior knowledge.

The following are some suggestions that teachers can use with their students to enhance their students' abilities to make inferences from read texts.

- Read the text for the big ideas.

- Generate some probes to get at those big ideas.

- Go from general to specific in talking and thinking about the story.

- Ask: What is important about this story?

- Is this story more about the place, the plot, or the characters?

- What does this story tell us about how people behave and relate to each other?

- Work for a unified understanding of the context, such as: What is the purpose of the writing, how does this make you feel, and what motivates or excites you from this story.

- What do you think is the theme or the message from this story/text?

WHOLE OF TEXT STRATEGIES

A number of researchers have noted what is called the post grade four slump in students' reading and reading comprehension. One suggestion is that this slump in reading is related to an increase in text complexity and an increase in the level of difficulty of the vocabulary in that text with more words across all subject areas becoming increasingly phonologically and morphologically complex (Leach, Scarborough, & Rescorla, 2003). Furthermore, readers are expected by their teachers to be more accurate in their reading and there is more of a need to decode written information rapidly with less assistance and support. The message here is that to enhance students' comprehension skills, post grade four, teachers still need to work with their students on strategies at both the word (vocabulary) level and at the text (structure) level.

It is claimed that students have traditionally been taught comprehension strategies as separate skills, making it difficult for some readers to know why, when, and where, to use these strategies when reading. The evidence is that effective educators explicitly teach their students a range of reading strategies by explaining and modeling those strategies, and encouraging their students to become independent users of those strategies. They do this by systematically withdrawing support and providing ample opportunities for their students to practice those strategies using a variety of texts (Afflerbach, Pearson, & Paris, 2008). Typically, these strategies have a planning, reflection, and reviewing focus. For example, if a reader is having difficulty with a word, the following reviewing strategies may be adopted. The reader is asked to read on to the end of the passage to see if the word makes sense in context, or the reader stops and checks how to say the word and the meaning of a word then, once the reader has worked out the word, the passage is re-read as a whole.

As the students read a text they can also be asked to picture in their mind what is occurring. The teacher can facilitate this by asking the reader to visualise the setting of the story, the activity, and the people and how they look and react to their situation in the plot. It is asserted that such discussions improve the linking of visual and verbal material in working memory (van Meter, Aleksic, Schwartz, & Garner, 2006). Thus, visual imagery has been shown to be a useful comprehension enhancing strategy because it helps to organise and build coherence within the text and the reader. This helps to relate the incoming read information to the reader's prior knowledge and affective experiential memory, which in turn increases the reader's involvement and enjoyment with the reading.

Across the grades, students need to be exposed to a rich variety of text including expository text (such as information about living things and the environment) as well as narratives (stories). Along with being exposed to more text forms, students need to be shown how to identify the main idea in a paragraph and how to summarise the read text. When students are asked to summarise a piece of text, teachers expect the students to make the length of the text shorter, but often when asked to do this, the reader typically expands on the meaning of the word he/she does not know and then notes the main points in the texts. When teachers see this behaviour they need to remember that until the reader understands the meaning of the words they are not in a position to write a meaningful summary. Summarisation involves two parts: the first where the text is expanded and the technical words explained, followed by the second which involves a more telegraphic and compact statement once the vocabulary is understood. Many readers are unable to get to the second stage without going via the expansion stage, and teachers need to teach these two processes if they want students to effectively comprehend and summarise the content of the text.

Graphic organisers can also help in the summarisation of the text for the reader. Such summarisations help when the student is required to talk about the text to others or recall the text for assessment purpose. Graphic organisers enable the reader to concentrate on the main ideas or specific words in the text. In terms of narrative text, a story frame can be used to highlight the setting, the characters, the plot, the problem, and how it was resolved (Roser, Martinez, Fuhrken, & McDonnold, 2007). This can be a way to tie together story ideas at the sentence level and also at the whole text level.

The following are some suggestions that teachers can consider with their students to increase the effectiveness of graphic organisers and story frames:

- Use card or a large piece of paper to write the main ideas in large writing.

- List contributing paragraph ideas on the same card under the main idea.

- Draw or divide a poster board into story frame sections that reflect the structure of the read text, such as introduction, developments, and conclusion.

- Use post-it notes to write ideas about the story and add these to the story frame.

- Imagine and describe sections of the story or passage to match each section of the story frame;

- The teacher should model the construction of a story frame graphic organiser by using think-aloud talk to reveal his/her thinking processes.

Typically, less-skilled comprehenders are less likely to use context to construct meaning because they are less confident in using their existing background knowledge and experiences in relationship to the text being read (Woolley & Hay, 2007). One way of encouraging comprehension and the application of reading comprehension strategies is to ask students to explain their thinking: before (infer and predict); during (revise and predict); and after (evaluate and extend) their reading of the text (Figure 1).

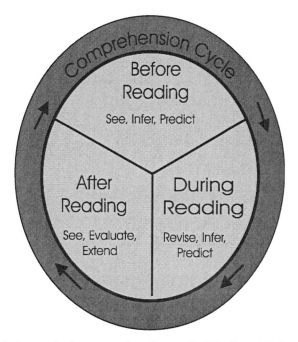

Figure 1 – The before, during, and after comprehension cycle (Woolley, 2006).

One way for students to evaluate and reflect on their progress during the reading of the text and afterwards is through the use of self-recording notes. For example, readers are instructed to predict possible outcomes before and during the reading of the text, and to note if these predictions come true at the conclusion of the reading. Before the reading, the students are instructed to scan: the illustrations, story title, and first paragraph. Next, they write their predictions on a post-it note and place it on the page near the title. During the reading they are asked to stop at an appropriate spot and reflect and revise their earlier predictions by noting how the story is similar or different. Students can also be encouraged to draw pictures on the post-it notes to illustrate their predictions and reflections at each stage, as a variation of this strategy. Alternatively, the notes can be placed on a graphic organiser instead of the reading passage. This strategy enables more independent learning because it promotes goal setting (prediction), monitoring (revision), and reflection (evaluation). Such predictions also provide an opportunity for group discussions about the text. When children and students share ideas around this type of activity they can compare and contrast their thinking with those of their peers.

Another activity that can be used to encourage discussion about the text is called TELLS. This is an advanced organisation strategy, which asks students to share their ideas with others as they progress through the five TELLS steps.

T   Study the story *t*itle.
E   *E*xamine and skim the story.
L   *L*ook for important words.
L   *L*ook for words that you don't understand, and work these out beforehand.
S   Decide whether the text i*s* fact or fiction.

ENGAGEMENT

Reading comprehension is closely linked with reading engagement. Engaged readers are motivated to read frequently out of curiosity and enjoyment of learning and to apply their knowledge gained from reading to answer new questions or to solve problems. Engaged readers are also readers who have a high degree of conceptual knowledge and are highly motivated.

The following are some suggestions to encourage student engagement with text, particularly for readers who are less motivated.

–   Focus on relevant texts, e.g., newspapers and magazines.

–   Include texts from the web.

–   Give your program a life skills focus.

–   Life skills are about independent living skills, money management, and work and leisure skills.

–   Use texts that relate to the readers' desire to know more about a topic.

–   Select texts that are age and interest appropriate.

–   Place reading and writing in social and community contexts, such as writing to a friend, using SMS texts, writing e-mails, shopping, and using timetables.

–   Encourage the reader to talk about what is working or not working in terms of their reading, and work on building strategies (such as using a thesaurus).

–   It is often a lack of confidence rather than a lack of strategies about reading that is the concern and so have the student self-monitor their reading improvement.

–   Avoid blaming questions, such as why don't you understand the text?.

- Work on reading tasks that have a clear purpose and outcomes that are relevant for that person.

- Treat the reader with respect and keep the reading or comprehension problem in perspective.

- Have short and long-term objectives that the reader and his/her family and others understand and support.

FEEDBACK AND RETELLING

In a teaching dialogue situation that is focused on readers' gaining meaning from the text, teachers can help shape the readers' motivation to read by providing effective feedback. Hattie (2009) has maintained that effective feedback adds to the student's sense of security, self-efficacy and confidence, which encourages the reader to take risks and attempt new tasks. Overall, the aim of reading performance feedback is to guide the student's learning, thereby reducing the need and amount of feedback as the student becomes more capable, confident, and in control. When providing corrective feedback it is also important to focus on the student's strengths rather than just his/her weaknesses or errors in performance. The claim is that negative or unrealistic expectancies and poor use of feedback can be harmful to the student's academic and social development. A highly effective procedure for monitoring comprehension is to ask the student to do a retelling of the text. The following is a sample of a student's level of reading at the start of an intervention that concentrated on students with comprehension difficulties. This program involved trained tutors who asked before, during, and after reading questions (Woolley & Hay, 2007). The reading tutors also encouraged students to: talk about the meaning of the words in the text; use visualised imagery about the setting, characters, and events in the story; and re-read the text a number of times until fluent reading was achieved and the text as a whole was processed into the reader's long-term memory.

The first retelling is based on the book *A Real City Kid* (Falk, 1971).

> There was a boy called Mark and Stephen and they became friends when they were little. And Stephen and his sister, Jane, and his mum and dad had to go in the country on a farm.

By the end of the intervention the same student's retellings were longer, and included more story detail and more elaborate descriptions, which included adjectives and adverbs. The example below,written towards the end of the program is based on the book *The Thirteenth Floor* (Juhren, 1974).

> The two children were trying to get to floor thirteen again and they got there and they heard a strange humming sound and they walked slowly toward it. The elevator door closed tightly on them and they couldn't get out. The elevator was dark inside and the children were feeling frightened because they could hear the strange sounds getting louder and closer to them.

CONCLUSION

In recent times there has been an increasing awareness that teaching of comprehension strategies has to be considered as an ongoing developmental processes for students. In particular, students in primary, middle and high schools need to be taught to use a repertoire of vocabulary enhancement and comprehension strategies to increase their comprehension of text.

Comprehension is more than testing; it is at the very core of the reading process - facilitating the understanding and meaning of texts. Educators need to provide their students with a rich set of opportunities so that the reader can gain a broad vocabulary and the necessary language skills, content knowledge, and reasoning skills to determine why, how, when, and where to use comprehension enhancing strategies. Effective reading comprehension requires the reader to have the following attributes: background knowledge of the text; fluent word recognition and decoding skills of the words in the text; knowledge of the vocabulary and meaning of the words in that text; an understanding of how the text is constructed; and ,finally, task persistence. These reading attributes can be both taught and encouraged and this is particularly important for students who come into our classrooms from disadvantaged backgrounds.

REFERENCES

Afflerbach, P., Pearson, D., & Paris, S. G. (2008). Clarifying differences between reading skills and reading strategies. *The Reading Teacher, 61*(5), 364 – 373.

Biemiller, A., & Boot, C. (2005). An effective method for building meaning vocabulary in primary grades. *Journal of Educational Psychology, 98*(1), 44.

Catts, H. W. (2009). The narrow view of reading promotes a broad view of comprehension. *Language, Speech & Hearing Services in Schools, 40*(2), 178 – 183.

Ehren, B. (2009). Looking through an adolescent literacy lens at the Narrow View of Reading. *Language, Speech & Hearing Services in Schools, 40*(2), 192 – 195.

Falk, I. (1971). *A real city kid.* Melbourne: Cheshire.

Hart, B. & Risley, T. R. (1995). *Meaningful differences in the everyday experience of young American children.* London: P.H. Brooks.

Hattie, J. (2009). *Visible Learning.* NY: Routledge.

Hay, I., & Fielding-Barnsley, R. (2009). Competencies that underpin children's transition into early literacy. *Australian Journal of Language and Literacy, 32,* 148 – 162.

Hay, I., Elias, G., Fielding-Barnsley, R., Homel, R., & Frieberg, K. (2007). Language delays, reading delays and learning difficulties: Interactive elements requiring multidimensional programming. *Journal of Learning Disabilities, 40,* 400 – 409.

Juhren, R. (1974). *The thirteenth floor.* N.Y.: Scholastic Inc.

Leach, J. M., Scarborough, H. S., & Rescorla, L. (2003). Late-emerging reading disabilities. *Journal of Educational Psychology, 95,* 211 – 224.

Nation, K., & Norbury, F. (2005). Why reading comprehension fails: Insights from developmental disorders. *Topics in Language Disorders, 25,* 21 – 32.

Pearson, P. D., Hiebert, E. H., & Kamil, M. L. (2007). Vocabulary assessment: What we know and what we need to learn. *Reading Research Quarterly, 42*(2), 282-296.

Perfetti, C. (2007). Reading ability: Lexical quality to comprehension. *Scientific Studies of Reading, 11*(4), 357 – 383.

Reutzel, D. R. (2007). Organising effective literacy instruction: Differentiating instruction to meet the needs of all children. In L. B. Gambrell, L. M. Morrow, & M. Pressley (Eds.), *Best Practices in Literacy Instruction* 3rd ed., (pp. 313 – 343). NY: The Guilford Press.

Roser, N., Martinez, M., Fuhrken, C., & McDonnold, K. (2007). Characters as guides to meaning. *The Reading Teacher, 60*(6), 548 – 559.

Ricketts, J., Nation, K., & Bishop, V. M. (2007). Vocabulary is important for some, but not all reading skills. *Scientific Study of Reading, 11*(3), 235 – 257.

Stanovich, K. E. (1986). Matthew effects in reading: Some consequences of individual differences in the acquisition of literacy. *Reading Research Quarterly, 21,* 360-407.

Van Meter, P., Aleksic, M., Schwartz, A., & Garner, J. (2006). Learner-generated drawing as a strategy for learning from content area text. *Contemporary Educational Psychology, 31,* 142 – 166.

Woolley, G.E. (2006*). The development, documentation, and evaluation of a strategy-training program for primary school students with reading comprehension difficulties.* Unpublished doctoral dissertation, Griffith University, Brisbane.

Woolley, G., & Hay, I. (2007). Reading intervention: The benefits of using trained tutors. *Australian Journal of Language and Literacy, 30,* 9 – 20.

In: Language and Literacy Education in a Challenging World   ISBN: 978-1-61761-198-8
Editors: T. Lê, Q. Lê, and M. Short   © 2011 Nova Science Publishers, Inc.

Chapter 17

TESTING ENGLISH AS A FOREIGN LANGUAGE (EFL) IN A COMMUNICATIVE CONTEXT

Kent McClintock

ABSTRACT

As teachers and test designers in an EFL communicative context attempt to create a balance between the test constructs of practicality, reliability, validity, washback and authenticity, focusing on one particular construct at the expense of the others may have a negative influence on the desired outcome of the test. It is realistic to expect that a test which focuses primarily upon hearing authentic language will have some reliability issues, and also a test that emphasizes reliability will have an impact upon the validity of the test. Striking a balance between each construct is desirable and the realization that these constructs are not separate entities, but are intertwined and rely on each other is essential. The following chapter addresses the pivotal requirements teachers and test designers are obligated to consider when formulating a communicative test for EFL learners in order to aid and ensure that an effective test, while maintaining the testing maxims, has been generated.

Keywords: foreign language, testing, practicality, reliability, validity, washback, authenticity.

INTRODUCTION

Testing is a necessary part of learning a given subject in an educational environment and the learning of EFL is no exception. Generally, tests are conducted for the purposes of eliciting meaningful feedback for not only the educator, but also the students, in that, they enable interested parties to evaluate the effectiveness of the teaching and learning process. Tests may also a great source in which to motivate students to further develop their language skills by allowing them to analyze their progression of knowledge and ability in the target language (TL). When it comes to language learning, the essential component of communicative ability, oral testing of learners may grant the valuable insight and prediction as to how the learner will perform using the language in a non-testing or classroom environment. The testing of language learners, rests upon the facts that they enable the educators and learners to "define course objectives, they stimulate student progress, and they evaluate course achievement" (Valette, 1977, p.3). This chapter hopes to elicit the theoretical aspects in test development, answer why they are of importance and highlight the fundamental shift in testing methods now taking place within the EFL community as they pertain to the educators and learners.

TEST DEVELOPMENT

In designing tests, educators are often concerned with ensuring that the said test provides for 'practicality', 'reliability', 'validity' and beneficial 'washback'. These maxims have plagued educators perpetually, yet in the EFL classroom, the modern maxim concerning 'authenticity', further complicates the equation. The ideal of authenticity relates to teaching learners 'real' and 'authentic' language in order to build their competence, which is limited for most learners. However, there is a non-consensus among educators and theorists what 'real' and 'authentic' mean with regards to testing. For tests to maintain the three standard maxims in test development: practicality, reliability and validity, Breen (1985) highlights the complexity involved for educators when he states, "(a) What is an authentic test?; (b) For whom is it authentic?; (c) For what authentic purposes?; and (d) In which particular social situation?" (p.61). Thus, for an educator, the answers to these questions can prove to be quite difficult to ascertain when it comes time to evaluate and test their learners, and further burdens theorists with giving a clear picture as to what they believe the terms 'real' and 'authentic' signify. Further complicating the equation concerning 'authenticity' is the fact that learners are learning the language in a foreign language (FL) environment, with most having minimal exposure to the language, generally only with the teacher in the classroom and for a brief amount of time. Lightbown (2000) believes that, "the most important reason for incomplete acquisition in foreign classroom settings is probably the lack of time available for contact with the language" (p. 449). In this era of global communication, with English being the dominant world language and the increasing need for competent speakers of English, the ability to design effective tests that distinguish capable individuals' who are communicatively competent in the language while maintaining the maxims involved with test development, is not a straightforward endeavour.

To assume that the testing maxims presented earlier were the only constraints placed on educators developing tests would be heedless. Also factoring into the equation is the opinion that there must be a "common understanding of what it is to know a language" (Omaggio, 1983, p. 331). Although, for English as a Second Language (ESL) and EFL theorists, the conception of what communicative competence and language proficiency consists of is a heavily debated topic and one that does not truly have a clear and common consensus. In order to capture a relatively general perspective of the mindset regarding this debate, and why it is of importance when constructing tests, Omaggio (1983) presents four categories which lay at the heart of the debate and may assist in identifying whether or not a learner is competent and proficient in the TL. The four categories which were distinguished consisted of grammatical competence, sociolinguistic competence, discourse competence and strategic competence. For an educator teaching in a FL environment, assessing whether a learner is adept in all competencies is highly improbable, particularly within their context and the fact that their learners in all likelihood have little understanding in regards to sociolinguistic competence and strategic competence, thus further elevates the educators' dilemma of ensuring that tests satisfy their end goals.

Within the last few decades, the accepted goal of language learning has become 'communicative competence' rather than strictly linguistically competent. The reason for such a change relates to Omaggio's four competences. When it comes to communicative ability in a second language (L2), learners are generally hoping to attain the skills and abilities necessary to communicate their thoughts and feelings in a cohesive and coherent manner, regardless of the situation presented. Being able to communicate competently in the course of discourse in the TL is the goal of most learners who undertake learning a new language, or so it is postulated. If that is not the goal of the learner, then, admittedly, there is a point in studying language other than for extrinsic reasons. Hence, when educators are developing a test to evaluate their learners, the dilemmas posed in how to actually measure what is communicatively competent or proficient, while at the same time maintaining the testing maxims (practicality, reliability, and validity) can be ambiguous at best. As educators have shifted towards the "aims of (a) make communicative competence the goal of language teaching and (b) develop procedures for the teaching of the four language skills that acknowledge the interdependence of language and communication" (Richards and Richards, 2001, p. 155), highlights the need to develop testing techniques that address these ideals in order to effectively evaluate course objectives, student progress and course achievement. Thus far, most FL education curricula have not been focused on the dual aims set forth by Richards and Richards. In most cases, the learning of a language has been geared towards succeeding on standardized tests such as the Test of English for International Communication (TOEIC) and the Test of English as a Foreign Language (TOEFL), yet until recently, the acceptable level of ability was not based on communicative competence. The focus of instruction in many educational contexts has been based on the teaching approaches of Grammar-Translation (GT) and Audiolingualism (ALM). While both approaches have been noted to increase one's English ability in terms of grammar and structure, and afford educators relative ease in constructing practical, reliable, and valid exams, both fail to address and examine the learner's communicative competence (authenticity), now the foremost requisite of FL curriculums.

TEST PRACTICALITY

There are many criteria an educator must address when developing and administering a test. However, the starting point of the test development process is essentially practicality. Practicality, in general, refers to how effectively and efficiently the test will be in regards to the factors Brown (2004) highlights: "not excessively expensive, stays within appropriate time constraints, is relatively easy to administer, and has a scoring/evaluation procedure that is specific and time-efficient" (p. 19). Until now, most testing that has taken place within the EFL world has been conducted in a relatively practical manner. This has been achieved by utilizing discrete-point testing (testing individual aspects of the language by itself) and norm-referenced type tests (the ranking of learners based on their test results) (Hughes, 1989). These test types have been utilized in large part based on the teaching approaches that educators have used in educating their learners, those being GT and ALM. The fact that both approaches strictly pertain to the teaching of the languages linguistical forms and not the communicative nature owes greatly to why the administering of these types of exams has persisted and is easy to comprehend, as they adhere, for the most part to the factors of practicality that Brown alluded to. The most commonly used example of such tests is the multiple-choice exam. The practicality of a multiple-choice exam is self-explanatory: it not only saves time in the administering of the exam, but also in its scoring, due to the ease of computer-generated scores. Also, economic constraints may be eased by reducing the amount of hours those educators or other individuals may have spent evaluating the tests.

However, in association with the new teaching approaches that are now becoming the norm within the EFL field, (Communicative Language Teaching (CLT); English for Specific Purposes (ESP); Content-based Instruction (CBI); and Task-based), the practicality issues in testing that seemed so straightforward with GT and ALM has been reversed and demand rethinking. As these approaches to teaching language do not separate it into its individual parts, but rather require learners to apply all the language parts and skills in combination with one another, new forms of testing are required to evaluate whether the learner is successful in acquiring the tasks learnt. In doing so, it has meant that educators have had to address the question of practicality once again when developing tests for these types of teaching approaches. The most commonly adopted testing techniques that educators have employed in doing so are 'integrative tests' (where learners are asked to apply a whole cross-section of their language skills, rather than individual items) and 'criterion-referenced' (the individuals actual ability to use the language) (Hughes, 1989). Concerns of practicality are readily apparent when these types of tests are manipulated. The foremost practicality concerns that relate to these types of exams are the cost effectiveness and time constraints. While discrete-point tests may take an exceptionally long time in development (the difficulty in writing quality multiple-choice questions), the administering of them is quite short, in contrast to integrative exams. Integrative exams are rather effortless to formulate and take little time to do so, but when administering the test, allotting enough time for each individual student, particularly if an interview is utilized, poses an enormous obstacle for educators, and the tests practicality. Not only may such an exam lack practicality time-wise, but it may not be economical if several teachers are required to administer the exam over an extended period of time.

It is incontrovertible that all tests have both positive and negative aspects in regards to practicality. What is of utmost concern therefore is to discern what purpose the test is attempting to serve - whether it is a learner's linguistic or communicative competence. Once this has been determined, the type of test can be decided. Doing so allows the educator to formulate a plan of action so that the practicality issues that are involved with developing and administering tests can be reduced and dealt with.

RELIABILITY

The common consensus among theorists (Brown, 1980; Bachman, 1990) maintains that in order for a test to be considered reliable, it must have consistency in measurement and also be dependable. Generally, the maxim of 'reliability' is concerned with two types: test reliability and scoring reliability. Test reliability is fundamentally attempting "to identify potential sources of error in a given measure of communicative language ability and to minimize the effect of these factors on that measure" (Bachman, 1990, p. 160). Although, what Bachman states is essentially correct, how an educator achieves identification and minimization of the effects, sources of errors and other factors can be overwhelming and complicated, because learners bring their own uniqueness into the testing environment. Factors which accompany learners into the test may ultimately affect the results, and are uncontrollable by the educator/tester, which may include such attributes as "illness, a 'bad day', or no sleep the night before" (Brown, 1980, p. 211). Traditionally, tests such as a written language exam adhere to the principal espoused by Hughes, by virtue of their focus on the linguistical aspects of the language and the testing approaches utilized in measuring the learner's skills. The employment of discrete-point tests are typically very systematic and thus produce highly reliable results among learners. Most learners have developed excellent memory skills when it comes to linguistical aspects of the language, thanks in part to rote-learning. Tests of this nature, routinely involve a number of pre-planned and a fixed number of questions which a student answers either right or wrong (Underhill, 1987). As a result of the rote-learning environment that most learners have been educated in, the likelihood of said test producing unreliable results could be seen to be negligible or at least minimized. However, one must not forget that people "simply do not behave in exactly the same way on every occasion, even when circumstances seem identical" (Hughes, 1989, p.29).

As the EFL community further distances itself from the traditional teaching practices of ALM and GT, the issue of test reliability is once again present, yet in a different form. This is due to the fact that the oral testing of learners is now becoming the accepted manner in which to assess their language abilities, and therefore producing new considerations for educators when manipulating the modern testing techniques that accompany the contemporary teaching approaches. In exploiting integrative testing formats such as interviews, peer-interaction, or responses to oral queues - involving "the student's ability to communicate in specific situations" (Valette, 1977, p. 12), three major problems arise. These are: "1) the large amount of tester's time required per student; 2) difficulty in scheduling the test; and 3) misgivings about rater objectivity in assessing student performance" (Mueller, 1987, p. 126). While the first two problems identified by Mueller are commonly acquainted with test practicality, it is the third concern of scorer reliability that is ordinarily identified as causing the greatest concerns about the reliability of oral testing. To minimize the effects of "human error, subjectivity, and bias" (Brown, 2004, p. 21) when scoring exams, an effort on the part of the educators themselves along with the educational institute to assure the adequate training in the evaluating system as it pertains to the communicative ability, as well as how to select the criteria that is to be evaluated has to be accounted for (Madsen, 1983). In the training of scorers, Madsen (1983) believes the characteristics and qualities of a good scorer that should be exemplified are, a "good interviewer is neither harsh, nor familiar, condescending nor intimidating." And that a, "sincere, open, supportive manner is most effective" (p. 163). In selecting criteria to be evaluated, one must absolutely return to the course objectives set forth at the beginning of the course for a guide with which to advance. "If we test directly the skills that we are interested in fostering" (Hughes, 1989, p. 45), then educators have a sound base whereupon they can certify that they are evaluating what is of essence, therefore optimizing the reliability of the test. When these two requirements (scorer training and selected criteria) are addressed, the concerns regarding test reliability should hopefully be minimized.

VALIDITY

Generally, in regards to testing, reliability and validity are commonly seen to be in conflict. As Brown (2004) perceives it, validity is "by far the most complex criterion of an effective test – and arguably the most important principle" (p. 22). However, Bachman (1990) views these two concepts as complimentary when he states that, "when we increase the reliability of our measures, we are also satisfying a necessary condition for validity: in order for a test score to be valid, it must be reliable" (p. 160). Accordingly, both concepts are important in designing practical and effective tests. Designing a highly reliable test may suffer due to difficulties in proving that test results are interpreted in a justifiable and accountable manner, therefore a balancing act between the two concepts is always in play. How to balance between the two will in large part come down to analyzing the course objectives, and determining what those objectives were at the beginning of the course. However, both concepts are concerned with "identifying, estimating, and controlling the effects of factors that affect test scores" (Bachman, 1990, p. 160). In tests of language, validity is the degree to which the test actually measures what is intended to be measured, and these measurements are then supported most convincingly by subsequent personal observation of the teachers themselves along with the learners peers, often referred to as a type of test validity, that of 'criterion validity'. The questions that arise for an educator when considering 'criterion validity' are: "Does the test accurately and sufficiently measure the testee for the particular purpose of the test? Does it enable the tester to reach his criteria?" (Brown, 1980, p. 212). The realm of 'criterion-validity' also encompasses two other types of validity that must be considered: 'concurrent validity' and 'predictive validity' (Brown, 2004; Harris; 1969; Hughes; 1989; Johnson, 2001). 'Concurrent validity', measurement is assessed by having the teacher acknowledge the learners test results with those of other tests, alongside the learners achievement or performance within the course itself (Harris, 1969). If it is observed that the correlation between these two measures appears to be high, the test may then be assessed as being valid. However, in the oral testing of learners, educators must be aware that when administering an oral test enough time is given to the learner to respond in order to represent the course objectives. For if a short amount of time is given for the learners to respond, as opposed to a lengthy period, then the results are not in unison, and the said test cannot be deemed valid (Hughes, 1989), or at least the validity is in question. For an educator to confirm that 'concurrent validity' is established, it essentially "depends in a large part on the reliability of both test and criterion measure" (Harris, 1969, p. 20).

The ability of the teacher to predict the future success of learners within the TL is the basis of 'predictive validity' (Bachman, 1990; Brown, 2004; Hughes, 1989). The most commonly practiced methods of predicting future language usage have consisted of proficiency tests and placements tests, whether to predict future communicative ability or to assess the learner's ability in assuring they enrol in the appropriate class level (Hughes, 1989). However, a common problem associated with these types of predictive tests lies in the fact that they may not be measuring the appropriate skills or abilities that the course is interested in, thereby becoming predicatively invalid. Given that most programs are focused on the communicative competence, predicting one's future communicative ability outside the classroom can be complicated. When predicting a learner's communicative competence, such evaluations and predictions are typically quite subjective in nature, based solely on the teachers perceived conceptions of how the learner will perform. In addition, the teacher must recognize that other factors are often in play when evaluating a learner's ability, "such as subject knowledge, intelligence, motivation, health, and happiness" (Hughes, 1989, p. 25). Clearly, the complexity of assessing future communicative competence is not as facile as administering a proficiency test. In order to predict the future language abilities somewhat accurately, educators and theorists must decide upon what it is to 'know a language', the likelihood of which is unrealistic, yet critical for the reason being "to find a way to measure outcomes against a common metric, and to predict accurately the degree of success with which an individual can handle a variety of needs in a whole range of situations" (Omaggio, 1983, p. 330), rather than the separate components that make up a language.

To further know whether or not a test is valid, largely depends on the 'content' of the test itself. When deciding on what to test, teachers must ensure "its content constitutes a representative sample of the language skills, structures, etc. with which it is meant to be concerned" (Hughes, 1989, p. 22). This can be achieved by considering the objectives set out at the beginning of the course. For if the course objectives were that of communicative competence, and the learner's ability to utilize the language then it is obvious that the content of the test will address the objectives related to speaking, which therefore promotes the validity of the test. However, supposing that the objective of speaking ability was measured by "asking the learner to answer paper-and-pencil multiple-choice questions requiring grammatical judgements" (Brown, 2004, p. 23) would not constitute validity. As well, an educator should design a test that will "include a proper sample of the relevant structures" (Hughes, 1989, p. 22) that were covered up to that point within the course. If the test omits certain relevant structures that were learnt and are required of the learners, then the test cannot be a valid representation of the course objectives. Ultimately, the best course of action for an educator to take in confirming that content validity has been satisfied is to directly test the structures learnt (Brown, 2004; Harris, 1969; Hughes, 1989). Of chief concern for educators is that content validity is essential in "defending the validity of classroom tests" (Brown, 2004, p. 24).

Establishing the validity of a test can be a daunting task for an educator. However, another type of evidence that must be addressed is the concept of 'construct validity'. Construct validity is essentially concerned with "the extent to which performance on tests is consistent with predictions that we make on the basis of a theory of abilities, or constructs" (Bachman, 1990, p. 255). For the most part, construct validity tends to fall within the realm of ESL/EFL research, as the theorists are attempting to perceive outcomes to validate their constructs. Within language learning pedagogy there are numerous constructs that encompass the process, such as 'proficiency', 'communicative competence' and 'writing' (Brown, 2004). Therefore, the concept of construct validation may be viewed in the same light as content validity (Underhill, 1987), due to the fact that both types of validity fundamentally address the common question (Bachman, 1998; Brown, 2004; Underhill, 1987). The importance of construct validity within EFL cannot be underestimated or paid a disservice in test development. The concept assures the advancement of the theoretical exploration on the part of EFL practitioners to further ameliorate the existing theoretical constructs in regards to language learning and teaching, or to elicit new ones to be manipulated in the future.

Having drawn attention to the distinct types (criterion, concurrent, predictive, content, construct) of test validity, test designers are ultimately evaluating these differing types in order to meet the perception of whether or not the learners themselves view the test as valid.

This is yet a further type of validity and is commonly referred to as 'face validity' (Brown, 2004; Harris; 1969; Underhill, 1989). The importance of 'face validity' is crucial for the learner, because it allows the learner to evaluate whether or not the test is actually testing what they learnt, and validates to them that the material learnt is of value in their language learning endeavour. For if the material that is being tested is not a clear indication of the tasks that were learnt, learners may question their motivation for studying the said course and the relevance of it (Harris, 1969). As well, if the learner's perception of the test is negative, "it may mean that they do not perform on it in a way that truly reflects their ability" (Hughes, 1989, p. 27). The followers of the construct 'face validity' argue that it "reminds us that the psychological state of the learner (confidence, anxiety, etc.) is an important ingredient in peak performance by a learner" (Brown, 2004, p. 27). Yet, because the construct itself cannot be measured since the importance of which is subjective in nature as viewed by the individual learners, administrators and general public, there is a vast amount of opposition against including the construct of 'face validity', into the development of a test. The opposition against stems from the fact that the concept of 'face validity' presents itself as being nothing more than an appeasement to the psychological state of individuals involved within the course.

As has been discussed, validity includes various distinct types which all need to be contemplated individually during the development of a test, so as to guard against the exclusion of crucial material from the course objectives as well as making certain that the test actually measures what it is intended to measure. In today's EFL environment, where oral tests have come to supplant those of written tests, it would be egregious on the part of the educator to completely hold value to the theoretical concepts of validity as set in stone, since dialogue between two interlocutors could be nearly impossible to validate statistically, unlike written tests. Thus, rather than viewing the oral testing of learners and the results that they produce along a strict theoretical and statistical plain, "common sense is the tester's best friend" (Underhill, 1987, p. 105) when it comes to validating an oral test.

AUTHENTICITY

The much bantered-about concept of authenticity within the EFL environment and its role in test formation is directly attributed to the modern teaching approaches of English for Specific Purposes (ESP), Communicative Language Teaching (CLT), Content-Based Instruction (CBI) or a notional/functional syllabus (n/f) that have become the general methods in which to educate learners in the TL. With curricula now emphasizing communicative competence, rather than the lingusitical components that make up the language, educators have also had to readdress the performance assessment methods utilized in the past. Ones which enable them to determine the communicative competence of the learners are now needed. These new forms of testing the learner, predominately integrative and criterion-referenced (such as interviews, information gaps, and using the telephone), represent a shift away from the traditional discrete-point norm-referenced tests, and 'authenticity' plays a central role.

As was discussed earlier, in reference to Breen (1985), the difficulty in identifying what language is authentic is rather problematic. A crucial practice that may allow the teacher to identify what language is deemed authentic would be eliciting from the learners themselves:

why they are learning the language. The practicality of which, is that the "decisions as to contact and method are based on the learner's reason for learning" (Hutchinson & Waters, 1987, p. 19). While it may be easy to identify the language needs of some learners (i.e. a businessperson or engineer), it may not be readily apparent as to what language needs other learners (i.e. junior or high school students) have for learning the language. Most certainly, this is the case "where students have divergent reasons for learning, or (as in many school situations) where we simply do not know what their eventual uses (if any) of the FL will be" (Johnson, 2001, p. 227). With that being the case, the teacher needs to clearly identify what their learner's needs are 'now' and what their needs will be in the 'future' in order for communicative approach to learning the language to be effective. In eliciting the learners to produce their reasons for learning the language, the teacher has a great resource on which to draw upon in determining the 'authentic' language for the course and at the same time providing a stimulus to the learners in that they will feel a greater sense of involvement within the course. In addition, by identifying the 'real' learning needs of the learners, the teacher has thus begun to establish a communicative teaching curriculum, starting with the 'needs analysis.'

An accompanying problem for learners when it comes to authenticity is that they are typically learning the language in a FL environment where they have minimal exposure to it outside the classroom. The only contact they generally have is either with their teacher or peers and only for a few minutes at a time. With the encouragement of actively engaging in dialogue, they will hopefully discover that "one linguistic form can fulfill a variety of communicative functions, and one function can be fulfilled by a variety of linguistic forms" (Widdowson, 1979, p. 119). This allows the learner to experience how the linguistic forms which they have learnt can be used in social and cultural contexts, other than their own, and supports the teacher's decisions when selecting what speech is authentic and will be tested. However, even though educators may not be able to provide authentic or real linguistic forms to the learner, educators can provide contextual norms with the tendencies of native speakers in different social contexts. Having learners use the language in as real a context as possible provides the learner with a practical opportunity to realize his or her abilities, and also provides the teacher with useful feedback concerning the student, the test, and whether the course itself has been a success or failure. If a teacher is testing for communicative competence, it is only fair to provide the learner an opportunity to use the language in the assessment situation. Although, it is imperative for the teacher to remember that the material used to form the test must coincide with that of the course content, in order to maintain a valid assessment. The question that then arises from this standard is how teachers can assure that the language test is attempting to validate the learner's ability in the language in an authentic manner. Brown (2004) believes that authenticity in a test could be achieved if the following are considered:

> The language in the test is as natural as possible. Items are contextualized rather than isolated. Topics are meaningful (relevant, interesting) for the learner. Some thematic organization to items is provided, such as through a story line or episode. Tasks represent, or closely approximate, real-world tasks. (p. 28)

Accordingly, because communicative type tests or task-based tasks attempt to mirror a 'real-life' context, this poses a threat to reliability for the fact that the situation is not 'real', and can only resemble an actual non-testing language scenario. Given the variety of teaching contexts, the probability of a consistent form of communicative testing that can be consistently measured in an accurate manner is highly unlikely. To guard against a communicative test being invalid and unreliable, Hughes (1989) points out three key ways in which to alleviate this dilemma, those being: "Clearly recognisable and appropriate descriptions of criterial levels are written and scorers are trained to use them. Irrelevant features of performance are ignored. There is more than one scorer for each performance" (p. 110). Hence, an authentic testing environment, although useful, practical and valid, will always remain a threat to the reliability of the test due to its authentic nature. Another concern that may jeopardize the reliability of an oral test or other alternative forms of assessment is that many of the tests vary considerably across a wide range of curricula and contexts, particularly when one considers the teaching method of ESP where learners are learning a more specific type of language that is employed within their field of study. Also complicating the matter is the fact that psychological, human error and a host of other factors have a significant influence on the results of the tests and, therefore, the reliability of the test. However, an oral test designed and utilized in such a fashion that it mimics the course objectives and in-class training would appear to be practical, reasonable and valid to the students, and could achieve a certain level of 'face validity'. In today's EFL environment, which is a multi-billion dollar industry, face validity goes a long way in satisfying the needs of the learners and the external parties involved, however groundless this supposed construct may be. For if the test does test a supposed authentic context in the learners eyes, 'face validity' can be assumed to have been achieved, and if it does not, vice versa. However, inferences from the test results are only significant in one testing context; therefore, an authentic oral test can only be reliable and valid within a specific context and any claims to expand the reliability of a test, which lacks validity shall occur. In exploiting a task-based test or a communicative type of assessment, the value to be had in determining a learner's ability to complete a language task, while employing a broad spectrum of the language components, rather than selected isolated parts is undeniable, not only for the teacher but more importantly the learners themselves. Communicative tests provide precious feedback to all parties involved in the learning process as to whether or not the course was a success, failure or just so-so. And they highlight what areas either need to be improved upon, relegated, or added in the learning process so that the learning of the language can be secured.

TESTING CONSEQUENCES

The construct of 'washback' or 'backwash' (both terms used interchangeably) within language testing theory is a response to the effects that the test has on both the teaching and learning process (Brown, 2004; Hughes, 1989, Johnson, 2001). As with any concept, there are both negative and positive outcomes that result from it. In regards to negative washback, "if the test content and testing techniques are at variance with the objectives of the course, then there is likely to be harmful backwash" (Hughes, 1989, p. 1). For example, if the objectives of the course were that of learner's communicative competence (oral ability), yet the testing method selected for assessment was a multiple-choice test, clearly the two are at variance with each other. The testing of those abilities that the course objectives set out to teach are the ones that should be tested. Therefore, if the course objectives were that of communicative ability, correspondingly the communicative ability of the learner should be tested in a fashion (i.e., oral test) that measures it. In doing so, the washback generated from the test would likely prove to be positive.

Another source of negative washback is when the content of the test measures too few of the specifications that were learnt throughout the course. "Good sampling is very important. It fails if the test items are regularly perceived of as covering just one small area of the total behaviour. If this happens, bad washback will occur…" (Johnson, 2001, p. 302). In order to avoid such a situation, a thorough sampling of everything that was included in the course objectives needs to be addressed when formulating the test, whereby the learners can attest to the fact that what they learnt was what they were tested on, and hence providing positive washback. Otherwise, a questioning on the part of the learners as to why they learnt certain aspects of the language, yet were not tested on them and whether or not they deem the course to be of benefit to them will come about, and negative washback will be present. Further hindering the outcome of positive washback from a language test is the fact that all too often in the learning environment, "teachers must often 'teach to' a test" (Johnson, 2001, p. 292). Such is the case where indirect, discrete-point and norm-referenced testing methods are practiced. Although, for many teachers who are teaching for communicative competence, these testing methods are also used, due to guidelines imposed by national curriculums and for the simple fact that they produce an objective outcome. Frequently, the instruction within the course is concerned predominately to the types of questions (multiple-choice exercises) that may be present on the exam and not on the objectives of the course, leading to negative washback for the teacher, learners and the course.

In today's EFL testing environment, where the measurement of communicative competence in authentic contexts is the goal, there are several schemes in which teachers can ensure that positive washback will hopefully be generated. As we have seen already, two methods that should be followed when formulating the test (those of: testing the abilities outlined in the course objectives; and selecting a comprehensive sampling of those abilities) helps create a foundation on which to foster positive washback. This is clearly demonstrated in Brown's (2004) statement that: "A test that achieves content validity demonstrates relevance to the curriculum in question and thereby sets the stage for washback" (p. 37). For the most part, the teaching methods and testing assessment methods that are presently used within EFL classes are generally new and foreign to the learners, as many of them are likely encountering them for the first time. The 'newness' of these methods is directly related to the more frequent teaching (ALM and GT) and testing (indirect, discrete-point, norm-referenced) approaches that the learners have grown up being taught in. That being said, the consequences of the learning and testing that teachers may presume to occur when utilizing communicative learning and direct, integrative and criterion-referenced testing methods may not be realized. For this reason, having knowledge of the learner's prior history will enable the teacher to better identify the potential consequences of the learning and the testing.

In determining what type of testing method one should exploit, either indirect, discrete-point and norm-referenced or that of direct, integrative and criterion-referenced, the best alternative is to proceed with the latter, given the probable communicative nature of the course. In combination with direct testing, criterion-referencing, where students are not ranked against each other, often proves to be a motivating factor for many learners. "If test specifications make clear just what candidates have to be able to do, and with what degree of success, then students will have a clear picture of what they have to achieve" (Hughes, 1989, p. 45). In knowing what they need to achieve, the learners can concentrate their efforts on producing the language skills they have learnt to the best of their abilities without the added burden of worrying how they compare to the rest of their peers, which is quite common amongst learners having been tested with indirect and nor-referenced tests.

Learner motivation and the fostering of it on the part of the teacher may result in creating positive washback for the course and the test. The degree to which an individual is motivated will directly impact whether one attains success or experiences failure at a given skill they wish to acquire. As well, the degree of motivation affects on how learners perceive failure: for example, a simple mistake or responding "correctly to fewer than half of the items (and yet be given a pass)" (Hughes, 1989, p. 46), may be perceived as a frustrating disaster, and therefore de-motivating and creating negative washback. Whereas, if the learner perceives that same mistake as an insight into what they need to improve upon, it may provide an impetus for further practice and study. Typically for the teacher, the concept of motivation is the appearance of enthusiasm and involvement that their learners display in relation to the activities that are utilized for teaching. However, no amount of enthusiasm or involvement shown by learners necessarily translates into whether the studying of the language is useful. When one undertakes the learning of a skill, in this case a FL, it is important on the part of the teacher to clearly delineate why the language would be useful for the learners. With a clear conception of how the learning of the skill will prove beneficial, it is hoped that the learners will then have a greater inclination to be motivated and learn. Additionally, another way to promote learner motivation and, as a result create positive washback, is through simply commenting "generously and specifically on test performance" (Brown, 2004, p. 29), pointing out errors and giving praise of good performance. In knowing where exactly one went wrong, the learner has the ability to adjust their learning focus and then endeavour to eliminate them. As well, the praise given for good performance enables the learner to realize that they do have the necessary ability to complete the tasks using the language in a meaningful manner. Overall, the construct of washback is one that is pivotal in ensuring the success or failure of the course and test.

CONCLUSION

In teaching for communicative competence, rather than strictly for linguistical competence, as has been the situation for many FL learners until recently, the need for new testing methods has been required in order to measure the communicative abilities of the learners set forth in the objectives of such courses. For if testing was to follow the testing methods used to test linguistical competence (i.e. indirect, discrete-point, norm-referenced) then "the relationship between performance on them and performance of the skills in which we are usually more interested tends to be rather weak in strength and uncertain in nature" (Hughes, 1989, p. 16). In addition, with the focus on providing learners with language that is 'real' and 'authentic', tests for these skills "cannot be captured in additive tests of grammar or reading or vocabulary and other discrete points of language" (Brown, 1980, p. 218). Therefore, in the testing of communicative competence where 'real' and 'authentic' language is being assessed, theorists (Bachman, 1990; Brown, 1980; Brown, 2004; Hughes; 1989) believe that the means in which this is made is through the usage of direct, integrative and criterion-referenced tests. Even though such tests are not likely very objective in nature, due to spoken language being a complex skill in which many language skills interact with one another, they are relevant to the communicative language classroom in that they allow "the students the opportunity to demonstrate their ability to communicate" (Valette, 1977, p.9). With communicative language tests being subjective, the threat to the basic test maxims of practicality, reliability, validity and washback is ever present. Thus, a great deal of responsibility for resolving the issues threatening these constructs is placed upon the educator and the institution. Attempting to design a language test that holds each maxim in account along with being authentic is not an easy task. Yet it is most certainly possible and should be the goal of every teacher.

REFERENCES

Bachman, L. F. (1990). *Fundamental considerations in language testing*. Oxford: Oxford University Press.

Breen, M. P. (1985). Authenticity in the language classroom. *Applied Linguistics*, *6*(1), 60-70.

Brown, H. D. (1980). *Principles of language learning and teaching*. Englewood Cliffs, NJ: Prentice-Hall.

Brown, H. D. (2004). *Language assessment: Principles and classroom practices*. White Plains, NY: Longman.

Harris, D. P. (1969). *Testing English as a second language*. New York, NY: McGraw-Hill Book Company.

Hughes, A. (1989). *Testing for language teachers*. Cambridge: Cambridge University Press.

Hutchison, T. & Waters, A. (1987). *English for Specific Purposes: a learning-centered approach*. Cambridge: Cambridge University Press.

Johnson, K. (2001). *An introduction to foreign language learning and teaching*. Essex: Pearson Education.

Lightbown, P. M. (2000). Anniversary article: Classroom SLA research and second language teaching. *Applied Lingusitics*, *21*(4), 431-462.

Madsen, H. S. (1983). *Techniques in testing*. Oxford: Oxford University Press.

Mueller, M. (1987). Interactive testing: time to be a test pilot. In W. M. Rivers (Ed.), *Interactive language teaching* (pp. 124-138). Cambridge: Cambridge University Press.

Ommagio, A. C. (1983). Methodology in transition: The new focus on proficiency. *The Modern Language Journal*, *67*(4), 330-341.

Richards, J. C. & Rodgers, T. S. (2001). *Approaches and methods in language teaching* (2nd ed.). Cambridge: Cambridge University Press.

Underhill, N. (1987). *Testing Spoken Language: A handbook of oral testing techniques*. Cambridge: Cambridge University Press.

Valette, R. M. (1977). *Modern language testing* (2nd ed.). New York, NY: Harcourt Brace Jovanovich.

Widdowson, H. G. (1979). The teaching of English as communication. In C. J. Brumfit & K. Johnson (Eds.), *The communicative approach to language teaching* (pp. 117-121). Oxford: Oxford University Press.

In: Language and Literacy Education in a Challenging World   ISBN: 978-1-61761-198-8
Editors: T. Lê, Q. Lê, and M. Short   © 2011 Nova Science Publishers, Inc.

Chapter 18

L2 Vocabulary Acquisition: Learning Vocabulary with L1 and L2 Learners

Shanthi Nadarajan

Abstract

This chapter looks at semester long study that examined the relationship between vocabulary instruction and second language (L2) learners' ability to increase their vocabulary when placed alongside first language (L1) speakers and L2 speakers. Three classes (L1, L2, L1 & L2) were provided with explicit rules about the target words while another three classes had the meanings of difficult words explained to them. A comparison of the pretest-posttest vocabulary size and word used in three essays indicated that a) L2 learners when placed with L1 speakers learned differently from the other groups; b) direct teaching of vocabulary does not necessarily increase all L2 learners' vocabulary growth, and c) L2 learners benefit from explicit vocabulary instruction in the writing class. The study suggests that systematic direct vocabulary instruction may have a role in the language classroom.

Keywords: explicit, implicit, academic vocabulary, vocabulary instruction, meaning based instruction, rule based instruction, prewriting, focus on form.

Introduction

Second language scholars agree that meaning based instruction is more important than form based instruction but the ideal lesson should (still) contain some attention to forms that are embedded in meaningful language (Adamson, 2004). While the debate on how to focus on form (conscious learning processes) continues, there is call from the second language (L2) vocabulary community stating that adult L2 learners need to be taught the most frequent words in the target language explicitly as vocabulary happens to be a prerequisite for language use (Schmitt, 2000) and the existing L2 environment limited to conversational language (Wong, 2005). There is added suggestion that vocabulary activities in class be based on focus on form (FonF) and focus on forms (FonFs) vocabulary activities (Laufer, 2005) that begin with learners first noticing select vocabulary forms and then consciously reflecting on its structure within a meaningful context. This chapter looks at a study that assessed L2 learners' ability to increase and use academic vocabulary alongside L1 speakers and L2 learners through a) rule based explicit vocabulary instruction, and b) meaning based implicit vocabulary instruction.

A RATIONALE FOR EXPLICIT VOCABULARY INSTRUCTION

The objective of this study is three fold. First is the issue of difference between first language (L1) and adult L2 acquisition process. Second is getting L2 learners to notice and attend to specific vocabulary. Third is the importance of sight vocabulary for vocabulary learning to take place.

The L1 and Adult L2 Language Acquisition Process

As Scheffler (2008) mentions, acquiring a foreign or second language for adult L2 learners 'naturally' means acquiring it in the way other cognitive skills are acquired which means beginning from an explicit declarative representation and accumulating a sufficient number of (partial) entities to perform the skill (p. 300). This concept has its origins in Bley Vroman's (1989) view on the L2 acquisition process which states that adults come equipped with general problem solving mechanisms which enable them to deal with abstract formal systems. It is these mechanisms that permit adults to learn through various forms of instruction and learning processes not shared by the L1 process. This position partially accounts for the varying degrees of L2 learner's success in the L2. It is unlikely that L1 speakers' language processes, which are largely implicit, are in need of explicit instruction and have developed through communicative use of the language.

Getting Learners to Notice and Attend to Vocabulary

Currently, vocabulary is seen as best acquired in purely meaning focused instruction (Doughty & Williams, 1998). This assumption is based on Krashen's natural learning hypothesis where vocabulary is said to be acquired through reading and comprehensible input. While reading undoubtedly facilitates, it is not possible to assume that words will be noticed and remembered. A word must appear a number of times within a specific span in order to become a part of the learner's internal vocabulary. As Laufer (1997) points out, few words are retained following an encounter especially when learners deal with long text and are in a hurry to arrive at overall meaning. L2 learners also overestimate their understanding of words and are confused by "deceptively transparent words" due to their imprecise word knowledge (p.25). As for the communicative classroom, though in theory, the L2 learner is said to have unrestricted access to target language input, in practice L2 learners have few opportunities to use the language. Interaction between speakers and learners happens to be crucial for language development as it provides learners with a) comprehensible input, b) elicits negative evidence, and c) pushes learners to modify their output which contributes to fluency. However, a number of second language acquisition (SLA) researchers (Swain &

Lapkin, 1989) have pointed out that, despite countless comprehensible input, L2 learners rarely speak out in the L2 classroom. Most L2 learners' utterances are confined to single word utterances with little attention to error correction. Teacher correction, if at all, is haphazard and lacking in focus. As for the immersion class, students' lack of oral proficiency rarely provides any opportunity for the monitor model to take over.

Importance of a Basic Vocabulary

For vocabulary learning to take place, L2 learners must also possess a threshold vocabulary in order to understand new words, attend to the various meanings and use them meaningfully. Laufer (1997) insists that learners must first have a threshold vocabulary (sight vocabulary) in order to recognise words and context automatically. Nation (2001) states that "following the 2,000 word level, learners need to specialise in their vocabulary learning in order to suit their language goals" (p.168). He further suggests that the 570 words of the Academic word list be made a useful learning goal for learners wanting help with their academic reading. For learners to increase their vocabulary, Laufer (2005) suggests that learners be taught through focus on form (FonF) and focus on forms (FonFs) activities. Incidentally, Long (1983) defined FonF as drawing students' attention to linguistic elements as they arise incidentally in lessons where the overriding focus happens to be on meaning or communication (Long,1991, pp. 45 – 46). This type of instruction differs from meaning focused instruction where learners attend to the message that they want to communicate and the "traditional" method (FonFs) that involves teaching discrete linguistic structures in separate lessons based on a predetermined syllabus. Ellis, Basturkmen & Loewen (2002) describe the FonFs approach as conditions where students view themselves as learners of a language while the language becomes the object of the study. As for FonF, the learner is the language user and language becomes the tool for communication. Currently, the concept of FonF includes planned FonF, which is the use of focused tasks "designed to elicit the use of specific linguistic forms in the context of meaning-centered language use" (p. 420). Regardless of whether FonF is planned, explicit or implicit, vocabulary instruction through FonF has to be carried out from within a meaningful communicative environment.

METHOD

The objective is to investigate a) the effect of explicit rule based vocabulary instruction on L2 learners' vocabulary acquisition and b) L2 learners' ability to learn to use academic words in their writings, and c) learner differences and its effect on L2 vocabulary development. The context for learning were six undergraduate academic writing classes: a) two L1 classes (baseline input); b) two ESL classes (L2 learners only), and c) two immersion classes (combination of L1 and L2 learners).

Research Questions

The three research questions were as follows:

1. Does rule based explicit vocabulary instruction help increase L2 learners' academic vocabulary?

2. Does explicit attention to rule based vocabulary forms help L2 learners' increase their academic word use?

3. Are L2 learners affected by differences within and between groups?

The design

The study involved 129 first year undergraduates (L1=65 students and L2 = 64 students) from an American University. The subjects came from six intact classes (3 treatment – rule based explicit instruction) and 3 (implicit – meaning based instruction). The instructors were 4 L1 teaching assistants who had volunteered to participate in the study. All teaching assistants had a Masters degree in English and were working towards their doctoral studies in an L2 program. All instructors were trained to teach ESL students. Three classes were identified as the control group that taught vocabulary in context (A2-, B1-, and C12-). The (-) sign indicates the control group and (1) indicates L1 subjects while (2) denotes L2 subjects. Implicitly in this context refers to focus on word meanings (semantics) and using a pre-determined set of words for the prewriting activities. The remaining three classes, (A1+, B2+, and D12+), where (+) indicates the treatment group, worked with a pre-determined set of words but instead of using them in their writings, the instructor checked on the correctness of the forms and explained their use for approximately 2- 4 minutes per session. These groups were categorised as the treatment intervention group. The L2 subjects were undergraduates from the China, Japan and Korea and Latin America. Of the total 129 subjects, 79 (61.2%) were males and 50 (38.8%) were females. The age of the subjects was between 18 to 27 years.

The study

In terms of vocabulary input, twenty high-frequency academic words were selected from the students' language textbook (The University Book, 2003) following a discussion with the instructors. The target words are as indicated below:

accurate	*appealing*	*brief*	*celebrate*	*considerable*
deceptive	*minute*	*wild*	*vivid*	*obscure*
essential	*peak*	*organic*	*overall*	*perpetual*
fine	*remote*	*powerful*	*prolonged*	*surplus*

Eight ten- minute vocabulary activities involving sentence completion and word association tasks were constructed as in (a) and (b). Each word was consciously recycled (six to eight times) during the semester in the various language classes through the various fonf, fonfs and meaningful activities.

    (a) Completion exercise
       i.   She decided to purchase a number of essen _____ oils to protect her skin.
       ii.   It must be noted that there is not a character in *Measure in Measure* that is not essen _____ weak and therefore human.
          (answers: essential, essentially)
    (b) Word association (Circle the next word)
       i.   Essential a) *proposition,* b) *nature,* c) *manpower,* d) *oil,* e) *organs*
          (answers: proposition, manpower, oil)

There was a pretest and a posttest. However, subjects were unaware that they had to take a posttest at the end of the study. This was to ensure that the students did not memorise for the post-test. All subjects had to complete two paper and pencil versions of the Productive Vocabulary Levels Test (Nation, 1993) during the first week and last week of the study (PVLT-Version A). The tests were given to determine the entry and exit level proficiency of all participants. In terms of instructors, instructors were required to allocate 10 -15 minutes of ten lessons for teaching vocabulary either through rule based explicit instruction or meaning based vocabulary instruction. All other instructions were carried out within a meaningful context. The treatment classes were required to work on 10 completion activities and 10 word association activities. Generally students took 6 to 8 minutes to complete the activities after which the instructor went through the difficult words by correcting specific errors or drawing attention to different meanings and forms. The instructors explained the various meanings of unfamiliar words based on learner needs either in context or explicitly by pointing out the various rules of the linguistic forms. Students involved in the control groups (meaning based instruction) were required to write free sentences with the target words (predetermined words) for the first ten minutes following which the instructor would discuss the words in context. As part of the coursework, students were required to write three academic essays. The first paper was a rhetorical essay (E1) discussing the various articles in the University Book. The second paper was a reflective essay (E2) describing the experience of the subjects and the third paper (E3) was a reflective essay. All students submitted an electronic copy of the papers which was then downloaded for analysis by the researcher.

Instruments

The study used Nation and Laufer's (1998) Productive Vocabulary Levels Test (PVLT) to measure vocabulary gains. The PVLT measure was used because it has been found to be a reliable measure of vocabulary level, that is easy to use and capable of providing reliable scores for learner performance at the 2000, 3000, UWL, 5000, 10,000 word level (Zimmerman, 2006). As for analysing the writings, Laufer and Nation's (1995) Lexical Frequency profile was used. In the explicit instructional tasks, 20 target words were used in various contexts (240 opportunities) throughout the semester. As they were high frequency words, the words were also available in their readings. So, there were plenty of opportunities for retrieval and pushed output. Completion exercises were selected for the explicit instructional tasks because sentence completion activities have been found to be more effective for learning vocabulary than any in-depth writing exercise, when time happened to be a constraint (Folse, 2006). Once the task had been completed or near completion, the instructors would prove oral feedback as indicated in situation 1. The explicit feedback varied in relation to quality and quantity of interaction within proficient and less proficient students, L1 and L2 learners and learning context.

Situation 1:

Explicit Vocabulary Instruction (FonF)
Class (B2+)
Tr: It says cultural movement. What is cultural movement?
  S1: Time difference
Tr: What do you mean by cultural?
  S1: ... people's culture, being different.
Tr: Yah. That's a noun. Its ... expressions of a particular community.
  S1: Yes... like how cultural changes.
Tr: Not cultural but culture changes. There is a difference between culture changes and cultural changes. One is a noun and one is an adjective.
  S2: Yes, like popular culture ... hip hop
  S1: It's like... to grow something and the culture changes.
Tr: Yes, when you grow something in a Petri dish and it changes... like culturing of micro-organisms as well.

As for the implicit instruction group, the students wrote brief paragraphs using the given keywords for five to eight minutes. It was already determined that the instructors would focus on the same words during the eight sessions. However, the associative words were not pre-planned and the words appeared as students used them in their writings and during the follow up discussion sessions. Students then wrote on a given topic or expanded on the target words without any further discussion as indicated in (b). This was considered pushed output (written form) within implicit instruction.

   (a) Free writing tasks
        Culture – Cultural wave
   (b) Sample (student's) writing:

The Korean Wave refers to the recent cultural phenomenon of South Korean popular culture sweeping through China, Japan, Taiwan, Vietnam, Singapore, Thailand and other Southeast Asian countries. As known, culture plays the central role in building one country's image. Therefore, Korea has to find for methods to keep this Cultural Wave.

As for written performance, the students were required to submit three separate essays. Essay one was collected four weeks after the session began and essay two was collected two weeks after the first assignment. The final essay was collected a month after the second assignment.

RESULTS

The results of the study can be summarised as follows:

RQ# 1: There was an increase in the posttest scores using the PVLT tests for both implicit (control) and explicit (treatment) groups as indicated in Table 1 below.

Table 1 – Mean and percentage of scores on PVLT (Prettest and Posttest)

Group	Pretest				Posttest			
	2K	3K	5K	AWL	2K	3K	5K	AWL
Implicit	13.78	9.36	9.38	9.02	13.76	13.12	9	**11.52**
%	76.56	52.0	52.11	24.44	76.44	72.89	50.00	**64.00**
Explicit	13.89	9.09	9.07	8.83	12.47	12.17	7.96	**9.49**
%	77.17	50.50	50.39	49.06	69.28	67.61	44.22	**52.72**

N (92)   Note: The increase at Posttest level is italicized in bold

The control groups subjected to meaning based implicit learning activities recorded an increase of 3.8 (20.89%) at the 3000 word level and 2.5 (13.89%) for the Academic Word level (AWL). The treatment group subjected to explicit instruction recorded a gain of 3.08 (17.11%) at the 3000 word level and 0.66 (3.67%) at the AWL level. The repeated mean ANOVA used to compare the difference between the treatment types indicated that the difference between scores for the various groups were statistically significant at $F(1,126) = 4.18921$ with $p < 0.001$. Meaning based implicit instruction was more effective for helping learners increase their vocabulary.

However, with success in L2 learning being gauged in relation to the different degrees of success rather than failure it was necessary to see if all groups increased their academic vocabulary similarly. Table 2 indicates the rates of achievement in the AWL for the various classes involved in the study.

The top two classes (B1- and C12-) had gained by more than 16% compared to D12+ which had lost by -9.7%. It was possible to state that the meaning based implicit instructional process was more efficient.

RQ#2: In terms of essays, there was a difference within the average percentage of academic words used for all three essays by both L1 and L2 learners. As indicated in the Table 3 below, it was evident that 5 % of the words in all three L1 essays happen to be academic words. As for the L2 subjects, except for the first essay (E1) which was 5.2%, less than 5% of the words happen to be academic words. To study the effect of instruction over L2 performance in relation to setting due to learner difference, a repeated measure analysis of variance (ANOVA) was conducted for the AWL of E1, E2 and E3 and for the instructional groups. The three essays were not totally independent of each other since the final essay (E3) was a revision of either E1 or E2.The alpha level for the analyses was set at 0.05 for test of significance. The results of academic word use (AWL) was statistically significant at $F (1, 123) = 1152.238$, $p < 0.001$. The level of word use between control (implicit) and treatment (explicit) group were statistically significant at F (1, 123) = 7.259, p< 0.05. The two-way interaction (See Figure 1) between the groups and L1 and L2 subjects were also statistically significant at F (1, 123) = 6.092, p < 0.05. From the interaction plot it was possible to deduce that the L2 subjects in the rule based explicit groups (D12+ and B2+) were responding to the formal instruction in a systematic manner.

Table 2 – Pre and Post AWL Scores

Group	UWL	Mean	%	SD	SEM	Gain (%)
B1-	Pre	11	61.4	4.92	1.03	
	Post	**14.5**	80.4	3.53	0.74	*19.1*
C12-	Pre	6.8	38	4.2	1.21	
	Post	**9.8**	54.2	3.61	0.9	*16.2*
A1+	Pre	11.3	63	3.21	0.67	
	Post	**13**	72.4	3.88	0.78	*9.4*
A2-	Pre	7.7	42.9	5.08	1.36	
	Post	**8.9**	49.6	3.47	0.9	*6.8*
B2+	Pre	5.4	30.2	4.88	1.3	
	Post	**5.9**	32.7	5.8	1.37	*2.6*
D12+	Pre	7.8	43.3	5.92	1.32	
	Post	6.1	33.6	6.12	1.44	*-9.7*
Instructors = A, B, C, D		Treatment = +		Control = -		
L1 students = 1		L2 students = 2		L1 + L2 students = 12		

Note: Gains are in bold

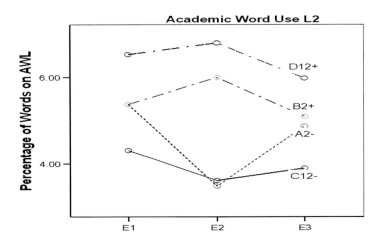

Figure 1: Academic Word Use for the 3 Essays (E1, E2 & E3)

RQ#3: To determine whether L2 learners vocabulary development is affected by learner differences, the pre-test and post-test results at the 2000 word level and the AWL level of the instructional groups were compared as in Table 3.

Table 3 – Differences between L1 and L2 Pretest and Posttest Scores

		2k				UWL			
		Pre	*SD*	Post	*SD*	Pre	*SD*	Post	*SD*
L1	Control	15.440	*2.083*	**15.966**	*1.210*	11.160	*4.732*	**13.724**	*3.844*
	Treatment	15.581	*2.754*	14.970	*3.046*	11.968	*2.601*	**12.545**	*4.206*
L2	Control	12.120	*3.551*	12.120	*3.707*	6.880	*4.447*	**9.077**	*3.346*
	Treatment	11.708	*4.428*	11.708	*4.796*	4.792	*4.890*	**5.292**	*5.409*

Note: Gains are italicized in bold

L1 subjects had begun with a higher 2000 word level and AWL (+15.5 and +11.5) while the L2 subjects had begun with a lower score for the 2000 word level and AWL (+6.8 and +4.8) The treatment groups for both L1 and L2 were heterogeneous in nature. To determine whether L2 subjects were affected by proficiency level (in terms of speakers and learners), a repeated mean measure was conducted for subjects who had scored above 14 (approximately 80%) at the 2000 level. There were 41 subjects for the control and 35 for the proficient L2 learners. There were 16 L2 students in the control and 19 L2 students in the experimental group. The main effect of language groups was significant $F (1, 52) = 16.066$, $p <0.001$. The results for testing the within subjects' effects and between subjects' effects were not significant and this could be related to the small effect size. There were less than 20 L2 students with a satisfactory level of basic vocabulary in the study.

DISCUSSION

The findings from this study suggests that formal instruction that integrate focus on form and focus on forms vocabulary activities have an effect on L2 learners' vocabulary development. While the findings revealed that meaning based implicit (incidental) instruction as more effective for helping learners increase their vocabulary, there were additional evidence in the study to suggests that systematic attention to rule based vocabulary instruction can help learners acquire key vocabulary knowledge at a faster rate compared to meaning based vocabulary input.

Marked Improvement when L2 Learners Placed with L1 Speakers

From the comparison of the instructional groups, it was evident that the strongest vocabulary gains were experienced by the classes in the meaning based implicit instructional group. The analysis of the various subgroups (6 classes) indicated that all groups increased their academic word level at the post test. However, the real differences came from the combination classes which had begun from almost the same initial level. The meaning based group gained more words while the rule based explicit instructional group did not increase their AWL, suggesting that L2 learners despite their initial level can still improve their vocabulary when placed in an L1 environment. Evidently, even the weak L2 learners benefit from the interaction of advanced speakers. However, the very fact that the initial level was actually based on the average scores of both L1 and L2 subjects need to be taken into consideration.

Vocabulary development is affected by initial vocabulary level and meaningful input. Learners who begin with a higher level of vocabulary knowledge at the pre test go on to increase their vocabulary as demonstrated by the L1 subjects. This is the progressive nature of vocabulary development. But it must be noted that the L1 language acquisition process is different from adult L2 acquisition. L1 speakers are viewed as invariably successful in the language. The L1 process does not make use of explicit formal instruction and speakers are not influenced by affective factors (Scheffler, 2008, p.300). However, with adult L2 learners, there is variation in their level of success. Adult learners make use of various forms of instruction and their learning is affected by personality and motivation. It is possible for L2 learners to benefit from meaning based implicit input because it involves conscious processing of associative words, but this does not work for all L2 subjects. Many of the L2 subjects in the experimental group began from a low initial vocabulary level and they did not increase their AWL vocabulary in the study and some even loose their vocabulary. The adult L2 learners' vocabulary development is dependent on threshold vocabulary level as often stated by researchers (Read, 2000; Meara, 2002). It therefore becomes difficult for L2 learners to increase their vocabulary when they lack a basic sight word recognition and are unable to guess or generalise meanings of unfamiliar word forms. From the study it could be said that the combination group involving implicit learning conditions gained more compared to the explicit learning groups.

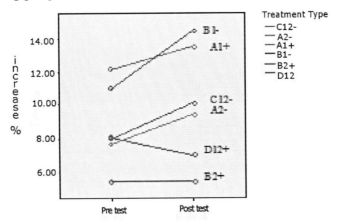

Figure 2: Interaction plot for the subgroups

It is possible that the L2 learners did gain from the interaction of L1 subjects as it provided additional knowledge about the word. The L1 speakers did most of the talking in class and L2 responses were limited to brief phrases and one word answers throughout the study. There were exceptions when there were proficient L2 learners in the class. The fact that the L2 classes began from a low initial level and did not increase their vocabulary size by the end of the study (See figure 2) is further evidence for L2 learners' need to have a threshold vocabulary for rules based explicit instruction to work.

Explicit Instruction is Effective in Helping L2 Learners use their Academic Vocabulary

In terms of academic word use, both implicit and explicit instructional groups academic word use were not very different. As for instructional group however, it was evident that the L2 learners in the treatment group had increased their academic word use for E2 and reduced it for E3 (See Figure 3a & 3b).

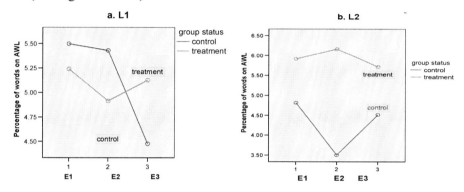

Figure 3a & 3b: Interaction plots for L1 and L2 subjects by essays

This rise for the L2 subjects second essay suggests that explicit form focused instruction has an immediate effect on L2 learners' word use. However as learners gradually learn to focus on grammar and syntax, the emphasis on vocabulary will change. The fact that the third essay was a reflective essay rather than academic essay (E1 and E2) could have contributed to the reduced use of academic words as well. Nevertheless, the performance of the L2 learners in the treatment groups was consistent and predictable. It cannot be ignored that it was the L2 learners in treatment groups who used the largest number of academic words for the second essay demonstrating that it is possible to get learners to increase their academic word use through vocabulary instruction.

L2 Learners Require Basic Vocabulary Competence to Learn New Academic Vocabulary

L2 learners were affected by the differences between and within groups. The L2 subjects in the meaning based implicit instructional group began from a higher 2000 word level. They had a much higher academic word level than the L2 subjects in the explicit instructional group. These differences resulted in a negative performance for rule based explicit vocabulary instructional group. However, when a modified group was used involving only students who obtained 80 per cent and above, it was found that the L2 subjects in the explicit instructional group despite starting from a lower level were capable of accelerating their vocabulary growth at twice the rate of that of the L2 subjects in the implicit instructional group (See figure 4). This improvement is noteworthy.

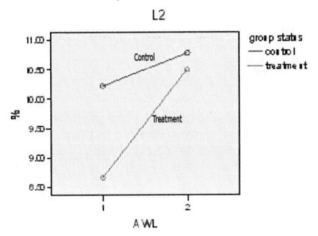

Figure 4: Performance of proficient L2 learners according to instructional groups

Formal instruction does have a positive effect on the L2 vocabulary learning process but it is solely not subject to L1 or L2 learning conditions rather to learners' initial vocabulary ability and instructional process. Learners may still notice words and meanings and be unable to express a word well because they are unsure of their vocabulary ability. So, regardless of whether pedagogic treatments are pre-planned or incidental, there is no guarantee that the learners to whom they are addressed have reached an appropriate level of development. However, getting learners to notice and attend to key words does help because word learning happens to be an accumulative process that learners need to retrieve and use them in order to make it a part of their active vocabulary.

CONCLUSION

Overall, L2 learners who begin from a larger vocabulary base have more words to work from during interaction. This vocabulary helps L2 learners develop an underlying competence in the language and enables them to progress. However, the assumption that the communicative classroom will trigger natural language processes leading to acquisition and development of the second language is no longer true. It works for L1 speakers but does not always work for less proficient L2 learners. While it is possible that some vocabulary can be taught explicitly, there is also the problem of getting students to use it. As Skehan (1998) says, "learners do not simply learn what teachers teach" (p.130). However, in the L2 classroom, less proficient learners do depend on teachers to learn their words. In that matter, the instructional approach and systematic practice of specific skills matter. L2 learners need to learn certain vocabulary directly and this can be done through a number of methods. Similarly, they need to be taught the strategies that will help them expand their vocabulary. At the end, it is not a question of how far they have reached alongside L1 speakers, rather it is a matter of what the L2 learners learning goal happens to be. As for a vocabulary syllabus, as

Scheffler (2008) states, describing a syllabus as both communicative and structural need not be a contradiction in the current language teaching system. A well planned vocabulary program that uses communicative activities to teach vocabulary uses drills in the form of information gap activities and association practice to help reinforce learning should be seen as relevant and necessary for L2 learners to become successful and fluent. The research has indicated that it possible to teach vocabulary through meaning based and rule based instruction in the classroom but it must be noted that not all words are amenable to explicit instructions. Similarly, not all L2 learners benefit from explicit instruction especially when they do have sufficient vocabulary to begin with. There are some words which are best explained in context while others can be explained through rules. Most of all, it is a matter of getting learners to acquire basic proficiency in the target language and learning to use it productively that matters.

REFERENCES

Adamson, H.D. (2005). *Language minority students in American schools: An education in English.* New Jersey: Lawrence Erlbaum & Associates Inc.

Bley-Vroman, R. (1989). What is the logical problem of foreign language learning? In S. Gass & J. Schachter (Eds.), *Linguistic perspectives on second language acquisition* (pp. 41-68). Cambridge: Cambridge University Press.

M. Gass & Jacquelin Schachter (eds.), *Linguistic Perspectives on Second Language Acquisition* (pp. 41-68). Cambridge, UK: Cambridge University Press.

Doughty, C., & Williams, J. (1998). *Focus on Form in Classroom Second Language Acquisition.* Cambridge: Cambridge University Press.

Ellis, R., Basturkmen, H. and Loewen, S. (2002). Doing focus on form. *System. 30*, 419-432.

Folse, K. (2006). The effect of type of written exercise on L2 vocabulary retention. *TESOL Quarterly, 40*(2), 273-293.

Laufer, B. (2005). Focus on form in second language vocabulary learning. *EUROSLA Yearbook, 5*, 223-250.

Laufer, B. (1997). The lexical plight in second language: Words you don't know, words you think you know, and words you can't guess. In J. Coady, & T. Huckin (Eds.), *Second language vocabulary acquisition: A rationale for pedagogy* (pp. 20-34). Cambridge: Cambridge University Press.

Laufer, B. & Nation, P. (1998). A vocabulary size test of controlled productive ability, *Language Testing, 16*, 307-322.

Laufer, B. & Nation, P. (1995). Vocabulary size and use: Lexical richness in L2 written production. *Applied Linguistics, 16*(3), 307-322.

Long, M. H. (1991). Focus on form: a design feature in language teaching methodology. In K. de Bot, R. Ginsberg, and C. Kramsch (eds.), *Foreign Language Research in Cross Cultural Perspective* (pp. 39-52). Amsterdam: John Benjamins.

Meara, P. (2002). Review Article: the Rediscovery of vocabulary. *Second Language Research, 18*(4), 393-407.

Nation, (2001). *Learning vocabulary in another language.* Cambridge: Cambridge University Press.

Nation, P. (1993), Measuring readiness for simplified reading: A test of the first 1000 words of English. *RELC, 31,* 193-203.

Scheffler, P. (2008). The natural approach to adult learning and teaching of L2 grammar. *IRAL, 46*(4), 289-313.

Skehan, P. (1998). *A cognitive approach to language learning.* Oxford: Oxford University Press.

Schmitt, N. (2000). *Vocabulary in language teaching.* Cambridge: Cambridge University Press.

Read, J. (2000). *Assessing vocabulary.* Cambridge: Cambridge University Press.

Wong, W. (2005). Input Enhancement: From theory and research to the classroom. New York: McGraw Hill.

Zimmerman, K. (2005). Newly placed versus continuing students: Comparing vocabulary size. *TESL Reporter, 38*(1), 52-60.

PART III

SOCIO-CULTURAL ASPECTS OF LANGUAGE AND LITERACY EDUCATION

In: Language and Literacy Education in a Challenging World   ISBN: 978-1-61761-198-8
Editors: T. Lê, Q. Lê, and M. Short   © 2011 Nova Science Publishers, Inc.

Chapter 19

TEACHING CULTURE THROUGH FOREIGN LANGUAGE: ISSUES AND CHALLENGES

Muhlise Coşgun Ögeyik

ABSTRACT

This chapter touches on the significance and challenges of culture in foreign language learning and teaching environments. Since culture has become an increasingly important component of foreign language teaching in recent times, discussion of some cultural issues in education is the core of this chapter. In common sense, learning cultural components of the target language is thought to be a pathway to communicate efficiently in the target language. In addition to providing access into communicative competency, learning culture helps language learners relate the abstract forms of a language to real people and places. Culture teaching may offer learners some opportunities to learn about their own cultural norms by comparing their own native culture with the target language culture. However, some challenges may come about while learning these cultural components. In culture teaching, learners may disrupt their own world view and self-identity as well as ways of acting, thinking and evaluating. As every culture has its own cultural norms and these norms differ from one culture to another, some of the norms can be completely dissimilar and conflicting with other cultural norms. While dealing with such dissimilar norms, some problems may arise among learners who do not know or share the norms of the other culture. It may also force learners to develop prejudices about otherness. In this chapter, some suggestions are recommended to overcome the potential problems and to boost intercultural competence.

Keywords: culture, culture teaching, language education, intercultural competence, cultural awareness.

INTRODUCTION

Culture is a complicated term to be defined as a specific or universal expression. In a general sense, the term culture refers to the system of shared beliefs, behaviors, and artifacts that the members of a society use to cope with their world and with one another, and that are transmitted from generation to generation through learning (Bates, 1990). The notion of culture, which can be assumed as a living entity, has an interaction and evolution in itself.

Peterson and Coltran (2003) define culture as a complex and interrelated pattern of human behavior that includes all thoughts, communication strategies and systems, languages, beliefs, values, customs, rituals, manners, interactive roles, relationships and expected behaviors of a racial, ethnic, religious and social group. What is clear in this definition is that all elements belonging to human life are interwoven within the notion of culture. In a parallel way, Kramsch (1993) states that culture is a notion through which a social group represents itself and others through its values such as works of art, literature, social institutions and artifacts of daily life. From these definitions of the term culture, it can be deduced that culture is an umbrella term that acts as a mirror reflecting the values of a community. Culture, then, is a dynamic entity with variable perspectives, and it is the connection of many passageways where the passengers attempt to learn their own and others' directions throughout their life. The main tool guiding people in the junctions of cultures is language. Then, cultural awareness and transfer can be best realized through language.

CULTURE AND LANGUAGE

Language is not the mere sum of static language items such as sounds, words, phrases or sentences, but it is a dynamic body with its flexible systems reflecting and being affected by other cultures. A language is a part of culture and a culture is a part of a language. The two are intricately interwoven so that one cannot separate the two notions. In other words, language and culture are two concepts which are strictly interrelated. It is difficult to mention one of these concepts when the other is absent.

All languages change through time (Fromkin & Rodman, 1993) and a new phrase or word can penetrate into a language through the interaction of the speakers of different cultures. Old fashioned words or phrases may replace new ones transferred from other languages, from other cultures and through any interaction. The words or phrases borrowed from other languages and cultures replace the older ones. For instance, there are many words in Turkish that came from English and penetrated into Turkish such as activity: aktivite; actual: aktüel; emblem: amblem; anarchy: anarşi; archive: arşiv; agenda: ajanda. On the other hand, some words came into English from Turkish; for instance, yoğurt: yoghurt. Such transfers are countless and occur due to interactions of cultures. This interaction can be viewed as enrichment within languages and cultures.

CULTURE AND LANGUAGE EDUCATION

It is well known that knowing a language means not only comprehension of linguistic features such as grammar, phonology, lexis and syntax of a language, but also certain characteristics of language related items such as culture. As the use of language in general is related to social and cultural values, language is presumed to be a social and cultural phenomenon. Therefore, the importance of the language proficiency level of a person calls upon the development of competency in the learner's language skills. The notion of competence has been valued in various ways in language teaching and learning practice. As consistent with the needs and expectations in language learning and teaching, the paradigms in terms of competency have changed. During the first half of the 20th century, linguistic competence was thought to be a complementary element of comprehended linguistic units. In this context, language learners are thought to be developing the necessary linguistic items and performing them in language skills; in other words, linguistic competence is what learners know about language (Fromkin and Rodman, 1993). Chomsky (1965) defines linguistic competence as what one knows about the language while linguistic performance is one's actual language use. However, what is known about a language is different from what people do with language knowledge. That is, the speakers of a language need more than grammatical competence in order to be able to communicate effectively in a language (Hymes, 1972). Since competence is accepted as an idealization, it is realized by an ideal speaker communicating in a homogenous situation (Brumfit and Johnson, 1991).

Therefore, with the 1970s, the paradigm of language teaching and learning shifted from a linguistic oriented paradigm to a communicative oriented one; thus, communicative competence became the foundation of language education. In communicative competence, learners are expected to know how language is used by the members of a speech community to accomplish their purposes. In order to accomplish all aspects of a language in a communicative way, learners need to have the ability to apprehend behavior from the cultural perspectives of the members of the target language. Thus, the paradigm has shifted to cultural competence which involves an understanding of all aspects of traditions of the target language, particularly the social structure, the values and beliefs of the people, and the way things are assumed to be done. Cultural competency means engaging in foreign culture and developing self-awareness; in this sense, cultural competency helps individuals see the world with the eyes of others and evaluate other beliefs, thoughts and life styles. Sercu (2005) stresses the importance of culture teaching and insists that teaching a foreign language means connecting learners to a world that is culturally different from their own. In that case, language learning is not merely the acquisition of communicative competence in the target language but also developing intercultural competence and engaging in the other culture. That is, cultural competence entails an understanding of the differences in interactional norms between different speech communities and an ability to reconcile or mediate between different existing modes (Byram and Fleming 1998).

CULTURE TEACHING

Language as mentioned above is not a mere code system dealing with simply grammatical functions to be acquired. On the contrary, languages are learned for communication, and effective communication requires the integration of multiple factors, including linguistic, cultural, and cognitive variables. If so, languages can be seen as the keys for opening the doors of other cultures (Byram, 1991). On the other hand, languages are not simple reflectors of cultures but instead could be considered central elements of cultures. In everyday language teaching and learning environments, language can be considered as a tool used for conveying meaning, and meaning is typically obtained by cultural awareness.

Traditionally, culture has been taught through the transfer of some cultural elements in different courses such as Landeskunde, Kulturkunde or Civilisation. However, in these courses, a penetration of the target culture in terms of information about history, geography, arts, religious, traditions, and life styles has been required (Tomalin and Stempleski, 1993). Instead, in recent years, multiculturalism and multilingualism have been determined as set of concepts in the changing notion of language teaching (CEF, 2001). The concept of culture in this perception has been accepted as interpreting cross-cultural awareness. The common cultural points are: everyday living, living conditions, interpersonal relations, social classes, values, beliefs, body language, social conventions, ritual behaviors, etc. These culture specific items correspond to knowledge of society and culture of community.

CULTURE CONTENT IN LANGUAGE EDUCATION

Until the late 1970s, the importance of teaching culture in language teaching environments was discussed, and since the 1970s as a paradigm shift, teaching of cultural components have been included into the language teaching curricula (Pulverness, 2003). With the great efforts and insistence of some intellectuals such as Byram (1991), Kramsch (1993, 2001) culture teaching has been included into the agenda of language educators and curricula in order to evoke cross-cultural awareness, consequently to lead to successful communication. Byram (1991) states two possibilities to be combined in the teaching process: the use of the learners' mother tongue for comparative analysis of their own and foreign cultural meanings can be combined with the teaching of the foreign language both as a subject and as a medium of experience of foreign cultural phenomena. Then, what is clear in this combination is that language awareness and cultural awareness are common points both in mother language and foreign language.

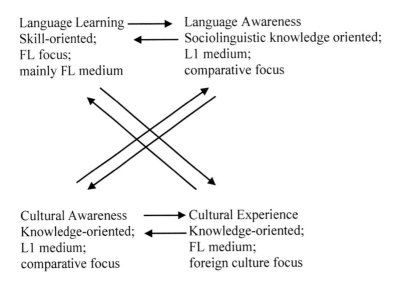

Language Learning ⟶ Language Awareness
Skill-oriented;   ⟵ Sociolinguistic knowledge oriented;
FL focus;   L1 medium;
mainly FL medium   comparative focus

Cultural Awareness   ⟶ Cultural Experience
Knowledge-oriented;   ⟵ Knowledge-oriented;
L1 medium;   FL medium;
comparative focus   foreign culture focus

Figure 1: The Language and Culture Teaching Process (Byram, 1991, p.20)

As indicated in the diagram of language and culture teaching process, there exists a mutual relationship between the dual concepts. Thus, language learning and language awareness cannot be separated from cultural awareness and cultural experience. In other words, there appears a mutually supportive link between the language and cultural meanings of the experience. Such mutual relationship between language and culture has been the core of many attempts to develop intercultural competence in language teaching and learning environments (Adorno 1993; Foucault, 1994; Wittgenstein, 1999). Thus, the facts of one culture can be interpreted by moving towards cross-cultural perception. It is a dialectical connection between a person's own culture and other culture(s) which can be understood by comparison.

WHY CULTURE TEACHING?

Foreign language education is an evolutionary process during which many approaches have been attributed great importance; among those approaches, culture appeals to refresh common assumptions with regard to intellectual individual transformations. In common sense, language is shaped by its user within the context in which the target language is used, and the context is by and large figured out through cultural norms. Therefore, language teaching and learning processes are linked to the cultural links of the language.

In a natural process, someone involved in teaching or learning a language is also involved in teaching and learning culture at the same time (Thanasoulas, 2001). In view of the fact that culture and language are acknowledged as inseparable concepts in language teaching, some scholars attempt to explain the interrelation between those concepts. In an attempt to demonstrate this relation, McKay (2003) contends that culture influences language teaching in two ways: linguistically and pedagogically. Linguistically, it affects the semantic, pragmatic, and discourse levels of the language. Pedagogically, it influences the choice of the language materials because cultural content of the language materials and the cultural basis of the teaching methodology are to be taken into consideration while deciding upon the language materials.

In addition, Kramsch (1993) focuses on the interrelation of language and culture and states that neither language nor culture can exist without the existence of the other. Damen (1987) also points out that language should be culture related and culture specific for the purpose of comprehending a message that has been conveyed. Then both language and culture are like the mirrors reflecting the values of any society. Brown (1994) insists that there are values, presuppositions, about the nature of life and what is good and bad in it, to be found in any normal use of language.

Whether culture is consciously or unconsciously a part of any educator's language syllabus, the transmission of culture is unavoidable. In this sense, culture learning or teaching is a natural process in which people internalize the knowledge needed to function in a society. When this process is carried out in a non-native language context, acculturation occurs (Damen, 1987). In the acculturation process, an individual involves in pulling out of the world view of the first culture and must learn a new way of comparing his or her own culture. In this process, each individual's path of acculturation may differ without following the same experiences. That is, interacting with the other culture inevitably occurs individually in an intercultural environment.

In some cases, educators may not be aware of the necessity of cultural orientation. Instead, they may think teaching a foreign language is just dealing with the common linguistic features of that language. However, interaction with culture is an automatic practice taking place in language teaching. For instance, even greeting types in any piece of dialogue denote the cultural aspects of the language learnt. That means, when learners are learning even the simplest or basic items of any language, they engage in intercultural communication by acquiring culture-specific and culture-general knowledge, skills and attitudes required for effective communication and interaction with the individuals from other cultures.

INTERCULTURAL COMMUNICATION IN LANGUAGE CLASSES AND MATERIALS

Intercultural communication is the foundation of interaction between two cultures- native culture and target culture in foreign language teaching. Intercultural pedagogy finds its dimension and evokes a superfluous aspect in language teaching and learning by understanding and comparing cultures of other people. It is the mobility of the objectives of language teaching in or out of the language class. In every aspect of life, engaging into different cultures is inevitable. For instance, satellite broadcast and mass media prompt this mobility and offer cultural opportunities to be engaged in. Furthermore, in language classes, the materials used to teach a foreign language convey cultural information and messages explicitly or implicitly.

Among those course materials, course books increasingly take part in the cultural transmission within the educational system and they are ascribed an increasingly central role. Course books have been the vital core of language courses due to the fact that they provide a variety of communicative tasks, drills, language situations, opportunities, and exercises. Cunningsworth (1995) reports some roles of course books such as a resource for presentation materials (spoken/written); a source of activities for learner practice and communicative interaction; a reference source; a syllabus; a resource for self-directed learning or self-access work; and a support for less experienced teachers. If so, course books can be attributed significant importance in the sense that they provide helpful tasks, strategic guidelines, and authentic examples of target language by serving learning styles and strategies. Those books give alleged genuine examples from real life and provide some pathways for choosing the suitable situational conditions for the learners of that language. Then, a course book should present cultural elements and open paths to different cultures. While dealing with such course books, learners inevitably engages in different cultures. Course books, in other words, should present a wider range of cultural topics to both educators and learners and provide a comprehensive picture of cultural knowledge in order to conduct appropriately in cross-cultural communication (Zu & Kong, 2009).

Literary texts as well as course books are the vehicles for conveying cultural items to target language learners. It is an unquestionable fact that literary texts make available the written and oral cultures of the target language or other cultures through the target language. Whatsoever the topic or genre of literary text, it stimulates awareness of cultural codes. While dealing with such texts, learners of a language both encounter different cultural items and may get the chance of comparing their own culture and the other culture(s). Then, reading literary genres leads to be familiar with culture specific points in language learning process. It is simply accepted as given that literature is a viable component of second language programs at the appropriate level and that one of the major functions of literature is to serve as a medium to transmit the culture of the people who speak the language in which it is written (Valdes, 1986). For instance, in the extract below, there exist many hidden cultural points from English culture.

Radiating to point men's feet and women's feet, black or gold-encrusted (This foggy weather. Sugar? No, thank you. The commonwealth of the future) the firelight darting and making the room red, save for the black figures and their bright eyes, while outside a van discharges, Miss Thingummy drinks tea at her desk, and plate-glass preserves fur coats. (Monday or Tuesday by Virginia Woolf, 1921)

In the extract, the custom emphasized implicitly in parenthesis indicates both the time expression in the story and cultural codes from a British tradition. "Miss Thingummy drinks tea" is another indicator for such tradition. Another implicit reference in terms of British habit is "This foggy weather" referring to one of the most common topics British people use in their daily conservations.

On the other hand, in some literary texts, cultural points are presented explicitly in order to evoke cultural awareness of readers. For instance, in *A Passage to India*, which is a masterly investigation of racial apprehension in colonial India, a deep association of British and Indian cultures in terms of Islamic and Christian beliefs, customs, and attitudes are repeatedly and explicitly presented:

...and then an Englishwoman stepped out into the moonlight. Suddenly he was furiously angry and shouted: -Madam, this is a mosque, you have no right here at all; you should have taken off your shoes; this is a holly place for Moslems. (E. M. Forster, 1942)

However, it is sometimes discussed that literature of the past cannot be used as a source to interpret contemporary society (Hammerly, 1982; Seelye, 1993). Such a view may be partially legitimate but culture is an extensive expression that deals with not only contemporary issues but also with a particular period, society, civilization or group. The main argument for using literary texts can be assumed as literature's ability to represent the particular voice of an author among the many voices of his or her community and thus appeal to the particular in the reader (Kramsch, 1993). For the reason that literary texts are richer and more diverse than factual texts, they offer learners the opportunity to explore both the multiplicity of language and culture (Fenner, 2001). In this context, cultural awareness shares with language awareness a dual purpose of supporting language learning and extending general understanding of the nature of culture.

As well as authentic literary texts, translated texts can be appraised as culture transmitting tools. Translation which has direct affiliation with the transformation of culture by means of different text types and is regarded as intercultural communication has mainly dual functions in foreign language learning environments, explicitly, both for comprehension and production in native and foreign languages. Regarding this idea, translation activities can be assumed as not only the contrastive analyses of languages but also comparing two cultures, namely native and foreign cultures. For instance, a written text referring to Moslem tradition in Turkish may reflect some common customs of that culture. The words Ramazan and Kurban Festivals, which cannot be translated for the readers from other cultures, are used in original forms and take the attention of readers towards those words. Hence, those words may be learnt as representative of Moslem culture. In order to convey meaning, some expressions can be added to those words: for instance, the former one is a festival which is celebrated after a month called Ramazan when eating and drinking during the daytime are avoided and the latter one refers to the festival whose roots are back to pagan ceremony lasts four days and some sacrificial animals such as lamb, sheep, or calf are immolated as a requirement of Moslem tradition. In the same manner, some meal names such as kadınbudu köfte, karnıyarık, imambayıldı, vezir parmağı, ali and nazik, which carry different and absurd meanings when translated are conveyed as in their original forms. Thus, the readers who face those meal names in a translation text can learn about different types of meals from the Turkish tradition.

Culture knowledge is also gained through mass communication tools, which include mass media. The development of the media has had considerable impacts on private life, and the media and mass communications have interacted and mixed with pre-existing cultures, forms and values, especially in the development of popular culture. That is, many people consume movies, radio, television, newspapers, magazines, and the internet in their private lives, and in doing so, they are confronted with different cultures. Facilities of the mass media, as tools for life-long learning, in education settings, therefore, can have learners to engage in cultures.

The matter of how the intercultural tools can be integrated into language education can be proposed by taking the advantages and disadvantages of culture teaching and learning into account. Although culture and cultural studies are accepted as integral parts of language education curriculum (Kramsch, 1993), some challenges may appear during the education process.

BENEFITS AND CHALLENGES OF CULTURE EDUCATION

In developing intercultural awareness in foreign language classrooms, students are subject to making a distinction between cultural norms, beliefs, deviations of their own culture and other culture(s). They compare their own native cultural norms with the target or other cultural norms.

In intercultural education, then, a learner begins to question, criticize and evaluate individual thinking by integrating both his/her own and other culture by defeating prejudices about the other or otherness. Thus, foreign language learning means changing learners' behaviours and integrating a new way of life and new values of life in his/her existing behaviors and life pattern. By assimilating many new codifications, learners develop cultural awareness. While integrating into new components, their consciousness about the world and humanity may change depending on various patterns. Furthermore, culture teaching in which learners observe similarities and differences among various cultural groups may trigger motivation towards the target language. Thus, they may have a tendency to judge the previous and inappropriate opinions and values of both their own culture and other cultures. By carrying out some culturally based activities such as searching about countries and peoples, singing songs, role plays, learners are motivated to cope with the difficulties in the sense of linguistic, communicative and cultural competences. Accordingly, culture education can boost learners' interest towards other culture(s) as well as their motivation towards learning and using the language they learn.

However, some language educators may be hardly aware of the requirement of culture orientation due to their lack of knowledge about the cultural components of the target language they teach, or their prejudices about the otherness. They may also see culture teaching and learning as a threat to the native values. Thus, students of such educators may face many problems both at the linguistic and communicative level. In order to find solutions to such problems, in the teacher training process, prospective language educators should be exposed to culture specific components.

Integration of intercultural aspects of language learning into the language teacher education curriculum can be supportive in establishing cultural awareness. In this sense, some opportunities can be recommended:

- both educators and learners of teacher education programs may have the chance to spend a period of residence in a country where the language they are studying is spoken;

- via the mass media, prospective language educators may construct their intercultural perceptions;

- through the internet, they may join some chat rooms of other countries as an integral part of some speaking or elective courses by corresponding with other colleagues on various issues of culture; this could lead to motivating discussions among them both for linguistic and, comprehensively, for cultural differences. Such an activity may enhance them to learn and respect the concept of the "other";

- prospective language educators may introduce culturally oriented materials into the literature and translation courses; in linguistic courses, cultural aspects may be discussed pragmatically under the attentive guidance of the teacher educator; or some newspaper reports on the world events can be used as course materials in linguistic, translation and elective courses;

- some research projects can be designed for making research and raising awareness on global culture as the extracurricular activities (Ögeyik, 2008).

It is increasingly becoming apparent that culture is the soul of any country and has a significant link with language. Thus, the inclusion and exclusion of culture in language curricula is an important issue and a challenge for language teaching. As culture is a deeply embedded part of language, and language is the expression of culture (Brown, 1994). An individual who is learning a language in a culture oriented course may use words and expressions more skillfully and authentically, use language appropriately and act naturally while dealing with language. In addition to those advantages, studying culture boosts learners' general and intellectual knowledge by learning about other cultures.

However, culture teaching may lead to some challenges in education settings. In culture education, learners may disrupt their own world view, self-identity, and even ways of acting, thinking and evaluating. Since every culture has its own cultural norms and these norms differ from one culture to another, some of the norms can be completely dissimilar and conflicting with other cultures' norms. While dealing with such dissimilar norms, some problems may arise among learners who do not know or share the norms of other culture. When they read a piece of writing in foreign language culture and if they do not know the presented cultural components, it may create hindrances for learners to read such texts. Such an obstruction may affect learners' linguistic competency negatively, and their attitudes towards reading authentic texts may be disrupted.

Most course books give genuine examples from real life without background knowledge for such real situations, so those examples may be considered as challenging to understand the situations. In some situations, when confronted with a different culture, learners may reject this new culture. What is more, if the values of other culture(s) are presented as dominant, learners may easily develop prejudice towards those values and ignore those components. Therefore, they may even reject to learn the language of such cultures. In addition, some ideological and religious items may be discarded by learners. Even if they may be eager to learn about such components of other cultures, they, after acquiring the knowledge about them, may begin to compare their own ideological and cultural norms with other cultures. If differences appear between the two cultures, they may react negatively and value the target culture as odd.

On the other hand, language learners may think their own cultural values are dominant values, so they may expect that their cultural identity should be appraised as the supreme one. If target culture or other cultures are valued as the dominant one(s), learners' communication competence is disrupted. Such a mismatch may affect their psychological comfort. In a classroom, even group isolation may appear due to such cultural mismatch. Some may support target culture and the rest may favor their own culture by rejecting otherness. The solutions to these possible problems can be accomplished by the references of educators and cooperation of some institutions such as families, schools and governments. Through authentic texts, mass media materials, course books and translated texts, cultural awareness can be raised; and through cultural awareness, linguistic and communicative competence in the target language can be developed. Therefore, educators should choose culture-oriented materials consistent with the expectations of learners.

Since there are real differences between groups and cultures, both learners and teachers of a second language need to understand cultural differences and to recognize openly that everyone in the world is not just like me, that people are not all the same beneath the skin (Brown, 1994). Therefore, individuals need to look at themselves from this perspective to overcome the limits of monocultural perception through contact with a multicultural perspective.

CONCLUSION

Culture means different things to different people in different situations. In foreign language teaching and learning processes, culture education prepares learners to be successful both linguistically and communicatively in using foreign language. Besides, such an education process is a socialization process in which learners are involved in learning about the culture of target language and recognize their own cultural norms. If learners have fun while learning cultural components of other culture(s), some of the challenges associated with foreign language learning processes are reduced. The students may have pleasure while learning about other families, living conditions, social relations, ceremonies, festivals, leisure time activities, food, social customs, geographical characteristics, historical periods and backgrounds, transportation facilities, clothing styles, education lives, and religious customs of different countries.. In this sense, learners can be directed to develop awareness of sociocultural differences as well as linguistic differences. In addition, presenting some cultural norms as dominant ones may cause unintended pragmatic disappointment in language classes while dealing with cultural components. To find a solution for these potential challenges, choosing appropriate materials and discussing different cultural norms might be offered. As each culture has its own cultural norms, cultural components should be conveyed as something triggering the socialization process in using foreign language pragmatically and communicatively. Educators need to be sensitive about the learners' positive or negative attitudes towards the cultural components they learn and motivate their students to develop knowledge about otherness to overcome prejudices.

REFERENCES

Adorno, T. (1993). *The culture industry: Selected essays on mass culture*. London: Routledge.

Bates, P. (1990). *Cultural anthropology*. New York: McGraw-Hill.

Brown, D. (1994). *Principles of language learning and teaching*. Englewood Cliffs, NJ: Prentice Hall Regents.

Brumfit, C.J.; & Johnson, K. (1991). *The communicative approach to language teaching*. Oxford: Oxford University Press.

Byram, M. (1991). Teaching culture and language: towards an integrated model. In Buttjes, D and Byram, M. (eds.). *Mediating languages and cultures*: *Multilingual matters* (pp. 17 –32). Clevedon: Multilingual Matters Limited.

Byram, M. & Fleming, M. (1998). *Language learning in intercultural perspective: Approaches through drama and ethnography*. Cambridge: Cambridge University Press.

Chomsky, N. (1965). *Aspects of the theory of syntax*. Massachussetts: Heinle& Heinle Publishing.

Common European Framework (CEF) (2001). *Reference for languages*. Cambridge: Cambridge University Press.

Cunningsworth, A. (1995). *Choosing your course book*. London: Macmillan.

Damen, L.(1987). *Culture learning: The fifth dimension in the classroom, reading*. Massachusetts: Addison-Wesley Publishing.

Fenner, B.(2001). *Cultural awareness and language awareness based on dialogic interaction with texts in foreign language learning*. Strasbourg: Council of Europe Publishing.

Forster, E.M. (1942). *A Passage to India*. London: Penguin.

Foucault, M. (1994). *The order of things: Archaeology of the human sciences*. USA: Vintage Books.

Fromkin, V. & Rodman, R. (1993). *An introduction to language*. Orlando: Harcourt Brace College Publishers.

Hammerly, H. (1982). *Synthesis in second language teaching: An introduction to linguistics*. Blaine, Washington: Second Language Publications.

Hymes, D. (1972). On communicative competence. In H.H. Stern (ed.) *Fundamental concepts of language teaching* (pp. 26-34). Oxford: Oxford University Press.

Kramsch, C. (1993). *Context and culture in language teaching*. Oxford: Oxford University Press.

Kramsch, C. (2001). *Language and culture*. Oxford: Oxford University Press.

McKay, S. L. (2003). *The cultural basis of teaching English as an international language*. Retrieved April 22, 2004 from *http://www.tesol.org/pubs/articles/2003/tm13-4-01.html*.

Ögeyik, M.C. (2008). English language teacher education and language related fields. *5th International Conference. The Language: A phenomenon without frontiers*, Varna, Bulgaria.

Peterson, E. & Coltran, B. (2003). *Culture in second language teaching*. Retrieved April, 2008 from *http://www.cal.org/resources/digest/0309peterson.html*.

Pulverness, A. (2003). *Distinctions and dichotomies: Culture-free, culture-bound.* Retrieved April 22, 2004 from *http://elt.britcoun.org.pl/forum/distanddich.htm.*

Seelye H. N. (1993).*Teaching culture: Strategies for intercultural communication.* Lincolnwood, IL: National Textbook Company.

Sercu, L. (2005). *Foreign language teachers and intercultural communication. An intercultural investigation.* Clevedon: Multilingual Matters Limited.

Thanasoulas, D. (2001). *The importance of teaching culture in foreign language classroom.* Retrieved August 18, 2003 from *http://radicalpedagogy.icaap.org/content/issue3_3/7-thanasoulas.html.*

Tomalin, B. & Stempleski, S. (1993). *Cultural awareness.* Oxford: Oxford University Press.

Valdes, J. (1986). *Culture bound.* Cambridge: Cambridge University Press

Wittgenstein, L. (1999). *Culture and value,* (translated by Peter Winch). Chicago: Chicago University Press.

Woolf, V. (1921). *Monday or Tuesday.* New York: Harcourt Brace Company.

Zu, L. & Kong, Z. (2009). A study on the pproaches to Culture Introduction in English Textbooks. *English Language Teaching, 2*(1),110-112.

In: Language and Literacy Education in a Challenging World   ISBN: 978-1-61761-198-8
Editors: T. Lê, Q. Lê, and M. Short   © 2011 Nova Science Publishers, Inc.

Chapter 20

STREET CHILDREN'S ENGLISH IN A TOURIST DISCOURSE

Mark Lê

ABSTRACT

English language teaching normally takes place in a class or school where students are presented with a specific syllabus which reflects their levels, abilities, and curriculum perspective. This chapter deals with a different learning discourse where English learning takes place but there is no apparent teaching. It discusses street children's English in a tourist discourse where children learn English mainly on the streets in their social interaction with foreign tourists. The chapter examines some characteristics of street children English and how they reflect some theoretical views on language learning.

Keywords: acquisition, code-switching, interaction, language, learning, pragmatics, stereotyped speech, street children.

INTRODUCTION

Terms about English learning and teaching to non-English speaking background people are many and their acronyms are widely used such as English language teaching (ELT), teaching English to speakers of other languages (TESOL), English as a second language (ESL), English as an added language (EAL), and English as a foreign language (EFL). Literature about language learning and teaching is maily about syllabus, curriculum, and other class-based activities and numerous teaching sources such as textbooks, computer-supported resources, workbooks, and English tests are commercially produced to meet the growing demand of learning and teaching English. In many bookshops in Asia, a big section is devoted to English language learning and teaching.

FROM THE TOUR TO THE RESEARCH JOURNEY

Children and adolescents who appear to be drifters can be found on streets of most developing countries. These youngsters wear shabby, dirty clothing and can be seen begging, performing menial chores, working, or just wandering apparently without a purpose. They share an appearance of abandonment that may lead researchers to single them out as street children. However, although these children look alike, they have different family characteristics, life histories, and prognoses. Researchers have attempted to classify samples of street children in many different ways. The broadest categorisations divide children into two groups: children on the streets and children of the streets.

Research has been carried out in second language learning with great attention given to English as a target language. This is manifested in active promotion at academic conferences, research journals, and on-line resources. Virtually there is no research on how 'street children' learn English from the street, where traditonal sources such as teacher, classroom, textbook, and testing are absent. It is often said "life is a school" and this metaphor is well suited to the discourse of street children who learn 'English as a tourist language'.

As tourists in some developing countries, many things strike us about some kids we see on the street. One of the most notable features is their English interlanguage. When approached by street vendors, it is a great surprise for many tourists to find out 'how much' these street children know English communicatively. In some cases this could be displayed in the very simplest form of a curious smile and a common greeting such as "How are you?", or "Where are you from?", and some expressions of fun used for novelty of interaction with strangers. However, in many cases, particularly those involving street vendors they appeared to display a broader and more sophisticated use of English. In some cases, street vendors' communication in English was impeccable, possessing an enthusiasm and willingness to engage in communicative interaction with tourists.

My research interest on street children's English started when I visited Vietnam as a tourist. Due to my academic background in applied linguistics, the visit to Vietnam was an eye-opener for me from a language teacher's perspective. When I was in Ho Chi Minh City and Hanoi, I was puzzled and inspired by street children's "ways with words" in English with foreigners. I prefer not to use the term 'English competence' or 'English ability' to describe the language use of these children when they interacted with English-speaking tourists. The expression "ways with words" is more appropriate when referring to the special English used by these children.

The following questions arose in my mind when I first met street children in Vietnam:

- What is the background of these children?
- How do they learn English?
- What is their English-in-use discourse?
- What are some characteristics of their English?
- What are pragmatic aspects of their English?
- How do language learning theories accommodate street children's English?

It is obvious that those questions have been raised and discussed in various academic forums by language educators. However, teachers are more concerned with institutionalised teaching where learners are presented with a carefully planned curriculum, whether it is teacher-centred or learner-centred. The common aspects of formal education are still there: syllabus content, teaching approaches, educational resources, assessment and evaluation. However, those street children that I met did not have formal teaching and learning. They function in a different way and their "school" was in a specific and real life context. They were "teacherless" in the sense that they did not have teachers to guide them through the curriculum. The learned English primarily through their peers and tourists, who were participants in a social discourse. The traditional dichotomy of teaching and learning did not exist. No assessment was imposed on them as they were their own assessors in terms of the success or otherwise of their selling services.

After the first visit, my curiosity about street children's English motivated me to visit Vietnam the second time after one year. The second visit was more focussed: to establish a strong base for mounting my ethnographic research on street children's English.

THE STUDY

The main aim of this study is to investigate the nature and functions of street children's English in two major cities of Vietnam Ho Chi Minh City (Saigon) and Hanoi where street children are very active due to the recent influx of tourists to Vietnam. The participants in this study are street children under 16 years of age who spend some of their time on the streets to sell goods to foreign tourists. The study focuses on three significant aspects of language use: form, meaning, and function. The specific objectives of this study are:

- to identify some linguistic characteristics of Street children' English, particularly in relation to stereotypical speech, code switching and linguistic interference;
- to identify the English conversational skills of street children in terms of: functions and strategies such as greeting, persuading, trapping, initiating, repairing, collaborating and terminating; and
- to identify the nature of the discourse(s) in which these street children used English..

There has been a strong rise of ethnography in research within anthropology and cognate fields in social sciences and humanities, particularly in dealing with social issues such as ethnic identify, prejudice and discrimination, gender equity, and intercultural communication. One of the main attractions of ethnographic research in linguistic and cultural studies is that researchers play both the roles of an observer and a participant in a real social and cultural context. The downside of traditional anthropology is the strong influence of the researcher's socio-cultural background in data collection and interpretation. This happens when researchers who study foreign cultures in an effort to provide comprehensive insights about them inevitably construct that knowledge within the discourse of their own cultures. In other words, the knowledge about the target culture is heavily mediated by the meta-discourse created by the researcher. This may easily lead to misinterpretation of cultural meanings and values (Creswell, 2003; Law, 2004)..

A study of street children cannot ignore the contexts in which these children live, play and work. Research should therefore show interest in the explication of the ways in which members of a discourse community, through their practices, produce the social structure of everyday activities (Leedy & Ormrod, 2005). The aim is to describe those practices and show how they work. The researcher should be interested in finding, describing, and analysing the structures, the machinery, the organized practices, and the formal procedures that produce orderliness.

To adopt ethnography as a research approach, I spent a year in two major cities of Vietnam for data collection. It was an essential way for the researcher to be totally immersed in the context where street children worked and it was a necessary experience which was useful for not only data collection but also data analysis and interpretation.

In this study, there are several types of quanlitative data collected in the fieldwork for this project: street children interview data, researcher's observation data, fieldwork notes, researcher' memo and foreign tourists' reflective notes on street children in Vietnam. Saldana (2010) treats analytical memo as data which can be coded, categorized, and searched. He points out the difference between field note and analytical memos as follows. Field notes are the researcher's "written documentation of participant observation, which may include the observer's personal and subjective responses to interpretations of social action encountered. Field notes may contain valuable comments and insights that address the recommended categories for analytical memo reflection" (p.33).

Researching street children in a different country, ethical consideration is important. For street kinds in large cities in Vietnam such as Hanoi and Ho Chi Minh City, they are often very keen to initiate conversation with tourists in public places. In the Vietnamese context, parental permission for research interview and observation does not exist. The social and cultural convention does not require it. On the contrary, it is could be intimidating for their parents to be required to sign consent forms. However, this does not mean that research should ignore the ethical issues which may affect the children as participants in research. It is essential that these children's safety, comfort, and freedom be absolutely maintained. My study was not an experimental study which required children to perform under some experimental conditions. It was an ethnographic study which took the social context as 'what it is', not 'what it should be'. In other words, the study focused on the real contexts in which these children carried out their daily activities. To maintain anonymity and privacy of these children, no video recording and photographing were used. The interviews in this study did not include topics which are socially and culturally insensitive, particularly those issues with reference to sex, politics and religion.

THE FINDINGS

Due to the limit of a book chapter, the findings are briefly presented here under broad themes and their sub-themes.

Social skills

Communicative Enthusiasm

Some street kids were very demanding and pushy. But generally, they were very friendly, persistent, and enthusiastic. They were genuinely interested in communicating with tourists. They often remained with the tourists and continued a conversation even after the selling had been completed. Their common strategy was to try to make tourists respond to their initiating verbal act. When this was successful, their next strategy was to maintain the conversation.

Humour

Smiling and laughing were common features of the kids in communicative interaction with tourists. They smiled and laughed at little things that tourists showed them. Their innocent laughing could be misinterpreted by tourists as unfriendly and nasty. For example, a tourist stepped on dog droppings or fell off a bike. Laughing can be interpreted as a demonstration of non-seriousness from the point of view of Taoism, which is important in Vietnamese culture. According to Taoism, life is too serious to be taken seriously.

Working collaboratively

Working collaboratively was a special feature of the street kids' sense of survival. I did not witness any fights, mild or violent, when they were engaged in selling with tourists. They were active in their selling task but did not show animosity as we often see among traders.

Linguistic skills

Code-Switching

An interesting phenomenon about street kids in Vietnam is that some of them were bilingual or multilingual. Apart from Vietnamese, their mother-tongue, they could speak English, French, and German. However, English was still their most widely used language with tourists. This could be due to the fact that most foreign tourists in Vietnam come from English-speaking countries. Their skill of code-switching was very impressive. In a conversation with a group of tourists, they could switch from one language to another.

Stereotypical speech

A fundamental aspect of grammar is its creativity. Language users have different ways to create a message. Even when we try to repeat a message, we can easily 'reconstruct' it as demonstrated in the language game "Chinese whispering", in which a message transmitted through a number of people tends to be distorted and can become a new message. However, in human languages, there are also expressions which are stereotypical in the sense that they are 'already made'. Proverbs are the best examples. When we want to express an idea, we may borrow a proverb to represent the idea. We do not need to create our own expression or linguistic form. Stereotypical speech is automatic in the sense that it is used without the act of deliberate encoding of a message. Words and expressions have already been fixed. Stereotypical speech is often used in rituals and celebrations such as marriage, church sermons and court cases. They are also widely used in greetings, emphasis, apology, addressing, and farewell. For example,

- How are you?
- Good morning.
- I'm sorry.
- You know!
- You know what I mean!
- I beg your pardon.

The street kids in this study used stereotypical expressions such as:

- Hey, you.
- Where you from?
- Welcome you.
- You like Vietnam.
- Cheap cards for you.

However, they use stereotypical speech in such a 'creative' way that it does not stifle the flow of a conversation.

Linguistic Interference

Linguistic interference occurs when the first language interferes with the second language. In this case, the Vietnamese interfered in the way the street kids used English with tourists. The word "you" was used by these street kids as a direct translation from a number of Vietnamese words of addressing. In English, the pronoun "I" indicates the addressor and "you" indicates the addressee. In Vietnamese, different words are used for the addressee and addressor depending on their social status and interpersonal relationship. The English word "you" can be translated as "em", "anh", or "ong" in Vietnamese depending on the two factors just mentioned. Misunderstanding could occur when the street kids uses 'hey you' to address tourists. It could be interpreted as rude or impolite.

Pragmatics

A number of publications about Asian students tend to stereotype them as passive learners. Their learning style tends to be suitable to a teacher-centred curriculum in which teachers are the source of knowledge and students are the sponges which absorb knowledge transmitted from teachers. This could be the case in a formal classroom discourse where explicit and hidden curricula are rigidly reinforced. However, the street kids did not show any signs of being passive children when they functioned in their own social context. Here, they were active and creative in conversation.

One of the important factors in engaging in a conversation is to initiate a conversation. Conversation initiation can be seen as a 'make or break' stage of conversation. In the West, conversation normally starts with a neutral and impersonal theme: the weather. It is safe to start with weather as a topic and other topics will develop gradually depending how comfortable one feels about the others. Here is an example:

- Speaker 1: Hello.
- Speaker 2: Hello.
- Speaker 1: The weather is so nice.

- Speaker 2: We're lucky. It hasn't rained for a long time.

The weather is not a popular topic in Vietnamese conversation. People talk about the weather only when there is a flood or storm. In contrast, a conversation normally centres on personal things such as family members, friends, and events relating to their existence. Here is an example:

- Speaker 1: Where are you going?
- Speaker 2: I want to buy a chicken.
- Speaker 1: Are you having a special guest at home?
- Speaker 2: My uncle from Nha Trang is visiting us.
- Speaker 1: Is he old? Is he married?

- Speaker 2: He is old, but not married.
- Speaker 1: Why isn't he married?

The street kids in Vietnam did not have any problem with initiating a conversation. They were always the first people who broke the ice. They did not need to beat about the bush with the weather. They could tell strangers things about their friends and families. They were more interested in human affairs than the weather.

Intercultural awareness

Here is a sample of a kid's initiation of a conversation:

- Kid: Happy you!
- Tourist: very good.
- Kid: You from where
- Tourist: Australia
- Kid: Welcome you!
- Tourist: Thank you.

The street kids tend to have a good intercultural awareness. Though some of them have never gone to school, they know names of cities in different countries and the languages of those countries. They know big names in sports, music, and cinema.

Personal praise

Street kids were very eager to praise tourists, particularly when an attempt was made to speak Vietnamese:

- Kid: You very beautiful!
- Tourist: Thank you!
- Kid: You speak Vietnamese.
- Tourist: No, I wish I could.
- Kid: Speak: "chao em"

- Tourist: Chao em.
- Kid (laughing): Very good. You number one.

Theoretical consideration

How do language learning theories explain street children's English? The following three major theoretical views are considered here in examining street children's English in this study.

Nativist view of language learning

The nativist theory emphasizes the unique ability of human beings in learning language, a complex system which is beyond the learning capacity of non-human creatures. Language learning is an outstanding achievement which is rooted in the biological foundation of human beings, particularly the brain. According to Chomsky (1968), children learn language as naturally as they learn walking. It happens naturally as they are born with some universal grammar within the language acquisition device (LAD) which triggers learning when young children are exposed to their mother tongue. During this critical stage of language acquisition, language learning is effortless. Street children in this study learned English at a young age, thus it is expected that they learn English without a great effort if they are exposed to an environment where English is used. In the context of their learning, the environment is very minimal and restrictive: tourists, brief encounter, narrow range of English use. Thus their English tends to be more 'stereotyped' than the language of children in a natural native language environment such as those in Australia, England or USA.

Krashen's view on acquisition and learning

Krashen (1981) made a distinction between language acquisition and language learning. Like Chomsky, he argues that language *acquisition* in children takes place without great effort in first and second language development, whereas *learning* takes place in adults who try hard to learn a second language. It is a conscious process. However unlike Chomsky, he pays more attention to language input provided by caretakers, parents and others in interaction with children during this process of acquisition. He states:

> Real language acquisition develops slowly, and speaking skills emerge significantly later than listening skills, even when conditions are perfect. The best methods are therefore those that supply 'comprehensible input' in low anxiety situations, containing messages that students really want to hear. These methods do not force early production in the second language, but allow students to produce when they are 'ready', recognizing that improvement comes from supplying communicative and comprehensible input, and not from forcing and correcting production." (Krashen, p.7)

The street children in this study were exposed to limited language input as their condition of learning was not perfect even it took place in a natural context. Their speaking skills and listening skills were developed simultaneously, as an integral communicative development. For these children, the comprehensible input was not made in high anxiety situations. Actually they were in charge of the situation of interaction, not the tourist.

Functional view of language learning

The functional view of language learning considers language functioning as the most important aspect or condition for language learning. Halliday (1994) thinks that children know what language is because they know what language can do for them. He introduced three major functions: ideational, interpersonal and textual. The ideational function is about our world and is concerned with clauses as representations. The interpersonal metafunction is about the social world, in terms of interpersonal relationship, and it is concerned with clauses as exchanges. The textual function is about the verbal manifestation in a text, and is concerned with clauses as messages.

Halliday's three functions (or meta-functions) are useful in examining the language use of the street children in this study. In their use of English with tourists, the ideational function is about the things that they wanted to sell to tourists. The interpersonal function is specifically about seller and buyer, about street children and tourists, and about Vietnamese speaker and foreigner. The textual function is the aspects of language such as words, phrases, clauses which are structured in 'their own ways with words' to create a text in their interaction with tourists as their clients.

CONCLUSION

Language learning has attracted a great deal of attention in theory as well as practice. Theoretical understanding of language learning is important for exploring the way in which the human mind works and for discovering the intricate relationship between language and its socio-cultural context as language structure cannot be divorced from its use. Pedagogically, educators are keen to find ways to enhance students' language and literacy competence. However, little attention has been given to language learning by some children whose school is the city streets where they learn language and learn how to use language for earning a living. This chapter provide some insights into these children's ways with words in English and their English is accommodated in major theoretical perspectives.

REFERENCES

Celce-Murcia, D. & McIntosh, L. (1989). *Teaching English as a second or a foreign language*. Rowley, MA: Newbury House.

Chomsky, Noam (1968). *Language and mind*. USA: Harcourt Brace Jovanovich.

Creswell, John W (2003). *Research Design: Qualitative, Quantitative, and Mixed Methods Approaches*. Second Edition. Sage Publications.

Halliday, M.A.K. (1994). *Introduction to functional grammar*, 2nd ed. London: Edward Arnold.

Krashen, Stephen D. 1981. *Principles and practice in second language acquisition*. London: Prentice-Hall International (UK) Ltd.

Law, John. (2004). *After Method: Mess in Social Science Research*. New York: Routledge

Leedy, P. & Ormrod, J. (2005). *Practical research: Planning and design*. New Jersey: Pearson Education

Leonard, D. C. (2002). *Learning theories, A to Z.* Santa Barbara: Greenwood Press.

Lightbrown P. M. & Spada N. (2003). *How languages are learned.* Oxford: Oxford University Press.

Saldana, J. (2010).*The coding manuals for qualitative researchers* .London: Sage.

In: Language and Literacy Education in a Challenging World   ISBN: 978-1-61761-198-8
Editors: T. Lê, Q. Lê, and M. Short   © 2011 Nova Science Publishers, Inc.

Chapter 21

LOCAL IDENTITY MEETS GLOBAL CULTURE: REFLECTIONS ON THE MYTHS AND REALITIES OF MEANINGFUL ENGLISH LANGUAGE ACQUISITION IN AUSTRIAN COMMUNITIES

Sibylle Gruber

ABSTRACT

In this paper, I explore the reasons why my attempts at learning English in an Austrian educational setting were largely unsuccessful. I show the importance of putting motivation and applicability of the newly learned language at the forefront of any language education method. I argue that learning a new language can provide an opportunity for students to expand their understanding of their positionalities and identities in an increasingly globalized environment. I highlight an example of foreign language learning and foreign language acquisition in present-day Austria. I conclude by showing that without understanding how individuals see their participation in learning or rejecting a foreign language, and without understanding how they are influenced by factors such as parental attitudes, community involvement, and cultural expectations, we will not understand the complexities involved with foreign language acquisition.

Keywords: foreign language acquisition, motivation, application, identity formation, constructivist learning.

INTRODUCTION

After learning English as a second language in Austria in the 1970s and 80s, and after teaching writing to English native speakers since the 1990s in the southwestern part of the United States, I have finally started to revisit my highly unpleasant second language acquisition experiences. Since my first English lesson in a small town--population 998--in Austria in 1974, I also studied French for five years, took a year of Latin, and am now studying conversational Spanish to make sure that I can communicate with my bilingual

English-Spanish-speaking students and their Spanish-speaking parents. I had been hesitant and nervous about committing to learning another language that was foreign to me since my previous experiences had been largely disastrous. My teachers made me believe that I had no talent for acquiring new languages, and my grades were concrete proof of their opinions. Learning a new language was arduous and painful, reminiscent of novacaine or lidocaine-free visits to the dentist. It also seemed futile because I didn't understand the applicability of English, French, or Latin outside the confines of the Austrian classroom.

Now, of course, I am very motivated to use English, and I apply my second language every day; I also apply my increasing knowledge of Spanish regularly. It is this motivation and application process, I argue in this paper, which can provide the needed incentive for foreign language learners to engage in the learning process and to take seriously the need for becoming proficient in a foreign language. I first explore the reasons why my own attempts at learning English in an Austrian educational setting were largely unsuccessful. I then show the importance of putting motivation and applicability of the newly learned language at the forefront of any language education method. I end by highlighting an example of foreign language learning and foreign language acquisition in present-day Austria. If students are motivated and can apply their newly acquired skills, learning a foreign language, even though it might be challenging, loses its reputation as being useless, pointless, and futile. Furthermore, knowledge of a new language, my example shows, provides opportunity for students to expand their understanding of their positionalities and identities in an increasingly globalized environment.

Much research has focused on language teaching practices, analyzing how different methodologies affect student learning of a foreign language (Lightbown & Spada, 1990; Lightbown, 2003; Lyster & Ranta, 1997; Lyster & Mori, 2006), how sequence and variability influence acquisition (Ellis, 1994; Fasold & Preston, 2007; Tarone, 2009), the relationship between input, intake, and output, the impact of corrective feedback (Lyster & Ranta, 1997; Lyster & Mori, 2006), and more recently the need for action-based classroom research to engage teachers in developing new language learning practices (Allwright & Hanks, 2009; Tarone & Swierzbin 2009). My contribution approaches language learning from an auto-ethnographical perspective. Like Norton and Toohey (2001), I look at situated practices to highlight the connections between the individual and the social. However, my work takes away the intermediary and takes seriously the importance of unmediated first-hand accounts of foreign language learners. Instead of learning about non-native English speaker through interviews, questionnaires, observations, or large-scale quantitative research, my research is driven by my strong conviction that first-hand narrative explorations and micro-level research can clarify and complicate theory-driven case studies and large-scale studies of foreign language learning. Without understanding how individuals see their participation in learning or rejecting a foreign language, and how they are influenced by factors such as parental attitudes, community involvement, and cultural expectations, we will not understand the complexities involved with foreign language acquisition.

RECOLLECTIONS FROM THE PAST

Close to 40 years ago, when I and all my classmates were required to study English, I saw no need for learning a foreign language, for learning a language that wasn't my own, and that wasn't my family's, my neighbors', or even my teacher's language. At 10, after a blissful 4 years of elementary school, we were introduced to two English-speaking cartoon characters whose life and travels through Britain were supposed to encourage us to learn how to speak a new language. Nobody around me spoke English; nobody around me thought that they would ever live in an English-speaking country; nobody around me thought that they would vacation in a country were English would be necessary for communication. My community was small. Farming was big, and the cows, pigs, and chickens just didn't get excited about being talked to in English. They didn't care about French either, another language that seemed abstract and unnecessary when we studied it for five years in middle and high school. No trips were planned that would lead us outside our home country where we were very proficient in switching from home dialects that everybody spoke and understood, to school German that also everybody understood but not necessarily spoke.

My English teachers were Austrians, just like me. But unlike me, they had a grasp on that new language that I didn't have. Looking back, they weren't fluent, nor did they know everything there is to know about the language. Their pronunciation of English words was very similar to Arnold Schwarzenegger's way of using and abusing the English language. But those teachers were invincible in the eyes of 10-year olds whose horizons hadn't yet been expanded beyond the small rural community east of the Alps that they called home. I could conjugate verbs, but I couldn't compose a sensible sentence even if my life had depended on it. Grammar was relatively easy to comprehend, but my mind went blank every time I was supposed to answer a question in class. Maybe it started when one of my teachers laughed at me after a spelling mistake that should have been minor. I wrote "god" instead of "good" on an exam, and my life was never the same after that. Was it because I didn't capitalize God, which, in a Catholic country might be considered a major offense? Or was it because the teacher didn't realize that her reaction would shut down my already very weak and bruised circuits? Was it because she was trained in an Austrian system were confirmation is writ small, and were we knew – intrinsically – that we should never stand out and never shine? I never shined, not even in my wildest imagination. My teacher always made sure that we never thought too highly of our language skills. Nobody did, and our collective grades showed it. I studied enough to squeak by and to show the teacher that I could pass, even if a good God was not on my side.

I didn't develop a love for English—not even a slight liking—until I was done with high school. My exit exam was one of the most nerve-wrecking experiences I have ever had. After oral exams in history, geography, and German, my English teacher looked at me with what I imagined to be the biggest smirk I had seen on a teacher's face. I knew that she knew deep down, where her corrupted mind met her extreme dislike of the one who mistook God for good, that I would miserably fail this portion of my exam. She knew that I froze—utterly and miserably—every time she looked at me. I can only assume that she thought I had no aptitude at all for learning a foreign language. She didn't know, however, that my inability to speak had little to do with aptitude and much to do with social factors, and some to do with how we were being taught and motivated. Maybe I couldn't speak because I was an introvert; maybe I couldn't comprehend why I would want to speak; maybe I didn't learn because no consideration was given to my learning style; maybe the method of teaching a foreign language through drill and kill exercises didn't encourage conversational English. But I had given myself a pep talk and had drunk herbal tea made of a soothing combination of calming chamomile, passion flower, peppermint, and lavender before I went into the exam room where seven teachers in suits were waiting unsmilingly for the next candidate.

My self-inflicted mantra was simple: "Keep breathing. No matter whether you think it's wrong, just say it. Just say it. Just say it." I made my mind go blank. "Nothing left to lose." I didn't know then that this was going to be the precursor to my yoga practices, where meditation allows me to go beyond the limits of my limited mind, finding tranquility, inner peace, and wisdom. It is highly recommended in the U.S. for stressed-out executives, teachers with too many papers to grade, and students who have too many papers to write. For me, it was a last resort before I would be led to the gallows where the henchwoman would gladly take the last ounce of self-confidence and step on it with her elegant shoes—forever denying me access to a university education, or, as I realized later, merely delaying my attempt to graduate for another year.

I looked at the teacher, but I didn't see her. I heard her voice, but I blocked out the speaker. "Just say it. Just say it," remained a constant in my otherwise emptied-out mind. Slowly, the words that formed the question that I needed to answer came into focus. "Give us an example of why Maria Theresia was so important for the well-being of the Austro-Hungarian Empire?" I didn't think. I just spoke. I don't know what I said; I don't know whether it made much sense. It made enough sense for the teacher to look at me in shock—or maybe it was pleasure—and to pass me for the English portion of my exit exam.

I was exhilarated that my fears didn't come true. My motivation to pass had been very high: I didn't want to repeat a year with the same teacher, and retake the exam with her. I didn't want to spend more time in a classroom environment that was not conducive to learning, but was conducive to self-doubt, feeling inadequate, and learning little that was useful. My motivation came from fear, and my application of my English language skills was induced by that same fear. Now I know that I had briefly overcome my "silent period" and engaged in formulaic speech (Krashen, 1985). This, however, didn't change the fact that I could not express myself successfully in English. I assume that if my motivation had been more positive—self-development, understanding another culture, communicating with those who speak another language, traveling to a country where the language is spoken, acquiring new cognitive processes (Cook, 2002; Coleman, 1996)—I might have been able to apply my knowledge more successfully and more continuously to the specific situations that encouraged foreign language use.

CHANGING DIRECTIONS

I often think about my experiences learning a foreign – and what I thought to be useless – language taught to children in a small rural community who were expected to work on the family farm, marry a farmer, work in local stores, or the service industry. Expectations weren't high, and didn't move beyond a 15 kilometer radius. Family members and neighbors knew of jobs; they put in a good word for new high school graduates; and hardly anybody left the small community they called home. Now, close to 40 years later and more than 10,000 kilometers from my original home, I teach English to mostly native speakers. Whether English is a first, second, third, or forth language, I now realize that engaging with language requires a framework that goes beyond the classroom and that students can understand, recognize, and identify with. When I learned English, I had no motivation to study the language except that I didn't want to fail the course. Any application of the knowledge we acquired was sorely missing. We were given no reason for studying vocabulary, conjugating verbs, or learning an obscure grammar rule. Even though we studied many vocabulary words, our unconscious mind merely tucked them away in the deepest recesses of the cranial vault, never to be brought back out again. We rehearsed the words, but we didn't know what to do with the acquired knowledge once the teacher finished her lesson, the test was over, and the next lesson was started. We didn't engage in conversations because there was nobody with enough English skills to listen and talk to. Our families provided little motivation, and our community was largely insular and uninterested in foreigners. The occupying powers after WWII included British and American forces, and even though Hershey bars became the coveted treat of the day that was shared and savored for days, Austria breathed a collective sigh of relief when the occupiers left in 1955, and when Austria's neutrality was finally established.

Motivation to learn English, then, was sorely missing. We didn't know how to look for it, nor did we know why we should be looking for it. We assumed that we would stay in our tight-knit communities, and we assumed that we would never move to a bigger city where we might meet non-German speakers. We didn't have many dreams, and we didn't dream of vacations to foreign lands. We certainly had no intentions to move to an English-speaking country and call it our home. Our teachers, like our parents, had no high hopes for any of the students in their classes. We would follow in the footsteps of our parents and our siblings who had respectable jobs. We would never aspire to a college education since it would mean more school and no income. In other words, my early language-learning experiences, and the socio-cultural system of my childhood, provided little motivation to reconstruct and renegotiate our identities, to move away from what we knew, and to entertain new ways of seeing and new ways of knowing.

What was missing from our education – at home and at school – was an interest in life outside our community, or new possibilities in our community. In the future, some of us might want to vacation abroad; we might want to live in a bigger city where we come in contact with English speakers; we might go to college; and we might even live outside of Austria. We took a school trip to Vienna and to the United Nations building, but we couldn't imagine that any of us might work there. We saw the big building that was part of the University of Vienna, but we didn't even walk the halls because our teachers knew that their charges weren't interested in higher education. My mother's brother lived in the U.S., but it never occurred to me that I could leave Austria and move away from home.

I did leave Austria when I was 19, and I had no choice but to engage in English conversation during my six months as a nanny in the U.S., taking care of two gregarious children whose only language was English. All of a sudden, the need for knowing some English and for being able to communicate in another language than my home language became quite important. Indeed, it became a survival skill. I could not complete simple tasks without knowing how to read instructions in a cookbook, or how to ask questions about when the kids needed to be picked up from school, or what lessons needed to be completed before play time. I also needed to learn the value of a dollar, and what it meant when somebody said that I still owed her a dime or a quarter. I learned how to spell with my two extroverted charges; I learned new words every day; and I became an expert in asking those around me to "please repeat" when I was dazed and confused. I desperately needed to be literate in English;

English wasn't foreign to my two little charges; and being literate in English was no longer a painful imposition that lacked meaning and was futile.

My 5-months stay in the U.S. convinced me that English was indeed useful. On my return home I enrolled at the University of Vienna. I, who had had extreme difficulties with English, wanted to become an English teacher. My stay in the U.S. had not only provided me with motivation and purpose to study English, but it had also taught me that I no longer identified myself as language-challenged, but that instead I embraced language as a new door that had opened new social and cultural identities and with it a newly developed self-esteem. Even though I didn't know at the time what processes I was going through, in Cote & Levin's (2002) typology of identity formation, I had moved from a drifter, searcher, and guardian to a resolver who started to desire self-growth, and who used her newly developed skills and competencies actively, searching out communities that provide opportunities for self-growth (pp. 3-5). My college work exposed me to study abroad opportunities through Fulbright, and my study abroad experiences in turn brought with them a desire to continue my foreign language learning in an English-speaking country. What I couldn't imagine for 19 years – whether it was because I had been apathetic towards changing implicit expectations or because I had a rigid sense of self-identity (Cote & Levin, 2002) – changed when my exposure to new communities helped me understand that my teacher's evaluation of my English-learning skills were restricted to her own understanding of how language should be taught and learned, and were hampered by the community's belief that foreign language acquisition did not contribute to the community's social and cultural values.

RECOGNIZING TEACHER LIMITATIONS AND COMMUNITY INFLUENCES

Our understanding of the best ways to acquire new language and literacy skills has changed dramatically over the last 20 to 30 years. We have grappled with questions of how home literacy influences school literacy, of how language is learned and understood by infants, of methodologies that can encourage meaningful literacy acquisition by using a structural, functional, or interactive model of second language acquisition, and of pedagogies that can promote confidence and can show the need for learning a foreign language.

Introducing meaning into language and literacy acquisition is a challenging proposition, especially when the new literacy skills seem far removed from a student's home literacies that define her social and cultural identities. It becomes even more challenging when there is little training for teachers on how to make literacy and language acquisition applicable for their students. Our Austrian-born and raised English teacher certainly knew the language better than we did. She had studied English in one of the academies in Austria. Her pedagogical training revolved around the theoretical knowledge that seemed acceptable 30 years ago, mostly focusing on a grammar translation method. Our teacher wasn't all-knowing, even though we thought she was. She also didn't have much experience teaching English beyond the confines of her own experiences as a student learning the language and then studying how to teach it from teachers who believed in a methodology that has long proved to be unsuccessful for second language acquisition. She did not have exposure to native English speakers before she took on a roomful of unwilling students who needed to be taught a language that was, in many ways, as foreign to her as it was to us, and that also had little meaning for her beyond the classroom. It was a subject to be taught, not a language to be lived. She certainly knew grammar better than we did, and she knew the English book that she was teaching. She gave us exercises directly from the book. She had us do translations directly from the book. Her corrections were always focused on spelling, on grammar, and on punctuation. She mostly encouraged rote-learning with the threat of a failing grade looming in the background. When we passed a test, we attributed it to luck, which was reinforced by our teacher who would point out that it was an easy test.

Motivation, in other words, was largely absent in our language-learning classroom. According to Ormrod (2003), motivation can have positive effects on learning outcomes, such as directing behavior toward particular goals; leading to increased effort and energy; increasing initiation of, and persistence in, activities; enhancing cognitive processing; and determining what consequences are reinforced. In the end, motivation can lead to improved performance (Ormrod, 2003). Although we didn't know this during our high school years, we weren't motivated to learn English; instead, because of how we interpreted our social environment, we did not see any connections between what was important in our communities and the study of English. Following Reiss's (2004) explorations of motivation, we should have been influenced by power, curiosity, status, acceptance and social contact (p. 187), to name just a few of the 16 motives that signify intrinsic motivation. But our mastery of English would not have brought us power; instead, it would have led to ostracism since nobody wanted to stand out and take on leadership roles. We were not curious about the intricacies of the English language because that knowledge did not help us with farm work, understanding weather patterns, or forming friendships. Our social status would not have improved if we had known enough English to communicate; quite contrarily, we would have been seen as strange and too involved in activities that were not useful in the short term. Our families and friends wouldn't have accepted us any more if we could have spoken a foreign language; and our peers would not have looked up to us if we had tried to use English words and phrases.

Paying attention to motivation, and with it the best way to acquire and apply new language skills while recognizing that learning a new language has lasting impact on a learner's identity development, has found increasing support in the L2 teaching community. Bonnie Norton (1997), in a special issue on language and identity in the *TESOL Quarterly*, makes it clear that "speech, speakers, and social relationships are inseparable" (p. 410). As she succinctly points out, "every time language learners speak, they are not only exchanging information with their interlocutors; they are also constantly organizing and reorganizing a sense of who they are and how they relate to the social world. They are, in other words, engaged in identity construction and negotiation" (p. 410). These new approaches to language and literacy acquisition supported by scholarship and research on motivation, application, and identity formation and intercultural competence have shown the importance of paying close attention to students' positionalities in their communities. Wenger (1998), for example, points out that researchers need to consider social participation which refers "not just to local events of engagement in certain activities with certain people, but to a more encompassing process of being active participants in the *practices* of social communities and constructing *identities* in relationship to these communities" (p. 4).

The connections between foreign language learning and identity have been largely accepted in research findings (Firth & Wagner, 1997; Norton, 1997; McNamara, 1997;

Schecter and Bailey, 1997; Sercu, 2006; Block, 2006; Block; 2007). In the classroom, this would mean that teachers would need to see themselves not only as transmitters of new information, but also as intermediaries to acquiring intercultural competencies. This, in turn, would increase students' openness to acquiring new language skills and to apply those skills in ways that changes their understanding of themselves and of the social and cultural communities around them. However, even though research has pointed out the need for such competencies, most teaching practices in EFL classrooms, according to Sercu (2006), still emphasize communicative competence, in part because teacher training emphasizes such competence, textbooks are focused on language learning and do not include intercultural competence, and in part because teachers are not exposed to intercultural and international environments, making it difficult for them to learn and teach about cultures in which English is spoken (p. 62, 68).

But the classroom is not the only place that can encourage 21st century students to gain intercultural competence and to see the value of becoming proficient in English. Globalization, the relative ease of travel, and increased internet use and online communication tools, including online social networking systems, have changed how our local communities understand their roles in an increasingly global organism that modifies a known way of life, transforms living spaces, and invariably changes cultural belief systems that have been revered for decades and often centuries. The European Union has brought more awareness to how individual countries are intricately connected to each other, creating a network that requires communication across nominal borders and across extensive language barriers. With 23 official languages, and about 150 regional and minority languages, members of the European Union are encouraged to learn a foreign language. Over half the population in the European Union can communicate in English, and over half the population can engage in a conversation using a language that is not their first language (European Commission, 2006).

With the many political changes in Europe, overwhelming internet access, and the ensuing globalization of Austria, one might assume that foreign language acquisition would no longer be as foreign as it was 40 years ago, when the insularity of Austria was often addressed in guide books, and when travelers were warned that they wouldn't be able to count on an English-speaking host in any of the small towns that are connected by one-lane roads and hiking trails. Austrians, the tour books warned, will not even talk to you in any form of German that you will be able to understand. Your four semesters of German language study will be useless, and your efforts to speak English slowly and more loudly will only result in uncomprehending responses in that language they think is German. Now, however, life for English-speaking tourists should be much improved since English language teaching in Austria has expanded to Kindergarten and elementary school. It can only have changed the life of English-speaking tourists for the better. The new generation of Austrians should now be able to participate in the increasingly English-speaking 21st century world. With 89 percent, it is the language most often taught as a foreign language in the European Union.

CREATING ENVIRONMENTS FOR MOTIVATION AND APPLICATION

I have been visiting an Austrian middle school for about six years now. I was invited by the English teacher of 5th graders in a small town in Lower Austria that is located about 10 miles west from my home town. I didn't know what to expect, but I didn't expect much. In fact, I wasn't sure that they would understand much of anything I was going to say. I remembered my own non-existent English comprehension when I was their age, and I couldn't fathom that the 11 to 12–year olds would know what I was talking about. And, mostly they didn't. My English was too foreign for them. I didn't speak like their teacher at all. I spoke with an American accent that I had acquired after many years in a dark and dreary language lab called "Plato" at the University of Illinois. I didn't sound at all like Arnold Schwarzenegger, the only Austrian they had heard from time to time on TV. Now they saw a life person, and even though I was Austrian, I spoke to them in English. I talked about my experiences in the United States; I told them about American schools and the differences in the Austrian and American education systems; I handed out flyers that gave more detailed information about how many students went to college. And I gave them brochures about Arizona's tourist attractions. I could hear the whispers while I was talking. "Was hat sie gesagt?" mostly followed by "Ich habe sie nicht verstanden," and sometimes by a one-word explanation in German.

"Any questions? Anything you want to hear more about?" was, quite naturally and expectedly, followed by nervous silence. My heart went out to them when I saw history repeat itself. I could have been any one of the 30 anxious students, nervous about speaking in a language that they didn't own, worried that the teacher or the stranger who spoke funny would call on them, fearful that they would say something wrong and be scolded for not knowing. But I was merely projecting. History was not repeating itself. The teacher, before I started talking to the class, had assured me that they had "studied America" so that the students would be prepared for me and could ask some questions. It was just that they hadn't expected me to talk first, and I hadn't talked about what they had learned. When I asked in German whether they had any questions for me, and when the teacher gave them an encouraging nod – she had prepared them by asking every student to write down a question for the visitor – one tentative hand went up and the student looked down and read from her note: "Have you seen the Statue of Liberty?" Another one wanted to know whether I had met Arnold – hero and villain. And had I been to Disneyworld? And somebody else was interested in American football. I answered the questions in English and then translated some unknown words into German. Anxiety, fear, and worry dissipated, and interest in using their English skills increased.

It was a short hour in the classroom with students who no longer reminded me of myself 40 years ago. It was followed by Kaffee und Kuchen in the teachers' lounge. The teacher who had invited me was excited because it was the first time the students showed genuine interest; two other English teachers wanted to know whether I could come and talk to their classes, and the principal invited me back for the following year. And I did come back the following year, and the year after, and again the next year. The following year, I no longer talked to one class but to three classes. The principal had dedicated the day as "English" day, with English activities throughout the day. No German was allowed in the hallways; students were enthusiastically searching specific objects that were part of an English scavenger hunt; teachers did their best to teach math, history, and geography lessons in English; and parents helping out in the cafeteria weren't sure whether to laugh or attempt their rusty English-skills when the kids asked them in their best English about the location of a hidden box that needed to be found for their scavenger hunt. For that day, the teachers had become facilitators, no longer giving lectures or testing grammar skills. Students had to apply their English skills to problem-solve, and they had to participate actively in meaning-making. It was a moment that Vygotsky (1978) would have considered a wonderful example of combining speech and action into a single activity, leading to a merging of intra- and interpersonal activities. Furthermore, the collaborative nature of the scavenger hunt provided scaffolding experiences (Vygotsky, 1978) that encouraged less-advanced English learners to practice their skills without fear of failure. Students were engaged in social activities that motivated them to apply the knowledge they had acquired in their English lessons.

The day of constructivist teaching and learning raised the anxiety level of some teachers who were used to more traditional methods. They thought of the day as a lost day because, as they put it, "no teaching happened." Even though they heard students communicate in English, they were concerned that it wasn't "grammatically correct" and that it would reflect badly on their teaching. This perception, however, shifted significantly during the following years of my visits. Last year, five years after the first "English day," I visited another group of 11-12 year olds at the same school. The school had hired a new English teacher who had finished her teacher-training program only the previous year. In her classroom, language teaching took into account the importance of interaction. In addition to a state-prescribed textbook, the teacher also used several of the principles emphasized by the ideologies of social constructivism in her day-to-day communications with the students, paying close attention to student engagement, student voice, and social interaction. When I visited her class, President Obama had been in office for a few months, and the students had learned about the first family in the U.S. Instead of talking about my background and my experiences first, I started with a stand-up exercise that led to enthusiastic participation. "What are the names of Barack Obama's kids?" Hands shot up, and before I could call on anybody, I heard "Malea and Sasha" over and over again. "Who was the first President of the United States?" was followed by brief consultations before hands went up. "George Washington," resonated through the room. In no time, every student had answered at least one question, and we were ready to talk about the geology of the Grand Canyon, the history of Navajos and Hopis, Schwarzenegger's governorship, and, of course, possible visits to Disneyland.

CONCLUSION

Foreign language education, in this small school in an Austrian rural community, has changed significantly since my own experiences. Students didn't see themselves as passive consumers of useless information; instead, they were motivated by the activities encouraged by the teacher and by the school, by a belief that they might travel abroad, by their use of English-speaking online social networking systems and "Youtube", and by the possibility that they could go on to higher education. Although only 18 percent of Austrians currently attend college (Kritik, 2010), the students I visit no longer believe that it could never be them. Parents are traveling abroad, and they talk about their lack of useful English when they try to ask directions, rent a car, or order a meal. Students, in the school I visit, apply their knowledge in the classroom without fear of being reprimanded for a grammar mistake. Because their families support them in acquiring English skills, they are also confident that their social and cultural identities will not be marred by knowing a foreign language. English, in other words, is no longer dreaded by this small group of students because teachers have adapted new pedagogies and new methodologies, students have embraced their roles as participants in the learning process, and the socio-cultural fabric of the community has changed enough to accommodate intercultural competence without fearing that such competence will undermine the foundation of Austrian beliefs, values, and identities.

REFERENCES

Allwright, D. & Hanks, J. (2009). *The developing language learning: An introduction to exploratory practice.* Basingstoke: Palgrave MacMillan.

Block, D. (2006). *Multilingual identities in a global city: London stories.* London: Palgrave.

Block, D. (2007). *Second language identities.* London: Continuum.

Coleman, J. A. (1996) *Studying languages: A survey of British and European students. The proficiency, background, attitudes and motivations of students of foreign languages in the United Kingdom and Europe.* London, Centre for Information on Language Teaching and Research.

Cook, V.J. (2002). Language teaching methodology and the L2 user perspective. In V.J. Cook (ed.), *Portraits of the L2 User* (pp. 325 – 344). Clevedon: Multilingual Matters.

Cote, J. E., & Levine, C. (2002). *Identity formation, agency, and culture.* New Jersey: Lawrence Erlbaum Associates.

Ellis, R. (2002). Does form-focused instruction affect the acquisition of implicit knowledge? *Studies in Second Language Acquisition, 24*(2), 223-236.

European Commission (2006). Europeans and their Languages (Survey). Retrieved 26 February 2010, from *http://ec.europa.eu/education/languages/pdf/doc629_en.pdf.*

Fasold, R., & Preston, D. (2007). The psycholinguistic unity of inherent variability: Old Occam whips out his razor. In R. Bayley & C. Lucas (Eds.), *Sociolinguistic variation: Theory, methods, and applications* (pp. 45-69). Cambridge: Cambridge University Press.

Firth, A., & Wagner, J. (1997). On discourse, communication, and (some) fundamental concepts in SLA Research. *Modern Language Journal, 81,* 286–300.

Krashen, S. (1985), *The input hypothesis: Issues and implications,* Longman.

Lightbown, P. (2003). SLA research in the classroom/SLA research for the classroom. *Language Learning Journal, 28,* 4-13.

Lightbown, P. M., & Spada, N. (1990). Focus-on-form and corrective feedback in communicative language teaching: effects on second language learning. *Studies in Second Language Acquisition, 12,* 429-48.

Lyster, R., & Mori, H. (2006). Interactional feedback and instructional counterbalance. *Studies in Second Language Acquisition, 28,* 269-300.

Lyster, R., & Ranta, L. (1997). Corrective feedback and learner uptake: Negotiation of form in communicative classrooms. *Studies in Second Language Acquisition, 19,* 37-66.

McNamara, T. (1997). Theorizing social identity: What do we mean by social identity? Competing frameworks, competing discourses. *TESOL Quarterly, 31*(3), 561 – 567.

Norton B., & Toohey, K. (2001). Changing perspectives on good language learners. *TESOL Quarterly, 35*(2) 307 – 322.

Norton, B. (1997). Language, identity, and the ownership of English. *TESOL Quarterly, 31*(3), 409 – 429.

ORF. (2010). Kritik an Bildundspolitik. *News@ORF.at.* Retrieved 10 February, 2010, from *http://www.orf.at/091125-45153/index.html.*

Ormrod, J. (2003). *Educational psychology: Developing the learners* (4th ed.). Upper Saddle River, NJ: Prentice Hall.

Reiss, S. (2004). Multifaceted nature of intrinsic motivation: The theory of 16 basic desires. *Review of General Psychology, 8*(3), 179–193.

Schecter S. R., & Bayley, R. (1997). Language socialization practices and cultural identity: Case studies of Mexican-descent families in California and Texas. *TESOL Quarterly, 31*(3), 513-541.

Sercu, L. (2006). The foreign language and intercultural competence teacher: the acquisition of a new professional identity. *Intercultural Education, 17*(1), 55-72.

Tarone, E. (2009). A sociolinguistic perspective on interaction in SLA, in A. Mackey & C. Polio (Eds.), *Multiple perspectives on interaction: Second language research in honor of Susan M. Gass,* (pp. 41-56). New York: Routledge.

Tarone, E., & Swierzbin, B. (2009). *Exploring learner language.* Oxford: Oxford University Press.

Vygotskii, L.S. (1978). *Mind in society: The development of higher mental processes.* Cambridge, MA: Harvard University Press.

Wenger, E. (1998). *Communities of practice.* Cambridge: Cambridge University Press.

In: Language and Literacy Education in a Challenging World   ISBN: 978-1-61761-198-8
Editors: T. Lê, Q. Lê, and M. Short   © 2011 Nova Science Publishers, Inc.

Chapter 22

RESPELLING AND CREATIVITY IN SMS: CHALLENGES FOR LITERACY IN THE DIGITAL AGE

Rotimi Taiwo

ABSTRACT

This study explores the increasing exposition of young people to digital writing and the challenges this poses for literacy in the contemporary world. Scholars have been divided on their attitude to the increasing practice of respelling and creativity in SMS. While some see it as portending danger for students' language performance, others see it as a practice that helps literacy. This chapter proposed that SMS can be used to enhance rhetorical competence in written discourse. The correlation between the social nature of text messaging and that of learning presents a good ground for using text messages to teach some basic aspects of language and literary competence. Teachers' role in the language classroom is to create awareness of the different contexts, style, purpose and audience and how to use these to create meaningful texts. Text messaging context is a novel context, which teachers need to help students understand. Real samples of SMS can be good repository for teaching some basic aspects of language like spelling, word order, word boundary, word formation, spelling, and the use of some major literary devices like imagery, rhyme, simile and metaphor.

Keywords: respelling, literacy, creativity, imagery, text, language, competence.

INTRODUCTION

The growing popularity of mobile-phone technology has been affecting the way people communicate through the medium. A major challenge to language teachers is the question of whether to incorporate the language of text messaging into the school syllabus. Scholars are divided on their attitude to this issue. While some have been concerned about the likely effects it will have on the written language performance of the generation of contemporary young people (Sunderland, 2002), for others, it is seen as a signifier of linguistic ability (Crystal, 2008). For Crystal, the fear that texting may have a negative impact on language performance is unfounded. According to Crystal, "there is increasing evidence that texting helps rather than hinders literacy" (p.8). This chapter addresses two major, but related aspects of SMS discursive practices: respelling and creativity. These two phenomena have different motivations in the context of SMS usage. Respelling is borne out of the constraint of space, which makes it impossible for text composers to use full orthographic forms. They therefore resort to the use of traditional and innovative short forms frequently accompanied by a relaxed use of punctuation and grammar rules. Creativity, on the other hand, is what text messages producers do, when they draw inspirations from their experiential knowledge of the context of language use to create messages that are meaningful within the socio-cultural context of their operation. Many times, respelling is seen as a form of creativity because it could be innovative and idiosyncratic, as text writers have different mechanisms for doing it. For the purpose of this chapter, we want to differentiate between creative text spelling and another kind of creativity, which employ symbolism as a major device to make the message more vivid to the addressees. In this chapter, we examine three major questions:

1. What are the major forms of respelling and creativity in SMS texts?

2. What challenges does the increasing exposure of younger people to digital writing through SMS have for language literacy in the contemporary world?

3. How can language teachers use the SMS register to teach some aspects of language and rhetoric?

TEXT MESSAGING

Text messaging, also referred to as short messaging system (SMS) is one of the social interactive technologies (SIL) which affords users the opportunity to communicate by sending short messages through mobile phones and computers, others being Instant Messaging, Internet Relay Chats (IRC), and so forth. It is the exchange of brief messages from one mobile phone or from computer connected to the Internet to another mobile phone. One common feature of text messaging is that users attempt to define themselves stylistically to their groups by playing with the language and creating new prescriptive rules for written language in the process. Text messaging is instant, location independent and personal. This makes it relevant for learner-centred approach and interactive language learning. Text messaging has attracted the attention of scholars from different disciplines and some of the issues that they have explored include the popularity of text messaging among the adolescents (Thurlow, 2003), and its effect on language learning and use (Taiwo, 2007, Bush, 2004).

The linguistic effect of electronic communications technology has attracted so much attention from language scholars. They have different dispositions to the growing popularity of text messaging, which is the most popular attraction for cell phone users. Thurlow (2003), who examines the use of SMS among young people, whom he sees as the driving force behind the growing text messaging culture describes it as 'communicatively adept' having 'linguistic creativity' and a 'robust sense of play', as it enhances and supports intimate relationships among them. In support of Thurlow, Reid & Reid (2002) underscore the role text messages play in helping to fulfil social-relational or phatic function of language use. Sunderland (2002) is one of the scholars who has expressed deep concern about the transformation text messaging is bringing to language. He noted an emerging register and concludes it is 'penmanship for illiterates.' In his articles that was published in *The Guardian* of November 11, 2002, he comments that

> As a dialect, text ('textese'?) is thin and – compared, say with Californian personalized licensed plates – unimaginative. It is bleak, bald, sad shorthand. Drab, shrink talk…. The dialect has a few hieroglyphs (codes comprehensible only to initiates) and a range of face symbols…. Linguistically, it's all pig's ear…. it masks dyslexia, poor spelling and mental laziness. Texting is penmanship for illiterates. (p. 11)

John Humphrys in September 29, in an article in *Mail Online* describes texters as "vandals who are doing to our language what Genghis Khan did to his neighbours 800 years ago." According to him, "they are destroying it: pillaging our punctuation; savaging our sentences; raping our vocabulary. And they must be stopped"(Crystal, 2008:9) Crystal however dispels this fear as he affirms that text messaging helps rather than hinders literacy. This chapter looks at two phenomena commonly associated with discursive practices in text messaging – respelling and creativity and their implications for literacy development all over the world.

RESPELLING AND CREATIVITY

Respelling is a term used in literature on orthography to refer to any form of non-standard innovative or alternative spellings, for example, 'ur' for 'your'; 'tmrw', '2mrw' for 'tomorrow', and so forth, which are common forms in digital writing. The term respelling is also specifically used to refer to an alternative form of spelling that emphasizes pronunciation (phonetic respelling or pronunciation respelling), e.g., *luv* for *love*. Respelling is not a new phenomenon in language use as many studies on netlinguistics made us to believe. According to Shortis (2007), it is a digital recycling of pre-existing popular practices which are all around us. Buttressing this point, Shorts observes that

> Digital technology has diffused the use of re-spellings and orthographic principles which were in previous use in vernacular literacy practices including trade names, children's transitional 'creative spelling' and graffiti. (p. 13)

Crystal (2008) in his book on the great debate on SMS says abbreviations and rebuses and other linguistic forms have a history as old as the written language (Crystal, 2008: 7). He cited instances of the use of such short forms in telegrams, telex and other earlier communication. Respelling just came back alive in text messaging and other digital writing because these media encourage it. For instance, the small screen of mobile phones has been designed to accommodate the fewest number of characters needed to convey a comprehensible message. Similarly, the limited space in an online video game does not encourage elaborate forms because you can only write one line at a time. This therefore encourages users not only to abbreviate, but also to ignore punctuation and grammar, which would normally extend the length of text.

Most of the earlier studies on SMS texts have emphasized the different linguistic strategies used in order to manage communication through this medium (Thurlow, 2003; Bush, 2004; Taiwo, 2008). These include the use of abbreviated forms, acronyms and initialism, letter/number homophones, non-conventional spellings, and accent stylization.

Werry (1996) identifies three major motivations for respelling: (i) economy and text entry reduction, (ii) simulation of spoken language, and (iii) graphical and iconic devices. SMS users have been experimenting with the written language in the context of SMS and manipulating it to fit the technological limitations of space and style. In the process, they have developed their own stylistic shorthand. Some of the stylistic devices commonly identified are homophonic single grapheme abbreviation *b* for *be* or *c* for *see*); numeric characters replacing homophones (*d8* for *date*, *b4* for *before*); aphesis and abbreviation (*attn* for *attention*, *lo* for *hello*); dropping vowels (*rcvd* for *received*, *mbrsd* for *embarrassed*); acronyms (*yw* for *you are welcome*, *ttyl* for *talk to you later*); grapheme changes (*cud* for *could*, *wot* for *what*); and contraction (*bday* for *birthday*, *werru* for *where are you*). Other scholars who have equally identified the typical linguistic characteristics of SMS are Thurlow (2003) and Sunderland (2002).

Creativity is a term that can be applied to a variety of issues that involves critical thinking and production or implementation of novel ideas. Creativity is one of the typical characteristics of human nature, and disciplines that study human social behaviour such as psychology, sociology, philosophy and linguistics have approached the concept from different perspectives relating it to the human nature. Creativity is often associated with the Arts, Literature and Language. Hockett (1966) in his "design features" of human language, identified "productivity", which can also be interpreted as creativity, as one of the thirteen design features of human language. One of the scholars who later worked elaborately on this feature of human language in the theory he formulated about language in the late 1950s and early 1960s is Noam Chomsky. In his book *Aspects of theory of syntax*, Chomsky observes that:

> Within traditional linguistic theory, furthermore, it was clearly understood that one of the qualities that all languages have in common is their "creative" aspect. Thus an essential property of language is that it provides the means of expressing indefinitely many thoughts and for reacting appropriately in an indefinite range of situations... The grammar of a particular language, then, is to be supplemented by a universal grammar that accommodates the creative aspects of language use and expresses the deep-seated regularities, which being universal, are omitted in the grammar itself. (Chomsky, 1965, p. 6)

Chomsky also talks about the freedom of thought, self-expression and imagination that humans possess, which enables them to use their mental power to generate an infinite number of sentences. To corroborate Chomsky's view on the creativity of humans in language use, Carter (2004) identifies linguistic creativity as a property of all language users, which they use "for expressing their social and cultural selves" (p. 214). Creativity in language use is further enhanced by a characteristic of language, called "openness" which enables users to create new lexical items (lexical creativity), as well as syntactic pattern (syntactic creativity). Creativity comes into play sometimes in the context of novel human experiences, such as the one we are examining in this study. The context of SMS is such that allows exhibition of creativity in language. One reason is because the medium is written but conceptually oral – a hybrid, which makes the linguistic experience entirely different. Another is that the space is limited, so language users have to be able to manage their discourse within it – this, essentially calls for their creative ingenuity in linguistic economy. The result of this is that composing in English in this medium has become more elastic and less rule-governed, therefore ellipsis, abbreviation and colloquialism have become common features of SMS text messages.

One important aspect of creativity is symbolism – the use of symbols to represent ideas and emotions. Creativity in text messaging is largely context-based, since whatever will be meaningful to the language users has to be part of their experience. Users of SMS use language creatively for different reasons, which includes, for painting a more vivid picture of their message, for humour, for critiquing, and for expression of cultural identity. Literary writers use different devices to tell their stories in poems, plays and novels. Likewise, advertisement copy writers provide catchy copy for advertising slogans. Newspaper editors also think of how to play on words to create catchy headlines. Texting follows the same principle of creativity.

Apart from the context of text messaging, creativity and respelling have also found expression on the Internet and other electronic devices. For instance, diary writing, which is almost an extinct form of literature, has been resurrected in the form of Web journals popularly referred to as Weblogs or simply Blogs. Emails, Instant Messaging (IM) and internet chats also contextually favour creativity and respelling.

TEXT MESSAGING AND LITERACY

Since people have been expressing concern on the potential negative effect of text messaging on children's writing, several studies have been carried out either to confirm or refute such concerns. The questions that are generally asked are: Is text messaging infecting or liberating the English language? Is text messaging ruining children's grammar and spelling? Some studies have shown that "textism" as it is called, is creeping into the formal school register language and affecting students' composition abilities. They see this as an indication of its negative effects on students' language performance (Brown-Owens, Lenhart, Arafeh, Smith & Mcgill, 2008).

Some studies have also shown that rather than being destructive, text messaging improves children's writing and spelling. David Crystal one of the scholars whose findings reveal this concludes that to disparage text language would be to disparage regional accents or dialects, since they are all part of the natural development of language. For him, people have to be highly literate to know how to abbreviate a word so the recipient knows what they mean. Also a group of researchers at Coventry University explored how the use of text abbreviations might be related to the skills children need in reading and writing and found out that the children who were better at spelling and writing used the most "textisms". This links the use of text message abbreviations positively with literacy achievements. A research similar to this was conducted at Melbourne University in Australia where the researchers tried to find out how mobile phones can boost learning, and their findings reveal that for some students who find writing difficult, the phones have improved their literacy. Plester, Wood and Joshi (2009) explored the relationship, in 10 to 12-year-old children in the UK, between the usage of textisms and school literacy attainment. They found that there was no association between overall textism use and the children's spelling scores. They therefore conclude that there was no evidence that using text messages damage the children's standard English ability. Also Wood, Plester & Bowyer (2008) carried out a research whose results indicated that the use of textism is positively related to the development of subsequent reading and phonological awareness. The general argument of scholars who see positive connection between text messaging and literacy is that to produce and read text abbreviations requires, in the texter a level of phonological awareness and orthographic awareness.

It is important to understand that the literacy practices that surround the use of SMS is multimodal in nature, combining strong components of oral, written as well as visual meaning. The nature of articulation manifests in the speed of typing, the complexity of text language, innovative use of alphabetic characters visually, and that of interpretation, which entails adequate experience at decoding the semiotics are part of the skills of this new literacy. These current demands for specific language competencies have shifted the definition of literacy. Literacy in the present age includes being able to articulate and decode these new language norms and conventions springing up in the digital media, new ways of reading and writing text and new attitudes to communication and language norms. As Reinking (2005) puts it, literacy in the present age is being able to communicate in a "post-typographic" world.

TRENDS IN THE USE OF TEXT MESSAGES

Since the beginning of the Millennium, there has been an unprecedented growth in the mobile market in developing countries. Despite the great variation in the rate of diffusion of cell phones around the world, its growth has been rapid. By the end of 2008, there were an estimated 4.1 billion mobile subscriptions, up from 1 billion in 2002. This represents six in ten of the world's population, although it is hard to make a precise calculation about how many people actually use mobile phones. For instance, a single mobile phone may have several users in poorer countries, where mobile phones are sometimes shared or rented out by their owners. The spread in the use of mobile phones has been having tremendous impact on the social life of the people all over the world. To buttress this, an ITU 2009 reports says by the end of 2008, there were over three times more mobile cellular subscriptions than fixed telephone lines. While fixed line global penetration has been stagnating at just fewer than 20% for the last years, there has been an unprecedented growth in mobile cellular lines subscription. Africa is the continent with the fastest growth. According to a Reuters' publication of March 2, 2009, two thirds of the world's cell phone subscriptions are in developing nations, with the highest growth rate in Africa where a quarter of the population now has a mobile. Apart from its use for personal and social relations, SMS has been adapted for other innovative purposes, which include its use for educational, health, agricultural, political and economic purposes. Scholars have identified why SMS should be adopted for learning. They believe modern technology promotes active learning. They also argue that since learning is a socio-cultural process, the use of SMS, which is a socio-cultural tool, having the potential for encouraging classroom interactivity, is one of the best means for teaching and learning. Research findings have shown significant improvements in the learner performance and in their attitudes towards using SMS in their vocabulary learning.

Text messaging is also deployed for health purposes. It is being used by health professionals to increase the level of support, education and information available to patients. For instance SMS has been applied in many ways to improve sexual health and there is enough evidence of its effectiveness. Due to people's accessibility to it even in the most remote parts of the world, with little or no basic healthcare facilities, it is being used to send basic prevention and other health messages. In Australia and South Africa, automated text messages are sent to patients as hospital appointment reminders (Doner, Meara & Da Costa, 2005; Maphan, 2008). Also, in Rwanda and Tanzania, critical health data and information on HIV are being delivered through SMS.

Likewise, in agriculture, a sophisticated market information system for efficient trading, connecting sellers and buyers over the mobile phone via SMS with necessary information about prices and crops is being used in West Africa. In Sierra Leone, Kenya and Nigeria, SMS was used to monitor elections. In the Philippines and Hong Kong people use their mobile phones as virtual wallets, making these countries leaders among developing nations in mobile transactions. SMS text messages in form of chain texts and prayer requests are helping to boost and encourage faith deepening in Nigeria and the Philippines. In Finland SMS is used to access roadside lavatory. The idea is to curb the growing unrestrained vandalism of toilets through graffiti. Finnish Road Administration feels people will be less likely to write graffiti in public toilets knowing that their mobile numbers are recorded for security reasons.

EXPLORING THE POTENTIALS OF SMS FOR LANGUAGE LEARNING

Until the advent of computer networking, speech and writing have remained distinctly separate linguistic skills. While speech is associated with orality and immediacy, accompanied with paralinguistic cues that help interlocutors to comprehend the message, writing, on the other hand is more conscious of distance and therefore better structured. These two aspects of language do not come as simultaneous experiences in the life of most language learners. Speech is naturally acquired by children, but writing has to be taught formally, usually when the child starts schooling. Apart from this, they are associated with different discourse contexts – speech, usually with contiguity and informality and writing with distance and formality. These two hitherto distinct aspects of language are now gradually merging in the context of digital discourse, such as online chats, discussion forums, Instant Messaging and SMS. In these contexts, writing is being used to capture patterns and techniques of speech - peoples' fingers are virtually become their voice. In view of the observation above, it is important to take a cursory look at the challenges the discourse practices in the language of SMS can pose to language literacy. From all indications it is clear that teachers in the digital age have grater responsibilities in teaching language.

In the sections that follow, I will demonstrate how text messages can be used to enhance language literacy, using samples of text messages composed by young people from all over the world. First, it is important to identify the correlation between the social nature of texting and that of language learning. Learning language is best done in a social and collaborative way. Using real instances of language use stimulates in learners better learning. This is particularly true when such examples are not far removed from the experience of such learners or when they come from the learners themselves. Text messaging may be an important tool to help students learn how different discursive contexts affect the choice of linguistic style. One of the major roles of teachers in language learning is to create awareness of content, style, purpose and audience and how these impact on style and usage. For instance, some aspects of word formation processes, like acronyming and clipping can be taught using SMS. These two processes create new words by reducing the length of the old ones to find accommodation for them on the mobile phone screen. In the past, acronyming and clipping were seen as processes that are not too productive, especially, when compared with other processes like affixation and compounding, which are more popular word formation processes in English. However, the context of text messaging has proved this to be incorrect or at least debatable. The predominant use of these two processes in text messaging is not unconnected with the need for brevity in the medium. The use of acronyms, such as *ASAP* (as soon as possible), *FYI* (for your information), *RU* (are you), *TTYL* (talk to you later) and clippings, such as g-clipping (*comin, mornin*), other forms of clipping (*bday, sis, congrats*) are common enough to attract some attention to their relevance as productive expressions in the digital communication register. They could then be taught as part of the growing register of SMS in language classrooms.

Imagery is one of the most prominent devices used in text messages. Imagery evokes the meaning and truth of human experiences. It is a device by which the poet makes his meaning strong, clear and sure. Image-making expressions in any poetic discourse appeal to some human senses like sight, touch, sound, taste, smell and so forth. The text messages below make use of imagery to project meaning.

T1. *Find arms that will hold u at ur weakest, eyes that will c u at ur ugliest, heart that will love u at ur worst, if you have found it, u've found love. I found love when I met u.*

T2. *God's luv 4 u is nt proud as GLO. It does not change ownership like CELTEL It is not expensive like MTN and does not have NAFDAC no, so it cant expire.*

T3. *As u've logged out of 2007 & begin 2 browse 2ru 2008 may u doubleclick goodness, mercy and download success, gud health & comfort. Happy New Year.*

T1 is a message of love that employs tactile, visual and perceptive imagery to construct the message. T2 uses Nigerian socio-cultural images combined with simile to capture the composer's perception of God's love. People who are familiar with contemporary events in mobile telecommunications in Nigeria will understand the context of the message. The background issues that will throw more light into the motivations for creating the text are:

(a) Glo Mobile, one of the mobile telecommunications providers has as its slogan "Glo with pride"

(b) A mobile telecommunication provider, which started in Nigeria as ECONET Wireless in 2001 has since change its name to Vodacom, Vmobile, Celtel and now Zain.

(c) MTN is known to charge the most expensive tariffs for its service among the service providers in Nigeria

(d) NAFDAC is the body that regulates and controls quality standards for foods, drugs and chemicals imported or manufactured locally and distributed in Nigeria. NAFDAC also assigns batch number, date of manufacture and expiry dates to products.

T3 is a new year's greeting imaging the experience of people as they move from one year to another. This is done through the use of computer terminologies – 'logging out', 'browsing', 'double clicking' and 'downloading.' These text messages are good resources for teaching students about how to create imagery in text. Exposure of students to real examples of imagery produced by young people like them can stimulate in them the ability to create their own texts using imagery.

The general impression created in literature on text messaging practices is that respelling is used when text composers want to achieve brevity. This may be true for many cases of respelling, but not for all cases. Some instances of respelling show that an alternative spelling is not always shorter than the conventional one. For instance, the use of phonetic spellings *mai* for *my*, *trai* for *try* and *laif* for *life* show that strategies for respelling are not motivated solely by the quest for brevity. In fact in the first two re-spelt expressions – *mai* and *trai*, they occupy more space than the original word. T4 below further proves this.

T4.   *Wishing u the merriest xmas 'n' the happiest new year. No 1 deserves it any more than a wonderful person like u.*

The use of *'n'* for *and* is apparently not for brevity, because this alternative form takes the same amount of space as the conventional form it replaces, being also three characters. From instances like this, one can conclude that sometimes respelling is just an indication of experimenting with an alternative spelling. The awareness of alternative spellings in the context of SMS and other CMC modes encourages creativity in students. It also helps them to learn pronunciation.

Text messaging language can also be used to teach word order and word boundary. In order to save space, text messages do not clearly define word boundaries – two separate words can be written together as if they were one. Some examples are seen in the messages below.

T5:   *We cn meet at 2. Willwait for u at d bustop. We can then goto any of the 2places u suggestd. Lookinfwd to seein u 2mrw*

T6:   *Smile u make & hello say 2 wanted just I dat out find u wen funny very it find wil u. CONFUSED? Read backwards. 4rm (name)*

Apart from the typical general use of abbreviation, T5 did not separate some words. For instance, *will* and *wait* are written together. Likewise, *bus* and *stop*, *go* and *to*, *2* and *places*, *lookin* and *fwd*, yet the messages are decodable for people who are competent in the knowledge of English word boundary. The practice here can be used to test the knowledge of word boundary and spelling in a language class. T6 is written backwards and the text instructs the addressee to read it in such manner to be able to understand it. This creative way of reversing English word order can be used to teach this phenomenon as well as test its knowledge.

Text messaging practice is a very good resource for teaching literary competence. Composers of text messages use a good number of literary devices without being necessarily aware of it. Teachers can use these to stimulate students' creative ability. Let us consider some text messages to illustrate these.

T7.   *Bcus u r humble & hate 2 fumble,u ll nt stumble nor grumble,ur enemies will mumble in double trouble,because its ur tyme to bubble.stay blessed*

T8.   *This new month, God will edify,identify,justify,modify , beautify,purify,gratify magnify,dignify,satisfy & GLORIFY you. Enjoy God's grace this mnt&4eva cha o*

The repetition of the sound of the final accented syllables of some words, which in the study of literature is a kind of rhyme, is the prominent feature of T7 and T8. The syllable *–ble* ending of *fumble, grumble, mumble, double, trouble,* and *bubble* in T3, as well as the *–ify* ending of *edify, identify, justify, modify, beautify, purify, gratify, magnify, dignify, satisfy* and *glorify* in T8 produces a rhyme. These texts may be good resources for teaching rhyme in poetic language. It also helps students in their vocabulary building to acquire words that associate as a result of some similar patterns in their orthography and pronunciation.

T9.   *Life is like music. It has high notes and low notes. No mater how high or low your notes may be, keep in tune with God and you'll never go out of tune in the music of life.*

T10.   *Life is like a piano, white keys are happy moments and black keys are sad moments, but remember both keys are played 2gether 2 give sweet music called LIFE*

T11.   *Prayer is the key that opens your day to every blessing. It also is a lock that closes the night to keep you safe while sleeping. So what you have to do is "use your key all the time. (metaphor)*

T12.   *Love is a WAR, easy to start but HARD 2 end.*

T9 – T12 produce good examples of similes and metaphors. While T9 and T10 compare two things each – *life* to *music* and *piano* respectively, using an explicit comparative expression (*like*), T11 and T12 also compare two things each – *prayer* and *key* and *love* and *war* respectively by direct associative comparison. Similes and metaphors are powerful tools for conjuring images and students can learn about how to use them to bring life and richness to what they have to say. Teachers can reproduce samples of text messages that make use of these devices and ask the students to identify the devices in them. They can also be encouraged to create their own SMS using the devices. Other literary devices, such as allusion, pun, irony and paradox are also known to be commonly used in SMS. In fact, it is usually the case that one hardly finds any creative SMS without one or more of these rhetorical devices, since by their very nature, creative SMS composers consciously or unconsciously deviate from the strict orthographic form and literal sense of a word in order to make meaning.

In order to use SMS language to teach standard spelling, teachers can present text messages that exhibit extreme respelling and abbreviation patterns and ask the students to change the re-spelt and abbreviated forms to the standard forms. This kind of exercise exposes students to both the standard and alternative spelling. Users have to be able to spell to know how to abbreviate. Each linguistic situation presents opportunities for using language in unique ways. Being elaborate and being brief are aspects of language skills learners need to know. Brevity may present some problems, especially when forms used are the ones the addressee is not familiar with. For instance, it may not be very clear sometimes what short forms to use for some words, as shown below.

> *nt not, night, net*
> *yr year, your*
> *wt with, what*

Whatever form is used, the ability to decode effectively similar short forms for different words is an indication of lexical competence. The role of the teacher is to ensure that students are exposed to the possibilities of language use by presenting these to them in the classroom. One way of creating awareness of registers in students is by asking them to identify a variety of settings in which they communicate regularly, such as at home with parents, in school with friends, with friends through SMS, and so forth. After drawing up a comprehensive list, student can then be asked how they would render some simple everyday greetings like "Hello, how are you?" in different settings considering the interlocutors. A variety of possibilities will be produced like:

> *Hello dad, how are you - with the father*
> *Hi, ao 're u?- text-speaking with a friend*
> *Hey, what's up? - conversation with a friend*
> *Good day Miss White, how are you - with a teacher*

With these varieties, the teacher can guide a discussion on similarities and differences and possibly dray a scale of formality to show how language use differ in contexts. Students' performance can be enhanced when the teacher uses such real life examples. The interactive situation also encourages the students to explore the open-ended nature of language and to create their own examples to reflect their stylistic peculiarities.

CONCLUSION

Respelling and creativity in language use have been identified as dominant strategies in SMS text messaging. The emerging linguistic style in text messages, which makes composition more elastic and less rule-governed, is a major issue being discussed by scholars, especially in regard to its effect on language learning. This practice in digital writing where orthography and speech are merged in one medium of communication is another aspect of language use that calls for the attention of teachers in the language classroom. As this practice takes hold of the linguistic sphere, it presents new challenges and opportunities for teaching and learning. I propose the use of real samples of text messages, which are very rich repository of respelling, creativity rhetorical devices as means of teaching some basic aspects of language, such as word order, word boundary, and word formation, spelling, and the use of some literary devices like imagery, rhyme, simile and metaphor.

ACKNOWLEDGMENT

My deep appreciation goes to the Humboldt Foundation for funding my research work on digital discourse. Between September, 2008 and August, 2009, I was a fellow of Alexander von Humboldt at the University of Freiburg, Germany. This work is one of the outcomes of my research stay in Germany.

REFERENCES

Brown-Owens, A.; Eason, M.; & Lader, A. (2005). *Hat effect does computer-mediated communication, specifically, instant messaging, have on 8th Grade writing competencies?* Retrieved February 12, 2009 from *http://web.archive.org/web/ 20030821214021 /http://w.usca.edu/medtech/course/et780/may03/groupprojects/cmc-im.html.*

Bush, C. (2004). Language beyond the text: Txt msgs 4 a new gnr8n. *The Journal of New Media and Culture,* Summer/Fall, *3* (2). Retrieved October 20, 2006, from *http://www.ibiblio.org/nmediac/summer2005/text.html.*

Carter, R. (2004). *Language and creativity: The art of common talk.* London: Routledge.

Chomsky, N. (1965). *Aspect of theory of syntax.* Cambridge: MIT Press.

Crystal, D. (2008) *Txtng: The Gr8 Db8.* London: Oxford University Press.

Doner, S. R. Meara, G. M. & La Costa, A. C. (2005). *Uses of text messaging to improve outpatient attendance. Medical Journal of Australia, 183*(7), 366-368.

Harris, P. Rettie, R. & Kyan, C. C. (2005). Adoption and usage of m-commerce: A cross-cultural comparison of Hong Kong and the United Kingdom. *Journal of Electronic Commerce Research, 6*(3), 210-224.

Hockett, C. (1966). The problem of universals in language. In J. H. Greenberg (Ed.) *Universals of language (2nd. ed.)* (pp. 1-29). Cambridge, MA: MIT Press.

Lenhart, A, Arafeh, S., Smith, A., & MacGill, A. R. (2008). *Writing, technologies and teens.* Retrieved January 30, 2009 from *http://www.pewinternet.org/pdfs/ PIP Writing Report FINAL3.pdf.*

Maphan, W. (2008). Mobile phones: Changing healthcare, one SMS at a time. *The South African Journal of HIV Medicine, 9*(4), 11-16.

Plester, B. Wood, C. & Joshi, P. (2009). Exploring the relationship between children' knowledge of text message abbreviations and school literacy outcomes. *British Journal of Developmental Psychology, 27*(1), 145-161.

Reid D. & Reid, F. (2002). *Insights into the social and psychological effects of SMS text messaging.* Retrieved October 2, 2004 from *http://www.160characters.org/.*

Reinking, D. (2005). Introduction: Synthesizing technological transformations of literacy in a post-typographic world. In D. Reinking, M. Mckenna, L. Labbo & R. Kieffer (Eds.) *Handbook of literacy and technology* (pp. xi-xxx). New Jersey: Lawrence Erlbaum Associates.

Sutherland, J. (2002). Can u txt? John Sutherland asks what texting is doing to the English language - and finds it all a bit. *The Guardian Newspaper*, November 1, 2002.

Shortis, T. (2007). *Gr8 Txtpectations: The creativity of text spelling. English Drama Media, June 2007.* Retrieved July 10, 2009 from www.articlearchives.com/media.../1480988-1.html.

Taiwo, R. (2007). Computer-mediated communication: Implications for the teaching and learning of English as a second language. In M. Olateju, R. Taiwo, & A. Fakoya (Eds), *Towards the Understanding of Discourse Strategies* (pp. 231 – 247). Ago-Iwoye: Olabisi Onabanjo University Press.

Taiwo, R. (2008). Linguistic forms and functions of SMS text messages in Nigeria. In S. Kelsey & K. St. Armant (Eds.), *Handbook of research on computer-mediated communication* (pp. 969-982). Hershey, Pennsylvania: IGI Global.

Thurlow, C. (2003). *Generatn txt? The sociolinguistics of young people's text-messagin – Discourse Analysis Online.* Retrieved October 2, 2004 from *http://extra.shu.ac.uk.daol/articles/vl/a3/thurlow2002003-paper.html.*

Werry, C. C. (1996) Linguistic and Interactional Features of Internet Relay Chat. In S. Herring (Ed.), *Computer-mediated communication: Linguistic, social and cross-cultural perspectives* (pp 47-63). Amsterdam, John Benjamins.

Wood, C., Plester, B., & Bowyer, S. (2008, September). *A cross-lagged longitudinal study of text messages and its impact on literacy skills: Preliminary result.* A poster presentation at the British Psychological Society Developmental Section Conference, Oxford, UK.

In: Language and Literacy Education in a Challenging World   ISBN: 978-1-61761-198-8
Editors: T. Lê, Q. Lê, and M. Short   © 2011 Nova Science Publishers, Inc.

Chapter 23

"YOU HAVE TO BE ALWAYS THINKING HOW TO TELL [YOUR] STORY ": ENGLISH LEARNERS AND DIGITAL STORIES AT A SOUTH CHINESE UNIVERSITY

Paul McPherron and Jen Nowicki Clark

ABSTRACT

Drawing on work that has emphasized the way students in divergent contexts use digital stories to tell stories and reflect on past and future experiences, this paper contributes a perspective on digital stories from English language classrooms at a university in southern China and analyzes the ways students and teachers use digital stories to create personal narratives and project global and local identities. By illustrating the implications of using digital stories in educational contexts, we argue that just as important as the semiotic power (c.f. Hull & Nelson, 2005) of digital stories in creating new forms of litearcy and meaning-making, this type of multimodal composing opens new spaces for cross-cultural dialogue and negotiation, particularly in English language classrooms around the world.

Keywords: digital stories, English language learning, China, multiliteracies.

INTRODUCTION

In 2007 at a university in southern China- named here as China Southern University (CSU), a foreign teacher[1], seven students, and four local teachers participated in a Digital Storytelling workshop. In recent years, digital storytelling and the use of various movie-making tasks have become popular in language and literacy pedagogy in the United States and elsewhere as part of the growing field of Computer Assisted Language Learning (CALL) (Lambert, 2002; Meadows, 2003; Tharp & Hills, 2004; Hull & Nelson. 2005; Davis, 2005),

---

[1] CSU generally considers native-English speaking teachers who have received higher education and training outside of China as foreign teachers. Local teachers are defined as Chinese citizens who may or may not have received higher education outside of China.

but this was the first movie-making activity of its kind at CSU. Facilitated by Jennifer Nowicki- one of the authors of this chapter- and one student assistant, the group learned different approaches and activities for preparing their personal story scripts, recording their narratives and combining their oral stories with visual images from their own lives.

Drawing on the digital stories created by the group, this chapter illustrates ways in which the creation and reading of digital stories are used as curriculum and teaching materials for literacy instruction at CSU and in language classrooms throughout the world. Further, the paper offers close readings of student and teacher digital stories, pointing out properties of multi-modal text design as well as key themes in how participants at a university in Southern China use digital stories to project and digitally "write" their global and local identities. Specifically, we analyze the digital stories in response to the following two research questions:

1. How do the students creatively use the various elements of digital stories (i.e., dramatic question, imagery, and audience) to mediate macro themes and identities in their larger narratives?
2. How do the production and viewing of digital stories support English language and literacy learning and open new spaces for cross-cultural dialogue in language classrooms?

Before analyzing the themes and examples from the digital stories in relation to the above questions, the next sections briefly review key notions in media literacy and work on English language teaching (ELT) in China, and we present a fuller description of the process of creating digital stories and the digital storytelling group at CSU.

Multiliteracies, Digital Stories, and CLT in China

In the 1990's, k-12 educators in the United States began to place attention on media literacy and the need to teach students to uncover messages and meanings in non-print as well as print "texts" (Cox, 1994; Alvermann, Moon, & Hagood, 1999). In addition, groups such as the Center for Media Literacy (CML) and the National Association for Media Literacy Education (NAMLE) linked the skill of reading non-print texts with the ability to create or "write" media texts. On their website, NAMLE offers a typical definition of media literacy:

> Within North America, media literacy is seen to consist of a series of communication competencies, including the ability to ACCESS, ANALYZE, EVALUATE, and COMMUNICATE information in a variety of forms, including print and non-print messages. Media literacy empowers people to be both critical thinkers and creative producers of an increasingly wide range of messages using image, language, and sound. (Original emphasis, NAMLE, 2008)

Academic and practitioner work in a variety of education and linguistics fields have pointed out that the "wide range of messages" are primarily located outside of formal schooling contexts and draw on popular culture and traditional cultural references, and much work argues that the ability to "read" and "write" in language education must incorporate these new literacy practices (Lankshear & Knobel, 2003; Skinner & Hagood, 2008; Ajayi,

2008), often referred to as *multiliteracies* (Cope & Kalantzis, 2000; Gee, 2003; 2007). In addition, Gee (2003), Street (1995) and others point out that the learning and use of *multiliteracies* is by definition a social practice and students as digital writers and readers "bring their own cultural resources, agendas, and purposes to literacy learning" (Skinner & Hagood, 2008, p. 13).

Ajayi (2008) notes that an expanded view of literacy and language entails a new conception of illiteracy and disadvantage for people who are not visually and media literate (p. 210); however, national and local education policies and curriculum around the world typically only address foundational literacy, based on print-based texts only. Further, Hull & Nelson (2005) note that traditional views on literacy often view the new literacy practices associated with media literacy and multiliteracies as a threat to our collective ability to communicate. Instead, they argue:

> The new media that afford multimodal composing might helpfully be viewed not as a threat to or impoverishment of the print-based canon or traditional means of composing, but rather as an opportunity to contribute a newly invigorated literate tradition and to enrich our available means of signification. (p. 226)

In the same way, we argue that the digital stories created and "read" by English language learners at a university community in southern China reinforce the traditional skills taught in language classrooms- reading, writing, listening, and speaking- as well as allow students to explore traditional narrative structure while learning new "means of signification," meaning-making, and story-telling techniques. Of equal importance for our study, the creation and reception of these stories provide new spaces for students and teachers to negotiate local and global identities and engage in cross-cultural dialogues.

Digital stories are short, 2-4 minute multi-media narratives told from the first person, accomplishing a variety of purposes depending on the author and context. Much has been written about the use of digital stories in community centers with adolescents (Davis, 2005; Hull & Nelson, 2005; Davis & Weinshenker, 2009); and some work has examined digital stories as part of classroom projects and identity construction for English language learners in the United States (Skinner & Hagood, 2008). In addition, there have been studies that document the overall effectiveness of using digital stories in EFL contexts (Wan, Tanimoto, & Templeton, 2008), but to our knowledge there is no work on digital stories in an EFL context that analyzes the intersection of digital text construction, the development of multiliteracies, and identity processes for English language learners. As we document in the next sections, CSU offers a particularly interesting setting to examine these issues because of its strong promotion of communicative language teaching (CLT) methodology and integration with Western-teaching methods and ideas about literacy instruction.

The CSU Context

The data for the paper are part of a larger study of English language reforms and classrooms at CSU that took place over a three-year period of teaching and researching at CSU from 2004-2007, but the eleven stories analyzed in this paper were created in the spring of 2007 as part of an extracurricular Digital Storytelling Group. The data primarily come from three sources: 1) the eleven finished digital stories that were collected onto one DVD; 2) teacher notes and transcripts from classrooms that used the stories as course content; and 3) interviews and written feedback from the authors of the stories. The paper follows participant-observer and ethnographic research traditions in TESOL in order to represent the complexity of the research questions and draw out key themes that emerge in the data in response to the two research questions (Watson-Gegeo, 1988; Richards, 2003).

The university where the study took place, CSU, was founded outside of a coastal city in Guangdong Province in 1981. In 2002, CSU administrators created the English Language Department (ELD) to teach all English language classes and promote "a high-level of communicative competence" which they write on their website is "the ultimate goal for our students." To achieve this goal, the ELD has set up multi-skill classes that emphasize language meaning and use, instead of traditional structure and form-focused teaching. They have also created numerous English clubs and discussion programs that emphasize using English outside of the classroom in immersion settings. The digital storytelling project described and analyzed here connects to these communicative language reforms and was supported by CSU and ELD administrators through allocation of classroom space and computer support.

THE DIGITAL STORYTELLING GROUP AT CSU

The digital storytelling group was facilitated by Jennifer Nowicki during the spring semester in 2007, and consisted of both students and teachers. The group met on five Friday mornings from 8am-12pm in order to learn various approaches and activities for preparing their personal story scripts, recording their narratives and combining their oral stories with visual images from their own lives. Examples of digital stories were used throughout the training to generate discussion of how to use multimedia purposefully. This process required critical formation of a personal narrative, which was negotiated with the support of other participants during the "Story Circle" part of the training on the first day. Over the following weeks, participants practiced writing and reading their scripts, paying special attention to appropriate vocabulary, grammar, intonation and pronunciation. As a working cohort, the group regularly listened to each other's stories to make suggestions about which images were most appropriate at which times, and provide feedback to each other in a natural conversational atmosphere.

In the CSU group, the trainer drew on the seven elements of digital stories described in Lambert (2002): point of view, dramatic question, emotional content, voice, soundtrack, economy, and pacing, but she narrowed these elements into point, audience, voice, economy, and shape to help students focus their stories. While students were free to create any type or genre of story that they wanted, all authors in the CSU storytelling group chose to create personal stories that fall under the category of autobiographical narrative as described in Hull and Nelson (2005). The stories do, however, represent different purposes for autobiographical stories as described in Lambert (2006) including: a tribute to family members or friends; a reflection on travel and cross-cultural experience; documentation of humorous or meaningful events; a representation of a place or community; and a moral lesson or life instructions.

When the stories were completed, participants explored potential applications of digital storytelling to their continued work as English language learners and teachers. As one participating local teacher noted, "It teaches us not only a new technology, but also improves our integrative skills such as listening, speaking, reading and writing skills. At the same time, the result brought me a great sense of achievement and success… It is a great way to promote students' interests in learning language." A DVD with all of the stories was produced for each of the participants and the ELC program to use for educational and outreach purposes. The completed stories were screened publicly 3 times: at the last day of the workshop, at the Faculty Lecture Series and at English Corner as a special presentation. These opportunities raised awareness among the CSU community about this project. They also allowed the students to be recognized publicly and to present their own reflections on the process in front of their peers, opening the learning process to a broader audience other than only classroom teachers and students, a key aspect of *multiliteracies* and multi-modal composing.

DIGITAL STORYTELLING ELEMENTS IN THE CSU DIGITAL STORIES

The following data sections offer detailed examples and discussion of a few key digital storytelling elements in stories as they relate to the research questions. We compare the ways authors incorporated these themes into their stories and how they contribute to each author's macro-themes and narrative structure. In particular, we perform close readings of three student stories that were particularly successful and triggered much discussion with audiences at CSU: Sue, a 3rd year English major who created a story narrating her experiences as a premature and small baby; Pan, a 2nd year Journalism student, who described her family unity through stories about her mother's cooking; and Timmy, a 2nd year Mathematics student, who told a unique narrative about the morning after a typhoon had caused flooding on the CSU campus.[2]

Explicit and Implicit Dramatic Questions

Many of stories revolve around a dramatic question as described in Lambert (2002). For example, Sue begins her story with a combination of pictures, starting with a recent picture of herself as a college student, and she then mixes images from when she was very young and small, and her parents were concerned with her health.

According to Labov's (1997) general structure of narrative, the first statements in the story "My name is [name omitted]" and "When I was born I was only 1.5 kilograms weight" represent the *abstract* of Sue's narrative, by describing what the story is basically about. The use of a black and white photo foreshadows the tensions and complications that arise in the rest of the narrative, but as introduction to her story, Sue, in effect, answers any question about whether she survived and if she is healthy now. Following Labov's (1997) structure of narrative in English, the next section of a typical narrative is the *orientation* which anchors a story in a specific cultural and physical space, and the rest of the text and images in Table 1 present the surrounding circumstances, preview the main complication in Sue's narrative, and hint at a dramatic question, specifically "How did Sue survive in 'Old China'" when she was so small and her father's parents wanted to give her up?"

---

[2] All names used in the paper are pseudonyms to protect anonymity.

Table1 – Introduction to Sue's digital story

Voice	Images
My name is [omitted] When I was born I was only 1.5 kilograms weight.	Recent picture of Sue in black and white.
You can imagine how little I was as a baby. My father also told me that I was as small as a chopstick.	Picture of Sue standing as a baby next to flower.
Three fingers together could cover my little face. My relatives thought I could not live longer.	Picture of Sue frowning next to play pen.
And my father's parents even had the thought of giving me up. Because at that period people preferred a boy to a girl.	Picture of Sue with her younger brother.
Boys are more important than girls at Old China.	Black and white picture of boys

After this introduction, Sue's main narrative follows a typical English narrative structure revealing how her maternal grandparents- living in a rural village- raised her from a young age. In her narrative, the complicating action is Sue's weight and her grandparents concern with feeding and raising her. Sue states:

> My grandma held me in her arm, in order to make me happy, and raise me easily. Because I was a 1.5 kilogram weight when I was born, and she was afraid that I could not be brought up healthy. And she even wept at night.

And she describes how her grandfather would cook her rice:

> I still can't forget the shadow of my grandpa's back. He cooked meals for me every day. And it always took him more than an hour to cook the rice by fire. To make it soft and a little bit wet. It was hot near the fire and he was sweating.

Throughout the main body of her narrative, Sue repeatedly thanks her grandparents and refers to her 1.5 kilogram weight, and she ends her story in with what Labov (1997) labels an *evaluation* in which she makes clear the importance of the story and answers the question "What happened in the end?" She states:

> Now, I am a grownup; healthy and happy; living in another city in a beautiful university. I have my new life and new friends. But this does not mean that distance will change my love towards my grandparents. I know that they love me more than I love them. They devote all their love for me for a 1.5 kilograms baby girl. I love you my grandma and grandpa.

In addition to pictures of her grandparents decorated with hearts and stars, Sue juxtaposes pictures of CSU campus buildings and herself with friends on campus with her final statement.

Sue's story follows the general narrative structure of English narratives described by Labov (1997) from abstract to orientation, to complicating action, to evaluation and coda, but responses to her somewhat implicit question about "how did she survive in these circumstances" reveal interesting comments about modern life and government policy in China. On one hand, this story is paying tribute to Sue's grandparents and pointing out how successful she is because of their love and devotion. On another level, however, the story is discussing the reproduction policy in China (such as the One Child Policy) and female and male gender roles including the notion that boys are more valued than girls. In the orientation to Sue's story, she does specifically mention "In that period people preferred a boy to a girl. Boys are more important than girls in Old China." It is interesting that she uses the phrase "Old China" in English to refer to the circumstances that would have allowed her parent's to "give her up" because she was a girl. The phrase "Old China" is commonly invoked to describe the time period before the formation of the Republic of China in 1911 and eventual creation of the People's Republic of China in 1949, but Sue uses this common term to describe the 1980's when she was born. In this somewhat *double voicing* (c.f. Bakhtin, 1952/1994) of a dominant term in Chinese historical discourse, she implicitly is adding 40 or more years to the timeline of "Old China." In this way, her response to the dramatic question "how did I survive?" is implicitly challenging the accepted narrative of modernity in China.[3]

Audience: Who is watching?

When creating their digital stories, the students and teachers in the group often discussed the audience for their stories and the question of "To whom are you speaking?" Indeed, according to Lambert (2002), the notion of audience awareness is central to all of seven elements of digital storytelling, and as described in Larsen-Freeman (2005), the skill of crafting your message to a specific audience is central to a communicative approach to language teaching. Though no explicit instructions were given to the participants about choosing an audience, all of the stories included aspects that appear to speak to a Western-audience. For example, Pan's story about food and her mother's cooking begins with the following explanation of campus life and Southern Chinese cuisine.

Her story goes on to explain her love for her mother's cooking, and she asserts, "without much knowledge, the best way that she can express her love for me is by making tempting food." Her story becomes a tribute to her mother's cooking and the love of her family, and she ends the story with a series of pictures of her family enjoying meals and parties.

In explaining the differences between the "mass-produced" food of the cafeteria and the lovingly prepared food by her mother, Pan appears to be explaining university life in China and comparing it to the love and care that she receives at home as an only child, a situation that resonates with many CSU students. However, it is unclear if her mother will ever be able to understand the story. In this way, the primary audience is clearly the larger CSU community of English learners and foreign teachers and students who can speak English.

---

[3] See Yu (2009) for a discussion of narratives and conceptions of Chinese modernity.

Table 2 – Pan's description of campus cooking

Voice	Images
Many people say campus life is quality time of the whole. That's true, however, not necessarily delicious.	Campus grounds and buildings
This is our dining hall; food here is cheap and popular. Every noon, after classes, students flow into here.	Students buying and eating food in dining hall
Most dishes in the student's dining hall are typical Guangdong food, without any spice, that's a little bit hard for me. Food here is just like "mass-production manufacturing".	Close shots of food on plates and in cafeteria line.

Table 3 – Pan's conclusion

Voice	Images
Being away from family, I miss home cooking more strongly than ever before. Not because school food is bad, but for warm feeling that only exists at home.	Picture of table with multiple plates of food. Three pictures of Pan with mom, and other family members smiling and eating together.
Mom told me that the secret recipe of cooking is heart and love. I will continue the family meals and pass the love to my children.	Text: "Wherever I go, family love will always play a major part of my love. I would like to hand down the lovely tradition to my future daughter"

Irene, an experienced teacher who has taught at CSU since 1983, added a further, instructive, dimension to a story that explained some of China's history to foreign teachers as well as instructed her Chinese students in the benefits of hard work and perseverance. In her story, she portrays herself as one who has overcome struggles and is an inspiration to her students. Her story begins:

> I was born in Beijing. When I was four years-old, my father was denounced as a rightist, and my family was forced to move to the intra Ningxia Hui autonomous region. There I got my primary and secondary education. Then, as millions of high school graduates did during the Cultural Revolution, I became a farmer working in the field. Two and a half years later I managed to find a job as a high school teacher. In 1977 after 12 years of being closed, universities resumed their examinations and opened the doors to the young students who wanted to study. Fortunately, I seized this chance and went to a local university. I could not enter the famous university that I had chosen because of my father's historical issue. And then, I became a teacher here at [CSU]. I f you ask me what is life? I would say life is a journey; you develop new eyes during your journey.

Interestingly, she never overtly instructs students to work hard or be diligent in studying, but through her story, she notes the successes of her diligent students and describes her joy in helping them succeed: "Students always show their shining potentials in my classroom. One of my strong points is I can always ignite their sparks into big flames." The main theme is clearly about expressing yourself through hard work overcoming any obstacles. In this way, the audience for Irene's story was not only the foreign teacher community, though her story resonated with foreign teachers who viewed it, as the story of the Cultural Revolution and its effects on education and teachers has been a popular topic of many recent books on China and Chinese culture.

Individualism and Personal Narratives

East Asian societies have stereotypically been framed as collectivist versus the individualism valued in Europe and the "West" (Sugimoto, 1997), but the digital stories created at CSU provide interesting examples in relation to this artificial dichotomy-particularly because the task of creating a story requires, on the surface, a personal story and each author is typically the protagonist of the story, as evidenced in the stories described above. Similarly, Timmy created a very personal story about how he was able to catch fish in the campus creek on the day after a typhoon. In the beginning of his story, he orients the audience through a series of pictures of the destruction caused by the storm and pictures of himself, with his shirt off catching fish. He pairs these pictures with the following description:

The next morning I went out to take a walk around campus. The morning sky was so beautiful! The campus was very serene! Why are there so many people? What are these two guys doing? It looks like they want to beat something. Wow, what a big fish! The water of the lake is overflowing. It's going through the channel and into the road! And I'm the first one who discovered there are many fishes swimming through the channel. And this is where the fish catching story happens.

It is interesting to compare Timmy's story with Pan's and Sue's stories, which are all personal narratives, but they move the focus of their story to family tributes. Alternatively, Timmy and his abilities and skills remain the center of his narrative. In classroom and public viewing of the videos, students often commented on Timmy's story as self-centered, but many students also found the images of the blue skies and clear water as an exciting documentation of a major weather event, and they marveled at the adventure and humor in Timmy's story.

Individualism and personal sacrifice were also themes that came up in discussing Irene's story as part of our English classroom curriculum. Each of the chapter's authors also used Irene's personal story as part of language learning exercises in classrooms and after public viewing, expecting students to be interested and challenged by Irene's personal of success, perseverance, and devotion to her education. In one of our classes, however, students argued that teachers should not be viewed as role models anymore or explicitly teach ethical standards. In class, one student noted that the story of overcoming the Cultural Revolution and struggling to learn at universities is "something we've heard many times before" from teachers and has become "boring." We did not expect this reaction, but these comments led to a deeper discussion about what students at CSU considered "old" and "modern" China, and it offered an important cross-cultural and cross-generational dialogue about individual success and community development.

CONCLUSION: LITERACY LEARNING AND CLT IN CHINA

And I've learned that you have to be always thinking how to tell [your] story no matter where you go. I haven't had that sense before this class, so it is hard for me to find a suitable picture to express my words. (Digital story-telling group participant)

We end our chapter with a brief discussion of the importance of incorporating multimodal composing and multiliteracies into school curriculum as well as the need to expand the goals of a communicative classroom. The group described here met multiple Fridays throughout a 16-week semester, but other school-based digital storytelling groups have worked as three-day workshops. Other timeframes may work as well, as long as the participants can provide feedback and support during an initial story circle and are given enough space and time to rehearse and alter their narrative before they record their story and pair it with images and animation. The unique aspect of digital stories and multimodal composing is the attention on group literacy development through listening to multiple drafts of a story, and facilitators in both the short and long formats should work to maintain group trust and a project-based learning environment. Further, the public viewing of stories at a university building showcases the work of the group, and brings in the larger context and audience of the participants to consider as well as open literacy practices to a group setting, a key aspect of multiliteracies as noted above.

We also highly recommend the use of stories as classroom material to teach aspects of spoken English such as intonation, pragmatics, and register, and as content for classroom discussion and listening activities. As we experienced through first-hand use of the stories in our own classrooms, we always learned a new interpretation from student perspectives on the finished projects. It is important to note that not all of the stories reveal a complex position on identity and new meaning creation, nor should they be expected to. In fact, there is often, what Lambert (2002) calls "helicoptering" in the stories of new participants, a feature of a story that tells many details without emphasis on a main point or dramatic question. This does not take away from the usefulness of digital stories as a language learning and literacy activity; as with all teaching activities in a communicative or community language learning setting, the role of the teacher is to facilitate and create the context for learning, not to dictate the type of story that students should tell. In fact, one of the key elements of many of the stories, for example Timmy's fish-catching story, is humor and the fun of creating and telling a story in English through a multi-modal process, and a teacher must be open to very local meanings and jokes that students tell through their stories.

CLT at CSU

Digital storytelling as a classroom project connects with communicative language teaching reforms in China that call for increased self-study, creativity, and integration of the four skills (Jin & Cortazzi, 2002; Liu, 2008), albeit with a more expanded view of literacy that includes images, videos, and a potentially large online audience. In reviewing the digital stories created at CSU, they certainly are part of this overall CLT approach to English learning in China, but, at the same time, the above examples from digital stories also reveal creativity, invention, and language play that is more a reflection of a *social-semiotic* perspective on language learning (Kramsch, 2006). In this way, inventions and re-appropriations of terms such as "Old China" or the purposes for telling stories are part of the process of student negotiation of their local and global identities in English and they point out the need to expand our understanding of communication as well as literacy in the second language classroom.

REFERENCES

Alverman, D.E., Moon, J., & Hagood, M.C. (1999). *Popular culture in the classroom: Teaching and researching critical media literacy.* Newark, DE: International Reading Association and National Reading Conference.

Ajayi, L. (2008). Meaning-making, multimodal representation, and transformative pedagogy: An exploration of meaning construction instructional practices in an ESL high school classroom. *Journal of Language, Identity, and Education, 7*(3/4), 206-229.

Adamson, B. (2004). *China's English: A history of English in Chinese education.* HongKong: HKU Press.

Bakhtin, M. (1952/1994). Speech genres and other late essays. In Morris, P. (Ed.), *The Bakhtin reader* (pp. 81-87). New York: Edward Arnold.

Cope, B., & Kalantzis, M. (Eds.). (2000). *Multiliteracies.* London: Routledge.

Cox, C. (1994). *Commission on media.* Urbana, IL: National Council of Teachers of English Press.

Davis, A., & Weinshenker, D. (in press). Digital storytelling and authoring identity. In C.C. Ching & B. Foley (Eds.), *Technology, learning, and identity.* Cambridge: Cambridge University Press.

Davis, A. (2005). Co-authoring identity: Digital storytelling in an urban middle school. *THEN Journal, 1.* Retrieved April 21, 2010 from *http://thenjournal.org/.*

Gee, J.P. (2003). *What video games have to teach us about learning and literacy.* New York: Palgrave MacMillan.

Gee, J.P. (2007). *Social linguistics and literacies: Ideology in discourse.* New York: Taylor and Francis.

Jin, L. & Cortazzi, D. (2002). English language teaching in China: A bridge to the future. *Asia Pacific Journal, 22*(2), 53-64.

Kramsch, C. (2006). The Multilingual Subject. *International Journal of Applied Linguistics, 16*(1), 97–110.

Labov, W. (1997). Some further steps in narrative analysis. *Journal of Narrative Life History, 7*(1-4), 395-415.

Lambert, J. (2002). *Digital storytelling: Capturing lives, creating community.* Berkeley, CA: Digital Diner Press.

Lambert, J. (2006). *Digital storytelling cookbook.* Berkeley, CA: Digital Diner Press.

Lankshear, C. & Knobel, M. (2003). *New litearcies: Changing knowledge and classroom learning.* New York: Open University Press.

Larsen-Freeman, D. (2005). *Techniques and principles in language teaching* (2nd ed.). New York: Oxford University Press.

Liu, J. (Ed.). (2008). *English language teaching in China: New approaches, perspectives, and standards.* New York: Continuum.

Hull, G. & Nelson, M. (2005). Locating the Semiotic Power of Multimodality. *Written Communication, 22*(2), 224-261.

Meadows, D. (2003). Digital Storytelling: Research-Based Practice in New Media. *Visual Communication, 2,* 189-93.

National Association for Media Literacy Education. (2008). Retrieved April 21, 2010 from http://www.namle.net/media-literacy/definitions.

Skinner, E. & Hagood, M. (2008). Developing literate identities with English language learners through digital storytelling. *The Reading Matrix, 8*(2), 12-38.

Street, B.V. (1995). *Social literacies: Critical approaches to literacy in development, ethnography and education.* London: Longman.

Sugimoto, Y. (1997). *An introduction to Japanese society.* Cambridge: Cambridge University Press.

Tharp, K. & Hills, L. (2004). Digital Storytelling: Culture, Media and Community. In S. Marshall, W. Taylor & X. Yu (Eds.), *Using community informatics to transform regions* (pp. 37-51). Hershey, PA: Idea Group.

Richards, K. (2003). *Qualitative inquiry in TESOL.* New York: Palgrave.

Wan, G., Tanimoto, R., & Templeton, R. (2008). Creating constructivist learning environment for Japanese EFL students: A digital story program. *Asian EFL Journal, 10*(2), 31-50.

Watson-Gegeo, K. (1988). Ethnography in ESL: Defining the essentials. *TESOL, 22,* 575-592.

Yu, H. (2009). *Media and cultural transformation in China.* New York: Routledge.

In: Language and Literacy Education in a Challenging World   ISBN: 978-1-61761-198-8
Editors: T. Lê, Q. Lê, and M. Short   © 2011 Nova Science Publishers, Inc.

Chapter 24

GENDER, SELF-PERCEIVED ENGLISH PROFICIENCY AND LANGUAGE LEARNING STRATEGIES OF KOREAN UNIVERSITY STUDENTS

Frans J. Kruger

ABSTRACT

The Language learning strategies have been identified as a significant variable in successful language learning. Although all language learners use language learning strategies, the use of these strategies differ among learners in the type of strategies employed and the frequency of strategy use. In this chapter I wish to contribute to our understanding of the language learning strategies Korean university students employ and how the choice and use of language learning strategies are influenced by the students' self-perceived English proficiency and gender.

Keywords: language learning strategies, self-perceived proficiency, gender.

INTRODUCTION

Some learners acquire English as a second or foreign language more effectively and quickly than other students (Dreyer & Oxford, 1996; Nisbet, Tindall & Arroyo, 2005). Since the 1970's language researchers have identified a number of factors that contribute to variation in second language acquisition (Rubin, 1975; Stern, 1975). One of these factors, language learning strategies, has been identified as a significant variable in successful language learning (Nisbet, Tindall & Arroyo, 2005). According to Oxford (1990, p.8) language learning strategies refer to "specific actions taken by the learner to make learning faster, more enjoyable, more self-directed, more effective, and more transferrable to new situations". Students employ language learning strategies not only to enhance their own learning (Scarcella & Oxford, 1992), but also "to promote their own learning success" (Franklin, Hodge & Sasscer, 1997, p.24). Most research has shown that language proficiency/achievement can be positively correlated with language learning strategy use (Green & Oxford, 1995; Oxford, 1989). Phillips (as cited in Rivera-Mills & Plonsky, 2007) has however found that although there was an initial correlation between language proficiency and language learning strategy use, the use of language learning strategies decreased as language proficiency continued to improve. Phillips' observations can partly be explained by the fact that different strategies are more helpful at different levels of language proficiency (Cohen, 1998). All language learners use language learning strategies, but the use thereof differ among learners in the type of strategies employed and the frequency of strategy use (Chamot & Kuper as cited in Su, 2005). It has been found that successful language learners combine different types of strategies to enhance their learning according to their personal learning needs (Oxford, 1990; Su, 2005). Put differently, "[w]hen the learner consciously chooses strategies that fit his or her learning style and the L2 task at hand, these strategies become a useful toolkit for active, conscious, and purposeful self-regulation of learning" (Oxford, 2003, p.2).

In this chapter I will investigate the language learning strategies that Korean university students employ, their self-perceived English proficiency, the role gender plays, and the interrelationship between these variables. English is seen as a very important subject in Korea, with the average Korean student studying English for at least 10 years: three years in middle school, three years in high school, and four years at university. In spite of the fact that so much time and effort is put into learning and acquiring English, most Korean students are only vaguely aware of language learning strategies, as well as how these strategies could help them learn English more efficiently (Lee & Oxford, 2008). As is the case with students in other English as a foreign language (EFL) context, 'the profile of Korean students' language learning strategies is not well researched (Lee & Oxford, 2008). In this chapter I wish to contribute to our understanding of what language learning strategies Korean university students employ and how the choice and use of language learning strategies are influenced by the students' self-perceived English proficiency, and gender.

WHAT DOES THE LITERATURE REVIEW SAY?

An area of basic research within the field of second language acquisition is the identification and description of language learning strategies. These strategies are also correlated with learner variables that include proficiency level, age, gender, cultural beliefs and values, and motivation (Chamot, 2004; Green & Oxford, 1995; Rao, 2006; Su, 2005; Wharton, 2000; Wu, 2008). In current research the effect of specific tasks on language learning strategy selection and use are being investigated (Cohen, 2003; Oxford, Cho, Leung & Kim, 2004). The majority of research on language learning strategies has been descriptive and geared towards "… identification procedures of learning strategies, terminology and classification of strategies, the effects of learner characteristics on strategy use, and the effects of culture and context on strategy use" (Chamot, 2004, p.15).

Identification and Classification of Language Learning Strategies

Although there has been a growing awareness of the usefulness of language learning strategies in cultivating independent, autonomous and lifelong learners (Allwright and Little as cited in Oxford, 2003), defining and classifying the various strategies is no easy task

(Griffiths, 2004). According to Rivera-Mills & Plonsky (2007, p.536) this is at least partly due to the fact that "… to date, there is no consensus as to which strategies should be included in the SLA research literature and under which categories to include them". A further difficulty is that language learning strategies are mostly unobservable and are mostly identified through student self-report which may take the form of retrospective interviews, stimulated recall interviews, questionnaires, written diaries, and journals (Chamot, 2004; Cohen, 1998; O'Malley and Chamot, 1990; Oxford, 1996; Wu, 2008).

Rubin (1975) was one of the first researchers to provide a definition for learning strategies, stating that it is the techniques and devices learners may use to acquire knowledge. Rubin (as cited in Griffiths, 2004) further divided learning strategies into direct learning strategies (clarification/verification, monitoring, memorisation, guessing/inductive inferencing, deductive reasoning, and practice) and indirect learning strategies (creating opportunities for practice, and production tricks). Also during the 1970's, Stern (1975) produced a list of ten language learning strategies that he believed characterised good language learners. O'Malley et al. (1985) identified 26 strategies that they divided into 3 categories: cognitive (specific learning activities), metacognitive (knowing about learning), and social. The addition of social strategies to language learning was an important step in the development of identifying and classifying language learning strategies (Griffiths, 2004). Not all researchers have subsequently identified social strategies in their classification systems. In the studies of Purpura (1997) and Gan, Humphreys, & Hamp-Lyon (2004) only cognitive and metacognitive strategies are used for the classification of language learning strategies.

A more recent distinction that has been made in identifying and classifying language learning strategies has been between strategies that are principally employed by learners for learning the L2, and those that are employed to enhance L2 usage (Rivera-Mills & Plonsky, 2007). Cohen (2003, p.280) defines language learning strategies as "…conscious or semi-conscious thoughts and behaviours used by learners with the explicit goal of improving their knowledge and understanding of a target language". These strategies are classified as being cognitive (manipulating and memorising target language structures), metacognitive (managing and supervising strategy use), affective (emotional reactions to learning and lowering associated anxieties), and social (cooperation with other learners and interacting with native speakers). In contrast to this, language use strategies are defined as those strategies that are "…used with an explicit goal of improving learners' knowledge of a given language …helping the students to utilise the language they have already learned to whatever degree" (Cohen, 2003, p. 280). Language use strategies include retrieving information stored in memory, rehearsing target language structures, covering strategies for classroom interaction, and compensating for gaps in target language knowledge (Cohen, 1998; Cohen 2003).

The most used language learning strategy classification has been produced by Oxford (1990). In attempting to redress the over-emphasis of cognitive and metacognitive strategies in strategy inventories (Griffiths, 2004), Oxford (1990) classified language learning strategies into six categories. These are memory, cognitive, compensation, metacognitive, affective and social learning strategies.

Memory related strategies help learner's link L2 concepts with one another without necessarily involving deep understanding. These types of strategies enable learners to retrieve information in orderly strings, through sounds, body movement, mechanical means, or location. Memory strategies do not always relate to proficiency in the target language, as these "strategies are often used for memorising vocabulary and structures in the initial stages of language learning, but that learners need such strategies less when their arsenal of vocabulary and structures has become larger" (Oxford, 2003, p. 13). Cognitive strategies are employed by learners to manipulate the target language material directly. Such strategies include note taking, summarising, outlining, practising sounds and structures formally, analysis, and reasoning. When learners lack knowledge of the target language they employ compensation strategies. These strategies include guessing from context, using synonyms, and utilising gestures and pause words during speaking (Oxford, 2003). As pointed out earlier, Cohen (1998) viewed compensation not as a language learning strategy, but rather as a strategy that is employed during language use. When learners utilise strategies to manage their overall learning process, they are engaged in metacognitive strategies. Examples include identifying learning needs, planning, monitoring, and evaluating (Oxford, 1990). Research by Dreyer and Oxford (1996), in an ESL context in South Africa, has been used as evidence that metacognitive strategies positively relate to L2 proficiency. Affective strategies are defined as identifying one's mood and anxiety levels, rewarding oneself for good performance, deep breathing, positive thinking, and talking about feelings, while social strategies relate to strategies learners employ with others to gain knowledge of and understand the target language and culture (Oxford, 2003).

These six categories were further divided by Oxford (1990) into direct strategies that are comprised of memory, cognitive, and compensation strategies (directly involving the target language) and indirect strategies that are comprised of metacognitive, affective, and social strategies (indirectly providing support for language learning through actions such as planning and cooperation).

Oxford's (1990) classification for language learning strategies may be the most comprehensive (Ellis as cited in Griffiths, 2004), but it still does not cover all the learning strategies employed by students. Both Woodrow (2005) and Chamot (2004) pointed out that this is to be expected considering the range of possible contextual influences on students learning. Oxford (1990) also acknowledged that:

…there is no complete agreement on exactly what strategies are; how many strategies exist; how they should be defined, demarcated, and categorised; and whether it is – or ever will be – possible to create a real, scientifically validated hierarchy of strategies. (p. 17)

Woodrow (2005, p.90) argues that the use of instruments such as SILL that make use of standardised scales to measure language learning strategy use is not appropriate "because of the wide range of contextual influences, such as cultural and educational background". Instead of using quantitative methods to produce generalised descriptions of language learning strategy use, Woodrow (2005) and Wu (2008) call on researchers to generate richer descriptions by using qualitative research methods such as case studies, action research and interviews (see also LoCastro 1994; LoCastro 1995).

In spite of the critique raised against Oxford's (1990) classification of language learning strategies, I have retained its use in the present study, as it can provide a useful base for understanding and investigating language learning strategies (Griffiths, 2004). I recognise that the results will reflect general, standardised information about the whole group that partook in the research.

Factors Affecting the Choice and Use of Language Learning Strategies

For the purpose of this study, I will briefly review research results that investigated the effect of gender and proficiency on the use of language learning strategies.

Gender

The results of research on the differences in strategy use between females and males have been varied (Chamot, 2004). Most studies have found that a significant difference exist between the strategy use of females and males, with females showing a greater use in the variety and frequency of language learning strategies as compared to males (Ehrman & Oxford, 1989; Green & Oxford, 1995; Lee, 2003; Oxford & Nyikos, 1989; Oxford, Park-Oh, Ito & Sumrall, 1993). One study has found that among bilingual foreign language learners in Singapore, males used more strategies than females (Wharton, 2000). Two previous studies that were conducted in Korea found that no significant difference existed in the strategy use of females and males (Kim, 1995; Oh, 1996), whereas one study (Lee, 1994) found that among Korean middle school, high school, and college students, females made use of learning strategies more than males did.

Proficiency

In contrast to gender, the relationship between learning strategies and learner proficiency is clearer. Research has shown that language proficiency/achievement can be positively correlated to language learning strategy use (Green & Oxford, 1995; Griffiths as cited in Griffiths, 2004; O'Malley & Chamot, 1990; Oxford, 1989; Park as cited in Su, 2005; Wharton, 2000; Wu, 2008). According to Chamot (2004, p.18): "Differences between more or less proficient language learners have been found in the number and range of strategies used, in how the strategies are applied to the task, and the appropriateness of the strategies for the task". Phillips (as cited in Rivera-Mills & Plonsky, 2007) however found that although there was an initial correlation between language proficiency and language learning strategy use, the use of language learning strategies decreased as language proficiency continued to improve. Phillips' observations can partly be explained by the fact that different strategies are more helpful at different levels of language proficiency (Cohen, 1998). Green & Oxford (1995) identified 23 "bedrock strategies" that were used equally frequently by all students that participated in their study, whether they were more or less proficient in their L2.

THE STUDY

Research Questions

The following research questions were designed for the purpose of this study:

1. What is the self-perceived English proficiency of EFL Korean university students, overall and in terms of gender?
2. What language learning strategies (LLS) do the students employ, overall and in terms of gender?
3. What is the relationship between the student's self-perceived English proficiency and LLS employed?

4. Is there a significant difference by gender in terms of the relationship between the student's self-perceived English proficiency and LLS employed?

This chapter deals with research questions 1 and 2.

Research Design

To gain understanding of the relationship that exist between self-perceived English proficiency, language learning strategies, and gender, a quantitative research design was utilised. Self-perceived English proficiency and language learning strategy preferences were measured through the administration of a Background questionnaire, including a learners' self-perceived English proficiency, and the Strategy Inventory of Language Learning (SILL).

Setting and Participants

The participants in this study were 69 Korean students that were attending a university in Gyeonggi Province, South Korea. At the time of the study all the students that participated were enrolled in a compulsory English class and have been studying English for at least six years. All the students participated voluntarily in the study. Of the 69 participants, 37 (53.62%) were females, and 32 (46.38%) were males. The ages of the participants ranged from 19 to 28 at the time the data was collected.

Instrumentation

Two questionnaires were used in the study. A background questionnaire was developed to gather data regarding the participants' demographic information, including age and gender, study major, and self-perceived English proficiency. For the self-perceived English proficiency section, the participants had to rate their English proficiency in the skills of reading, writing, listening, speaking, and overall proficiency. They responded to each skill item using a Likert scale of 1 through 5, with 1 representing "Very bad" and 5 representing "Very good". The self-perceived English proficiency section was included because "... All of these self-perceptions have motivational properties, with competence in a task more directly influenced by task-limited self-perceptions than global self-esteem" (Pressley et al as cited in Lee & Oxford, 2008, p.14).

To measure the participants' language learning strategy preferences, the SILL Version 7.0 (Oxford, 1990) was used. Version 7.0 was designed specifically for speakers of other languages that are learning English (ESL/EFL). The SILL is a self-report survey consisting of 50 items that was designed to determine and assess frequency in language learning strategy use (Nisbet et al, 2005; Oxford, 1990). The participants responded to each item using a Likert scale of 1 through 5, with 1 representing "Never or almost never true for me" and 5 representing "Always or almost always true for me". Examples of SILL Version 7.0 items are: "To understand unfamiliar English words I make guesses", and "I try to learn about the culture of English speakers". The SILL contains six factor-analytical strategy categories –

memory, cognitive, compensation, metacognitive, affective, and social - that are based on the language learning strategies identified by Oxford (1990).

The SILL is the most widely used instrument of its kind (Woodrow, 2005) with researchers also having highlighted the validity and reliability of SILL (Oxford & Burry-Stock, 1995). It should be noted that this instrument has been criticised (Woodrow, 2005) but it has been retained in the present study for determining language learning strategy use and frequency. The reliability of the SILL, as assessed by Cronbach alpha for internal consistency, has been reported as .86 - .98, depending of whether the SILL was taken in the participants L1 or L2 (Green & Oxford, 1995; Oxford, 1996). For the current study the Cronbach alpha reliability index for the overall scale was .899, N=69.

Data collection and Analysis Procedures

The researcher administered the two questionnaires. The purpose of the study was explained, and the instructions for completing the questionnaires were explained both verbally and in writing. Additional benefits and potential uses of the data were explained and discussed, with the participants having the chance to raise any questions or concerns. The questionnaires were completed in confidentiality. After completion, the researcher gathered the questionnaires and conducted quantitative analysis using PASW Statistics 17.0. To answer the research questions independent t-tests and ANOVA were performed to determine the effect of self-perceived English proficiency, and gender on language learning strategies. The standard of significance that was adopted in the study was p<0.05.

RESULTS

To describe and interpret the means obtained for the SILL the following key was employed: 1-2.49, low use; 2.5-3.49, medium use; 3.5-5, high use.

Results by Research Question

Research question 1: What is the self-perceived English proficiency of EFL Korean university students, overall and in terms of gender?

It is evident that the majority of participants view their overall English proficiency as being medium. Interestingly, 24.637% of the participants thought their English proficiency was either very bad or bad, compared to only 8.696% participants who though of themselves as being good at English. No participants thought their overall English proficiency were very good.

Male participants had a more positive perception than female participants in terms of their self-perceived proficiency in reading, writing, listening, speaking, and overall skills. Both male and female participants thought writing, followed by speaking, were the skills they were least proficient in, whereas reading and listening were seen as the skills they were most proficient in. Concerning their overall proficiency in English, 28.125% of female participants thought they were either very bad or bad, while 21.622% of males felt the same way. The majority of female and male participants thought they were of medium proficiency overall. Only 1 female (n=37) and 5 male (n=32) participants thought their overall English proficiency were good.

Research question 2: What language learning strategies (LLS) do the students employ, overall and in terms of gender?

The overall learning strategy use of the participants was 2.974, which indicate medium strategy use. The mean scores for the six categories were also in the medium-use range, ranging from 2.694 to 3.341. The most frequently used strategies were compensation strategies, mean=3.341, followed by metacognitive, mean=2.972, memory, mean=2.955, and cognitive strategies, mean=2.905. The two less frequently used strategy categories were social learning, mean=2.838, and affective strategies, mean=2.694. The frequency of use for metacognitive, memory, cognitive, and social strategies were fairly similar. In contrast, affective strategy use was substantially lower, and the use of compensation strategies was a fair bit higher.

Females, mean=3.009, more frequently made use of language learning strategies as compared to males, mean=2.935. The range of strategy use of female participants was 2.684 to 3.334, and those of males were 2.707 to 3.35. Compensation strategies were used most frequently by female, mean=3.334, and male, mean=3.35, participants. Whereas metacognitive strategies were rank second by females, mean=3.123, males ranked memory strategies, mean=2.898, second. The frequency of use of the various strategy categories followed the same ranking order for female participants as for the whole group. In contrast to this, males made use of affective strategies least followed by metacognitive, social, and cognitive strategies.

The five most frequently used strategies used by the participants as a group, as well as those used by females and males were determined. All of the five most often used strategies had means greater than 3.5, indicating that they were usually used. The most frequently used strategy was "When I can't think of a word during a conversation in English, I use gestures", followed by "If I don't understand something in English, I ask the other person to slow down or say it again", If I can't think of an English word, I use a word or phrase that means the same thing", and the memory-related strategies "I connect the sound of a new English word and an image or picture of the word to help me remember the word", and "I think of the relationship of things I already know an new things I learn in English".

Both female and male participants indicated that they usually made use of the five strategies they used most frequently with means for these strategies ranging between 3.595-4.027 and 3.565-3.938 respectively. The most frequently used strategy was the compensation-related strategy "When I can't think of a word during a conversation in English, I use gestures" for both females and males.

The two least used strategies by the participants, overall, and for females and males, were the affective strategies of "I write down my feelings in a language learning diary" and "I talk to someone else about how I feel when I'm learning English". All the strategies that were indicated as being used the least fall within the low-use range (mean=1 – 2.49), and are generally not used. The least used strategies included not only affective strategies, but also the memory-related "I physically act out new English words", the cognitive-related "I write notes, messages, letters, or reports in English", and social-related "I ask questions in English" and "I practice English with other students" strategies.

CONCLUSION

Based on the results of this study, the following conclusion can be drawn about the interrelationship of gender, self-perceived language proficiency and language learning strategy use among Korean university students. The most frequently used category of LLS of the participants was compensation related strategies. This was true for both females and males. The least frequently used category of LLS was affective related strategies. Again, this was the case for both the female and male participants. The order of strategy frequency for the participants was compensatory, metacognitive, memory, cognitive, social, and affective strategies. This is very similar to the results reported by Lee and Oxford (2008). In their study, only the order of memory and cognitive strategies were different, with cognitive strategies bring used more frequently than memory strategies. It was found in the present study that although females made use of language learning strategies more frequently than males, no statistical significant difference existed in the language learning strategy use of the two groups. This finding is similar to that reported by Lee and Oxford (2008), Kim (1995), and Oh (1996) among Korean language learners.

Surprisingly, in contrast to the results obtained by Lee and Oxford (2008) and Su (2005), there existed no linear relationship between self-perceived English proficiency and the frequency of LLS use. In both these studies it was found that an increase in positive self-image related positively to an increase in LLS use. For the present study, the opposite seemed to hold true. Males had a more positive perception of their English proficiency for the skills of reading, writing, listening, speaking, and overall proficiency than females did. Yet, apart from compensation related strategies, females used language learning strategies more frequently than males. What is apparent from the present study is that the use of LLS is not only determined by the variables of self-perceived proficiency in a L2 and gender. Rather, a host of factors influence learners as to what strategies to use, how frequently to use them, and when to use them.

ACKNOWLEDGMENTS

I would like to express my thanks to all the participants in this study and for Dr. Thao Lê for helpful comments on this chapter.

REFERENCES

Chamot, A.U. (2004). Issues in language learning strategy research and teaching. *Electronic Journal of Foreign Language Teaching, 1*(1), 14 – 26.

Cohen, A.D. (1998). *Strategies in learning and using a second language.* New York: Addison Wesley Longman.

Cohen, A.D. (2003). The learner's side of foreign language learning: Where do styles, strategies, and tasks meet? *International Review of Applied Linguistics, 41,* 279 – 291.

Dreyer, C. & Oxford, R.L. (1996). Learning strategies and other predictors of ESL proficiency among Afrikaans speakers in South Africa. In R.L. Oxford (Ed.), *Language learning strategies around the world: Cross-cultural perspectives* (pp.61 – 74). Honolulu: University of Hawaii at Manoa.

Ehrman, M.E., & Oxford, R.L. (1989). Effects of sex difference, career choice, and psychological type on adult language learning strategies. *Modern Language Journal, 73,* 1 – 13.

Franklin, L., Hodge, M.E. & Sasscer, M.F. (1997). Improving retention with strategy-based instruction. *Inquiry, 1*(2), 21 – 27.

Gan, Z., Humphreys, G., Hamp-Lyon, L. (2004). Understanding successful and unsuccessful EFL students in Chinese universities. *Modern Language Journal, 88,* 229 – 244.

Green, J.M. & Oxford, R.L. (1995). A closer look at learning strategies, L2 proficiency, and gender. *TESOl Quarterly, 29,* 261 – 297.

Griffiths, C. (2004). *Language learning strategies: Theory and research.* Occasional Papers No.1. School of Foundational Studies, AIS St. Helens, Auckland. Retrieved April 14, 2009, from *www.crie.org.nz/research_paper/c_griffiths_op1.pdf.*

Kim, Y.M. (1995). The effect of gender and learning context on the use of language learning strategies. *English Teaching, 50*(2), 331 – 345.

Lee, H.W. (1994). Investigating the factors affecting the use of foreign language learning strategies and comparing the strategy use of EFL and ESL students. *English Teaching, 48,* 51 – 99.

Lee, K.O. (2003, September). The relationship of school year, sex and proficiency on the use of learning strategies in learning English. *The Asian EFL Journal, 5*(3). Retrieved April 20, 2009, from *http://www.asian-efl-journal.com/sept_o3_ok.php.*

Lee, K.R. & Oxford, R.L. (2008). Understanding EFL learners' strategy use and strategy awareness. *The Asian EFL Journal, 10*(1), 7 – 32.

LoCastro, V. (1994). Learning strategies and learning environments. *TESOL Quarterly, 28*(2), 409 – 414.

LoCastro, V. (1995). Comments on Virginia LoCastro's "Learning strategies and learning environments": The author responds. *TESOL Quarterly, 29*(1), 172 – 174.

Nisbet, D.L., Tindall, E.R. & Arroyo, A.A. (2005). Language learning strategies and English proficiency of Chinese university students. *Foreign Language Annals, 38*(1), 100 – 107.

Oh, J.I. (1996). The effects of attitude and sex on use of EFL learner strategies. *English Teaching, 51*(2), 35 – 53.

O'Malley, J.M. & Chamot, A.U. (1990). *Learning strategies in second language acquisition.* Cambridge: Cambridge University Press.

O'Malley, J.M., Chamot, A.U., Stewner-Manzanares, G., Kupper, L., & Russo, R.P. (1985). Learning strategies used by beginning and intermediate ESL students. *Language Learning, 35*(1), 21 – 46.

Oxford, R.L. (1989). Use of language learning strategies: A synthesis of studies with implication for strategy training. *System, 17,* 235 – 247.

Oxford, R.L. (1990). *Language learning strategies: What every teacher should know.* Boston: Heinle & Heinle.

Oxford, R.L. (1996). Employing a questionnaire to assess the use of language learning strategies. *Applied Language Learning, 7*(1&2), 25 – 45.

Oxford, R.L. (2003). Language learning styles and strategies: An Overview. Retrieved April 2, 2009, from *http://www.web.ntpu.edu.tw/~language/workshop/read2.pdf.*

Oxford, R.L., & Burry-Stock, J.A. (1995). Assessing the use of language learning strategies worldwide with the ESL/EFL version of the strategy inventory for language learning (SILL). *System, 23*(1), 1 -23.

Oxford, R.L., Cho, Y., Leung, S., & Kim, H-J. (2004). Effect of the presence and difficulty of task on strategy use: An explanatory study. *International Review of Applied Linguistics, 42*, 1 – 47.

Oxford, R.L., Green, J.M. (1995). Comments on Virginia LoCastro's "Learning Strategies and Learning Environments": Making Sense of learning strategy assessment: Toward a higher standard of research accuracy. *TESOL Quarterly, 29*(1), 166 – 171.

Oxford, R.L., Nyikos, M. (1989). Variables affecting choice and language learning strategies by university students. *Modern Language Journal, 73*, 291 – 300.

Oxford, R.L., Park-Oh, Y., Ito, S., & Sumrall, M. (1993). Learning a language by satellite television: What influences student achievement? *System, 21*, 31 – 48.

Pupura, J.E. (1997). An analysis of the relationships between test takers' cognitive and metacognitve strategy use and second language test performance. *Language Learning, 47*, 289 – 325.

Rao, Z. (2006). Understanding Chinese Students' use of language learning strategies from cultural and educational perspectives. *Journal of Multilingual and Multicultural Development, 27*(6), 491 – 508.

Rivera-Mills, S.V.; & Plonsky, L. (2007). Empowering students with language learning strategies: A critical review of current issues. *Foreign Language Annals, 40*(3), 535 – 548.

Rubin, J. (1975). What the 'good language learner' can teach us. *Tesol Quarterly, 9*, 41 – 45.

Scarcella, R.; & Oxford, R.L. (1992). *The tapestry of language learning: The individual in the communicative classroom.* Boston: Heinle & Heinle.

Stern, H.H. (1975). What can we learn from a good language learner? *Canadian Modern Language Review, 34*, 304 – 318.

Su, M-H.M. (2005). A Study of EFL Technological and vocational college students' language learning strategies and their self-perceived English proficiency. *Electronic Journal of Foreign Language Teaching, 2*(1), 44 – 56.

Wharton, G. (2000). Language learning strategy use of bilingual foreign language learners in Singapore. *Language Learning, 50*(2), 203 – 243.

Woodrow, L. (2005). The challenge of measuring language learning strategies. *Foreign Language Annals, 38*(1), 90 – 99.

Wu, M.M-F. (2008). Language learning strategy use of Chinese ESL learners of Hongkong – Findings from a qualitative study. *Electronic Journal of Foreign Language Teaching, 5*(1), 68 – 83.

Wu, Y-L. (2008). Language learning strategies used by students at different proficiency levels. *Asian EFL Journal, 10*(4), 75 – 91.

NOTES ON THE AUTHORS

Esin Akyay is a Research Assistant at the Faculty of Education, Foreign Languages Education Department, Trakya University, Turkey. She has been working at ELT Department since 2007 after completing her undergraduate education.

Idris Aman (PhD) is an Associate Professor of Linguistics at the School of Language Studies and Linguistics, Faculty of Social Sciences and Humanities, Universiti Kebangsaan Malaysia, Malaysia. His main research interests are discourse analysis, sociolinguistics, and functional – discourse grammar.

Rosemary Callingham (PhD) is an Associate Professor in mathematics education at the University of Tasmania, Australia. She is the Coordinator of the M.Ed coursework in the Faculty of Education. She has an extensive background in mathematics education in Australia. Her research interests include statistical literacy, mental computation and performance assessment of mathematics and numeracy.

Geraldine Castleton (PhD) is an Associate Professor and the Head of School of Education at the University of Tasmania, Australia. She began her professional career as a primary teacher before moving into teacher education. She has been involved in undergraduate and postgraduate teacher education in four Australian universities and one university in the UK. Geraldine's area of expertise and passion is literacy education and she has worked as a teacher educator, researcher and consultant to governments and industry in this area in Australia and overseas in primary, secondary, post-compulsory schooling as well as adult literacy contexts, including workplaces. Geraldine is an active researcher and has an extensive list of publications that include edited books, book chapters, journal articles, published conference papers and reports.

Nur Cebeci is a Lecturer at the ELT Department of the Faculty of Education, Trakya University, Edirne, Turkey. She graduated from Trakya University, English Language Teaching Department in 2002. In the same year, she started to work as a research assistant at the same department. She holds an M.A. degree at the Social Sciences Institute from the same university. Her expertise is teaching English to young learners. She has attended national and international conferences held in Turkey and abroad as a presenter.

Clement Dlamini (PhD) is a Lecturer in mathematics education at the University of the Witwatersrand, South Africa. He is a leader of the Marang Language Thrust. He worked as a mathematics teacher at senior secondary level and a curriculum evaluator in Swaziland before joining the University of the Witwatersrand. In Swaziland, he was involved in the Southern and Eastern African Consortium for Monitoring Educational Quality (SACMEQ) as a Deputy National Coordinator. His research interests relate to issues of access to tertiary education and employment of learners who learn mathematics in a second language, including examination of the post colonial language policies. His PhD investigated discourse practices of mathematics high achieving learners with limited English language proficiency.

Ruth Fielding-Barnsley (PhD) is an Associate Professor in the Faculty of Education, University of Tasmania, Australia. She has been researching and teaching in the area of literacy for the past 25 years. She has written 2 book chapters and over 100 journal and conference papers. Ruth is also an advisor for the new National English Curriculum. Her main research interests include the role of metalinguistics in the process of learning to read, children's acquisition of reading, family support of literacy in the home, dyslexia and Asperger's Syndrome.

Sinem Doğruer is a research assistant in the Faculty of Education, Foreign Languages Education Department, Trakya University, Turkey. She has been working at English Language Teaching Department since 2008. She holds a B.A. degree from Faculty of Letters, Department of English Linguistics at Hacettepe University, Turkey. She began her MA studies at English Language Teaching Department at Trakya University. She is completing her MA thesis on critical discourse analysis and second language education. She worked as a teacher of English Language at a private high school in Edirne, Turkey. Her primary interests include linguistics, discourse analysis, critical discourse analysis, second language education and methodology.

Judith Falle (PhD) is a Lecturer in mathematics education, University of New England, Armidale, NSW, Australia. Judith has taught secondary mathematics and science in NSW for many years before moving to the university. Her interest in language and mathematics was fostered by listening to her students and trying to understand the connections between what they said and their mathematical responses.

Sibylle Gruber (PhD) is a Professor in rhetoric and writing of Northern Arizona University, Flagstaff, USA. Her research and teaching interests include cybertheories, feminist rhetorics, writing program administration, language and cultures, literacy practices, literacy studies, rhetoric and cultures, computers and composition, writing theory and practice. She has published many research books such as *Weaving a virtual web: Practical approaches to new information technologies* (2000), *Literacies, experiences and technologies (2007)*.

Ian Hay (PhD) is the Dean of the Faculty of Education, University of Tasmania. Before coming to UTAS, he was Professor and Head of the School of Education, University of New England. He has also held Associate Professor positions at the University of Queensland and Griffith University. Prof Hay has published more than 200 book chapters, refereed journal articles, reports, and other articles in a range of international and national peer review publications as well as various conference presentations. As a chief investigator, he has been awarded competitive research funds in excess of 1.25 million dollars, and has supervised some 20 higher degree research students. His main research interests include students with reading difficulties, children's literacy practices, motivation, and self-concept.

Lauren Hoban is a research assistant in the Faculty of Education, University of Tasmania. She is an instructional designer.

Alireza Karbalaei is a TEFL teacher at different universities in Iran. Now, Alireza is a PhD candidate in TEFL in University of Mysore, India. Alireza has published 12 articles in the area of language learning strategies, reading strategies, bilinguality, affective variables at EFL and ESL contexts. Alireza has also done some research on metacognitive reading strategies training such as summarization, underlining, note-taking, context clues, and paraphrasing strategies.

Frans Kruger has been living and working in South Korea for the past four years where he has been actively involved in the field of TESOL. He is currently teaching a course in practical English skills at Hankuk University of Foreign Studies. His research interests include linguistic landscapes, issues of globalization and TESOL, and investigating how aspects of peace education can be successfully incorporated into EFL curricula.

Thao Lê (PhD) teaches applied linguistics in the Faculty of Education, University of Tasmania, Australia. He graduated from the University of Saigon, Vietnam, and Monash University. He is the chief editor of the International Research Internet Journal *Language, Society and Culture*. He has been invited to give lectures at various universities such as University of Vienna, University of Western England, and University of Stuttgart. He was a keynote speaker at international conferences in Lisbon, Iloilo, Phuket, and Penang. He received the *University of Tasmania's Teaching Excellence Award* and *Award for Excellent Contribution to Graduate Supervision and Research*. He has organised major conferences in developing countries to promote empowerment, resource sharing and a paradigm shift in the educational discourse of globalisation.

Quynh Lê (PhD) is the Lecturer and the Coordinator of Graduate Research in the Department of Rural Health, University of Tasmania, Australia. She started as a mechanical engineer in Vietnam and gained her M.AppComp from the University of Tasmania, M.Ed at the University of South Australia, and PhD from Curtin University. She has participated in a number of Department research projects. Her research-enhancing activities include co-editor of the online international research *Journal Language, Society and Culture*, Assistant Director of the International Conference on Science, Mathematics and Technology Education in Hanoi, Vietnam. She has a wide range of publications in rural health, intercultural health, health workforce issues, social epidemiology, spatial statistics and the application of information technology in education and health.

Mark Lê is a teacher of English and currently undertaking PhD research on street children's English at La Trobe University, Australia. He has taught English in Australia, Vietnam, France, and England. He was awarded a Rotary Club scholarship to visit France and Africa for intercultural enhancement and international understanding. Apart from research, his interests include music and travelling.

Charlotte Hua Liu (PhD) is an Assistant Professor at the Faculty of Education, University of Canberra, Australia. Before her academic career, she was also an experienced secondary school teacher in mainland China. Her research areas are Vygotsky's educational psychological semiotics, micro educational sociology, language education, mathematics education, and educational research of qualitative and quantitative methodologies.

Jingxia Liu is an Associate Professor in the English Department, School of Foreign Languages, Three Gorges University, in Hubei Province, China. Her major fields of research are discourse studies, sociolinguistics and English teaching.

Kent McClintock is a foreign language educator currently residing and teaching in Kwangju, South Korea. He has been an EFL educator for the past 14 years. He currently holds the position of Program Supervisor of the ESL Program at Chosun University. His research areas of interest include: testing, intercultural communication, and acculturation.

Paul McPherron (PhD) is an Assistant Professor of Linguistics and TESOL at Southern Illinois University, Carbondale USA, where he teaches courses in TESOL Methods and Materials, Cross-cultural Communication, and Language Assessment. He has extensive experience teaching English at universities and secondary schools in China, Romania, and the United States. His research interests include communicative language teaching reforms, teacher and learner identity processes, and the use of digital stories in the English classroom.

Sally Mibourne (PhD) is a school principal in Tasmania. She taught in the M.Ed program at the University of Tasmania while she was a visiting principal at the University of Tasmania.

Tim Moss (PhD) is a lecturer in Education: English-Literacy at the University of Tasmania, teaching in the areas of literacy, practitioner research and critical thinking across multiple programs in the Faculty of Education. His research interests include literacy leadership, narrative and arts-based research methodologies, teacher identity, academic literacies and teaching/ learning/ assessment issues in higher education. He has also successfully supervised higher degree research students in fields as diverse as curriculum reform in medical education, student experiences of cross-cultural exchange, and autoethnographic studies of beginning teaching. In the context of the profession, Tim is past president of Drama Tasmania and former Director of Research for Drama Australia.

Rosniah Mustaffa (PhD) is an Associate Professor of English language studies at the School of Language Studies and Linguistics, Faculty of Social Sciences and Humanities, Universiti Kebangsaan Malaysia, Malaysia. Her primary research interests include learning styles, students with limited English proficiency, and language and society.

Shanthi Nadarajan (PhD) is a Senior Lecturer at the Centre for Language Studies in Universiti Malaysia Sarawak where she is also the English Language Course Coordinator. She received her PhD in second language acquisition and teaching from the University of Arizona, United States. She is currently teaching English for professional purposes. Her areas of interest are second language vocabulary acquisition processes, reduplication and language studies.

Jennifer Nowicki-Clark is a Co-Director of the consulting firm Creative Narrations where she has worked as an instructor, program coordinator and technology trainer in adult education since 2000. Currently based in Oakland, California, USA, she received her BA in Sociology from Boston College and her Masters degree in Linguistics from the University of Arizona.

Muhlise Coşgun Ögeyik (PhD) is an Assistant Professor at the Faculty of Education, Trakya University, Turkey. She has been working at English Language Teaching Department. She holds an MA degree in English Language Teaching from Trakya University and a PhD degree in English Language Teaching from Istanbul University, Turkey. Her special research interest areas are foreign language teacher training, literature education, linguistics, methodology, culture teaching, research design and methodology. She teaches linguistics, translation, culture, and literature at BA and MA programs. She has many published articles and papers in the related fields. She also has published books on intertextuality and poetry teaching.

Megan Short (PhD) is a Lecturer in language education and human development in the Faculty of Education, University of Tasmania, Australia. She was awarded a travel scholarship to participate in education program at Harvard University. Her teaching includes child development focusing on developmentally appropriate practice in early childhood, primary and middle school teaching and learning. She is also involved in literacy education, including educational linguistics and the need to promote language awareness in pre-service teachers. Her current research interests are investigating how beliefs about the role of grammar in language and literacy education can shape teaching practice.

Rotimi Taiwo (PhD) attended the University of Benin, Benin-City and Obafemi Awolowo University, Ile-Ife, Nigeria. He holds a PhD degree in English language and he has been teaching in the Department of English, Obafemi Awolowo University since 1997. His main research focuses on the application of (critical) discourse analytic theories to a wide range of discourse contexts, such as media, religion, popular culture, computer-mediated discourse and students' composition.

Paul Throssell (PhD) is a Lecturer in applied linguistics in the Faculty of Education, University of Tasmania, Australia. He has taught in primary schools and high schools in Australia and England. His research interests include learning styles, intercultural communication, and lifelong learning. He has presented numerous research papers at seminars and conferences. His PhD thesis was on life-long learning. He enjoys writing stories and poems.

Gary Woolley (PhD) is currently a Lecturer in literacy and learning difficulties with the inclusive education program at Griffith University, Australia. His particular professional interests include reading comprehension difficulties, memory, cognition and learning engagement. Gary's PhD. thesis focused on the design of training programs for volunteer tutors to assist students with reading comprehension difficulties. In recognition of the production of an exceptional work, which advances knowledge in the field of learning difficulties Gary was awarded the Tertiary Student Award for 2007 by Learning Difficulties Australia (LDA). Gary has taught primary and high school children in public and private school systems. He was the Learning Assistance Coordinator in a large private school for over fifteen years. He has written a number of articles and taken part in several research projects in literacy and inclusive education. In 2006 he was part of a team of five lecturers from the University of Canberra that won a Carrick Institute Citation for Teaching and Learning.

Yun Yue is a PhD candidate in the Faculty of Health Science, University of Tasmania. She taught English and business studies in China. She has presented papers at major conferences in China and Australia. Her research interests include second language learning, linguistic interference, health literacy and pragmatics.

Suxian Zhan (PhD) holds a PhD in education at Macquarie University, Australia. She is an Associate Professor and Director of the Centre for International Education and Communication, based at Baoding University, China. Her research interests are in applied linguistics, English language education, and teacher professional development programs. She has presented research papers in major conferences in China and Australia.

INDEX

D